Advancing the Legal Status of Women in Islamic Law

International Studies in Human Rights

VOLUME 136

The titles published in this series are listed at *brill.com/ishr*

Advancing the Legal Status of Women in Islamic Law

By

Mona Samadi

BRILL
NIJHOFF

LEIDEN | BOSTON

Library of Congress Cataloging-in-Publication Data

Names: Samadi, Mona, author.
Title: Advancing the legal status of women in Islamic law /
  by Mona Samadi.
Description: Leiden ; Boston : Brill/Nijhoff, 2021. | Series: International
  studies in human rights, 0924-4751 ; volume 136 | Includes bibliographical
  references and index.
Identifiers: LCCN 2021011113 (print) | LCCN 2021011114 (ebook) |
  ISBN 9789004446939 (hardback) | ISBN 9789004446953 (ebook)
Subjects: LCSH: Women (Islamic law) | Muslim women–Conduct of life.
Classification: LCC KBP526.3 .S26 2021 (print) | LCC KBP526.3 (ebook) |
  DDC 342/.1670878–dc23
LC record available at https://lccn.loc.gov/2021011113
LC ebook record available at https://lccn.loc.gov/2021011114

Typeface for the Latin, Greek, and Cyrillic scripts: "Brill". See and download: brill.com/brill-typeface.

ISSN 0924-4751
ISBN 978-90-04-44693-9 (hardback)
ISBN 978-90-04-44695-3 (e-book)

Copyright 2021 by Koninklijke Brill NV, Leiden, The Netherlands.
Koninklijke Brill NV incorporates the imprints Brill, Brill Nijhoff, Brill Hotei, Brill Schöningh, Brill Fink, Brill mentis, Vandenhoeck & Ruprecht, Böhlau Verlag and V&R Unipress.
All rights reserved. No part of this publication may be reproduced, translated, stored in a retrieval system, or transmitted in any form or by any means, electronic, mechanical, photocopying, recording or otherwise, without prior written permission from the publisher. Requests for re-use and/or translations must be addressed to Koninklijke Brill NV via brill.com or copyright.com.

This book is printed on acid-free paper and produced in a sustainable manner.

Contents

Acknowledgments IX
Glossary X

1 **The Legal Status of Women: An Introduction** 1
    1   Historical Aspects   4
    2   The Dictonomy Between Classical Islamic Law and the State   7
    3   Justice and Gender Equality   11
    4   Crucial Developments of Law   12
    5   Outline   19

2 **Foundations of Islamic Law**   24
    1   Immutable Law?   29
        1.1   *Sharia*   29
        1.2   *Fiqh and Usul al-fiqh*   32
    2   Sources of Islamic Law   33
        2.1   *The Quran*   34
            2.1.1   Authoritative Interpretations   36
            2.1.2   Dealing with Contradictions   37
        2.2   *Sunnah*   38
            2.2.1   Hadith Compilations   44
            2.2.2   Validity of Hadiths   45
        2.3   *Ijma*   50
        2.4   *Legal Reasoning*   52
            2.4.1   Ijtihad   52
            2.4.2   Other Forms of Legal Reasoning   57
    3   Who Has the Right to Interpret the Law?   59

3 **Women and Islam**   63
    1   The Pre-Islamic Status of Women According to Muslim Sources   64
        1.1   *The Pre-Islamic Status of Women According to Historical Sources*   67
    2   The Wives of Muhammad   70
        2.1   *Khadija*   71
        2.2   *Aisha*   72
    3   The Influence of Islam on Women   76
        3.1   *The Ethical Voice*   80

3.2 *Marriage* 83
    3.2.1 Temporary Marriages 88
    3.2.2 Polygyny 90
3.3 *Sexual Relations* 93
3.4 *Fornication and Adultery* 95
3.5 *Testimony* 98
3.6 *Compensation for Death* 104
3.7 *Inheritance* 108
3.8 *Divorce* 112
3.9 *Political Positions* 114
3.10 *Veiling* 118
3.11 *The Consequences of the Death of the Prophet on the Status of Women* 122

4 Guardianship of Women 125
1 Guardianship of Minors 126
2 Legally Incompetent but Financially Independent 130
    2.1 *Men Are the Managers of Women* 132
        2.1.1 Marriage Based on Cooperation or Supervision? 133
    2.2 *Correcting Women* 144
3 The Marriage Contract 148
    3.1 *The Guardians Right to Conclude the Marriage Contract* 151
    3.2 *Mahr* 155
    3.3 *The Analogy to a Sales Contract* 158

5 Advancing the Legal Status of Women in Islamic law 162
1 Gradual Changes 164
2 Could the Abolition of Slavery Be a Model for Advancing the Rights of Women? 167
    2.1 *The Status of Slaves* 169
    2.2 *Female Slaves* 170
    2.3 *Abolishing Slavery* 172
        2.3.1 Egypt 174
        2.3.2 India 176
        2.3.3 Persia 178
    2.4 *Is There an Ijma on Slavery?* 179
3 Does the Principle of Justice Include Female Autonomy? 180
    3.1 *The Concept of Justice* 181
    3.2 *An Unjust God?* 183

	4	Political Reform 186	
		4.1 *State Law* 188	

6 Concluding Remarks 193

Bibliography 195
Index 215

Acknowledgments

This book would not have been written without the help and active support of many individuals, colleagues, friends, and family. First and foremost, I want to express my deepest gratitude to Professor Mohammad H. Faghfoory at the Department of Religion, George Washington University. I am indebted for his support, not only while working on this book but for over a decade of generous support and inspiring conversations.

I have had the pleasure of researching much of the material for this book in such inspiring environments. George Washington University is where I started and finished this book. Time spent at Princeton University was very valuable for my research. I want to thank Professor Hossein Modarressi and Julia Buelow-Gilbert at the Department of Near Eastern Studies. They made sure I could make the most of my time at Princeton University.

Special thanks are due to Professor Said Mahmoudi, Stockholm University, and Professor Joakim Nergelius, Örebro University, who both reviewed early drafts of this text. Their perceptive comments on various chapters were most useful. I'd also like to thank Professor Mohammad Fadel at Toronto University for providing me with valuable material for this book.

This research project would not have been possible if it wasn't for the generous contributions of the Sweden-America Foundation, Johan & Jacob Söderbergs Foundation, Birgit and Gad Rausings Foundation for Humanist Research, Emil Heijnes Foundation for Law Research, and the Wallenberg Foundation for Jurisprudence Research.

To my incredible friends; the Londoño family; Rosario, Patricia, and Chiara, Ph.D. candidate Therese Johnstone, Karin Karlsson, Negar Sedghi Altieri, Tara Horne, Haleh Rahjoo, Ph.D. candidate Niousha Nademi, and Martin Runosson – I am so inspired by and grateful for every one of you. Without the endless encouragement and support from my parents Farhad and Zohre, and my brothers Milad and Mahyar, I would never have finished this.

Glossary

Agd   agreement

Aql   reason

Ayah   a verse of the Quran

Ayatollah   Islamic priest

Bid'ah   innovation, usually pernicious innovation as opposed to the valid precedent. Bid'ah is often used in contradistinction to the Sunnah.

Closing of the gate of ijtihad   ijtihad is the maximum effort expended by the jurist to master and apply the principles and rules of usul al-fiqh (legal theory) for the purpose of discovering God's law. The activity of ijtihad is assumed by many to have ceased about the end of the ninth century, with the consent of the Muslim jurists themselves.

Darurah   a legal instrument applicable in cases of extreme necessity or vital interest by which a person is allowed to act in a manner that would normally be forbidden.

Daruriyyat   indispensable benefits or rights – comprising: (right to) life, intellect, religion, family and property.

Fatwa   considered opinion given by a qualified scholar, a mufti (jurisconsult) or a mujtahid (one who is competent enough to conduct ijtihad) concerning a legal/religious issue: a religious edict. As there is generally no priesthood or the equivalent recognized in Islam (except in Shia Islam), a fatwa is necessarily not binding on believers. Fatwas need to be based on Islamic sources and it is not uncommon for Islamic scholars to hold different opinions on the same matters.

Faqih   jurist

Fiqh   Islamic jurisprudence. The term is often used synonymously with Sharia; the main difference being that Sharia bears a closer link with the divine revelation, whereas fiqh mainly consists of the works of religious scholars and jurists.

Fitnah   sedition; affliction and tumult. In the Quran it is often used to imply oppression and persecution which denies its victim the freedom of religion.

Fuqaha   the religious lawyers of Islam

Hadd   an obligatory Islamic punishment laid down in the Quran

Hadith   saying; traditions of the Prophet Muhammad

Halal   that which is permissible and legal

Haram   that which is forbidden and unlawful

Hudud   limits; the fixed punishments for certain crimes under Islamic law

Hukm   legal ruling; injunction; decision

Huquq   plural form of haqq, meaning rights

GLOSSARY XI

Ibadat plural form of ibadah. It refers to Islamic jurisprudence on "the rules governing worship in Islam" or the "religious duties of worship".
Iddah waiting period after divorce has been pronounced
Illah ratio legis, or reason for law
Ijtihad legal reasoning, by independent reasoning
Ijma scholarly consensus
Imam leader in prayer; leader of the Muslim community
Istishab finding a link. Legal term for the presumption of continuity, where a situation existing previously is presumed to be continuing at present until the contrary is proven.
Istishan Arabic term for juristic "preference". In its literal sense it means "to consider something good". Muslim scholars may use it to express their preference for particular judgements in Islamic law over other possibilities.
Jahili ignorant; non-Islamic
Jahiliyyah ignorance
Jihad struggle; often used for war in defense of Islam and Muslims
Kabah square building at the center of Islam's most important mosque, the Great Mosque of Mecca. Muslims face the Kabah, no matter where they are in the world, to do their daily prayers.
Mahdhab school of Islamic jurisprudence
Mahdi the guided one. The Shia are awaiting his return.
Makruk disapproved
Mandub recommended
Maslahah welfare; benefit. The rules of the Sharia are all deemed to be for the realization of the general benefit of the people. A part of extended methodological principles of Islamic jurisprudence, it bestows legitimacy on interpretations of Islamic law where there cannot be found a basis in the scriptural sources.
Maqasid al-shariah the aims or goals intended by Islamic law for the realization of benefit to mankind.
Mubah neutral, indifferent
Mujtahid scholar qualified to formulate independent legal or theological opinion based on the sources and methods of Islamic law.
Mufti an official who can issue Islamic legal rulings.
Muhsan a married Muslim of upright character who is not guilty of zina or riddah; a chaste person; of unblemished reputation.
Naskh doctrine of abrogation
Qadfh slanderous accusation (of illegal intercourse, adultery or fornication)
Qadi Islamic judge
Qiyas legal reasoning, by analogy
Ra'y in early fiqh (Islamic jurisprudence), a personal opinion in adapting Sharia law.

Riwaya narration
Sahih authentic; a hadith which is considered authentic
Sharia 'Islamic law' in the nearest English translation of Sharia, yet the latter is not confined specifically to legal subject matters and extends to much wider areas of moral and religious guidance.
Shahada testimony
Shura consultation
Shia branch of Islam comprising of sects believing that Ali is the rightful successor to Muhammad.
Sunnah practice; the practices of the Prophet Muhammad
Sunni branch of Islam that acknowledges the first four caliphs as rightful successors to Muhammad.
Surah chapter of the Quran
Tafsir or exegesis. An important Islamic science of delivering interpretations or commentary on the Quran.
Talaq unilateral pronouncement of divorce
Taqlid legal conformism, the obligation to recognize and respect the authority of the classic interpretations of Islamic law
Tawhid worshipping God alone
Tazir discretionary punishment under Islamic law
Ulama a member of an Ulema, a body of Muslim scholars who are recognized as having specialist knowledge of Islamic sacred law and theology.
Ummah the Muslim community
'Urf term referring to the custom, or knowledge, of a given society
Wajib obligatory
Wujub necessary
Wilaya in the Quran the term primarily refers to mutual support or help and cooperation.
Zina adultery and fornication, sexual intercourse outside marriage

CHAPTER 1

The Legal Status of Women: An Introduction

Gender was, then, the most enduring aspect of legal personality. Both slavery and minority were legal disabilities of a sort, as was – in a different respect – being non-Muslim. However, only female-ness permanently limited a person's legal capacity. A slave might be manumitted; a non-Muslim could convert; a child would reach maturity. A woman, however, would remain female, with the "whiff of disability" attached to her legal capacity.[1]

∴

The relationship between Islamic law and gender is a complex and at times contradictory system of religious tradition.[2] A historical overview shows that in places where, culturally, women have held power, Islam has both allowed and accepted women as equal to men. There are cases of powerful women who lead wars and nations without apparent social reservations or lack of trust in pre-Islamic Arabia.[3] Wealth was a source of power and influence, even

---

1   Kecia Ali, *Marriage and Slavery in Early Islam* (Cambridge: Harvard University Press, 2010), p. 47. See also, Judith E. Tucker, *Women, Family, and Gender in Islamic Law* (Cambridge: Cambridge University Press, 2008), p. 222.
2   The term "Islamic law" is somewhat ambiguous as it gives the connotation that it is a mere legal norm. However, the term includes more than law in the strict western sense, which in modern legislations is produced by legislative or parliamentary assemblies. In the Islamic legal tradition, the "law" includes not only the sources, which are regarded divine, but also the methods of interpreting the sources, see Jasser Auda, *Maqasid al-Shariʿah as Philosophy of Islamic Law: A Systems Approach* (London: The International Institute of Islamic Thought London, 2008), p. 57.
3   Numerous reports record the role of Nusaybah Bint Kaʿab al-Ansiriyyah al-Maziniyyah in the battles of Uhud, al-Hudaybiyyah, Khaybar, and Hunayn. See Ibn Hajjar al-ʿAsqalani, *Fath al-bari* (Beirut: Dar al-Maʾrifah, 1989), 6:93; Abu'l Faraj Ibn al-Jawzi, *Safwat al-sawfah* (Beirut: Dar al-Maʾrihah, 1989); 2:23 and Abd al-Malik Ibn Hisham, *As-Sira An-Nabawiya* (Beirut: Dar Ihys al-Thurat al Arabi, n.d.). For a brief overview of Muslim women who assumed political power and authority, see Bouthaina Shaaban, "The Muted Voices of Women Interpreters", in *Women and Islam, Critical Concepts in Sociology*, Vol. I, ed. Haideh Moghissi (New York: Routledge, 2005), pp. 210–211. See also, W. Robertson Smith, *Kinship and Marriage in Early Arabia*

for women.[4] The life of Prophet Muhammad's first wife, Khadija, supports the presence of high status for females among pre-Islamic Arabs. Khadija was a wealthy widow who employed Muhammad to oversee her caravan which traded between Mecca and Syria. She belonged to Mecca's social elite, was 15 years older than Muhammad and educated to a higher standard since she could read and write, unlike Muhammad. She had been married twice before she proposed marriage to Muhammad.[5] Muhammad himself accepted the position that free Arab women enjoyed before Islam, Khadija being the prime example of that, and strove for the improvement of the economic and legal status of all Muslim women. Nevertheless, there was a distinction between free Arab women and Muslim women, a distinction that would portray women as being inferior to men in Islamic legal theory.[6]

The question of equality in Islamic legal tradition has been regarded as meaningless, as Islam envisages the role of the man and woman as not competing, but complementary.[7] The Quran teaches that women and men are equal in their relationship with God,[8] and grants women the complete and independent possession of ownership of property and competence in economic transactions, including the right to inherit (although the share is half of a man's) and a dower during marriage and after divorce.[9] Nevertheless, the Quran also acknowledges adult Muslim men as privileged members of society, by imposing upon them the responsibility to care for and exercise authority over not only women, but also children, orphans, and the needy. The understanding is that men are intended to be the providers of the family and therefore enjoy

---

(Cambridge: Cambridge University Press, 1985) and W. Montgomery Watt, *Muhammad at Medina* (Oxford: Clarendon Press, 1956).

4 Wealthy women exercised authority and handled property, see Amira Sonbol, "Marriage Contracts in Islamic Society", in *Changing God's Law: The Dynamics of Middle Eastern Family Law*, ed. Nadjma Yassari (London: Routledge, London, 2016), p. 226. There are even reports of women reaching a position of superiority over men, because of their wealth, see Wiebke Walther, *Women in Islam* (Princeton: Wiener, 1993), chapter 3.

5 From her first marriage, Khadija had two sons, and she was entrusted her second husband's daughter when he died. For a brief overview of her life, see Resit Haylamaz, *Khadija – The First Muslim and the Wife of the Prophet Muhammad* (New Jersey: The Light, Inc., Somerset, 2007); Natalie Maydell and Sep Riahi, *Extraordinary Women from the Muslim World* (Lancaster: Global Content Ventures, 2007), chapter 1.

6 Nadia Abbott, "Women and the State in Early Islam", *Journal of Near Eastern Studies* Vol. 1 (1942), pp. 106–126.

7 Ziba Mir-Hosseini, Kari Vogt, Lena Larsen, *Gender and Equality in Muslim Family Law: Justice and Ethics in the Islamic Legal Tradition* (London: I. B. Taurus, 2013), p. 1.

8 Quran 16:97.

9 Asma Barlas, *"Believing Women" in Islam: Unreading Patriarchal Interpretations of the Qur'an* (Austin: University of Texas Press, 2002), p. 148.

legal rights of authority inside and outside the home, whereas women are freed from all financial obligations. Classical interpretations of Islamic law engaged in discussions about gender differences and the legal status of women uphold that "there are three grounds under the Sharia for being placed under guardianship: minority, insanity, and, within limits, *the state of being female*".[10] This guardianship manifests itself in a manner that subject women to the oversight of a father, husband, or another male relative. While the guardian is expected to act in the best interests of the woman, the guardianship of women undeniably limits a woman's legal status to that of a child, someone insane or incompetent. What is inconsistent with how the concept of guardianship is constructed in Islamic law, is that the ward, the woman, is incapacitated by the fact that she is a woman, but somehow that incapacitation does not involve her ability to enter into contracts, manage property or finances.[11]

The varying commentaries of the Quran confirm that over time, the status of women decreased as the commentaries on the verses regarding women became more and more restrictive. In a culture where misogyny was a norm and a part of the social and cultural environment in which religious scholars were engaged in, demeaning descriptions of women and their capabilities were not only tolerated — along with the social realities of women where they depended on men — they also influenced the interpretations of the verses of the Quran.[12] The paradoxical nature of Islamic law, shows that the construction of the Islamic legal theory stems not only from the Quran, but also from subjective interpretations based on social constructions of its time. Islamic law seems to condition the perception and the rights of women based on men's view of women and their character, while the perception of men and their rights are just acknowledged. Once the codification of the Quran and its traditions were considered to be the divine revelation to the Prophet, the enforcement of the verses in a society where the predominant view considered women as having no role in public life and bound to be secluded and veiled; the inferior status of women was accentuated and maintained. These descriptions also extend beyond the legal rulings concerning male-female

---

10 Jamal J. Nasir, *The Islamic Law of Personal Status*, 3rd ed. (Leiden: Brill, 2009), p. 186.
11 It is only when it comes to contracting their marriage contract and managing the property and finances of their children, that the incapacity starts to have an effect. That she is trusted with managing her property, but not that of her child, seems illogical. However, it also ensures that a woman does not manage the affairs of the husband, of which the child is a part, according to Islamic law.
12 Mohammad Fadel, "Is Historicism a Viable Strategy for Islamic Legal Reform? The Case of 'Never Shall a Folk Prosper Who Have Appointed a Woman to rule Them' ", *Islamic Law & Society* Vol. 18, No. 2 (2011), p. 36.

segregation.[13] Consequently, legal differences arise between the sexes in the social context of the family[14] and include—alongside guardianship—divorce, inheritance, polygyny and witnessing.

Acknowledging equality in the moral sphere of Islam, while upholding discriminatory views in the social and legal area is questioned more and more by modern scholars as it stands against the principle of *tawhid*, God's unity.[15] Some scholars rather question if the Quran sanctions these powers or if it actually attempts to restrict them in an effort to "protect women from the power of men already possess[ed] by virtue of the customs and practices of the society in which Islam was revealed".[16] They believe, for example, by establishing the role of women as witnesses in economic transactions, "the Quran seeks … to end the traditional perception by including them … the matter of witnessing served merely as a means to an end or a practical way of establishing the concept of gender equality".[17]

1 Historical Aspects

It is repeatedly argued in the Islamic tradition that the status of women and rights afforded women were vastly improved by the expressed commands in the Quran, as "the principal aim of the Quran was the removal of certain abuses to which women were subjected",[18] especially when studied against the

---

13   Abdulaziz Sachedina, "Woman, Half-the-Man? Crisis of Male Epistemology in Islamic Jurisprudence", in *Perspectives on Islamic Law, Justice, and Society*, ed. R. S. Khare (Lanham: Rowman & Littlefield Publishers, 1999), p. 146.
14   The term "family" and the legal connotation it has, is a modern concept. Pre-modern literature does not describe the family as the centre of social discourse, instead, the literature focuses on clans and tribes, where many of the marriage rules developed are based on the notion of the best interest for the tribe or clan. See Amira Sonbol, "Marriage Contracts in Islamic Society", in *Changing God's Law: The Dynamics of Middle Eastern Family Law*, ed. Nadjma Yassari (London: Routledge, 2016), p. 225.
15   Asma Barlas, argues that such a separation is un-Quranic, see *"Believing Women" in Islam*, p. 142.
16   Khaled Abou El-Fadl, "The Pearls of Beauty", in *A Search for Beauty in Islam: The Conference of the Books* (Lanham: University of America Press, 2001), p. 275.
17   Quote taken from Adis Duderija, "A Case Study of Patriarchy and Slavery", in *Maqasid al-Shari'a and Contemporary Reformist Muslim Thought*, ed. Adis Duderija (New York: Palgrave Macmillan, 2014), p. 234. See also, Taha Al-Alwani, *Issues in Contemporary Islamic Thought* (London: International Institute of Islamic Thought, 2005).
18   Quote taken from Fatima L. Adamu, "A Double-Edged Sword: Challenging Women's Oppression Within Muslim Society in Northern Nigeria", in Moghissi, *Women and Islam*, p. 367. An overview of the changes that occurred can be found in Norman Anderson, *Law*

background of *jahiliyya*—the period before Islam.[19] The predominant view among Muslims is that Arabs lived in ignorance and barbarism before Islam and that the Quran established a great step forward for society as a whole.[20] In particular, for women that came from poor conditions or lacked wealth were exploited, and slavery was widely practiced. Difficulties for social groups to break economic and cultural barriers meant that children born to poor parents were more likely to be considered a burden, and therefore not raised, resulting in the practice of female infanticide, which was prohibited by the Quran.[21]

While, it is certain that the position enjoyed by women underwent major changes during the early period of Islam, most likely, these changes varied depending on particular tribes.[22] Our historical knowledge of the pre-Islamic times is scarce and contains serious gaps; this is because most of the knowledge about the period before Islam that survived, has often been appropriated by Islam. The claim that Islam fundamentally transformed the social structures and gender roles, by prohibiting female infanticide, guaranteeing inheritance rights for women and removing extensive, unrestrained polygyny and incestuous relationships in the newly converted Arab tribes, is first and foremost a religious assertion and not a historical one.[23] Instead, it is difficult to distinguish whether women were mistreated because of their gender, or because of their economic and social status.[24] At the time of Muhammad, the family structure within the Arabian tribal system went through a transition from a combination of matrilineal-matrilocal and patriarchal-patrilocal, to patriarchal-patrilocal, the dominant form in Mecca even before the time of

---

Reform in the Muslim World (London: Athlone, 1976). See also, Tahir Mahmood, *Personal Law in Islamic Countries* (New Delhi: Academy of Law and Religions, 1987).

19 The term is usually translated as, "age of ignorance" and is the name Muslims gave to that period.

20 Nikki R. Keddie, "The Past and Present of Women in the Muslim World", in Moghissi, *Women and Islam*, p. 57.

21 Quran 6:151; 16:58; 17:31. The fear that a girl child would increase the economic burdens, as well as the fear of the humiliation that would arise if the girl child was captured by a hostile tribe and preferred to remain with their captors instead of their parents and brothers, are considered to be the underlying factors for these practices, see Asghar Ali Engineer, *The Rights of Women in Islam* (New York: St. Martin's Press, 1992), p. 21, and Ahmed, E. Souaiaia, *Contesting Justice: Women, Islam, Law and Society* (New York: State University of New York Press, 2008), p. 4 and chapter 3.

22 Sonbol Amira, "Rise of Islam: 6th to 9th Century", in *Encyclopedia of Women 38: Islamic Cultures*, ed. Suad Joseph et al., Brill Reference Online. Accessed 17 January 2018.

23 Alfons Teipen, "Jahilite and Muslim Women: Questions of Continuity and Communal Identity", *The Muslim World* Vol. 92 (2002), pp. 437–459.

24 See Hatoon al-Fassi, Allen Fromherz, and Barbara F. Stowasser in *Gulf Women*, ed. Amira Sonbol (Syracuse: Syracuse University Press, 2012), pp. 25–47, 48–68 and 60–103.

Muhammad.[25] The pre-Islamic social structure in which Islam was revealed, endorsed various forms of confrontation where Islam, on the one hand, criticized and refused parts of the norms and values of jahiliyya, but on the other, endorsed or partially modified other values. What we know for sure is that the status of women was, at least, different before the development of agriculture and deteriorated over time, due to male absence in case of long periods of warfare or long-distance trade.[26] Tribal life was disintegrating as a result of a new mercantile class in urban centers. Women and children were among those who were most affected by the changes in society, and the insecurities produced as a result of the disruption of the tribal structure led to provisions created for their care.[27]

It is hard to conclude whether Islam improved the status of women or is responsible for keeping them oppressed now, or both; as the Quran was, after all, written in a time and place with different levels of sexual inequality, both among Arab tribes and non-Arab empires.[28] Islam did not remove all traces of the past; traditions that were reformed or prohibited by Islam made their way back into Sharia through *adat*, pre-Islamic customary practices.[29] In fact, in the absence of other provisions, many Sharia provisions were based on custom.[30] The modest modification to women's status in Islamic law can partly be explained by the extreme importance of tradition and custom among the pre-Islamic Arabian community.[31] The significance of custom by the Arabs

---

25 Suan Spectorsky, *Themes in Islamic Studies: Women in Classical Islamic Law: A Survey of the Sources* (Boston: Brill, 2009), p. 24.
26 Peggy R. Sanday, "Toward a Theory of the Status of Women", *American Anthropologist* Vol. 75, No. 4 (1973), pp. 1168–1170. Sanday argues that there are three possibilities of what will happen after a prolonged male absence in society: women may occupy the sphere temporarily, or they may become the predominant labourers and remain in this sphere, or they may continue to occupy the sphere together with men and it may result in a balanced division of work. In the first instance, women's status does not change, in the second instance women gain power in the economic and political field where men develop an independent control sphere, where women in the end are treated as slaves. In the third instance, where women stay in the public sphere after the men return, is argued to be the strongest factor in elevating the status of women, or at least, changing it.
27 See Watt, *Muhammad at Mecca* and *Muhammad at Medina* (Oxford: Clarendon Press, 1956).
28 Keddie, "The Past and Present of Women in the Muslim World", p. 57.
29 Alfons Teipen affirms that "verses in the Quran about women are best understood as a procedure of standardization of certain already prevalent practices, not as a radical departure from pre-Islamic practice", see "Jahilite and Muslim Women", p. 441.
30 Engineer, *The Rights of Women in Islam*, p. 20.
31 Joseph Schacht, *An Introduction to Islamic Law* (Oxford: Clarendon Press, 1964), p. 17.

meant that "custom was mightier than what was right".[32] It was, after all, these Muslims who came to interpret the words of God. It is not likely that laws other than patriarchal laws were accepted by those men, despite the teachings of Islam. However, given the importance of the topic and its deep influence on the lives of women, the Quran could have opposed such views and suggested new regulations which would have included a more independent role for Muslim women.[33] The early history of Islam does speak of powerful women, whose authority was respected by men, but Islam did not uphold such a position for women despite it being not unfamiliar to the newly converted Arabs. Instead, patriarchal norms are imbedded in the Quran and the Islamic legal tradition, with the transition from various forms of relations to one centered around men, as upheld by the Prophet, being the greatest example of that. Therefore, whether the establishment of the Quran resulted in a great improvement for women's rights or not, is not of relevance, as it is fairly simple to determine that women do not have rights *equal* to those of their male counterparts in many areas of Islamic law.

2 The Dictonomy Between Classical Islamic Law and the State

Formulating Islamic doctrine today means confronting circumstances where Muslims are seeking relief from oppression and discrimination from governments with unprecedented power, calling for greater freedom and respect for their rights. Consequently, this has encouraged the support of democratization and human rights, and in some respects, secularization, which has threatened those in power, who legitimize their authoritative rule by referring to Islamic authority and law. Some governments are using Islam as a way to inhibit the growing demand for reforms, and by supporting the production of Islamic human rights,[34] they are maintaining their power and position.[35] At the same time, other governments are referring to other aspects or interpretations of

---

32 Samuel Ives Curtiss, *Primitive Semitic Religion Today: A Record of Researchers, Discoveries and Studies in Syria, Palestine and the Sinaitic Peninsula* (Oregon: Wipf and Stock Publishers, 2004), p. 65.
33 Abbas Mehregan, "Islamo-Arabic Culture and Women's Law: An Introduction to the Sociology of Women's Law in Islam", in *International Journal for the Semiotics of Law* Vol. 29 (2016), p. 412.
34 See the Cairo Declaration of Human Rights in Islam, Aug. 5, 1990, U.N. GAOR, World Conf. on Hum. Rts., 4th Sess., Agenda Item 5, U.N. Doc. A/CONF.157/PC/62/Add.18 (1993).
35 Ann Elizabeth Mayer, *Islam and Human Rights: Tradition and Politics* (Boulder: Westview Press, 2007), pp. 1–2.

Islamic law, to justify legal amendments that allow for men and women to have equal rights in the field of personal status laws, as is the case in Tunisia.[36]

Calls concerning the reformation of Islamic law increasingly occurred as a response to the challenge of the escalating Western impact in the Islamic world by the end of the nineteenth century.[37] The concern among some Muslim scholars was that the methods of interpreting, applying, and implementing Islamic law, was inadequate for the needs of Muslim societies. Their objective was to demonstrate that Islamic law was capable of not only functioning within a modern state, but also, it could adjust according to the circumstances of society. Sunni reformers call for abandoning the legal order as established by the legal schools over centuries, in favor of *ijtihad*, independent reasoning, to revive Islamic law and increase its flexibility under contemporary conditions. Such an approach is sternly challenged by traditional Sunni Muslim scholars, who usually describe legal rules as settled precedents that cannot be changed. This has, however, not been the case in many other areas of Islamic law. During the past centuries, whole categories of Islamic law have been made inoperable in various countries, without causing significant resistance.[38] Re-interpreting Islamic interpretations of the sacred text has often supported progressive views on other aspects of Islamic law. However, when

---

36 The Tunisian system, however, is still pluralistic in the sense that judges apply Sharia and custom alongside the legislation. For a review of the implementation of personal status laws in Tunisia, see Maaike Voorhoeve, *Gender and Divorce Law in North Africa: Sharia, Custom and the Personal Status Code in Tunisia* (London: I. B. Tauris, 2014).

37 Felicitas Opwis, Maslaha in "Contemporary Islamic Legal Theory", in *Islamic Law and Society* Vol. 12, No. 2 (2005), pp. 182–223. See also, Rudolph Peters, "Ijtihad and Taqlid in 18th and 19th Century Islam" in *Die Welt des Islams* Vol. 20 (1980), pp. 131–144, and Ahmad Dallal, "Appropriating the Past: Twentieth Century Reconstruction of Pre-Modern Islamic Thought", in *Islamic Law and Society* Vol. 7 (1999), pp. 333–342.

38 See, for example, the development of using modern scientific calculations instead of witnesses when it comes to crescent sighting. Traditionally, the testimony of two trustworthy men were enough to establish that the crescent had been sighted and that the next day would be the day to celebrate Eid al-Fitr. Nowadays, the testimony of witnesses, usually conflict with precise astronomical calculations about crescent visibility. As a consequence, jurists began to revisit the issue of traditional evidence, and a majority of jurists now rely on scientific calculations to determine the end of Ramadan. Saudi Arabia follows the traditional route and allows for moon-sighting reports even when calculations show that the moon is not visible at all. Likewise, Iranian courts rely on forensic science more than on traditional types of evidence as established historically by Islamic law. See Mohammad Samei, "Between Traditional Law and the Exigencies of Modern Life, Shia Responses to Contemporary Challenges in Islamic Law", *Journal of Shi'a Studies* Vol. 11, No. 3 (2009), pp. 256–259, 267. The same applies for intellectual property, which is not mentioned in the material sources of Islamic law, ibid., 259–262.

it comes to the rights of women, tradition has historically been granted an elevated status within Islamic law, which is justified and legitimized by reference to the Quran and the traditions of the Prophet.[39] The idea of complementary rather than egalitarian spousal and parental rights and duties continue to be the norms, but patriarchal norms in aspects of family law other than guardianship have been modified to some extent. The application of *takhayyar*, eclectic choice, has allowed the incorporation of specific clauses within the marriage contract.[40] The husband's unrestricted right to divorce has been inhibited in most Muslim countries, by the introduction of registration requirements, judicial supervision and compensation entitlements that the divorced wife has a right to.[41] This was achieved as Muslim states adopted a more contextual and methodological interpretation of Quranic injunctions.[42] State legislators are not bound by the results of legal reasoning as established by the schools of law, and could even choose to disregard any specific problematic opinion of Muslim jurists.[43]

Two significant changes of direction within the history of Islamic law are of importance. One was the introduction at an early date of a legal theory which not only ignored, but also denied the existence of all elements that were not, in the narrowest possible sense, Islamic, by reducing its material sources to the Quran and the narrated traditions of the Prophet, Sunnah; the second significant change, which began only in the present century, is the legislation made by Islamic states.[44] Nation states, especially during the last century, have played a greater role in how Islamic law is to be constructed and integrated within the

---

39 Fatima Mernissi, "Women in Muslim History: Traditional Perspectives and New Strategies", in Moghissi, *Women and Islam*, p. 37.
40 Such clauses were, for example, only permissible within the Hanbali school, but not the Hanafi school, see Rehman Javaid, "The Sharia, Islamic Family Laws and International Human Rights Law: Examining the Theory and Practice of Polygamy and Talaq", *International Journal of Law, Policy and the Family* Vol. 21 (2007), p. 116. Javaid, further argues that "the usage of *takhayyar* doctrine authorized Islamic jurists from all schools of thought to specifically incorporate provisions in marriage contracts prohibiting polygamous marriages".
41 Lynn Welchman, "Qiwamah and Wilayah as Legal Postulates in Muslim Family Laws", in *Men in Charge? Rethinking Authority in Muslim Legal Tradition*, eds., Ziba Mir-Hosseini et al. (London: Oneworld, 2015), pp. 107–132.
42 Javaid, "The Sharia, Islamic Family Laws and International Human Rights Law", p. 116.
43 Oussama Arabi, "The dawning of the third millennium on Shariʿa: Egypt's law No.1 of 2000, or women may divorce at will", *Arab Law Quarterly* Vol. 16 (2001), p. 19; and Javaid, "The Sharia, Islamic Family Laws and International Human Rights Law", p. 120.
44 Schacht, *An Introduction to Islamic Law*, p. 3. Some scholars argue that this development is catastrophic, as it will lead to the rise of tyrannical governments, see Wael B. Hallaq, *Sharīʿa: Theory, Practice, Transformations* (Cambridge: Cambridge University Press,

state. The resurgence of orthodox Islam, as a counteraction to these developmental changes in Muslim societies, with the Muslim Brotherhood, and the establishment of Islamic states such as the Islamic Republic of Iran, is undeniably challenging the call for reformation of the legal status of women. Despite these significant changes of direction, there seems to be an understanding of what constitutes an Islamic rule versus an un-Islamic one. "If a rule can be found in the historical doctrines of Islamic law as articulated by the schools of Islamic law, or can be derived using the reasoning techniques developed by theoretical jurisprudence, *usul al-fiqh*, it is 'Islamic.' A rule that originates in the will of the state, by contrast, is 'secular' and therefore is non-Islamic, and of dubious Islamic legitimacy. Indeed, it remains dogma that there is no conceptual room for human legislation in Islamic jurisprudence."[45] Some scholars argue that, in order to meet the needs of the Muslim community today, a new hermeneutic, a new usul al-fiqh, where new methods of interpreting the Quran are necessary to generate modern Islamic norms.[46] Calls for a new and expanded usul al-fiqh "shows the crisis that faces male-dominated epistemology in coming to terms with the demands about the recognition of a woman's personal status and the substantive-cognitive role of their person in reversing prejudicial decisions that deny her dignity as a full person."[47] Essentially, these calls for reforms propose the substitution of an old jurists' law with a new one.[48] However, Muslims scholars have written about positive law, without any reference to usul al-fiqh, as they "assumed the necessity and legitimacy of rules derived from practical reason ... many of the substantive reforms which are rightly demanded could be accomplished in a morally compelling fashion if promulgated through the positive law of a properly constituted representative state, without any need to advance implausible claims about the meaning of revelation".[49]

    2009) and Noah Feldman, *The Fall and Rise of the Islamic State* (Princeton: Princeton University Press, 2008).

45 Mohammad Fadel, *Islamic Law Reform: Between Reinterpretation and Democracy* (Leiden: Brill, 2017), p. 45.

46 Joseph Schacht, "Problems of Modern Islamic Legislation", *Studia Islamica* Vol. 12 (1960), p. 129 and Hallaq, *Sharī'a: Theory, Practice, Transformations*, pp. 500–542.

47 Sachedina, "Woman, Half-the-Man", p. 149.

48 Fadel, *Islamic Law Reform*, p. 50.

49 Mohammad Fadel uses the attempts to re-interpret the meaning of *da-ra-ba* in verse 4:34, from "beating" to "go away", as an example of such an instance. He argues that if positive law could be based on moral duties, rather than scriptural sources, the adoption of a law prohibiting wife-beating would be feasible, rather than resorting to debates about the interpretation of the verse. See *Islamic Law Reform*, pp. 47, 49. Fadel refers to Rifaʿa Rafiʿ al-Ṭahtawi, *al-Murshid al-Amin li'l-Banat wa'l-Banin* (Cairo: al-Majlis al-Aʿla li-l-Thaqafa,

The codification of Islamic law in Muslim states has thus challenged how Islamic law was traditionally interpreted and applied. The fall of the Ottoman Empire after World War I, and the establishment of nation-states in Muslim countries, where legal codes adopted were either based on Western law or to a great extent inspired by Western law, were factors leading to the marginalization of Islamic law.[50] The codification of Islamic law deprived Muslim jurists of their authority in the law-finding process and transferred it to secular administrations.[51] Islamic law was largely reduced to matters of personal status, where the legal autonomy of women is not recognized. Some Muslim states, such as Turkey and Tunisia, abolished their Sharia courts and the growth of secular legislation increased. The status and rights of Muslim women under secular regimes are undoubtedly greater than their status and rights under Islamic law.[52] Consequently, the status of women in modern Muslim countries varies, as the legal systems are mostly dual systems, and Islamic law is interpreted differently in these countries.

3   Justice and Gender Equality

Overcoming the widespread prejudices against Islam while examining the very real problems Muslim women face because of Islam, is challenging. The political climate post 9/11 is not in any way to the benefit of Muslims and Islam in general; the issue of women's rights and the use of feminism in military aggression, has become a cynical tool for the West to fight for rights and dignities of women in Muslim countries. At the same time, the perception of Muslim culture as inherently or inevitably patriarchal which oppresses its women is relatively common, even though most societies across the globe have been and still are patriarchal.[53] The history of the West proves that misogyny, inequality, or patriarchy is not exclusive to Islam. The potential implications of the Arab Spring on future feminist movements and expected gains for Muslim women at large, appear to be of a paradoxical nature. Tunisia's new constitution includes

---

2002); Khayr al-Din al-Tunisi, *Aqwam al-Masalik fi Ma'rifat Aḥwal al-Mamalik* (Tunis: al-Dar al-Tunisiyya li-Nashr, 1972) and Muḥammad Rashid Riḍa, *al-Khilafa* (Cairo: al-Zahra' li-l-I'lam al-'Arabi, 1988).

50   Ibid.
51   Aharon Lawish, "The Transformation of the *Shari'a* from Jurists' Law to Statutory Law in the Contemporary Muslim World", in *Die Welt des Islams* Vol. 44 (2004), pp. 85–113.
52   Abdullahi Ahmed An-Naim, *Toward an Islamic Reformation* (Syracuse: Syracuse University Press, 1987), p. 9.
53   Engineer, *The Rights of Women in Islam*, p. 1.

the adoption of a clause which guarantees gender equality and demonstrates great promise for those who argue that gender equality could be based on contemporary interpretations of Islamic law. Tunisia is also reviewing a law based on a verse of the Quran that stresses that a man receives twice the share of inheritance compared to a woman. The Tunisian inheritance law that is now proposed, is to ensure that men and women inherit equally. This prospective new clause has been the cause of controversy, not only in Tunisia, but also in other Muslim countries as many believe that such a change would be against Islam. Egypt's highest religious institution, Al-Azhar, issued a statement declaring that "the concept of equal inheritance is against Islamic teachings. Equality in inheritance is *unjust* for women and is not in line with Islamic Sharia" and also stated that "there is no room for re-interpretation, and it is not accepted by the public or non-specialists".[54] The statements provide two central questions of importance for the future role of women; first, who has the right to interpret the compatibility of gender equality with the sources of Islamic law, and second, does the Islamic principle of justice include gender equality?

4   Crucial Developments of Law

In no other area of law regarding human relationships does the treatment of women present challenges of rethinking past rulings of Islamic law. While most Muslim states disagree politically with fundamentalists about almost everything, they do agree with them on the position of women and their place in society.[55] Feminist movements within Islam are regarded as threatening the core of the Muslim society, that is, the family. Muslim women are increasingly part of the public sphere, but gender inequality in the private sphere, the family, is usually not challenged. Many of the social conditions regulating the family and women in society have changed, for example, both men and women work and share the financial responsibilities of the household in millions of marriages. The social reality of Prophet Muhammad or the developments in society ever since, have generally not been factors in how the law has been constructed or interpreted in Muslim societies. Ijtihad has been avoided as a tool of jurisprudence by the Sunni schools of law for centuries,

---

54   See, http://www.egyptindependent.com/calls-gender-equality-inheritance-islamic-teachings-al-azhar/ and http://english.ahram.org.eg/NewsContent/1/64/275762/Egypt/Politics-/AlAzhars-grand-imam-says-Islamic-inheritance-law-i.aspx (accessed 6 September 2017).
55   Mernissi, "Women in Muslim History", p. 37.

consequently obstructing a contemporary interpretation of the legal status of women in Islamic law.[56] While Islamic Sunni law began to seriously decline after the closing of the gate of ijtihad,[57] the Shia schools of law continued to develop and grow. Contrary to the Sunni schools of law, the Shia schools of law have always allowed for interpretation through ijtihad. Women have, in some respects, more rights under Islamic Shia Law, but there are still discriminatory regulations.[58] Thus, the trust many modern Sunni scholars place on the possibilities of ijtihad as a feasible method to advance women's rights in Islam, seems a bit far-fetched and over-enthusiastic.[59] While ijtihad is intended to allow for interpretations necessary to meet the legal needs of individuals and society, it is a method only to be used when there is no clear reference in the material sources of law. In other words, ijtihad is restricted to matters not governed by the Quran and Sunnah, although there are instances of this not being upheld.[60] The Quran declares that "men are the managers of the affairs of women for that God has preferred in bounty one of them over another".[61]

---

56   Jasmine Moussa, *Competing Fundamentalisms and Egyptian Women's Family Rights: International Law and Reforms of Shari'a-Derived Legislation* (Leiden: Brill, 2011), p. 30.
57   By the ninth century, it was considered that the Sunni schools had fully exhausted all possible subjects of law, and resulted in what was termed the "closing of the gate of ijtihad", see Wael B. Hallaq, "Was the Gate of Ijtihad Closed?" *International Journal of Middle East Studies* (1984), pp. 3–41.
58   For the Shia, a father does not hold guardianship over an adult woman. While a young man is presumptively emancipated from the control of the father upon reaching the age of majority, discriminatory standards were developed for women in Sunni Islam. In contrast, an adult woman must prove that she is capable of managing her affairs to be emancipated. Until such a time, she remains subject to the control of the father and treated as a minor, until her first marriage, see Mohammad Fadel, "Reinterpreting the Guardian's Role in the Islamic Contract of Marriage: The Case of the Maliki School", *The Journal of Islamic Law* Vol. 3, No. 1 (1998), p. 4.
59   The only way ijtihad could be a feasible method to address this issue, would be to allow for extending the meaning of key terms, beyond the definition of early jurists. This approach is used by several Muslim feminists, who argue that the word *qawwamun*, should be interpreted in different ways than it has been historically. This would, in turn, lead to new understandings of the whole verse as such, which has occurred in other cases. This has been done for verse 9:28, which describes the uncleanliness of unbelievers. While it historically was understood that this meant physical uncleanliness, later it was interpreted as spiritual uncleanliness, see Samei, "Between Traditional Law and the Exigencies of Modern Life", p. 268.
60   'Umar, the second caliph exercised ijtihad in matters where there existed textual rulings in the Quran and Sunnah. For examples of 'Umar's *ijtihad* see Muhammad Bultajiy, *Manhaj Umar ibn al-Khatab fi al-Tashri* (Cairo: Dar al-Fikr al-Arabi, 1970).
61   The traditional dictum that the Quran cannot be translated is cause for debate still, since Muslims regard the Quran as miraculous and inimitable. It is said that the word of God cannot be reproduced by the word of man. There are those who argue that it is

Yet, scholars argue that there are no clear verses in the Quran; thus ijtihad can be employed for every verse in the Quran.[62] Another inhibiting factor is that the right to carry out ijtihad technically lies in the hands of *mujtahids*; scholars qualified to interpret the Sharia by ijtihad.[63]

Feminist Muslim scholars maintain that the misogynist view of women is a consequence of the patriarchal interpretations of the sources of Islamic law, which construct men's superiority over women.[64] They assert that the arrival

permissible to translate the Quran, while others argue that it is absolutely prohibited, or only permitted under certain conditions. The question arises whether the translation of the Quran should be termed as translation of its meanings or a translation of its interpretation? Generally, it is argued that translations are interpretations and consequently no longer possess the divine character of the original Arabic. While this study will not discuss questions on the validity of translations, it will use the officially recognized translation of Arthur Arberry, scholar of Arabic and Islam. He acknowledges the orthodox Muslim view that the Quran cannot be translated, but only interpreted, see *The Koran Interpreted – a Translation* (Oxford: Oxford University Press, 1964), p. 24. The translation is directly from Arabic and strives in portraying the language in the best manner and does not make use of Islamic interpretations. It is regarded as one of the most authoritative translations. See Khaleel Mohammad, "Assessing English Translations of the Qur'an", *The Middle East Quarterly* (2005), pp. 58–71, for a description of the different translations of the Quran.

62 See Nasr Abu-Zayd, "The Status of Women Between the Qur'an and Fiqh", in *Gender and Equality in Muslim Family Law: Justice and Ethics in the Islamic Legal*, eds., Ziba Mir-Hosseini, Kari Vogt, Lena Larsen and Christian Moe (London: I. B. Tauris, 2013), p. 165. Abu-Zayd quotes Mohammad Mojtahedi Shabestari, stating that "there is not one single word in the Quran that is clear by itself".

63 Idb Rushd, *The Distinguished Jurist's Primer, Bidâyat al-Mujtahid wa Nihâyat al-Mugtasid*, trans. Imran A. K. Nyazee (Doha: Center for Muslim Contribution to Civilization, 2000) Vol. 1, p. xxxv. For a description of the shortcomings of ijtihad as a method of reforming Sharia, see An-Naim, *Towards an Islamic Reformation*, pp. 50–51.

64 Islamic feminism can be described as a principally diasporic group of feminist academics and researchers of Muslim background living and working in the West. Engaging in critically reviewing the Islamic tradition has proved to be difficult, especially for those who live in Muslim countries. Liberal voices are silenced, such as Nasr Hamid Abu Zayd, who was forced into exile after being found guilty of apostasy. He was also forced to divorce his wife as a Muslim woman cannot be married to a non-Muslim man. He argued a hermeneutic approach to the reading of the Quran, which challenged the mainstream views in Egypt. Sudanese Mahmoud Mohamed Taha was executed in 1985 for the same crime. Thus, the most productive environment for the Muslim women's movement challenging the traditional understandings of Islam is in a diasporic context, see Roxanne D. Marcotte, "Muslim Women's Scholarship and the New Gender Jihad" in *Women and Islam*, ed. Zayn R. Kassam (Santa Barbara: Praeger, 2010), p. 156. See also, William Safran, "Deconstructing and Comparing Diasporas", in *Diaspora, Identity and Religion: New Directions in Theory and Research*, eds., Waltrud Kokot, Khachig Tölölyan and Carolin Alfonso (London: Routledge, 2004), p. 10. Leila Ahmed argues that in countries where freedom of thought and speech is guaranteed, the possibilities of analysing fundamental assumptions responsible for the

of Islam improved the condition of women and that women were active participants at various levels of community affairs in the early Islamic community. The practices of the Prophet were distorted, by attributing cultural views of other peoples' views on women, to the Quran and the Prophet.[65] Patriarchal tribal practices, such as the rules on inheritance, and the adoption of the customs of the Byzantines and Persians, like veiling, were read into Islamic law and led to female subjugation.[66] They advocate a return to the Quran and specific parts of the Sunnah, emphasizing the egalitarian principles integral in them, to reform discriminatory laws.[67] These scholars are skeptical of the claims that Muslim interpretations of Islamic law, as found in the Quran, are a barrier to women's equal rights and argue that a return to "true" Islam will lead to justice for women.[68] They are actively claiming the right to interpret not

patriarchal readings of the Islamic tradition which hold women inferior to men, is different than in countries where Islamic traditionalism or fundamentalism is rooted, see *A Border Passage: From Cairo to America - A Woman's Journey* (New York: Penguin Books, 1999), p. 9.

65   Fazlur Rahman asserts that "although women's inferior status has been written into Islamic law, it is by and large the result of prevailing social conditions rather than of the moral teaching of the Quran", see "Status of Women in the Quran" in *Women and Revolution in Iran*, ed. Guity Nashat (Boulder: Westview Press, 1983).

66   Keddie, "The Past and Present of Women in the Muslim World", p. 59. Mernissi finds that through an arguably overwhelming male interpretation of Islamic law since its founding, many now consider Islam and Islamic law as sexist, although Islamic legal texts do not support it. She maintains that at the level of the Quran, Islam is progressive for women and blames the Arabian male elites for inheriting their sexist views from pre-Islamic customs. She asks herself if it is possible "that Islam's message had only a limited and superficial effect on deeply superstitious seven-century Arabs who failed to integrate its novel approaches to the world and women? Is it possible that the hijab, the attempt to veil women, that is claimed today to be a basic Muslim identity, is nothing but the expression of the persistence of the pre-Islamic mentality, the jahiliyyah mentality that Islam was supposed to annihilate?" Mernissi challenges traditional Islamic interpretations of women's rights by criticizing the interpreters of Islam, see *The Veil and the Male Elite: A Feminist Interpretation of Women's Rights in Islam*, trans. Mary Jo Lakeland (Reading: Addison-Wesley, 1991), p. 81.

67   Moussa, *Competing Fundamentalisms and Egyptian Women's Family Rights*, p. 27.

68   Reza Afshari, on the other hand, upholds that "Islamic reformism contends that traditions are layers of societal experiences accumulated under specific circumstances obscuring the true meaning and spirit of Islam. The argument is based on an ideological assumption that there are two types of Islam: the good Islam, as reflected in the lay Muslim's understanding of ethical and egalitarian messages of the Quran, and the bad Islam of Sharia as interpreted by the ulama. That ideological assumption is itself a result of refurbishing a pre-modern paradigm with the trappings of modernity. Thus, the neo-feminist discourse converges with the Islamic reformist's attempt to construct a new Islam outside its historical framework and free from its traditional confines of Sharia. This insertion of feminist consciousness into the mindset of a revealed religion has further embellished

only the Islamic tradition but also its sacred texts, to focus on examining the gap between the Quran and Sunnah, and describe how a conservative society, historically unfavorable to the rights of women, was responsible for putting traditionalist interpretations into practice.[69] The restrictive interpretations discriminatory to women are, historically, the result of men acting as commentators and interpreters of the religious texts as well as legislators, jurists and judges and those in power.[70] According to them, a reinterpretation of the Quran and a critical review of the secondary sources, would renew the position of women in Islam.[71]

---

and mystified the past. The most potentially iconoclastic discourse, secular feminism, is harnessed to the worn-down wheels of Islamic reformism", see "Egalitarian Islam and Misogynist Islamic Tradition: A Critique of the Feminist Interpretation of Islamic History and Heritage", *Critique: Journal of Critical Studies of Iran and Middle East* (1994), pp. 1–2.

69 See, for example, Amina Wadud, *Inside the Gender Jihad: Women's Reform in Islam* (Oxford: Oneworld, 2006); Fatima Mernissi, *Beyond the Veil: Male-Female Dynamics in Modern Muslim Society* (Bloomington: Indiana University Press, 1987); Fatima Mernissi, *Women and Islam: An Historical and Theological Enquiry*, transl. Mary Jo Lakeland (Oxford: Blackwell, 1991); Leila Ahmed, *Women and Gender in Islam: The Historical Roots of a Modern Debate* (New Haven: Yale University Press, 1992); Kecia Ali, *Sexual Ethics and Islam: Feminist Reflections on Qur'an, Hadith, and Jurisprudence* (Oxford: Oneworld, 2006) and Barlas, *"Believing Women" in Islam*. June O'Connor argues that at the heart of what could be described as Islamic feminism lies the process of "rereading, reconceiving and reconstructing traditions". Rereading texts and traditions must entail focusing on the presence and absence of women, their influences, and ways they have been excluded. Reconceiving seeks "the retrieval and recovery of lost sources and suppressed visions". Finally, reconstructing women in Islam is "the reconstruction of the past on the basis of new information and the use of historical imagination with new paradigms for thinking, seeing, understanding and valuing the past, in order to rethink the whole tradition". See "Rereading, Reconceiving and Reconstructing Traditions: Feminism Research in Religion", *Women's Studies* Vol. 17 (1989), pp. 102–104. See also Moussa, *Competing Fundamentalisms and Egyptian Women's Family Rights*, p. 30 and Marie-Aimee Helie-Lucas, "What is your tribe? Women's Struggles and the Construction of Muslimness", in *Religious Fundamentalisms and the Human Rights of Women*, ed. Courtney W. Howland (London: Palgrave Macmillan, 1999), p. 25.

70 See Leila P. Sayeh & Adriaen M. Morse Jr., "Islam and the Treatment of Women: An Incomplete Understanding of Gradualism", *Texas International Law Journal* (1995), p. 321; Aziza al-Hibri, "A Study of Islamic Herstory: or how did we ever get into this mess?" *Women's Studies International Forum* Vol. 5 (1982); John L. Esposito, *Women in Muslim Family Law* (Syracuse: Syracuse University Press, 1982); Rahman, "Status of Women in the Quran"; Ahmed, *Women and Gender in Islam*; Mernissi, *Beyond the Veil* and Haideh Moghissi, *Feminism and Islamic Fundamentalism: The Limits of Postmodern Analysis* (Oxford: Oxford University Press, 1999), p. 126.

71 Moghissi, *Feminism and Islamic Fundamentalism*, p. 126. See also, Ahmed, *Women and Gender in Islam* and Barbara Stowasser, *The Status of Women in Early Islam, in Muslim Women*, ed. Freda Hussain (New York: St. Martin's Press, 1984), p. 38. Amina Wadud

While it is true that women have generally not partaken in the historical interpretations relating to women's issues, and even if they have, it has not been enough, as the juridical deliberations that affect their rights remain unreformed. Without women's participation "in legal-ethical deliberations, women's rights will always depend on a 'representational discourse' conducted by male jurists who, in spite of their good intentions, treat the subject as 'absent' and hence lacking the necessary qualification to determine her rights in a patriarchal society".[72] The establishment of Muslim women's seminars in Iran, whose curriculum in Islamic Shia juridical studies is controlled by male jurists, has achieved negligible progress in making women's representation in matters affecting their rights fair and effective. Until now, an institutional development that includes women's voices in legal and ethical deliberations has been, at most, formal without any substantive result in protecting women from abuse. Thus, advocating some form of female inclusion to protect Muslim women's equal rights is insufficient. "Without a thorough overhaul of the traditional seminary culture, which is dominated by the patriarchal and even Arab tribal values that are part of the religious textual heritage of Muslims, it is impossible to create the necessary awareness among the majority of Muslim women about their basic dignity as human beings. As long as the male-dominated seminary curriculum ignores the sociological and psychological evaluation of a woman's personhood in the context of a family or society, the violation of women's rights in Muslim societies will continue unabated."[73]

---

suggests a "hermeneutics of tawhid" and argues that her approach allows for a fuller reading of the Quran and the conflicting verses concerning women's rights, stressing that "the attitudes towards women at the time and place for revelation helped to shape the particular expressions in the Quran", see *Quran and Women: Rereading the Sacred Text from a Woman's Perspective* (Oxford: Oxford University Press, 1999), p. 95. Asma Barlas employs hermeneutics in challenging the patriarchy of Islamic tradition and argues that "women have a stake in challenging its patriarchal exegesis". See *"Believing Women" in Islam: Unreading Patriarchal Interpretations of the Quran* (Austin: University of Texas Press, 2002), at xi. These scholars reach the conclusion that the Quran allows for a strong reading of gender equality.

72   Sachedina, "Woman, Half-the-Man?", p. 146. Abdulaziz also asks if "the male-dominated religious epistemology [can] provide an authentic voice in the interpretative process connected with the female "other"? How can male jurists undertake to map the subjective experience of the silent "other" of a Muslim society? Without participating, Muslim women stand little chance of overcoming being reduced to the legally silent, morally segregated, and religiously veiled half-the-man", ibid., 159.

73   Abdulaziz Sachedina, *Islam and the Challenge of Human Rights* (Oxford: Oxford University Press, 2009), p. 124.

The doctrine of *naskh*, abrogation, might be a more feasible method of achieving the goal of advancing the rights of women in Islamic law. The doctrine technically allows for the replacement of one verse in the Quran for another, and has historically been a valid method of interpretation in Islamic law.[74] The abrogation of verses was a technique used by the jurists to deal with the inconsistencies in the material sources, to decide which verse to follow. While the verse that was revealed at the later date has been the verse upheld, it has been questioned if this process is final.[75] Some scholars argue that Islamic law should instead be based on the revelations of Mecca, replacing the revelations in Medina. Verses emphasizing equality and justice were revealed in Mecca. The persecution of the Prophet and his allies, which eventually lead to the migration to Medina, brought about verses authorizing the use of force, first as a measure of self-defense, and later for the spreading of Islam and the Muslim state. In some instances, the use of force to compel non-believers to convert or to suffer cruel consequences such as death or enslavement are even acknowledged. By applying the doctrine of abrogation again, verses that abrogated earlier verses could be revoked, and Islamic law would be based on the spiritual aspects of Islam, rather than verses that were revealed based on a historical and situational context of the Muslim society from that time.[76] Even the Quran acknowledges that some readings are better than others: "[those] who give ear to the Word and follow the fairest of it."[77] The verse indicates

---

74 On the difference between ijtihad and naskh it is said that "'reinterpretation' is not the 'replacement' of a legal principle but rather its retention with some modification, if dictated by contemporary conditions". See Mohd Altaf Hussain Ahangar, "Crime and Punishment in a Modern Muslim State: A Pragmatic Approach", *The American Journal of Islamic Social Sciences* Vol. 3, No. 1 (2014), p. 52.

75 Abdullahi Ahmed An-Naim questions why modern Muslims should "be denied the opportunity to rethink the rationale and application of naskh so they can implement verses of the Qur'an which have hitherto been deemed abrogated, thereby opening up new possibilities for developing alternative principles of Islamic public law?" See *Toward an Islamic Reformation* (Syracuse: Syracuse University Press, 1987), p. 59. There have been attempts by modern Muslim scholars to answer these questions; some have attempted to harmonize conflicting verses, whereas others have rejected the doctrine of abrogation completely. See Muhammad Abduh, *Tafsir al-Manar* (Cairo: Dar al-Manar, 1367 Hijri), 2:138ff; Sayyid Ahmad Khan, *Tafsir al-Qur'an* (Lahore, n.d.), pp. 137–140 and Ahmad Hasan, *Early Development of Islamic Jurisprudence* (Islamabad: Islamic Research Institute, 2016), pp. 70–79.

76 An-Naim suggests that this would "produce an authentic and genuine modern Islamic law", see *Toward an Islamic Reformation*, p. 49. See also Mahmoud Mohamed Taha, *Second Message of Islam*, transl. Abdullahi A. An-Naim (Syracuse: Syracuse University Press, 1996), pp. 40–41, 49, 54.

77 Quran 39:18.

that while the Quran can be interpreted in various ways, not all interpretations are necessarily good. The Quran repeatedly assures its believers that God does not love wrongdoing and oppression.[78] Arguably, interpretations that lead to oppression should reasonably not be considered good interpretations that are relevant to uphold.[79]

5 Outline

This book examines the sources of gender differences within the Islamic tradition, with particular focus on the guardianship of women, which constitutes the greatest obstacle for recognizing the legal autonomy of women. The purpose is to identify the basis for the assumed normativity of male authority and hierarchical gender relations and analyze the challenges and opportunities for advancing women's rights in Islamic law. The book examines the historical and legal context for reform, to determine the origins and analyze the development of the guardianship of women in Islamic law. Achieving meaningful reform will require social and political action in addition to a strong legal basis in Islamic law. Still, demonstrating the possibility of strong women's rights within the Quran is imperative. Genuine women's rights reform must occur within the Islamic tradition, as most Muslims will not consider such reforms legitimate without a grounding in Islamic law.

As will be described in this book, the woman as politically passive, barred from the public sphere, secluded and estranged from the society she lives in, is a construction derived from, and legitimized by history and tradition.[80] Gender segregation and confinement to the home, as a general rule, tends to diminish the practical value of Muslim women's theoretical entitlement to certain rights and limit their abilities to realize economic independence as well as educational and other public achievements.[81] The custom of veiling

---

78 See, for example, Quran 4:9; 6:21; 6:45; 6:47 and 23:41.
79 The Quran warns against those who include their own intentions with interpretations and warns against "those who are bent on denying the truth attribute their own lying inventions to God. And most of them never use their reason", and that "there are among them illiterates, who know not the Book, but (see therein their own) desires, and they do nothing but conjecture". See verses 2:78–79.
80 Mernissi, "Women in Muslim History", p. 40.
81 The subject of the veil and gender segregation is complex and has clear cultural variations. See generally Hanna Papanek and Gail Minault, *Separate Worlds: Studies of Purdah in Southeast Asia* (India: Chanakya Publishers, 1982); Rahman, "Status of Women in the Quran", chapter 7 and Mernissi, *Beyond the Veil*.

perpetuated the notion that women are to obey men and are responsible for covering up their body to prevent men from being tempted and not being able to control themselves, and possibly, therefore, harassing them—after all, some of the social occurrences Islam sought to counterbalance were the promiscuous relationships that were part of the pre-Islamic society. To the broad understanding of the qualities of women, such as the traditions describing women as intellectually inferior, and that instead, men should be tolerant of women's defects and not rush to divorce their wives,[82] in the case of marital problems,[83] are the many references to men being "a degree above" women.[84] Primarily, the construction of the guardianship of women is based on the view of women as morally and religiously flawed. Many of the historical commentators of the Quran affirm men's superiority as apparent and obvious: "the superiority of

---

82   According to one tradition, the Prophet said "treat women well! They are created from a curved rib, and the curved part is the best. If you try to straighten it, it will break, but if you leave it, it will remain curved. Treat Women well!" In another version of the same event, it is described that a "woman is like a rib which will snap if one tries to straighten her natural crookedness," see Al-Bukhari, *Sahih*, 3:383, *Kitab al-nikah*, no. 5186. See also, Shaheen Sardar Ali, *Gender and Human Rights in Islamic and International Law* (The Hague: Kluwer Law International, 2000), p. 46.

83   These traditions are also used in excluding women from participating in public life and imposing the veil. As it is argued that women are not able to control their emotions and are not as wise as men are, therefore they should not work outside of the home, take a position of leadership, travel without a male companion and so forth, laying the foundation of patriarchal interpretations of Islamic law, see Khaled El Fadl, *Speaking in God's Name: Islamic Law, Authority and Women* (London: Oneworld, 2014), n. 68 and 74.

84   See the Quran 2:228, 4:34. There are several narrated traditions that describe the deficient mind of women, for example, "O people, women are inferior to men in faith, in wealth and in reason. The proof of their deficiency in faith is that they do not pray nor fast during their menses, the proof of their deficiency in reason is that the testimony of two of them equals that of one man, and the proof of their deficiency in wealth is that their share in inheritance is half of that of men. So keep away from bad women and be careful with the good ones, and do not give in to them when they are good, so that they do not expect you to obey them when they are bad." Quote taken from Mohsen Kadivar, "Revisiting Women's Rights in Islam: 'Egalitarian Justice' in Lieu of 'Desert-based Justice' ", in *Gender and Equality in Muslim Family Law*, p. 213. See also, *Nahj al-Balagha,* ed. Subhi Saleh (Beirut, 1967), Sermon 80, p. 125. Barbara Stowasser argues that "symbolic images of the female's defective nature", the themes of "woman's weakness" and "woman as threat to the male and society" were all integrated into Islamic theologian commentaries and interpretations from Bible-related traditions, see *Women in the Qur'an: Traditions, and Interpretation* (Oxford: Oxford University Press, 1994), pp. 23–25. It is also argued that medieval Islamic society was patriarchal to a far greater degree than had been the early Islamic community in Mecca and Medina, see 'Imad al-Din Khalil, *Ḥawla i'adat kitabat al-tarikh al-Islami* (Qatar: Dar al-Thaqafah, 1986), p. 23.

men to women is nothing hidden to [anyone with] good sense".[85] Although generalizing, most jurists' accounts "of male authority, women's deficiencies, and gendered public space represent a coherent picture of a 'natural' social hierarchy and gender roles",[86] which privilege men and influence the interpretation of the Quran.[87] "While assumptions that misogyny was a universal Islamic norm are clearly erroneous,[88] evidence of entrenched androgyny that at times bordered on misogyny was certainly a part of the general cultural and social ambiance of the religious intellectuals …[89] Indeed, openly androcentric and misogynistic statements were tolerated within public discourse, as evidenced by various Muslim authors' use of demeaning language to describe women and their capabilities."[90] From such a perspective, verses and interpretations that provide a patriarchal family structure, where women are in the hands of men to be controlled and maintained do make sense. In a tradition of patriarchy, where the father is the head of the family, with all the rights and obligations that follow, it is logical to construct and legitimize male guardianship as a necessary means to protect the weaker women and children.[91] The greatest obstacle for the advancement of women's rights is thus the notion that developed historically about their deficient minds, their intellect and men being "a degree above" that justifies most of the misogynist interpretations of the verses of the Quran relevant to the rights of women.

The scope of harmonization between Islamic law and women's rights depends largely upon the type of approach that will be adopted in the interpretation of the Sharia. The textual sources, although conflicting between the

---

85 Muḥammad b. ʿAbd Allah Ibn al-ʿArabī, *Aḥkam Al-Qurʾan*, ed. Muḥammad Bakr Ismaʿil, 4 vols. (Cairo: Dar al-Manar, 2002), 1:230.

86 Karen Bauer, "The Gender Hierarchy and the Question of Women as Judges and Witnesses in Pre-Modern Islamic Law", *The Journal of the American Oriental Society* Vol. 130, No.1 (2010), pp. 1–2.

87 Fadel, "Is Historicism a Viable Strategy for Islamic Legal Reform?", p. 36. Barbara Stowasser argues that Bible-related traditions such as the "symbolic images of the female's defective nature", "woman's weakness" and "woman as threat to the male and society" were all integrated into Islamic theologian commentaries and interpretations. See *Women in the Qurʾan*, pp. 23–25.

88 Mohammad Fadel, "Two Women, One Man: Knowledge, Power and Gender in Medieval Sunni Legal Thought", *International Journal of Middle East Studies* Vol. 29 (1997), p. 196.

89 Suzanne Stetkevych, *Abū Tammam and the Poetics of the ʿAbbasid Age* (New York: Brill, 1991), p. 239; D.A. Spellberg, *Politics, Gender, and the Islamic Past: The Legacy of ʿAʾisha bint Abi Bakr* (New York: Columbia University Press, 1994), pp. 140–149.

90 Fadel, "Is Historicism a Viable Strategy for Islamic Legal Reform?", p. 36.

91 Ziba Mir-Hosseini, *Men in Charge? Rethinking Authority in Muslim Legal Tradition* (London: Oneworld, 2015), p. 88.

egalitarian message of the Quran, do confirm that men excel women, to some extent. However, even if the egalitarian verses in the Quran speak of equality, it speaks of equality in the eyes of God. To argue that the Quran includes equality in the aspects that describe the relationship between men and women is implausible. However, "like many other religious texts, the Quran can be used as a document of equality or a document of repression".[92] My objective is to show a spectrum of views regarding the position of women in Islamic law. It ranges from traditional interpretations to modern or reformist interpretations. I do not try to cover all the points in between. I will argue that a contemporary and pragmatic interpretation of Islamic law on the legal status of women is essential; however, while many modern commentators have focused on hermeneutical approaches to reviewing the material sources of law, I will also describe other methods of Islamic law which can be deployed in the case of women. Many of the issues related to guardianship, or more specifically, the authority men have over their wives, can practically and individually be improved through the strategic use of the marriage contract. No general theory of contracts or explicit definition of a contract exists in Islamic law;[93] instead Islamic contract law is one of particular contracts, where different types are defined in terms of their ends.[94] While each contract had its own distinctive rules, there were plenty of overlaps between the sales-contract model and other forms such as the marriage contract, which obviously poses several problems. Yet, the format of the marriage contract is not in any sense holy, and there are no legal reasons not to review its format. While the Prophet ensured that Islam acknowledged rights for all women, the marriage contract today only really benefits a group of elite women, who are aware of the fact that they can stipulate the conditions of the marriage within the marriage contract, to include terms that are important to them. It is, however, not an opportunity all women have. Instead, many women only focus on giving up their *mahr*, or dower, for the right to initiate divorce. Nevertheless, the marriage contract can be a useful tool for the individual woman to ensure she has the legal rights she wants in a marriage, and if necessary, when dissolving the marriage.

92 Katherine M. Weaver, "Women's Rights and Sharia Law: A Workable Reality? An Examination of Possible International Human Rights Approaches through the Continuing Reform of the Pakistani Hudood Ordinance", *Duke Journal of Comparative and International Law* Vol. 17 (2007), pp. 483, 506.
93 The Quran allows for property to be exchanged through trade and mutual consent, see Quran 4:29. See also 9:71 on fulfilling all contracts and 2:219 and 5:93–94 on the prohibition of *gharar*, speculative uncertainty.
94 Hussein Hassan, "Contracts in Islamic Law: The Principles of Commutative Justice and Liberty," *Journal of Islamic Studies* Vol. 13, No. 3 (2002), pp. 282–283.

Most importantly, commentators have historically focused on successfully advancing legal theories on various issues within the realms of usul al-fiqh, without turning to the re-interpretation of the textual sources.[95] In certain areas, it has led to the complete abandonment of upholding Quranic verses. While Islamic law technically still allows for slavery, several factors have led both Muslim scholars and Muslim states to completely reject the practice. The modern abandonment of the institution of slavery within the Islamic tradition, is not confirmed by the sources of law. Instead, Muslims have, from a moral perspective, assumed that slavery is not in adherence with the will of God. Very few Muslims would maintain the position of the institution today. While ijtihad was part of the techniques to rationalize and explain why slavery was no longer compatible with the norms of society, it was not the reason for abandoning the practice. The moral aspects of Islam were in this aspect greater than the legal justifications for it, as can be found in the material sources of Islamic law. If verses from the Quran are no longer applicable, what is there to say that the same approach cannot be employed with the verse that stipulates that men are the managers of the affairs of women?

95 Fadel, "Is Historicism a Viable Strategy for Islamic Legal Reform?", p. 36.

CHAPTER 2

Foundations of Islamic Law

> [Legal schools have produced] a body of legal texts that are arguably superior in evidence, detail, range, and in sheer usefulness to virtually any recent attempt to present Islam as a unified system of human life.[1]

∴

Like any system of law, Islamic law is the product of its sources and methods. The construction of the sources of law and what have been accepted as sources of law, as well as the methods used to justify interpretations, need an in-depth examination to understand how the legal position of women is constructed.

The theory and practice of Islamic law is complex and a series of diverse positions must be considered. There are several versions of the Sharia, largely stemming from the Sunni and Shia split; and within these two factions there are different schools of law applicable to respective populations. While all the schools generally recognize the Quran and the Sunnah—the sayings and teachings of the Prophet—as the primary sources of Islamic law, their differences lie in their different interpretation of verses in the Quran and Sunnah, reflecting the sympathy to different cultures within which the schools thrived.[2] Sunni means, "People of Tradition and Community" and reflects the particular importance that the Sunni believers attach to the Sunnah. They revere the first four "rightly guided" caliphs, who were Companions of the Prophet, and as the immediate successors of him, accordingly the rightful leaders of Islam.[3] "Rightly guided" indicates that these men governed by the principles

---

1 Statement by the contemporary American scholar Shaykh Nuh Ha Mim Keller (who is Shafi'i), see Ibn al-Naqib, *Reliance of the Traveller*, trans. Nuh ha Mim Keller (Beltsville, MD: Amana Publications, 1999), pp. vii–viii.
2 See generally, Bello Daura, "A Brief Account of the Development of the Four Sunni Schools of Law and Some Recent Developments", *Journal of Islamic and Comparative Law* Vol. 2 (1968), p. 1.
3 These four caliphs were Abu Bakr (r. 632–634), Umar ibn al-Khattab (r. 634–644), Uthman ibn Affan (r. 644–656) and Ali ibn Abi Talib (r. 656–661).

established by Muhammad. The Sunni population composes a vast majority of the Muslim population and has four so-called *mahdhabs*, schools, namely Hanafi, Maliki, Shafi'i and Hanbali.[4] The founders of the schools Abu Hanifa (d 767/150), Malak ibn Anas (d 795/179), Muhammad ibn Idris al-Shafi'i (d 820/204) and Ahmad Hanbal (d 855/241) codified Sharia and established legal principles by their understanding of Islam.[5]

Historically, Sunnis have regarded Shiites as second-class citizens since the split originated in the first Islamic civil war in 661.[6] There are Sunni-Shia differences in areas such as the prayer ritual, inheritance laws, marriage ceremonies, and in the use of ijtihad. The Shia alternative of Islam distinguishes itself on certain fundamental theological questions, as it retains some of the philosophical, reflective and even mystical elements of medieval Islam. It is divided into three branches: the Ja'fari or Twelvers, Isma'ili and Zaidi. The Shia believers maintain that Muhammad wanted his only male blood relative, Ali ibn Abi Talib, the fourth caliph for the Sunnis, to be his successor. They revere him as the First Imam, leader of the community, and believe that all other imams are the direct male descendants of Ali and his wife Fatimah, Muhammad's daughter. Furthermore, the Shia consider the Twelfth Imam, also referred to as the Hidden Imam, to have been divinely inspired. Muhammad ibn al-Hasan al-Mahdi is believed to have been hidden from view by God in 878 and Shiites are still awaiting his return.[7]

---

4   Derived from the Arabic word *dhahabal yadhhabu*, which literally means "went" or "to go", *mahdab* generally means that which is followed and more specifically, the opinion or idea one chooses to adopt. Nearly 500 schools of legal reasoning developed in the early years, but only a few survived to current times. The four Sunni schools are the Hanafi School (Turkey, Syria, Lebanon, Jordan, India, Pakistan, Afghanistan, Iraq and Libya), the Maliki School (North Africa, West Africa and Kuwait), the Shafi'i School (Southern Egypt, Southern Arabia, East Africa, Indonesia and Malaysia) and the Hanbali School (Saudi Arabia and Qatar). The major Shia Schools are the Ja'fari or Twelvers (Iran and Southern Iraq), the Zaydi (Yemen), the Isma'ili (India) and the Ibadi (Oman and parts of North Africa).
5   Javaid, "The Sharia, Islamic Family Laws and International Human Rights Law", p. 112.
6   Even though numerous historical minorities have disagreed with the Sunni majority, for example, the Mu'tazila and Kharijites, the only major minority which has survived are the Shia, see Joseph Schacht, *Origins of Muhammadan Jurisprudence* (Oxford: Clarendon Press, 1976), pp. 40–44, 128, 258–259, 260–261.
7   *Mahdi* literally means the "divinely guided one" or "messiah", see Montgomery Watt, *Islamic Philosophy and Theology* (Edinburgh: Edinburgh University Press, 1962), pp. 20–26, 50–56, 99–104. The imam "is the mysterious logical and spiritual principle which binds the whole universe together and, therefore, the final authority in both law and religion". The Imam is seen as the "living entity of the infallible divine law", with the non-transmittable authority of interpreting the will of God. Under this theory, only Imam Mahdi can reform (and interpret) Shiite Islamic law, see Asaf A. A. Fyzee, Shi'i Legal Theories, in *Law in the Middle East*, eds., Majid Khadduri and Herbert J. Liebesny (Washington DC: The Middle East Institute,

In essence, all of the schools of law have a myriad of positions to justify their legal position on various issues. The certainty of the law-finding methods is weak, since scholars within same schools of law, utilizing the same method to interpret the material sources to construct the law, have reached different conclusions. Consequently, Islamic law does not have a unanimous standpoint with regard to many issues, and the sources of law include many contradictions.[8] Thus, the debate about the correct interpretation of Islamic law is not new; it has always been part of the Islamic tradition and can generally be divided into the two incompatible views of traditionalists and reformists. At the center of the debate is whether Islamic law should be based on reason or tradition. For most classical interpretations of Islamic law as well as contemporary traditionalist thinkers, doctrine and law are absolute and immutable. For them, the application of classical Islamic law is the application of God's legislation. To the extent that Islamic law embodies women's equal rights, it will be said by traditionalists that such law is not compatible with the literal wording of the Quran. Reformists on the other hand, rely on the context of the revelations, and allow for interpretations to be based on developments in society. Basically, any significant change in the conditions of society would allow for a change in the law. Even from the beginning, Muslims interpreted the eternal wordings of the Quran in light of specific socio-economic and political situations, validating the reformist standpoint.[9] Nevertheless, traditional scholarship is inclined to maintain the view that Sharia is immutable and not subject to change, even when the socio-political circumstances for a ruling have changed or if the context of revelation is culturally specific. Advancing

---

1955), p. 115; Majid Khadduri, "Nature and Sources of Islamic Law", *George Washington Law Review* Vol. 3, No. 22 (1953–1954), p. 23; Joseph Eliash, "Ithna 'ashari Shi'i Juristic Theory of Political and Legal Authority", *Studia Islamica* Vol. 29 (1969), p. 27 and Noel J. Coulson, *History of Islamic Law* (Edinburgh: Edinburgh University Press, 1964), pp. 106–108.

8 To control the vast interpretations, the established schools compiled both aspects of worship (*ibadat*) and inter-human relations (*mu'amalat*) to legal treaties, which became accepted as established material sources of Islamic law. Islamic law is generally divided into three subjects; *ibadat*, which entails worship issues and relates to the relationship between God and man, such as the rules for praying, fasting and hajj pilgrimage; *muamilat*, transactions, concerned with legal acts between individuals such as marriage, divorce, custody and inheritance; and finally, *siyasat*, literally meaning politics, addressing issues related to inter-state and state-individual relations, like laws of war and penal law. See Kamran Hashemi, *Religious Legal Traditions, International Human Rights and Muslim States* (Leiden: Martinus Nijhoff, 2008), p. 8.

9 Barbara Stowasser, "Gender Issues and Contemporary Quran Interpretation", in *Islam, Gender and Social Change,* eds., Yvonne Yazbeck Haddad & John L. Esposito (Oxford: Oxford University Press, 1998), p. 30.

the rights of women in Islamic law, calls for the examination and evaluation of the structure of a legal theory and reasoning that regulates and justifies interpretations, which to some extent, is considered divine and undisputable.[10] Thus, this chapter will evaluate the "superiority" of legal texts produced and the quality of the supporting evidence used by the different schools to reach a specific standpoint on the status of women.

The struggle, between which interpretation of Islamic law women should be reviewed against, can also be seen in the different constitutions and legislation in Muslim countries. In the majority of nation-states, the definition of personal status is vague, and many legislative provisions related to personal status are left to classical Sharia texts. Personal Status, *Al-Ahwaal Ash-Shakhsiya*, is a recent legal term; it is non-existent in classical Islamic jurisprudence and unknown to classical Islamic jurists.[11] A majority of modern Arab Islamic states still have no legislative representation on personal status.[12] While Saudi Arabia and Iran have legally implemented the notion of the male guardian in their legislation, Tunisia's new constitution, view women and men alike. Not surprisingly, this has led to criticism from the Islamic world claiming that the Tunisian path is "un-Islamic".

At the same time, it is argued that "whatever consensus existed in the pre-modern era about Islamic legal authority has collapsed. Muslims in every country today are contesting basic questions of Islamic law—questions of Islamic authority, questions of interpretive method, and questions about what types of law a state can legitimately enact without violating the fundamental principles of Sharia".[13] Countries that have constitutions with the requirement that

---

10   Scott C. Lucas, Justifying Gender Inequalities in the Shafi'i Law School: Two Case Studies of Muslim Legal Reasoning, *Journal of the American Oriental Society* Vol. 129, No. 2 (2009), p. 258.
11   Nasir, *The Islamic Law of Personal Status*, p. 34. The term was first used in Egypt in 1890s, however, its first definition was given in a ruling from the Egyptian Court of Cassation in 1934: "personal status is the sum total of the physical or family descriptions of a known person which distinguish him from the others, and gives legal effects under the law in his social life, such as being male or female, married, widowed or divorced, a parent or a legitimate child being of full capacity or defective capacity due to minority, imbecility or insanity, being of absolute or limited legal capacity. As for matters related to property, they are all by nature real status questions. But the Egyptian legislator, finding that *waqf*, gift and will, all being contracts without consideration, are based on the religious concept of charity, and includes them in the personal status issued ...", see Civil Cassation on 21/6/1934, Appeal No. 40J. Year 3, Published in Al Muhamat, year 13, p. 87.
12   Sharia Law in accordance to traditional legal manuals is still applied in most Arab Gulf States, Saudi Arabia, Yemen, Libya and Sudan. See Nasir, *The Islamic Law of Personal Status*, p. 35.
13   Lombardi, *Designing Islamic constitutions*, p. 644.

legislation should be in compliance with Sharia, struggle to determine "what institution should be entrusted with the power to develop an official interpretation for the state and impose it".[14] However, it would be oversimplifying matters not to consider the multiple factors causing unequal gender relationships or belief that the legal status of women in Muslim societies is solely based on historical readings of the Quran. Quranic verses validating the creation and reinforcement of hierarchies within the Islamic tradition are the verses entitling men to be the maintainers of women in conjunction with the testimony of women, verses permitting polygyny, the right for men to terminate the marriage and so forth. These verses are few, and the position of women in Islam appears to be determined solely on rules derived from a literal, but also contextual, reading of these few verses. Reviewing the interpretations of the sources of Islamic law that have found men to be the maintainers of women will not put an end to patriarchal practices. It will, however, provide the basis for questioning its legitimacy from within the Islamic tradition.[15] The secluded and estranged woman, barred from the public sphere and politically passive, is a construction derived from and legitimized by history and tradition.[16] The traditionalist version of Islam portrays women as having a strong sexual power over men, which needs to be concealed and constricted and institutions such as gender segregation and polygyny are perceived as strategies to constrain women's sexual powers.[17] However, such a view of women contradicts many of the verses in the Quran, or how society was constructed during the lifetime of the Prophet, and most importantly, completely disregards the fundamental principle of justice in Islam.

---

14 Ibid.
15 Barlas, *"Believing Women" In Islam*, p. 3.
16 Mernissi, "Women in Muslim History", p. 40.
17 Generally, segregation is based on the concept of ʿawra, meaning indecent to expose. In the Quran (24:57) it also refers to times of the day, where it is improper for an adult child to be in her parents' bedroom. Orthodox jurists regard a woman's body, including her face as ʿawra and there are disputed hadiths asserting that the Prophet and some of his Companions regarded even a woman's voice as ʿawra. Such an interpretation of ʿawra advocates a position in which a woman is not only segregated and veiled, but also legally silenced. The issue of whether or not a women's voice is part of ʿawra has been debated amongst jurists. See, for example, Mohammad al-Ghazali, who rejects the notion that a women's voice is part of ʿawra in *Qadaya al-marʾa bayna al-taqlid al-rakida wa al-wafida* (Cairo: Dar al-Shuruq, 1992), pp. 164–165. See Sachedina, *Islam and the Challenge of Human Rights*, p. 124. This restrictive view has been challenged by scholars, arguing that the Quran does not advocate the veil or segregation, instead it focuses on sexual modesty, see Rahman, "Status of Women in the Quran", p. 40 and Mernissi, *Beyond the Veil*, p. 16.

1   Immutable Law?

Islamic law is considerably different from other forms of law,[18] and is far from being coherent; the subject-matter from which it was created varied from place to place and the geographical differences account for much of the deviations between the ancient schools of law.[19] As described, there can be numerous different juristic opinions on the same legal matter, even in the same time and place, within the same Sunni and Shia schools of law. We know that influences from culture and tradition have tended to be rather strong in constructing the law, which is not exclusive to the Islamic tradition. The history of every state in the world shows that women have been, and still are, subject to various discriminatory legislations. The debate about the mutability or immutability of the revealed verses in the Quran is triggering the questioning of the relevance of inherited traditions and its negative impact on efforts to advance the rights of women within the Islamic tradition. Despite what traditionalists often defend, Islamic law is not wholly divine or immutable. This usually arises from not separating the terms Sharia, the source from which the law is derived, and *fiqh*, Islamic jurisprudence.[20]

1.1   *Sharia*

To Muslims, Sharia encompasses all aspects of life and includes detailed ritualistic observance as well as moral, ethical, and spiritual aspirations.[21] Its religiously based prescriptions actually have little in common with the practical legal needs of everyday life. Muslims are obliged to respect and follow the Sharia, as it represents the will of God. The term "Sharia", as such, appears only once in the Quran: "Then We set thee upon an open way (Sharia) of the Command; therefore follow it."[22] The term means "a

---

18   Islamic law is even sensibly different from the other two forms of sacred law: Jewish law and Canon law. Both Jewish law and Canon law are more uniform than Islamic law. See Stephen Vago, *Law and Society* (New Jersey: Pearson, Prentice Hall, 2006), pp. 17–18.

19   Schacht, *An Introduction to Islamic Law*, p. 4.

20   In the Quran (45:18) the word *Sharia* is used as "straight path" or "right path"; "Then We put you on a right way (*Sharia*) of the affairs, so follow it ..." and the Prophet Mohammed used *fiqh* in one of his sayings to mean "understanding": "To whomsoever God wished good, He gives the understanding (*fiqh*) of the faith". *Fiqh* is also use in the Quran to mean understanding, see Quran 9:87.

21   S. G. Vesey-Fitzgerald, "Nature and Sources of the Shari'a", in *Law in the Middle East*, eds., Majid Khadduri and Herbert J. Liebesny, (Washington DC: Middle East Institute, 1955), p. 85. See also, Fazlur Rahman, *Islam* (Chicago: Chicago University Press, 1979), pp. 101–109.

22   Quran 45:18.

path to be followed" and signifies not legal norms but the route or the way.[23]

A majority of Muslims believe Sharia is divine and to suggest that the Sharia is in any part inadequate could be regarded as heresy.[24] It is a widespread misconception however, that Islamic law is a divine, absolute law, which typically occurs when the terms Sharia and fiqh are understood to be corresponding with each other.[25] Fiqh, literally meaning "understanding", can be described as a "collection of juridical opinions"[26] or an "interpretative law"[27] and is the human interpretation of Sharia; the method by which the law is derived and applied covering the legal aspects of the Sharia.[28] In a strict legal sense, Sharia

---

[23] The verb *shari'a* in the Arabic language signifies to go to water, and the names *shi'ra* and *shari'a* mean either to give a drink or the road or the slope leading down to the water. It can also be found as three other terms from the same root, 42:13; 5:48; 42:21. Some modern scholars argue that the word "*sharia*" did not originate with the Muslims. More likely, it had already become common in Arabic speaking Jewish and Christian communities. For example, an early tenth century translation of the Old Testament to Arabic uses sharia to translate the Hebrew word *torah,* meaning a significant set of rules, while a Christian trait directed against the Jews in the tenth century used sharia to refer to a system of laws brought by a prophet. See Norman Calder and M. B. Hooker, *Sharia. Encyclopaedia of Islam* (Leiden: Brill, 2003), p. 1.

[24] In some Muslim countries, for example Sudan, heresy, or apostasy, is a crime punishable by the death penalty..

[25] While the Quran is divine and not subject to amendment, individual hadiths are generally neither divine nor infallible, and even further away from a divine origin are ijma and qiyas. Nevertheless, the tendency to exaggerate the divine aspect of these secondary sources is quite imbedded: "the Quran is the primary source of law. The three other sources, i.e., the Sunnah, ijma and qiyas have been stamped with the revelatory character. ... Qiyas derives its value from these sources; hence it is indirectly infallible". It is through ijma that the sanctity of Islamic laws and codes has been established, including those based on qiyas. See Hasan, *The Doctrine of Ijma,* p. 2; Farooq, "Analogical Reasoning (Qiyas)", pp. 154–244. Musa Usman Abubakar argues along similar lines: "opinions of Islamic jurists, particularly the four Sunni eponyms, have been glorified and sanctified as infallible to the extent that adherents of various schools of thought are ready to defend the position of their respective Imams no matter how implausible it is. Anybody who differs from the opinion is often considered heretic for simply holding a dissent[ing] opinion", *Gender Justice in Islamic Law*, p. 11.

[26] Jasser Auda, *Maqasid al-Shari'ah as Philosophy of Islamic Law: A Systems Approach* (London: The International Institute of Islamic Thought London, 2008), p. xxiii.

[27] Ali Khan, "The Reopening of the Islamic Code: The Second Era of Ijtihad", *University of St Thomas Law Journal* Vol. 1, No. 1 (2003), p. 352.

[28] See Said Ramadan, *Islamic Law: Its Scope and Equity* (London: Macmillan, 1970), p. 36, Abu Ameena Bilal Philips, *The Evolution of Fiqh: Islamic Law and the Madh-dabs* (Riyadh: International Islamic Publishing House, 1988), pp. 1–4, and Mashood A. Baderin, *International Human Rights and Islamic Law* (Oxford: Oxford University Press, 2005), p. 34.

differs from fiqh as it is the corpus of the revealed law as contained in the Quran and the authentic traditions of the Prophet Muhammad, Sunnah. Sharia refers to the primary sources of the law, which are divine, or semi-divine as regards the Sunnah, and final; covering the moral, legal, social and spiritual aspects of a Muslim's life. Fiqh is the science of Islamic jurisprudence, deriving both its *raison d'être* and substantive form from the primary sources of Islam, the Quran and the Sunnah. In principle, Sharia and its sources can neither be abrogated nor subjected to the limitations of time and circumstance.[29] Its interpretation, fiqh, however, may change according to time and circumstances.[30]

While the dichotomy between theory and practice has varied over time, it is generally recognized that it was strongest during the earliest stage of the Medina state. The state is viewed as the political expression of religion, though it was never supported by an organized power, it never had a "Church"; instead, there was and still is a conflict between the sacred law and the reality of actual practice. For the Umayyads, the office of the *qadi* (magistrate or judge of a Sharia court), gained increasing importance and prestige, instead of the strict observance of Sharia.[31] The Abbasids, on the other hand, challenged the rule of the Umayyads, legitimizing the effort on the assertion to have a greater commitment to the implementation of the Sharia.[32] The Sharia courts never accomplished the position of supreme judicial authority independent of political control.[33] Subsequently, there has been an unceasing fluctuation between greater and lesser compliance with Sharia in practice.[34] This led to a system where the jurists, concerned with the relationship between the individual and God, formulated standards of private law, rather than public law.[35] This is also

---

[29] Mohammad H. Kamali, *Principles of Islamic Jurisprudence* (Cambridge: Islamic Texts Society, 2003), pp. 7–8.

[30] See Said Ramadan, *Islamic Law: Its Scope and Equity* (London: Macmillan, 1970), p. 36 and Baderin, *International Human Rights and Islamic Law*, p. 34. Al-Sam'ani, eleventh century scholar, also argued that fiqh is subject to change "of circumstances and conditions of men, without an end or interruption", cited by George Makdisi, *Religion, Law and Learning in Classical Islam* (Aldershot: Ashgate, 1991), p. 35. See also, Wael B. Hallaq., *Law and Legal Theory in Classical and Medieval Islam* (Aldershot: Ashgate, 1994), p. 197.

[31] For an overview of the Umayyads, see Patricia Crone, *Medieval Political Thought* (Edinburgh: Edinburgh University Press, 2005), chapter 3.

[32] For an overview of the Abbasids, see Crone, *Medieval Political Thought*, chapter 8.

[33] Coulson, *History of Islamic Law*, p. 121.

[34] Bryant W. Seaman, "Islamic Law and Modern Government: Saudi Arabia Supplements the Shari'a to Regulate Development", *Columbia Journal of Transnational Law* Vol. 18, No. 3 (1980), pp. 424 ff.

[35] Coulson, *History of Islamic Law*, p. 120.

the reason why the formulation of Sharia principles is rather more of a moral character than something that constitutes legal rights.

Essentially, it can be said that the greatest weakness of Sharia is that it is a jurist's interpretative law. It has never been statute law, evolved from national legal traditions. Its religiously based prescriptions have little in common with the practical legal needs of everyday life. Muhammad himself was more interested in founding a new religion than establishing a comprehensive legal system.[36]

1.2   *Fiqh and Usul al-fiqh*

The rules of fiqh are derived from the Quran and Sunnah in compliance with a body of principles and methods which are collectively known as usul al-fiqh.[37] Fiqh, as such, is the end product of usul al-fiqh; and yet the two are separate disciplines. While fiqh is concerned with the knowledge of the detailed rules of Islamic law, usul al-fiqh are the methods that are applied in the deduction of such rules from their sources. Essentially, usul al-fiqh is concerned with the sources of Islamic law, their order of priority, and the methods by which legal rules may be deduced from the sources of the Sharia. Usul al-fiqh refers mainly to methods of reasoning and the rules of interpretation and deduction and is also concerned with regulating the exercise of ijtihad.

The need for the methodology of usul al-fiqh did not arise until the second Islamic century. When the Prophet was alive, his rulings were the source of the necessary guidance to problems that arose. Similarly, in the period after the Prophet's death, the Companion's decisions were mainly inspired by the teachings of the Prophet. It was with the territorial expansion, that the possibility of confusion and error in the interpretation of textual sources when unqualified persons attempted to carry out ijtihad became more apparent, and the need for the methodology of usul al-fiqh was recognized.[38] As an instrument of legal construction and ijtihad, usul al-fiqh allows for further adaptation and refinement in order to meet the changing needs in society that develop over time.[39] Historically, this gave Islamic law flexibility and adaptability within

---

36   Janin Hunt and Andre Kahlmeyer, *Islamic Law. The Sharia from Muhammad's Time to the Present* (Jefferson: McFarland & Company, Inc. Publishers, 2007), p. 31.
37   Mohammad H. Kamali, defines *usul al-fiqh* as "the science of the sources and methodology of the law", see *Principles of Islamic Jurisprudence*, p. 2.
38   Ibid., 5.
39   Ibid., 2. See also, An-Naim, *Towards an Islamic Reformation*, p. 291, who argues that Sharia is derived from human interpretation "reflecting what fallible human beings are able to comprehend and seek to comply with given the limitations of their own specific historical context".

different societies and the ability to develop over time, by opting for opinions more suitable for particular circumstances, and when necessary, creating new opinions.[40]

2 Sources of Islamic Law

Classical Islamic law recognizes four principal sources: the Quran, Sunnah, scholarly consensus, *ijma*, and various forms of legal reasoning, by analogy known as *qiyas* or independent reasoning, ijtihad.[41] Of these four sources of law, consensus and legal analogy are derivative sources; the function of consensus is to sanction rulings, and through legal analogy, rulings in the Quran and Sunnah are extended to new situations.[42] Ijma and qiyas are not expressly mentioned in the material sources of Islamic law; but are the product of an expressly sanctioned source—the ijtihad of the founding scholars of Islam.[43]

The essence of interpreting these sources fall within categories of what acts are regarded permissible, obligatory,[44] recommended,[45] neutral or indifferent,[46] disapproved[47] or prohibited.[48] Engaging in prohibited activities or

---

40   Wael B. Hallaq, *An Introduction to Islamic Law* (Cambridge: Cambridge University Press, 2009), p. 27.
41   The schools of law differ on the number of sources that can be used or emphasized, although they all agree that the Quran and the Sunnah constitute the two primary sources of Islamic law, see Abdul Hamid Abu Sulayman, *The Islamic Theory of International Relations: New Directions for Islamic Methodology and Thought* (Herndon VA: International Institute of Islamic Thought, 1987), p. 2. The Shia emphasize the human intellect and reason. A. Ezzati argues that "the position given to reason as a source of law is obviously correct because not even the Qur'an and Sunnah can be proven without use of the intellect; it is only once the intellect establishes their authority that they may be understood and interpreted by the human intellect", see "Islamic Law and the Challenges of Modern Time", *Journal of Shi'a Islamic Studies* Vol. 3, No. 1 (2010), pp. 51–52. References to the human intellect can be found in the following verses in the Quran; 47:24, 16:43, 9:122, 4:59, 29:69.
42   Opwis, "Maslaha in Contemporary Islamic Legal Theory", p. 190.
43   Hasan, *Early Development of Islamic Jurisprudence*, p. 40.
44   Acts that fall within this category are considered *wajib,* such as prayer and payment of pecuniary debts.
45   Acts that fall within this category are considered *mandub,* such as helping the poor.
46   Acts that fall within this category are considered *mubah,* such as consuming particular lawful foods.
47   Acts that fall within this category are considered *makruh,* such as unilateral divorce by the husband.
48   Acts that fall within this category are considered *haram,* such as breach of contract and theft.

failing to abide by the obligatory activities, will lead to punishment, whereas non-compliance to the other norms does not involve reprimand. A jurist must first of all decide to which of the legal norms a word in the Quran or Sunnah that has an imperative or prohibitive form belongs.[49] Generally, unless specifically prohibited, the default view in the Quran is permissibility.[50] In addition, the fundamental features of Islam, such as conceptions of justice, fairness, being good to others, compassion and moderation are emphasized in all matters concerning human conduct in the Quran.[51] These aspects, however, seem not to have been utilized when deriving laws concerning women from the sources.

2.1   *The Quran*

The Quran forms the foundation of Islamic law and is divine. Muslims regard it as the exact, uncorrupted words of God transmitted to human beings by the archangel Gabriel to the Prophet Muhammad, over a period of 23 years and in two phases, generally described as the Meccan and Medinan verses.[52] The verses in Mecca are more prophetic and ideological in nature and were revealed before the migration to Medina. The verses proclaimed in Medina focus on the establishment and survival of the Islamic community.[53]

The Quran calls for the raising of righteous and pious people who will participate in the struggle against injustices. Yet, the Quran "is not and does not profess to be a code of law or even a law book, nor Muhammad a lawgiver in any Western sense"[54] and it can even be questioned whether God has a legislative function,[55]

---

49   Wael B. Hallaq, *Law and Legal Theory in Classical and Medieval Islam* (Aldershot: Ashgate, 1994), p. 20.
50   Yusuf al-Qaradawi, "The Lawful and the Prohibited in Islam", undated, available online at: http://www.usislam.org/pdf/Lawful&Prohibited.pdf (accessed 6 September 2019), pp. 14–15.
51   Mohammad Hashim Kamali, "Islamic Family Law Reform: Problems and Prospects", *Islam and Civilizational Renewal* Vol. 3, No. 1 (2011), p. 39.
52   That the Quran is divine speech is proclaimed by the Quran itself, for example, see 9:6. The scripture came to be called the Quran, or recitation, as most of the believers, like Muhammad, were illiterate, and would listen to its teachings by public "readings". The verses of the Quran were revealed to the Prophet over a duration of 23 years, see Karen Armstrong, *Islam: A Short History* (New York: Random House, 2002), pp. 4, 14.
53   Abu Ameena Bilal Phillips, *The Evolution of Fiqh (Islamic Law and Madh-habs)* (Riyadh: International Islamic Publishing House, 2005), pp. 29–31.
54   Vesey-Fitzgerald, "Nature and Sources of the Sharia", p. 87.
55   Muhammad Mujtahed Shabestari, *Hermeneutic, the Scripture and the Tradition* (Tehran: Tarh-e No Publisher, 2000), p. 114.

FOUNDATIONS OF ISLAMIC LAW   35

as God describes it as a book of guidance.[56] Out of over 6,000 verses, it is estimated that merely around 350 to 500 verses contain legal elements.[57] Others argue that "no more than approximately eighty verses deal with legal topics in the strict sense of the term".[58] It is questionable if the legal injunctions in the verses fall within the obligatory or permissive categories, or if they are subject to a private or public sanction, as very few verses stipulate criminal sanctions.[59] Instead, the overwhelming majority of the verses in the Quran are of a moral character where the relationship between the believer and God is regulated.[60] As described, Muhammad was more interested in founding a new religion than to establish a comprehensive legal system. He did not establish the different schools of law, or prescribe the sources of law or methods of interpretation. Even the authoritative scriptural version of the Quran itself, was produced after the death of Muhammad.[61] The editing process of the Quran has been the object of disagreement among scholars, but by most accounts, it was finished, or almost completed, during the reign of the third caliph 'Uthman, although later dates have been suggested.[62] The integrity of the Quran has been the cause for debate and cause for accusations between Sunni and Shia in the early Islamic community. Shi'ites have been accused of rejecting the present version of the Quran, because of supposed manipulations carried out under the third caliph 'Uthman. There were, and still are, Sunni accusations against Shi'ites of having produced additions to the Quran, to promote the rights of the fourth caliph, Ali, for the leadership of the Islamic community.[63]

---

56   See e.g. Q2:2 which says: "That is the Book, wherein is no doubt, a guidance to the god-fearing."
57   Mohammad H. Kamali, "Law and Society. The Interplay of Revelation and Reason in the Shariah" in *The Oxford History of Islam*, ed. John L. Esposito (Oxford: Oxford University Press, 1999), pp. 19–20 and p. 41.
58   Coulson, *A History of Islamic Law*, p. 12.
59   Javaid Rehman, "The Sharia, Islamic Family Laws and International Human Rights Law: Examining the Theory and Practice of Polygamy and Talaq", *International Journal of Law, Policy and the Family* No. 21 (2007), p. 110. See also, David Pearl and Paul Menski, *Muslim Family Law* (London: Sweet and Maxwell, 1998), p. 3.
60   Coulson, *A History of Islamic Law*, p. 12.
61   Hunt and Kahlmeyer, *Islamic Law*, p. 16.
62   Albert Hourani, *A History of the Arab Peoples* (London: Faber and Faber, 1991), pp. 20–21. Others argue that the Quran was documented by caliph Ali and the Shia, see Vago, *Law and Society*, p. 110.
63   Muhammad Ismail Marcinkowski, "Some Reflections on Alleged Twelver Shi'ite Attitudes Toward the Integrity of the Qur'an", *The Muslim World* Vol. 91 (2001), pp. 137–153. Several reports validate both sides of the debate regarding the integrity of the Quran, and it is argued that the Quran itself addresses parts of these allegations, see Quran

2.1.1 Authoritative Interpretations

Even from the beginning, Muslims have interpreted the Quran in light of specific socio-economic and political situations. *Tafsir*, or exegesis, is an important Islamic science of delivering interpretations or commentary on the Quran, and can be broadly divided into two methodological approaches: interpretation by traditions, and interpretation by personal opinions.[64] The Quran has, as such, been the subject of various human interpretations,[65] which have been far from coherent but have shaped and become Islamic law. Legal pluralism was, and is, a part of the Islamic legal system; the question was rather, how to decide which is the most authoritative opinion. The science of *tarjih,* is a methodological approach, developed to assess dissenting legal opinions through a systematic examination of their sources, modes of transmission, and reasoning. However, it failed to achieve its intended purpose—to reach agreement on authoritative opinions in most cases.[66] The differences are instead considered as different manifestations of the same divine will and described as "diversity within unity".[67] The appreciation of the differences is an important principle of Islamic law, and as of today, there remains no will to find unity in Islamic law, since, "the blessing of the Muslim community lies in the jurists' differences of opinion".[68] This generally indicates that the jurists' differences of opinion in the interpretation of legal sources on certain matters offer a broad and equally legal scope from which judges may appropriately choose from time to time in cases before them. On this basis, the doctrine of *takhayyur* or *takhyir,* eclectic choice, evolved, and advocated to allow for movement within the different schools of Islamic law. The doctrine allows for the opportunity to provide more reasonable and just solutions in situations where the insistence on applying

---

9:15. See also, John Burton, *The Sources of Islamic Law: Islamic theories of abrogation* (Edinburgh: Edinburgh University Press, 2007), pp. 53–55.

64   Stowasser, "Gender Issues and Contemporary Quran Interpretation", pp. 30, 32.

65   Another method of interpretation used to understand the Quran is ta'wil. While tafsir "places the meaning of the Quran in historical context, using grammar, the *ahadith,* plain meaning, logic and reason", ta'wil focuses on the allegorical and poetic parts, to understand the unknown or hidden aspects of the Quran. It is by this method that Sufists read the Quran. See L. Ali Khan and Hisham M. Ramadan, *Contemporary Ijtihad: Limits and Controversies* (Edinburgh: Edinburgh University Press, Edinburgh, 2011), p. 20.

66   Wael B. Hallaq, *Authority, Continuity, and Change in Islamic Law* (Cambridge: Cambridge University Press, 2001), chapter 5.

67   Bert Breiner, "A Christian View of Human Rights in Islam" in *Two papers on Shari'ah,* ed. Bert Breiner (Birmingham: Centre of Islam & Christian Relations, 1992) p. 3.

68   The maxim says: *"Rahman al-Ummah fi Iktilâf al-A'immah".* See e.g. Coulson, *History of Islamic Law,* pp. 20–39.

principles from a specific school of law would lead to injustice.[69] In particular, with regard to Islamic family laws, this doctrine could prove to be a practical method of incorporating more equalitarian and fair interpretations of different schools of law for the advancement of the rights of women.[70]

2.1.2 Dealing with Contradictions

The Quran itself was the product of discussion, argument, acceptance, and denunciation, of both pre-Islamic norms, and with its previous assessments and claims, as it consists of quite a few contradictions.[71] While the Quran claims that it has no contradictions,[72] it has been acknowledged by the jurists to include apparent contradictions. To determine which of these textual contradictions should be followed, the doctrine of abrogation was developed, where latter verses are understood to abrogate earlier verses.[73] As a result,

---

69 Wael B. Hallaq, "Can Sharia be restored" in *Islamic Law and Challenges of Modernity*, eds., Yvonne Y. Haddad and Barbara F. Stowasser (Walnut Creek: Altamira Press, 2004), pp. 21–53.
70 Rehman, "The Sharia, Islamic Family Laws and International Human Rights Law", p. 116.
71 Nasr Abu Zayd, *Reformation of Islamic Thought: A Critical Historical Analysis* (Amsterdam: Amsterdam University Press, 2006), p. 99. For a more detailed description, see Alfred-Louis de Prémare, *Aux origines du Coran* (Paris: Éditions du Téraèdre, 2004). See also, Quran 2:109, 6:106, 10:109; 15:85; 29:46 regarding showing patience when Muslims were mocked or ridiculed by unbelievers. These verses are believed to have been abrogated for the so-called "sword-verses", which allow for the killing of unbelievers, Quran 9:5. See also Burton, *The Sources of Islamic Law*, pp. 1–2.
72 Quran 4:82.
73 The doctrine was based on verses in the Quran dealing with the issue; "And for whatever verse We abrogate or cast into oblivion, We bring a better or the like of it; knowest thou not that God is powerful over everything?" See 2:106 and 16:101. The doctrine came to be restricted to conflicting verses concerning commands and is divided into different types, where most Muslim jurists accepted abrogation of both the ruling and the wording of the text, and abrogation of the ruling but not the wording of the text. The first type concerns verses in the Quran which the Prophet explicitly declared that they should not be considered. The second one allows for the verse to remain as part of the Quran, though its legal implications are overruled by a later revealed verse. For example, jurists found that verses acknowledging the freedom to choose a religion were abrogated for verses legitimizing the use of force and compulsion. See Mustafa Zaid, *Al-Naskh fi al-Qur'an al-Karim*, 2 vols. (Cairo: Dar al-Fikr al-Arabi, 1963); Hasan, *Early Development of Islamic Jurisprudence*, chapter 4; Burton, *The Sources of Islamic Law*, chapter 3. The Quran provides for a number of verses relating to jihad, which is often invoked by Islamic extremists. The verses are referred to as the "sword verses", which are quoted in order to legitimize unconditional warfare against unbelievers and used to justify the Islamic territorial expansion. Supporters of violent jihad are convinced that their belief is absolutely right and divinely sanctioned, see Devin R. Springer, James L. Regens and David N. Edger, *Islamic Radicalism*

when two (or more) revelations conflict with each other, the latter replaces the earlier. While the jurists relied on the Prophet to determine which verses could be repealed or abrogated, the Prophet did not provide explicit instructions for the doctrine.[74] Where the revelations are located within the Quran matters little as the verses are not presented in a historically chronological order that correspond to how they are thought to have been revealed to the Prophet. Of importance is their place within the chronology of Muhammad's life.[75] The different schools of law came to deploy abrogation on different evidence, to justify the selection of which verse was considered to have trumped the earlier, leading the schools to oppose the reached conclusions of abrogation as made by rivalling schools.[76]

The theoretical necessity to be able to trace the revelation of specific verses, to relative dates, is based on a gradual process of revelation. Remarkably, the discussion of why an All-Knowing God did not disclose all the revelations at a single time, meant that the All-Knowing God, potentially did not know everything at once, but needed to gradually grow the divine knowledge to reveal to humans, or most importantly, why the divine mind changed over this period of time, is not really discussed within this doctrine. Such assumptions were met with arguments that time was of no difference to God.[77] In some instances, it was also upheld that God needed to gradually introduce the Arabs to the new norms of the Islamic society, as they would not have followed all of the rulings if God had revealed the final verses at once.[78]

2.2 *Sunnah*

At an early period, the ancient Arab idea of Sunnah, precedent or normative custom, reasserted itself in Islam and became one of the central concepts of Islamic law. The Prophet's words and deeds were recorded in a large number of verbally documented reports known collectively as *hadith*, literally meaning report.[79] The authority of the Prophet was conferred by the Quran, which

---

      and Global Jihad (Washington DC: Georgetown University Press, 2009), p. 18. For theories on *naskh*, see Burton, *The Sources of Islamic Law*, chapter 2 and 6 and An-Naim, *Toward an Islamic Reformation*, p. 21.

74   Hasan, *Early Development of Islamic Jurisprudence*, p. 67.

75   Michael Bonner, *Jihad in Islamic History: Doctrines and Practice* (Princeton: Princeton University Press, 2008), p. 24.

76   Burton, *The Sources of Islamic Law*, pp. 27–31.

77   Ibid., 21.

78   See, for example, verses in the Quran related to wine 16:67; 2:219; 5:90–91.

79   *Hadith* is a verbal noun derived from the Arabic root verb *hadatha*, which means "to occur", "to relate", "to speak" and "to report", see Edward William Lane, *Arabic English*

stated that obedience to him was part of obedience to God.[80] It was considered that the Prophet, being the receiver of the revelations, was in the best position to interpret the Quran. The collection of hadiths constitutes the second source of Islamic law, Sunnah, which means a well-trodden path. In the Islamic legal tradition, it became defined as "a word spoken or an act done or confirmation is given (thereof) by the Prophet" and was associated with all practices ever attributed to Muhammad, in the form of words, actions, approvals or even silence.[81] This was despite the first Caliph, Abu Bakr, who ordered Muslims—after the death of the Prophet—to not write anything on the authority of the Prophet, and ordered them not to make a habit of narrating.[82] At the same time, there are also traditions that describe the Prophet encouraging the companions to write down his statements.[83] It did, however, take about one hundred and fifty years after the revelations in the Quran, for the Muslim jurists to start documenting these traditions.[84] The period between the revelation of

---

Lexicon (New York: Ungar Publishing Co., 1956), p. 527. The term *hadith* appears in the Quran 20:9 translated as "has thou received the story [*hadith*] of Moses?"

[80] See Quran 4:65, which reads: "But no, by thy Lord! they will not believe til they make thee [Muhammad] the judge regarding the disagreement between them, then they shall find in themselves no impediment touching thy verdict, but shall surrender in full submission." See also, verses 2:151, 3:164, 4:115, 16:44 and 62:2.

[81] Doi, *Introduction to the Hadith*, p. 13.

[82] "You narrate on the authority of the Prophet things that you disagree upon amongst yourselves, and people after you are in further disagreement. So do not narrate on the authority of the Prophet anything, and whoever asks you about an issue, say 'between you and us is the Book of Allah, permit what it permits, and forbid what it forbids' ", see Nimat Hafex Barazangi, *Woman's Identity and Rethinking the Hadith* (Surrey: Ashgate Publishing Limited, 2015), p. 94.

[83] The hadith describes one of the companions of the Prophet, 'Abdullah ibn 'Amr declaring: "I used to write everything which I heard from the Messenger of Allah with the intention of memorizing it. However, some Qurayshites forbade me from doing so saying, 'Do you write everything that you hear from him, while the Messenger of Allah is a human being who speaks in anger and pleasure?' So I stopped writing, and mentioned it to the Messenger of Allah. He pointed with his finger to his mouth and said: 'Write! By Him in whose hand is my soul, only truth comes out of it'." Quote taken from Abubakar, *Gender Justice in Islamic Law*, p. 15. See also, Abu Ameenah Bilal Phillips, *The Evolution of Fiqh (Islamic Law and Madh-habs)* (Riyadh: International Islamic Publishing House, 2005), pp. 29–31.

[84] Burton, *The Sources of Islamic Law*, p. viii; Abubakar, *Gender Justice in Islamic Law*, p. 16; Abu Ameenah Bilal Phillips, *The Evolution of Fiqh*, p. 57. It is held that "researchers knew it by intuition that the Shiite are well-advanced in the documentation of sciences than the other because none, except for 'Ali and the scholars of his following, undertook the process of documentation in the first era of Islam. The reason might be centred on the disagreement between the Sahaba of the Prophet about the legitimacy of documentation. 'Asgalani in introduction of his book *Fath al-Bari* and other scholars did not like

the Quran and the collection of traditions is not well-documented, but when the documentation began, they rapidly multiplied.[85] It was even suggested that the Sunnah should be codified, but the proposal was itself not established within Islamic law.[86]

In the early period, the law was not predominantly derived from hadiths about the Prophet and his Companions, at least, not in the circles from which the earliest surviving legal traditions appeared—specifically the Hanafi[87] and the Maliki[88] school of law.[89] Rather, an early division emerged between those who argued that hadiths should be the main source for answering new questions, whereas the latter group maintained that the opinion of learned scholars, based on reason, should be the main source.[90] At first, there was some interaction between the two groups; however, by the mid-eighth century, their division had become solidified. Occasionally, ruling caliphs would engage in these disagreements, supporting one group over the other. For example, the

---

documentation. 'Umar ibn al-Khattab and other groups did not like it for fear of mixing up Hadith with the Qur'an." Quote taken from Vago, *Law and Society*, pp. 109–110. See also Al-Imam 'Abd al-Hussain Sharaf al-Din al-Musawe, *al-Muraja'at* (Beirut: Mua'sasat al-'Alamai lil-Matboat, 1411H), p. 326.

85   Burton, *The Sources of Islamic Law*, p. viii.
86   Schacht, *An Introduction to Islamic Law*, p. 22. Some Muslim groups objected to the view that the collected material should even be seen as an extension of the Quran, see Burton, *The Sources of Islamic Law*, pp. 22–25.
87   The Hanafi school was characterized by the "inhibited use of personal reasoning, *ra'y*" to regulate issues not specifically addressed in the Quran or by the Sunnah, see Coulson, *A History of Islamic Law*, pp. 40–51.
88   The Maliki School valued the traditions of the Prophet more than ra'y. The schools also emerged at different geographic locations, Hanafi in Medina (796 AD) and Maliki in Kufa (797 AD). Ibid.
89   Behnam Sadeghi, *The Logic of Making Law in Islam: Women and Prayer in the Legal Tradition* (Cambridge: Cambridge University Press, 2013), p. 3. The author argues that traditionalists (i.e. those transmitting hadiths and scholars) and jurists (*fuqaha*) formed distinct but overlapping groups. Most traditionalists were not jurists, and many jurists were poor traditionalists. Therefore, the two groups could develop independently from each other. A jurist such as Abu Hanifa, who lived in Kufa, worked with the traditions that were known in Kufa. Knowledge of traditions' circulation in other cities reached Kufa gradually and it was not until the 8th century that traditions reached Kufa on a massive scale. While some scholars identify that the hadith movement occurred in Medina and *ahl al-ray* in Kufa, Joseph Schacht and 'Abd al-Majid Mahmud argue that the both movements were present in both cities. See Schacht, *Origins of Muhammadan Jurisprudence*, pp. 228–257, and 'Abd al-Majid Mahmud, *al-Madrasa al-fiqhiyya li-al-muhaddithin* (Cairo: Maktabat al-Shabab, 1972), pp. 19–79.
90   Christopher Melchert, *The Formation of the Sunni Schools of Law, 9th–10th Centuries CE* (Leiden: Brill, 1996), p. 1.

Abbasid caliph al-Mamoun supported the Mu'tazilis, the most rationalist group.[91] However, as his support was complemented by the persecution of those Muslims who did not adhere to this school, it eventually proved detrimental to the position of the rationalists and finally led to the demise and disappearance of the Mu'tazilis. However, the ideas of the Mu'tazilis continue to influence Islamic jurisprudence and theology, especially within Shi'ism.[92] With the support of caliph al-Mutasim, who succeeded al-Mamoun, the traditionalists, who viewed the Mu'tazilis and their perspective as blasphemous, became dominant. The success of the traditionalists meant that mainstream Islam only allowed the role of reason within strict limits and mostly about secondary issues of jurisprudence.[93] Nevertheless, reasoning was inherent in Islamic law from its very beginning, moving from being vague and without direction and method, to later turning into an increasingly strict discipline.[94]

Islamic law, as such, did not yet exist during the greater part of the first century and the use of the term "Sunnah of the Prophet" is presumed to have been used in the theory of Islamic law towards the end of the first century. Originally, Sunnah had more political implications than legal, as it referred to the policy and administration of the caliph. In the time of the Prophet, the law fell outside of the sphere of religion, and as long as there were no religious or moral objections to specific occurrences, the technical aspects of the law were a matter of indifference to Muslims.[95] During the first century of Islam, many distinctive features of Islamic law came into being, and an emerging Islamic society created its legal institutions. The caliphs were political leaders and acted as legislators of the community, as there was no separation between the administrative and legislative activities of the Islamic government. The objective of the administrative law was not to modify customary law; its purpose was to organize the newly conquered territories for the benefit of the Arabs. In many cases, the legal and administrative institutions of conquered territories were adopted. Examples of this are the treatment of tolerated religions

---

91 For an overview of the Mu'tazilis, see Crone, *Medieval Political Thought*, chapter 6.
92 Iranian reformist thinker Hassan Yussefi Eshkevari sees Mu'tazili thinking as a historical precedent for religious rationalism. Reformist thinkers in Indonesia have also been influenced by the Mu'tazili, such as Harun Nasution and those belonging to the organization Jarangan Islam (Liberal Islam). Many reformist thinkers also find the Mu'tazili perspective interesting, as it ascribes justice in various social, economic and political dimensions, an important position. See Shireen T. Hunter, *Reformist Voices of Islam: Mediating Islam and Modernity* (New York: M. E. Sharpe, Inc., 2009), p. 24.
93 Hunter, *Reformist Voices of Islam: Mediating Islam and Modernity*, p. 25.
94 Schacht, *An Introduction to Islamic Law*, p. 37.
95 Ibid., 17–19.

and the methods of taxation. Along with the preservation of legal institutions and practices, legal concepts and maxims, even methods of reasoning of other civilizations, were used as models by the ancient schools of Islamic law. The Roman law concept of *opinion prudentium*, the opinion and decisions of lawyers, seems to have provided the model for the consensus of the scholars or, ijma, the third source of Islamic law.[96] The transmitters were non-Arab converts to Islam, who had an education in Hellenistic rhetoric which was normal in the areas of the Near East which the Arabs conquered. Concepts and maxims originating from the Canon law of the Eastern Churches, from the Talmudic and Rabbinic law, and Sassanian law, entered Islam and Islamic law during its period of development.[97] The method of qiyas, analogy, as well as other legal methods such as *istishab*, finding a link, and *istislah* or *maslahah*, public interest, are derived from Jewish law. Jewish law has particularly influenced religious worship.[98]

It is also likely that the question of whether the administrative acts of the first two caliphs, Abu Bakr and 'Umar, should be regarded as binding standards, arose at the time when a successor to 'Umar was to be appointed. There was discontent with the policy that the third caliph 'Uthman had enforced, as it had departed from the policy of his predecessors.[99] The political differences between the fourth caliph Ali and Mu'awiyah,[100] which caused the Sunni and Shia division in Islam, led to the emergence of fabricated and distorted hadiths. It is therefore recognized that although elements of the Sunnah are divine, not every hadith is authentic. The most controversial example, mostly denounced by Muslim historians and theologians, is the disputed tradition

---

[96] For more examples see ibid., 20.

[97] The office of the "clerk of the court", *katib*, who appears together with the judge, *qadi*, was introduced by Sassanian law. The Umayyads later took over this tradition from the Sassanian administration and appointed the Islamic judges. Ibid., 21.

[98] Ibid.

[99] "In this connexion, there appeared the concept of the '*Sunnah* of the Prophet', not yet identified with any set of positive rules but providing a doctrinal link between the '*Sunnah* of Abu Bakr and 'Umar and the Quran' ", ibid., 17–18.

[100] For an account of the power struggle between Ali and Mu'awiyah see Maulana Muhammad Ali, *The Early Caliphate* (Lahore: Ahmadiyya Anjamun Isha'at Islam, 2001). The civil war between Mu'awiyah, the governor of Damascus, and Ali, resulted in the death of thousands and the assassination of Ali. Mu'awiyah established the first Umayyad dynasty, and murdered the son of Ali, Hussein. See Ahmet T. Kuru, *Islam, Authoritarianism, and Underdevelopment: A Global and Historical Comparison* (Cambridge: Cambridge University Press, 2029), p. 71. For an account of the power struggle between Ali and Mu'awiyah see Maulana Muhammad Ali, *The Early Caliphate* (Lahore: Ahmadiyya Anjamun Isha'at Islam, 2001).

referring to a passage of the Quran, supposedly deleted by Muhammad and referred to as "satanic".[101] Due to the emergence of fabricated hadiths, a technique of authenticating the Sunnah was developed and generated six recognized books of Sunnah of the Sunni Schools.[102] The Shia rely on their collection of hadiths,[103] and do not accept a tradition unless it has been recorded or acknowledged by one of their Imams.[104] The application of criteria by which the subject matter of the hadiths might be transmitted from one generation

---

[101] Early Muslim historians such as Ibn Ishaq, al-Waqidi, al-Zuhri, Ibn Sa'd, al-Tabari and Ibrahi have disputed the history of this event. Ibn Hisham, Ibn Ishaq's editor, omits the passage but it is preserved as a quotation from al-Tabari in Guillaume's translation of Ibn Ishaq. See Ibn Ishaq, *The Life of Muhammad: A translation of Ishaq's Sirat rasul Allah*, ed. 'Abdu'l-Malik Ibn Isham, transl. Alfred Guillaume (Karachi: Oxford University Press, 1990), pp. 165–166. See also, William Muir, *The Life of Muhammad* (Oxford: Oxford University Press, 2002), pp. lxxix–lxxx. Most non-Muslim and some Muslim commentators have accepted the story of Muhammad's momentary acceptance of the verses. However, the prevailing Muslim view is that the event is a fabrication created by the unbelievers of Mecca in the early days of Islam. See Muhammad H. Haikal, *The Life of Muhammad* (Plainfield: American Trust Publications, 2005), p. 105. The verse declared that "these are exalted females whose intercession is to be desired". The tradition states that for Muhammad to obtain conversions from successful members of his tribe, he must accept three idolatrous goddesses Al-Lat, Al-Manat and 'Uzza as divine intercessors. The tradition says that these verses were later withdrawn and referred to as "satanic", see Joel Kuortti, "The Satanic Verses" in *The Cambridge Companion to Salman Rushdie*, ed. Abdulrazak Gurnah (Cambridge: Cambridge University Press, 1997), p. 134. It appears as though the Quran addresses and recognizes the notion of Satan trying to interfere: "We sent not ever any Messenger or Prophet before thee, but that Satan cast into his fancy, when he was fancying; but God annuls what Satan casts, then God confirms His signs – surely God is All-knowing, All-wise." See, Quran 22:52. See also, William Muir, *The Life of Muhammad* (Oxford: Oxford University Press, 2002), pp. lxxix–lxxx and Watt, *Muhammad at Mecca*, pp. 102–105.

[102] A technique of authenticating the *Sunnah* was developed; the traditions were divided into three categories according to the degree of their reliability. The classification was based on three criteria: 1. The perfection or imperfection of the chain of transmitters, 2. The freedom of the texts from any concealed defects, 3. Acceptance or rejection of any hadith by the Companions, their followers and their successors. The three categories of hadith are: 1. The *Sahih*: genuine Traditions declared so after all tests. 2. The *Hasan*: fair Traditions, although quite genuine, inferior in the matter of authenticity to the *Sahih* and 3. The *Da'if*: weak Traditions that are not so reliable. See 'Abdur Rahman I. Doi, *Introduction to the Hadith* (Erasmina – Pretoria: Al-Madinah Publishers, 1996), p. 42. It generated to six recognized books of *Sunnah* of the Sunni School; Al-Bukhari (d. 870 AD), Muslim (d. 875 AD), Abu Dawud (d. 888 AD), al-Tirmidhi (d. 892 AD), al-Nasa'i (d. 915 AD) and Ibn Majah (d. 886 AD).

[103] Such as, *al-Kafī* by Abu Ja'far al-Kulayni al-Razi (d. 939 AD) and *al-Istibar* by Abu Ja'far al-Tusa (d. 971 AD).

[104] Coulson, *History of Islam*, p. 105.

to another in a reliable manner resulted in the acceptance of not more than a few thousand hadiths. A hadith that had been passed down "via a defective or interrupted chain of transmitters" had no legal effect. As the entire community of Muslims participated, the transmissions of hadiths are regarded as altogether certain, stemming from the theory of consensus, ijma, making it inconceivable that the entire Muslim community would conspire to produce a falsehood.[105]

2.2.1 Hadith Compilations

The scholars who compiled the hadiths in the ninth and tenth century, are commonly most valued for their efforts to authenticate the traditions attributed to the Prophet. However, "rigorous historical authentication of the Prophet Muhammad's teachings was not their exclusive goal".[106] The hadiths could include comments or changes, in particular with regard to what background facts were included in the compilations. Most importantly, depending on where in the compilation the hadith was placed, it could mean a difference in how the hadith was interpreted. As such, the compilers were inclined to present traditions in a certain manner to affect the way they wanted their texts to be understood. "When close attention is paid to the narrative context in which this incident appears, one can speak meaningfully of the reports having materially different implications."[107] The compilation of hadiths can be divided into three genres: *musannaf, musnad* and *sahih*. The musannaf genre was developed in the second half of the eighth century and contain material on theology, the history of the early Muslim community, and law. Hadiths in this category are compiled topically. The concern of including hadiths that had been cleared by a reliable chain of transmitters is, however, absent.[108] The second genre, musnad, was developed during the late eighth and early ninth century, as a means of ensuring authentic traditions were attributed to the Prophet. Here, the hadiths were arranged alphabetically.[109] The sahih genre, also developed during the late eighth and early ninth century, organized by

---

105 Hallaq, *An Introduction to Islamic Law*, p. 17. See also, Mohammad H. Kamali, *A Textbook of Hadith Studies, Authenticity, Compilation, Classification and Criticism of Hadith* (Leicestershire: The Islamic Foundation, 2005).

106 Mohammad Fadel, "Is Historicism a Viable Strategy for Islamic Legal Reform? The Case of 'Never Shall a Folk Prosper Who Have Appointed a Woman to rule Them' ", *Islamic Law & Society* Vol. 18, No. 2 (2011), p. 20.

107 Fadel, "Is Historicism a Viable Strategy for Islamic Legal Reform?", pp. 21–22.

108 Such as the collection of Ibn Abi Shayba, see Jonathan Brown, *Hadith: Muhammad's Legacy in the Medieval and Modern World* (Oxford: One World, 2009), pp. 25–28.

109 Brown, *Hadith: Muhammad's Legacy in the Medieval and Modern World*, pp. 28–31.

topic, was a combination of the other genres, where the focus was to ensure that the hadiths included were reliable.[110] Other compilations were produced during the fifteenth and eighteenth centuries but they served more as encyclopedias.[111]

2.2.2   Validity of Hadiths

While it is difficult to evaluate the charges of forgery and examine the validity of those hadiths accepted and not accepted by the schools of law, it does put a shadow on the validity of Sunnah as a sacred source of Islamic law. Somewhat unrecognized is the fact that the individuals who collected the hadiths are not in any way infallible human beings, and that their collected works do not amount to a divine text.[112] Especially since "this apparatus suffered from the cardinal defect which is inherent, even to this day, in the Islamic theory of evidence – the presumption that a respectable man who would not willingly tell a lie is therefore necessarily telling the truth. Of faulty memory, wishful thinking, reading back the present into the past, casting the colour of one's opinion on the facts, and the effect of leading questions ... they [Muslim scholars of Sunnah] were in the main completely unconscious".[113] This displays the attribution of trust and the trustworthy person in Islam, thus the remarkably important position that the hadiths have received. A transmitted tradition was considered reliable if the person transmitting the tradition was considered reliable. At a period where political factions were fighting over political power; it was through the use of hadiths that jurists and rulers came to decide how to govern people. While the Quran is silent on such matters, recourse to hadiths became the best manner to claim legitimacy to any political claims. Controlling hadiths against other competing groups became "itself a conditioning factor for the legitimacy of caliphal authority".[114] In spite of opposition, traditions were "eagerly invented, collected, and transmitted by the early Muslims, and

---

110   The collections of al-Bukhari, al-Tirmidhi and al-Nasa'i fall within this category, ibid., 31–34.
111   Such as *Kanz al-'Ummāl*, *Majma' al-Zawā'id*, *Kashf al-Khafā'* and *al-Jāmi'al-Ṣaghīr*, see Fadel, "Is Historicism a Viable Strategy for Islamic Legal Reform?", p. 22.
112   Bukhari's compilation is regarded by Sunnis to be one of the most authentic collections of the Sunnah. However, as Mohammad Ali Syed correctly points out, not even Bukhari can claim infallibility as he is merely human and his collection of hadith is based on *isnad*, a chain of authority. See Mohammad Ali Syed, *The Position of Women in Islam: A Progressive View* (Albany: State University of New York, 2004), p. 22.
113   Vesey-Fitzgerald, "Nature and Sources of the Sharia", p. 63.
114   Mohammed Arkoun, *Rethinking Islam: Common Questions, Uncommon Answers*, trans. Robert D. Lee Boulder (Colorado: Westview Press, 1994), p. 45.

later on the process developed into an academic discipline [with] thousands of people [being] engaged in it".[115]

Many hadiths were introduced as time passed by, long after the Prophet had died. In particular, many of the hadiths that describe women as morally and religiously defective, *fitna*, a temptation for men, the larger part of the inhabitants of hell and having weaker intellectual powers and therefore not suitable for political rule, were introduced in the eleventh century.[116]

> It is ironic that even though there are only about six misogynist *Ahadith* accepted as *Sahih* (reliable) out of a collection of 70,000, it is these six that men trot out when they want to argue against sexual equality, while perversely ignoring dozens of positive *Ahadith*. Among the latter are *Ahadith* that emphasize women's full humanity; counsel husbands to deal kindly and justly with their wives; confirm the right of women to acquire knowledge; elevate mothers over fathers; proclaim that women will be in heaven, ahead, even of the Prophet; record women's attendance at prayers in the mosque during the Prophet's lifetime, including an incident where a girl playing in front of him as he led the prayer; affirm that many women (including women from the Prophet's family) went unveiled in the later years of Islam; and record that the Prophet accepted the evidence of one woman over that of a man.[117] When Muslims do refer to these *Ahadith*, they do so to emphasize Islam's egalitarianism, but they rarely question why the *Ahadith* have been erased so wholly from communal memory as to preclude the possibility of evolving a counterhegemonic discourse on sexual equality based on them.[118]

Much like the Quran, the Sunnah contains a vast number of contradictions. The contradictions within the Sunnah are actually so common that it is difficult to conclude that "one is dealing with a single, unitary body of information".[119] Even with this source, abrogation was employed to handle all the contradictions. What we see in the compiled collections of traditions, is the

---

115 G. H. A. Juynboll, *The Authenticity of the Tradition Literature: Discussion in Modern Egypt* (Leiden: Brill, 1969), p. 5.
116 Spellberg, *Politics, Gender and the Islamic Past*, p. 13.
117 See Fatima Mernissi, *Dreams of Trespass: Tales of a Harem Girlhood* (New York: Addison-Wesley, 1994) and Kaukab Siddique, *Liberation of Women Through Islam* (Kingsville MD: American Society for Education and Religion Inc., 1990).
118 Barlas, *"Believing Women" in Islam*, p. 46.
119 Burton, *The Sources of Islamic Law*, p. 3. See also, Ignaz Goldziher, *Muslim Studies* Vol. 2 (London: Allen and Unwin, 1971).

end-product, where the conflicting views have to some degree been harmonized. In many instances, the Sunnah even contradicted the verses in the Quran and in some of those cases, it was held that the Sunnah had replaced the Quran.[120] Remarkably, "the number of instances in which the Quran had superseded the Sunnah that can be mustered is minimal, compared with the number of instances of the alleged naskh of the Quran by the Sunnah".[121] For instance, the Sunnah affirms that the Prophet had declared the death penalty for adultery. The Quran on the other hand mandates that female fornicators should be locked up for life.[122] In this case, it was regarded to be a clear case of abrogation of the Quran by the Sunnah.[123]

One consequence of abrogating the Quran with the Sunnah, in particular with the emergence of distorted and fabricated hadiths, was that it would lead to the questioning of the credibility of Muhammad:[124] "if the Sunnah had naskhed the Quran, the unbelievers might have argued that Muhammad was saying or doing the opposite of what he alleged was being revealed to him by God; if the Quran has naskhed the Sunnah, they could have taunted Muhammad by pointing out that God was belying the man who claimed to be his Prophet".[125] It is claimed that the Quran addresses this by declaring "And when We exchange a verse in the place of another verse and God knows very well what He is sending down -- they say, 'Thou art a mere forger!' Nay, but the most of them have no knowledge."[126] The issue was dealt with by the jurists by claiming that the Sunnah was also revealed to the Prophet, abrogation was therefore simply a way to replace one revelation with another, again, by referring to the Quran: "your comrade is not astray, neither errs, nor speaks he out of caprice".[127] Paradoxically, the Quran is contradictory with regard to the divinity of the Prophet's actions as it also declares that "it is not for me to alter it of my own accord. I follow nothing, except what is revealed to me".[128] Consequently,

---

[120] The Shafi'i uphold the notion that verses in the Quran can only be abrogated for other verses in the Quran, and traditions can only be abrogated by other traditions. Ibid., 32–37.
[121] Ibid., 4–5.
[122] Quran 4:15–16.
[123] Burton, *The Sources of Islamic Law*, p. 4.
[124] On reviewing the authenticity of hadiths, the Prophet stated "compare what purports to come from me with the Book of God. What agrees with it, I have said; What disagrees with it, I have not said", see Muhammad bin Idris Shafi'i, *Kitab Al-Umm* (Cairo: Nabu Press, 2010); Syed, *The Position of Women in Islam*, p. 22.
[125] Burton, *The Sources of Islamic Law*, p. 5.
[126] Quran 16:101.
[127] Quran 53:2–3. See also, 59:7.
[128] Quran 10:15.

human understandings of actions ascribed to the Prophet came to supersede the revelations of God in some instances. Even more disconcerting are the hadiths referring to verses in the Quran that cannot be found in the Quran.

> Succeeding generations of Muslims, devoted followers and defenders of Shafi'i mahdhab, or system of ideas, and members of other, rival madhahib alike, would, in discussing naskh, soberly adduce reported instances of naskh of the verses of the surviving Quran by verses of the 'original' Quran.[129]

One hadith deals with the issue of when breastfeeding establishes a barrier for the marriage of a man to women who he is related to by *milk*, formed during nursing by a non-biological mother. While the hadith is dismissed by the Maliki, the Shafi'i accept this tradition. By doing so, they are in fact also accepting the possibility that there may be verses that were never included in the Quran, which might have included commands that would have abrogated earlier commands or current understandings of which verse in the Quran has abrogated the other ones. There are several hadiths that speak of the loss of the revealed verses, which acknowledges the Shia claim of the current Quran missing specific verses, although the Sunni do not agree on what those verses contained. Some of those reports describe the divine intervention removing verses, not only from the memories of the believers, but also from the scriptural source itself.[130]

> Two men recited a sura [unspecified] which the Prophet had taught them to recite and which they had been in the habit of reciting. One night, they stood up to pray, but could not recall a syllable. Next morning, they repaired first thing to the Prophet and informed him of what had happened. He replied, 'That sura is part of what has been withdrawn – so pay no further heed to it'.[131]

In fact, most of the Sunnah does not consist of the Prophet's praxis; rather it is "the free-thinking activity of early legists of Islam who had made deductions from the existing Sunnah or practice and—most important of all—had

---

129   Burton, *The Sources of Islamic Law*, pp. 7–8.
130   Ibid., 7, 50–55.
131   Quote taken from Burton, *The Sources of Islamic Law*, p. 49. Burton includes several traditions describing how several verses of the Quran were lost. Some even describe up to three hundred verses being lost.

incorporated"[132] into it foreign elements, including many of the pre-Islamic practices.[133] It is often argued that believing Muslims would not want to abandon the Sunnah, but if the Sunnah is not correct—why should it still be upheld? Only a few Muslim scholars advocate the complete rejection of the usage of hadiths as the basis for Islamic law, instead, most scholars argue that only specific parts of hadiths and the Sunnah should be upheld.[134] Nevertheless, it is difficult to maintain with certainty that the Sunnah as a whole is correct, or that genuine Sunnah were not included (for various reasons). Rather, it appears as if the Islamic system and the theories and methods of Islamic law, were constructed to deal with the inconsistencies which were evident in the Quran, the Sunnah, and in between these sources. Many times, the subjective opinions were used as political tools to govern in a specific manner, or to make sure other rivaling groups would not be able to gain the power to rule and influence.

For a system that prides itself in changing the ways of jahiliyya, it is remarkable that the notion of the custom of the Prophet (and the caliphs) has received such an important virtue in the interpretation of the words of God, a God who according to Muslims intended to end pre-Islamic norms. However, custom, or 'urf, is generally not a recognized source of classical Islamic theory, unlike almost every other legal system that includes custom as a source for the development of law. In Islamic terms, custom reflects human behavior, and since Muslim jurists argue that their legal system is superhuman, revealed by God to remain for all time, any human intervention in the legal process, particularly for purposes of revision is, ipso facto, unlawful. Historically there is evidence of controversy among Muslim jurists about according custom a formal status as a source of law, but the view that prevailed was the refusal to recognize custom as a formal source.[135] Instead, attempts were made to identify custom with Sunnah, ijma or to treat it as if it was a written stipulation. The attempt to identify custom with Sunnah seems natural, as Sunnah is the custom and practice

---

132 Fazlur Rahman, *Islam and Modernity: Transformation of an Intellectual Tradition* (Chicago: University of Chicago Press, 1965), p. 5 and John L. Esposito, *Women in Muslim Family Law* (Syracuse: Syracuse University Press, 1982), p. 103.
133 Barlas, *"Believing Women" in Islam*, p. 65.
134 Junyboll, *The Authenticity of the Tradition Literature*, pp. 13–18.
135 'Urf is recognized, within limits, by the Hanafi and Maliki schools of law but rejected by the Shafi'i school of law. Hanafi does not allow for 'urf to prevail over the Quran or Sunnah, but might over qiyas. See An-Naim, *Towards an Islamic Reformation*, p. 26. For more on the development of custom in Islamic law see Gideon Libson, "On the Development of Custom as a Source of Law in Islamic Law: Al-rujū'u ilā al-'urfi ahadu al-qawā'idi al-khamsi allatī yatabannā 'alayhā al-fiqhu", *Islamic Law and Society* Vol. 4, No. 2 (1997), p. 136.

of the Prophet; in other words, Sunnah is the product of custom. However, as jurists became aware of the inadequacies of the methods to deal with specific questions, there was a tendency to treat custom as a material source of law, without directly recognizing it as a formal source.[136]

2.3 Ijma

It was the need for a successor after the death of the Prophet that led to the development of ijma, or consensus, which came to be the third source of Islamic law.[137] Consensus ratifies any particular rule as certain if it is based on probable textual evidence, but does not allow for the abrogation of verses in the Quran, and some even argue that it does not allow for abrogation of Sunnah.[138] It is only when the ijma does not contradict the primary sources, that it is considered to be binding.[139] While difficulties and controversies were defining its scope and operation, the reasoning for justifying this doctrine is that if consensus was attained on probable evidence, the evidence could not be subject to error as the community cannot err.[140] The doctrine was supported

---

136   Ibid., 131, 149–150. See also, Ayman Shabana, *Custom in Islamic Law and Legal Theory: The Development of the Concepts of 'Urf and 'Adah in the Islamic Legal Tradition* (New York: Palgrave Macmillan, 2010), describing the shift in the status of custom in the modern period.
137   The ijma doctrine passed through four stages: *ijma' al-sahabah* (consensus of the Companions of the Prophet), *ijma' al-tabi'in* (consensus of the Successors), the period of ijtihad and the period of blind following [taqlid] by the different schools of jurisprudence.
138   Kamali, *A Textbook of Hadith Studies,* pp. 228–263.
139   Abubakar, *Gender Justice in Islamic Law,* p. 19.
140   Hasan, *Early Development of Islamic Jurisprudence,* chapter 7; Ahmed Hasan, "The Classical Definition of 'Ijma': The Nature of Consensus", *Islamic Studies* Vol. 14 (1975), pp. 261–270; and Schacht, *Origins of Muhammadan Jurisprudence,* pp. 82–94. An-Naim asks several important questions relating to this doctrine: "What constitutes *ijma*? Does it require complete unanimity or can it be formed despite some disagreement or minority dissent? Whose *ijma* is binding and upon whom? Is the consensus of the Companions and their community of Medina, that of Muslim scholars and jurists in general (or in a given locality), or that of the totality of Muslims? Is it the *ijma* of a single generation (or either scholars or the Muslim community) or that of several generations? Is the *ijma* of an earlier generation (or generations) necessarily binding on all subsequent generations?" see An-Naim, *Towards an Islamic Reformation,* p. 24. It was established that "only interpretation and application of the Quran and Sunnah are correct which have been taken over by the consensus ... Only those men and writings are regarded as authoritative whom the consensus of the community has acknowledged as such, not in synods or councils, but through a nearly subconscious voice of the people which in its universality was regarded as not being subject to error", see Ignaz Goldhizer, *Vorlesungen über den Islam* (Wissenschaftliche Buchgesellschaft, 1963), pp. 52–53, as translated and quoted in Herbert J. Liebesny, *The Law of the Near and Middle East* (Albany: State University of New York Press, 1975), p. 17.

FOUNDATIONS OF ISLAMIC LAW 51

by the report of the Prophet declaring "my people shall never be unanimous in error".[141]

Ijma is divided into two categories: explicit or implicit, depending on the process of its emergence. Ijma is explicit when qualified scholars reached consensus after deliberating on an issue brought before them; it is implicit when an issue is brought before one qualified scholar, and their contemporaries do not object to the ruling.[142] Deliberation is then not needed. Ijma can be definite and binding when there is clear textual support for the ijma, or speculative and non-binding when it addresses an issue for which there is no clear or ambiguous textual support.[143]

Once formed, the ijma is considered infallible, it constituted heresy to contradict it and while in theory it was possible to repeal an ijma of an earlier generation by a later generation, it was highly unlikely in practice.[144] In particular, the consensus reached by the companions of the Prophet have a special standing, as their consensus is seen by a majority of jurists, as binding, and later generations are restricted to follow its ruling and cannot depart from it.[145] Fiqh literature contain many claims of the ijma of the companions of the Prophet, which in practice restricts and denies later scholars from thoroughly analyzing them, and by doing so, questioning the legality of the ijma claimed.[146] Further discussion was precluded not only on those points which were the subject of a consensus but also on those matters where the jurists had agreed to differ: "for

---

141 Majid Khadurri, "Nature and Sources of Islamic Law", *George Washington Law Review* Vol. 22 (1953), p. 14. See also, Quran 4:115.
142 The principle of *shura*, mutual consideration, is established in the Quran 42:38: "their affair being counsel between them". Boseworth, C. E., states that shura is an advisory council, not a participatory one. This does not necessarily mean that the supreme leader is required to consult with only a few of his companions, see *The Encyclopaedia of Islam* (Leiden: Brill, 1960), Vol. 9. As affirmed by the Sunnah, the verse explicitly states that shura requires participation from all believers. If participation doesn't include all believers, there is no shura, and consequently no ijma. An ijma done only by the fuqaha (legal scholars), even when claimed to be supported by the Quran and the Sunnah, is not binding on everyone and will not constitute law until approved by the entire Muslim community, ummah. See Michael Mumisa, *Islamic Law. Theory and Interpretation* (Beltsville, Maryland: Amana Publications, 2002), p. 84; and Bernard, M., *The Encyclopaedia of Islam* (Leiden: Brill, 1960), Vol. 3, stating that ijma does not express the consensus of the community at large, but only the elders and established leaders.
143 Abubakar, *Gender Justice in Islamic Law*, pp. 17–18.
144 Consequently, some scholars argue that ijma is a primary source of law, see M. Izzi Dien, *Islamic Law from Historical Foundations to Contemporary Practice* (Indiana: University of Notre Dame, 2004), p. 40.
145 Kamali, *A Textbook of Hadith Studies*, p. 313.
146 Abubakar, *Gender Justice in Islamic Law*, p. 18.

if the ijma covered two variant opinions, to adduce a third opinion was to contradict it ... Ijma had thus set the final seal upon the process of increasing rigidity of the law".[147]

2.4 Legal Reasoning

The last source of law rests upon a concept of a divine intention of the law, *maqasid al-shariah*. Sharia has certain aims and purposes which are apprehended by the realization of people's welfare and their protection from corruption and evil.[148] As Islam expanded in the world and time passed by, many new cases that were not covered by the Quran or the Sunnah arose. Also, the language of the Quran and hadiths were not always obvious. The concept of ijtihad, independent reasoning, was developed as a method of Islamic law through which formal sources could be extended to cover interpretations and new developments of life. From ijtihad, other legal methods developed such as ijma and qiyas, as well as doctrines such as istihan, istislah or maslahah (welfare), 'urf and *darurah* (necessity), which are the most prominent. The interpretive methods constituting ijtihad, the process of reasoning, is considered as subsidiary sources of Islamic law, as they are the products of human reasoning.

2.4.1 Ijtihad

Except for a relatively few Quranic and Prophetic statements, containing a clear and specific normative ruling, the overwhelming part of the Islamic law is a product of ijtihad, a domain of interpretation resting on probability.[149] Ijtihad as such, is striving to solve new legal problems, and is only to be used when there is no clear reference of how to solve a legal issue in the textual sources of Islam, that is the Quran or the Sunnah.[150] It cannot be used to modify the textual sources and requires knowledge and competence to derive new rules of law through reasoning from the textual sources.[151]

There are various forms of legal reasoning, or ijtihad, some listed under the general term qiyas, or analogy.[152] The function of qiyas or ijtihad is to discover *illah*, the ratio legis of law. Qiyas is a restricted form of ijtihad: it is reasoning

---

147 Quoted in Wael B. Hallaq, *The Origins and Evolution of Islamic Law* (Cambridge: Cambridge University Press, 2005), p. 104.
148 Hashim Kamali, *Shari'ah Law: An Introduction* (Oxford: Oneworld, 2008), pp. 32–33, 232.
149 Hallaq, *An Introduction to Islamic Law*, p. 27.
150 Taha, *The Second Message of Islam*, p. 23.
151 L. Ali Khan and Hisham M. Ramadan, *Contemporary Ijtihad: Limits and Controversies* (Edinburgh: Edinburgh University Press, 2011), p. 1.
152 Shiite law does not recognize *qiyas* as a legitimate source of law, see Wael B. Hallaq, *The Origins and Evolution of Islamic Law* (Cambridge: Cambridge University Press, 2005), p. 21.

by analogy.[153] Similarly, ijma, is reasoning through consensus. To perform strict analogical deduction, the community must have in mind the intent of the law, since it is only then that the intention can be shifted to cover a related, similar situation.[154] The classic example of legal analogy is the case of wine. Only grape wine is explicitly forbidden in the Quran.[155] The ratio legis is the attribution of intoxication. Hence jurists have declared that all intoxicating beverages are prohibited.

Qiyas, as a methodology was developed to eliminate the free use of reason and independent value judgments. It is not a material source, but provides a set of methods through which the legal scholars extract legal norms. Historically, it provided Muslim scholars with a way to apply traditional religious law to contemporary issues. It has been suggested that the companions of the Prophet were unanimously in agreement over the use of qiyas.[156] However, there is little evidence to suggest that such a position was a deliberate act of the companions.[157] Eventually, the frequent use of qiyas in law led to a widespread disagreement on the use of qiyas.[158] Ijtihad was also restricted to matters not governed by the Quran and Sunnah, although there are instances of this not being upheld,[159] and technically not allowed on matters decided through ijma.

Scholars have not been able to agree upon a verse in the Quran, which could prove the validity of qiyas, see Hasan, *Analogical Reasoning in Islamic Jurisprudence*, chapter 3.

153 Qiyas is also closely related to ijma, as no qiyas can attain the status of law unless it is validated by ijma, see Mohammad Muslehuddin, *Philosophy of Islamic Law and the Orientalists* (New Delhi: Taj Company, 1986), p. 148.

154 Mumisa, *Islamic Law. Theory and Interpretation*, p. 15.

155 Quran 2:219 and 5:90.

156 Muslehuddin, *Philosophy of Islamic Law and the Orientalists*, pp. 136–137.

157 Farooq, "Analogical Reasoning (Qiyas)", p. 158. See also, Mohammad Omar Farooq, *Toward Our Reformation: From Legalism to Value-Oriented Islamic Law and Jurisprudence* (Herndon: International Institute of Islamic Thought, 2011).

158 The frequent use of qiyas in law led to a widespread disagreement on the use of *ra'y*, opinions, and qiyas. To control the vast interpretations, the established schools compiled aspects of worship and inter-human relations to legal treaties, which became accepted as established material sources of Islamic law. They divided Islamic law into three general subjects: *ibadat*, which entails worship issues and relates to the relationship between God and man, such as the rules for praying, fasting and hajj pilgrimage; *muamilat*, transactions, concerned with legal acts between individuals such as marriage, divorce, custody and inheritance and finally *siyasat*, literally meaning politics, addressing issues related to inter-state and state-individual relations, like laws of war and penal law, see Hasan, *Analogical Reasoning in Islamic Jurisprudence*, p. 424 and Hashemi, *Religious Legal Traditions*, p. 8.

159 'Umar, the second caliph exercised ijtihad in matters where there existed textual rulings in the Quran and Sunnah. For examples of 'Umars *ijtihad* see Muhammad Bultajiy, *Manhaj Umar ibn al-Khatab fi al-Tashri* (Cairo: Dar al-Fikr al-Arabi, 1970).

However, this notion is questioned by scholars, who argue that "there is not one single word in the Quran that is clear by itself".[160]

By the ninth century, it was considered that the Sunni schools had fully exhausted all possible subjects of law, and resulted in what was termed the "closing of the gate of ijtihad".[161] The use of the doctrine of independent reasoning diminished and from the ninth century, Islamic jurisprudence has been marked by *taqlid*, legal conformism. Taqlid is first and foremost a legal method for not fully qualified mujtahids—scholars qualified to interpret the Sharia by ijtihad—to be able to decide on cases in light of precedent rulings. Taqlid effectively limited "the influence of independent value judgments on the content of the revealed law", where jurists focused not on the revision of laws, but on justifying existing laws.[162] This obligation is however questioned by some modern scholars:

> A cardinal mistake in the subsequent history of Islam was an insistence upon taqlid or imitation. Although not without its controversies, for centuries the dominant voices within Muslim societies continued to argue that the doors to ijtihad had been closed. Such an argument undermined the essence of Islam, which is based on change, reform and re-interpretation.[163]

> What led to the blockage of ijtihad in the face of Muslims when ijtihad was wide open through the first three centuries of Islam? Who was that who would have agreed to allow the issues of religion to end in the hands of these madhahib (schools) so that they would monopolize ijtihad for themselves and would prevent ijtihad if it wouldn't go in their way, as if Islam with its books and traditions, with all the knowledge and evidences they carried, would have become their private property? Were these madhahib the heirs of the Prophet, or was it that God sealed off with them the patrons and the imams and made these madhahibs the

---

160 Nasr Abu-Zayd quotes Mohammad Mojtahedi Shabestari, see The Status of Women Between the Qur'an and Fiqh, in *Gender and Equality in Muslim Family Law: Justice and Ethics in the Islamic Legal Tradition,* eds., Ziba Mir-Hosseini, Kari Vogt, Lena Larsen and Christian Moe (London: I. B. Tauris, 2013), p. 165.
161 For a discussion on the issue of closing the gate of ijtihad, see Hallaq, "Was the Gate of Ijtihad Closed?", pp. 3–41.
162 Andra Nahal Behrouz, "Transforming Islamic Family Law: State Responsibility and the Role of Internal Initiative", *Columbia Law Review* Vol. 103, No. 5 (2003), p. 1147.
163 Quote taken from Rehman, "The Sharia, Islamic Family Laws and International Human Rights Law", p. 123.

only ones to know the past and the future knowledge, that they might have received what no one else ever had?[164]

Even though scholars have challenged the perception of closing the gate of ijtihad,[165] legal conformism persists.[166] From this time, which proceeded from the starting point of the decline of Muslim civilizations, Sunni Islamic law has had no considerable development.[167] Fear of inappropriate independent judgment and interpretation of the text led to blind-following of earlier interpretations. Consequently, jurisprudential problems have been arising for which there is no clear precedent or reference in the Quran or Sunnah. Islamic law thus became restricted to the legal findings of the jurists dating back to the ninth century.

The closing of the gate of ijtihad for the Sunni schools of law, basically curtailed any major development of Islamic law, imposing a dogma of limited religious interpretation, where interpreting the Sharia is limited.[168] For the advancement of the rights of women, the matter of re-interpretation is often argued by Muslim feminists to be the best option. According to them, since Sharia is based on these sources, much of it is contextual and needs to be re-assessed in a modified context.[169] There are however difficulties with re-interpretation based on ijtihad, as it is technically not allowed in any matter that is based on a definite text of the Quran or Sunnah. While that notion has been tested by scholars,[170] the right to exercise ijtihad is still in the domains of the mujtahid, and there needs to be serious discussions on the requirements of becoming a mujtahid, as the corpus of Islamic law, is becoming so great, it is nearly impossible for any person today to be able to fulfil the requirements.[171]

---

164 Quote taken from Vago, *Law and Society*, p. 111. See also, al-Musawe: *al-Muraja'at*, p. 326.
165 See Wael B. Hallaq, W., "Was the Gate of Ijtihâd Closed?" in *Law and Legal Theory in Classical and Medieval Islam*, ed. Wael B. Hallaq (Aldershot: Routledge, 1995), pp. 3–41.
166 However, even after the closing of the gate of ijtihad, rulings were deduced for new cases using qiyas, without claiming to exercise ijtihad, see An-Naim, *Towards an Islamic Reformation*, p. 25.
167 Hashemi, *Religious Legal Traditions*, p. 7.
168 See Sobhi Mahmassani, "Adaptation of Islamic Jurisprudence to Modern Social Needs" in *Islam in Transition, Muslim Perspectives*, eds., John Donohue and John L. Esposito (New York: Oxford University Press, 1982), p. 15 and M. Iqbal, *Reconstruction of Religious Thought in Islam* (Lahore: Sh. Mohammed Ashraf, 1971).
169 Engineer, *The Rights of Women in Islam*, p. 12.
170 Nasr Abu-Zayd, "The Status of Women Between the Qur'an and Fiqh", p. 165.
171 Mohammad Iqbal argues: "The transfer of the power of ijtihad from individual representatives of schools to a Muslim legislative assembly, which in view of the growth of opposing sects, is the only form ijma can take in modern times, will secure contributions to legal discussions from laymen who happen to possess a keen insight into affairs. In this way alone we can stir into activity the dormant spirit of life in our legal system, and give

While Sunni scholars restricted the possibility of using ijtihad as a method of interpretation by the 9th century, ijtihad has been and still is a method used by the Shia schools of law. While women do have a better legal standing in some aspects in the Shia schools of law—an adult woman does not need a guardian for the marriage contract, inheritance rights are more beneficial and there is an opportunity for the husband to bequeath one-third to his wife—there are still discriminatory provisions justified by ijtihad in the Shia schools of law. The Shia also have a hierarchical system of religious leadership, where the highest position is held by the *marja'*. The marja' is responsible for re-interpretation of the relevance of Islamic laws to contemporary issues and has the authority to announce religious edicts.[172] Re-interpretations can only come about through

it an evolutionary outlook," see *Reconstruction of Religious Thought in Islam* (Delhi: Kitab Publishing House, 1974), p. 138. Similar to this line of thought, Abdul Hamid A. Abu Sulayman states that "we must realize, however, that modern knowledge has expanded immensely and has become so complex that it is impossible for a single person to acquire a command of the multiple aspects of even one branch of knowledge. This means that the ability necessary for ijtihad in any one of the various branches of knowledge requires specialization in and absolute mastery of that branch. In view of this multifariousness of knowledge, and the multifariousness of the fields of specialization, it is clear that ijtihad, insights, solutions and alternatives, in the domain of social and scientific knowledge cannot be provided by the specialists in legal studies alone. But the task and the expectation are impossible. This is most noticeable in the case of legislators who formulate and categorize the laws and regulations covering economics, politics, information, industry and scientific research or transformation. It cannot be assumed that they are the masterminds of the knowledge from which the laws and regulation have been derived. In view of the achievements and progress made in the modern fields of knowledge, we need to bring to bear the expertise of economists, politicians, administrators and others who are well-versed in the various affairs of social life. Such specialists should at the same time have first-hand knowledge of the Qur'an and the Sunnah, which give them proper insight into the morals, values and purpose of existence as understood in Islam and validate their activities and contributions," see "Islamization of Knowledge: A New Approach toward Reform of Contemporary Knowledge," in *Islam: Source and Purpose of Knowledge* (Herndon, VA: The International Institute of Islamic Thought, 1988), p. 102.

172 Such a concept of religious leadership entitled with the monopoly to interpret religious texts, is not recognized by the Sunni, see Liyakat Takim, "Reinterpretation of Reformation? Shi'a Law in the West", *Journal of Shi'a Islamic Studies* Vol. 3, No. 2 (2010), pp. 143–144. Takim also notes that "the view that a stratified and hierarchical leadership is a recent phenomenon in Shi'ism is refuted by Devin Stewart who finds abundant evidence of strong hierarchical religious leadership in both Shi'a and Sunni legal establishments in pre-modern times". See Devin Stewart, "Islamic Juridical Hierarchies and the Office of Marji' al-Taqlid", in *Shi'ite Heritage: Essays on Classical and Modern Traditions,* ed. Lynda Clarke (New York: Binghamton Global, 2001), p. 149. However, according to Ayatollah Taskhiri, a number of Shi'a scholars who lived after Shahid al-Thani (d. 1558) did not hold *a'lamiyyah* to be a necessary requirement in following a religious leader. See Ayatollah Muhammad Ah Taskhiri, "Supreme Authority (Marji'yah) in Shi'ism", in *Shi'ite Heritage,*

FOUNDATIONS OF ISLAMIC LAW   57

the endorsement of the highest-ranking religious authorities, although it may be facilitated by others.[173] Basically, the right of interpretation lies only in the hands of the highest religious leader, which, historically, has not generally been favorable for the rights of women.

2.4.2 Other Forms of Legal Reasoning

Other forms of legal reasoning are istishab, finding a link, and istishan, juristic preference.[174] The doctrine of istishab is a stricter doctrine that tends to ensure that the law of God is not tampered with. Here it is presumed that practices are legitimate and have a legitimate origin until the contrary has been proven.[175] The doctrine of istishan on the other hand, allows for a conclusion that presumably starts from a revealed text but differs from one reached using qiyas, and represents the intention of creating an exception to the law.[176] For example, if a person by mistake eats while he is supposed to be fasting, qiyas dictates that the fasting is void. However, this interpretation is disregarded in favor of a hadith pronouncing fasting valid if the act of eating was the result of a mistake.[177]

Some istishan exceptions were justified by sacred texts, while others were based on consensus or the principle of necessity, darurah. The principle is found in the Quran and allows for the impermissible to become permissible, such as eating pork, committing unlawful acts to save his or her life, or demonstrating disbelief in Islam under coercion, as long as the believer remains faithful at heart, if it should be necessary.[178] Another example might be washing

---

p. 169. After reviewing arguments for and against following the most learned, Taskhiri concludes, "while taqlid is certainly necessary, following the most learned is not". (176) See Takim, "Reinterpretation of Reformation? Shi'a Law in the West", note 6.

[173] Mohammad Samei, "Between Traditional Law and the Exigencies of Modern Life, Shia Responses to Contemporary Challenges in Islamic Law", *Journal of Shi'a Studies* Vol. 2, No. 3 (2009), p. 269.

[174] The principles are mainly used as a basis of evidence rather than of general law, see S. G. Vesey-Fitzgerald, "Nature and Sources of the Shari'a", 102.

[175] Ibid., 101.

[176] The principle of istishan literally means "choosing the better" and is similar to the concept of equity. It was used most extensively by the Hanafi School, especially when it was considered that the use of qiyas would lead to an excessively strict result, see S. G. Vesey-Fitzgerald, "Nature and Sources of the Shari'a", p. 94 and Wael B. Hallaq, *An Introduction to Islamic Law* (Cambridge: Cambridge University Press, 2009), p. 25.

[177] Aron Zysow, "Mu'tazilism and Maturidism in Hanafi Legal Theory", in *Studies in Islamic Legal Theory*, ed. Bernard G. Weiss, *Studies in Islamic Legal Theory* (Leiden: Brill, 2002), p. 248.

[178] Quran 2:239; 2:173; 5:3; 16:115 and 16:106.

with ritually impure water that would invalidate prayer according to qiyas, but not with istishan. Here, qiyas would lead to hardship as it is not always easy to produce clean water. The application of the principle of necessity as legitimizing departure from strict reasoning is seen as derived from and sanctioned by the Quran and the Sunnah, since necessity, when not acknowledged, can cause nothing but hardship.[179] Ultimately, the doctrine of istishan, inspired by the principle of fairness, allows for departure from the rule of positive law, if its application challenges the fundamental Islamic principle of justice and the objectives as laid down by the Sharia, and leads to unfair results.[180]

Among the legal methods developed, istislah or maslahah,[181] are considered as "containing the seeds of the future of the Sharia" and being the most feasible in bringing the ideals of Islam closer to apprehension for contemporary issues.[182] The terms mean "benefit" or "welfare" and have been understood to represent the benefit or welfare of the Muslim community as a whole. Whatever seemed useful for society could be justified as being in accordance with, and part of Sharia.[183] Rulings based on maslahah can be found in legal writings as

---

179 Hallaq, *An Introduction to Islamic Law*, p. 26. See also, Quran 22:78 and 2:185.
180 Mohammad Hashim Kamali, *Principles of Islamic Jurisprudence*, p. 383; Ezzati, "Islamic Law and the Challenges of Modern Time", p. 47. See also, Quran 16:90 and 57:25.
181 Maslahah is the term generally used under Maliki jurisprudence. Istislah or maslahah considers the spirit of the law, which is, maintenance of religion, life, reason, descendants, and property. Nevertheless, the principle was criticized for allowing too broad a human interpretation and intervention. It has been said that the concept of istislah or maslahah seem to be similar to the English idea of "public policy" or "the policy of the law", see S. G. Vesey-Fitzgerald, "Nature and Sources of the Shari'a", p. 101.
182 Kamali, "Law and Society. The Interplay of Revelation and Reason in the Shariah", p. 288.
183 A hierarchical classification for the determination of the scope of maslahah are benefits considered as indispensable or necessary, and those that improve life generally. The indispensable benefits, which have been described as universal and equated with fundamental rights by contemporary Muslim scholars, are the protection of life, religion, intellect, family or offspring and property. These rights must not only be promoted but also protected, see e.g. Mohammad H. Kamali, "Fundamental Rights of the Individual an Analysis of Haqq (Rights) in Islamic Law", *American Journal of Islamic Social Sciences* Vol. 10, No. 3 (1993), pp. 340, 362. There are actually four models of maslahah, which were developed over the course of four centuries. Over this period of time, the method developed from a subsidiary legal principle to constituting a central principle upon which legal theory and the construction of laws were built. If the feature of public interest in a case can be shown to be unquestionably connected with these universal principles, the reasoning must proceed in accordance with maslahah, see Opwis, "Maslaha in Contemporary Islamic Legal Theory", p. 197. While the potential of this concept is debated, Al-Tawfi maintains "that maslahah is decisive over even the text of the law and ijma if the latter cannot be reconciled with regard for the general welfare insofar as the legal aspects of everyday life are concerned", see Paret, Istishan and Istislah, in *Encyclopaedia of Islam* 4:255–59 (Leiden: Brill, 1978), p. 104. According to Al-Tawfi, maslahah could overturn

FOUNDATIONS OF ISLAMIC LAW 59

far back as the eighth and ninth century. During the last century, discussions about maslahah have formed a large part of the question of how to tackle the inherent problem of a legal system which is based on a determinate text, and apply it to everyday life in an ever-changing society.[184] It has been regarded as a vehicle of legal change, in bestowing legitimacy on interpretations of Islamic law where there cannot be found a basis in the scriptural sources.[185]

3   Who Has the Right to Interpret the Law?

As described, Islamic law poses a complex, pluralistic system of law based on a divine message amassed in the Quran, causing the disagreement on the distinction between law and the interpretation of the law. The conditions of validly exercising legal interpretation within the Islamic legal theory raises the important questions of what justifies interpretation, and who has the right to interpret the (sources of) law?[186] With the societal developments of the past centuries, some Muslims began to question whether the *fuqaha* could be trusted to distinguish Islamic laws from non-Islamic,[187] and whether only the fuqaha had the authority to interpret the sources of law.[188] The statement by

---

existing interpretations in parts of Sharia, as long as it does not fall within the category of ibadat, religious rituals, see An-Naim, *Towards an Islamic Reformation*, p. 26. See also Heiner Bielefeldt, "'Western' Versus 'Islamic' Human Rights Conceptions?: A Critique of Cultural Essentialism in the Discussion of Human Rights", *Political Theory* Vol. 28, No. 90 (2000), p. 106.

[184] However, the technical term used was, istislah, see Opwis, "Maslaha in Contemporary Islamic Legal Theory", pp. 183, 187.

[185] See John L. Esposito and John O. Voll, *Makers of Contemporary Islam* (Oxford: Oxford University Press, 2001), p. 192.

[186] Joseph E. Lowry, "The First Islamic Legal Theory: Ibn al-Muqaffa' on Interpretation, Authority, and the Structure of the Law", *Journal of the American Oriental Society* Vol. 128, No. 1 (2008), pp. 25–40.

[187] Lombardi, *Designing Islamic Constitutions*, p. 618. For a general overview of these debates see Sami Zubaida, "Contemporary Trends in Muslim Legal Thought and Ideology", in *The New Cambridge History of Islam: Muslims and Modernity: Culture and Society since 1800*, ed. Robert W. Hefner (Cambridge: Cambridge University Press, 2010), Vol. 6, p. 270.

[188] Robert W. Heffner, *Shar'ia Politics: Islamic Law and Society in the Modern World* (Bloomington: Indiana University Press, 2011), introduction and the subsequent case studies. For detailed analysis of debates in Southeast Asia and Egypt, see generally, R. Michael Feener, *Muslim Legal Thought in Modern Indonesia* (Cambridge: Cambridge University Press, 2007). For Shia debates on Sharia adherence in the Iranian constitution, see Naser Ghobadzadeh, *Religious Secularity, a Theological Challenge to the Islamic State* (New York: Oxford University Press, 2015).

Al-Azhar, that interpretation lies in the hands of the jurists, proves the view the traditionalists have historically had and continue to uphold. This view is not exclusive to al-Azhar; all traditionalist groups, Sunni and Shia, claim that the right to interpret lies in the hands of a traditionally trained jurist. However, no authority in Islam can claim to own the right interpretation, as the Quran declares that no one can interpret the verses but God:

> It is He who sent down upon thee the Book, wherein are verses clear that the Essence of the Book, and others ambiguous. As for those in whose hearts is swerving, they follow the ambiguous part, desiring dissension, and desiring its interpretation; and *none knows its interpretation, save only God.* And those firmly rooted in knowledge say, 'We believe in it; all is from our Lord,' yet none remembers, but men possessed of minds.[189]

As no one but God can know which interpretation that is correct, no interpretation is exclusive. Islam has always emphasized the direct relationship between the individual believer and God. There is no mentioning of a distinct class of men with the ability to interpret the Quran, equivalent to Christian priests.[190] The principle of God's unity, tawhid, symbolizes the idea of a God who is indivisible, and whose sovereignty is indivisible. Theories of a religious elite with the right to act as an extension of God's sovereignty would be incompatible with the doctrine of tawhid.[191] It was the Islamic political theory of the leader, the caliph, which came to provide an exception to this notion. The question of how to rule, given the assumption that no one could exercise power over another, laid the ground for a theory of political power in Islam, based on the principle of representation through agency, that is, the belief that the caliph is the ideal public agent, *wakil*, acting on behalf of the community.[192] Ever since, the *ulama*, Muslim scholars who are recognized as having specialist knowledge of Islamic sacred law and theology, have gained a significant role and influence in Islamic societies. Unlike other religions, where the religious scholars are theologians, in Islam they are acting as sacral jurists.[193] In classical Islamic law,

---

189   Quran 3:7.
190   Gibreel, G., "The Ulama: Middle Eastern Powers Broken", *The Middle East Quarterly* Vol. 8, No. 4 (2001), pp. 15–23.
191   Barlas, *"Believing Women" in Islam*, p. 13.
192   Fadel, *Islamic Law Reform*, p. 48.
193   Bassam Tibi, "The Return of The Sacred to Politics as Constitutional Law: The Case of Shari'atization of Politics in Islamic Civilization", *Theoria: A Journal of Social and Political Theory* No. 115 (2008), p. 103.

"it was the jurists who granted themselves the right of authoritative interpretation, in their capacity as the sole authorized practitioners of legal interpretation, ijtihad".[194] The interpretation was influenced by education, personal position, and historical environment.[195] This led to the development of different, and at times, conflicting doctrines of positive law during the earliest period of Islamic legal history. The conflict between scholarly and caliphal authority was a central and a producing factor in the development of early Islamic legal thought.[196] While the caliphs found them competing with the law as embodied in hadiths, historically the ulama did not insist on the implementation of full Sharia, as long as it was recognized as a religious ideal.[197] Although a characteristic feature of Islamic law, the inconsistent legal doctrines do not in any real sense allow for a measure of certainty of the law, as certainty is not built into the law itself. Consequently, the classical interpretations made by jurists of Islam are nothing more than a man-made construct and most importantly, not the only possible interpretation.[198] Religion cannot be defined by a mere idea of a jurist or theologian as an interpreter of the text, making no single text in Islam unavailable for a different interpretation.[199] Essentially, traditionalists are maintaining adherence to a pluralistic legal system, which they believe is divinely inspired, but actually is the mere subjective construction of infallible men, biased by the prevailing trends in the societies they lived in.

Leaders in Muslim countries today are competing with calls for reform and secular notions of how the divine should be interpreted,[200] while at the same time, the modern revitalization of Islam has also paved the way for the rise and the demands of ultra-conservative and literal readings of the Quran and practices. The demand of a greater application of Sharia in modern Muslim societies, calls for examining the question to what extent the law should be subject to human interpretation and which aspects of the divine law require no such interpretation.[201] A contemporary version of the Sharia is essential for the social circumstances of present times, as the historical Islamic law

---

194　Lowry, "The First Islamic Legal Theory", p. 28.
195　Opwis, "Maslaha in Contemporary Islamic Legal Theory", p. 182.
196　Lowry, "The First Islamic Legal Theory", p. 39.
197　Schacht, *Origins of Muhammadan Jurisprudence*, p. 84.
198　Leila Ahmed, "Women and the Advent of Islam", *Signs* Vol. 11, No. 4 (1986), p. 679.
199　Shabestari, *Hermeneutic, the Scripture and the Tradition*, p. 114.
200　Lowry, "The First Islamic Legal Theory", p. 39.
201　Aron Zysow, *The Economy of Certainty: Introduction to the Typology of Islamic Legal Theory* (Cambridge: Harvard University Press, 1984), pp. 1–8, 493–511.

model fails to address emerging new questions, concerns and challenges successfully; particularly when it comes to the legal status of women. Muslim women should not be compelled to choose between religious belief and their autonomy.

CHAPTER 3

Women and Islam

Muslim scholars maintain that the supremacy of men over women was undisputedly the accepted way of living and the rule in pre-Islamic Arabia. The Quran came to support it by providing that "men are the managers of the affairs of women for that God has preferred in bounty one of them over another, and for that they have expended of their property",[1] and that "women have such honourable rights as obligations, but their men have a degree above them".[2] Based on these verses, the ulama did not make any changes to men's supremacy compared to jahiliyya as the social, political, and economic structures of jahiliyya had a decisive role in shaping laws regarding women.[3] The economic structure with financial dependency in pre-Islamic Arabia continued after the introduction of Islam. Women were generally not capable of surviving the harsh conditions without the physical strength and power of a man, and the Quran accepted the financial superiority of men. Consequently, the right to guardianship of underaged children was afforded men, as women did not have the economic capacity to take care of them. The permission of choosing a husband for an underage girl comes from the same premises; the financial burden of the family would decrease with one less child to feed. The blood-money of a woman was half that of a man, as the economic loss was greater if the breadwinner of the family was killed. The unchanged economic conditions after Islam led to the endorsement of not only blood money but other economically disadvantageous interpretations in Islamic law,[4] while simultaneously introducing property rights and the right to inheritance for females.

---

1   Quran 4:34.
2   Quran 2:228.
3   Jonathan Berkey, *The Formation of Islam: Religion and Society in the Near East, 600–1800* (New York: Cambridge University Press, 2003).
4   Abbas Mehregan, "Islamo-Arabic Culture and Women's Law: An Introduction to the Sociology of Women's Law in Islam", *International Journal for the Semiotics of Law* Vol. 29 (2016), p. 416.

1 The Pre-Islamic Status of Women According to Muslim Sources

Muslim scholars refer to the period before Islam as a period of barbarism and ignorance in which the Arabs were bound by tradition and precedent,[5] and the tribes followed polytheistic religions and worshipped many gods, goddesses, demons, animals and even stones.[6] Agriculture and trade were the main means of earning a livelihood; however, another method of creating considerable wealth was through plundering. Invasions and warfare between tribes, was completely determined by the economic gains in the Arabian Desert which had limited economic resources.[7] The socio-political, economic, and moral structure of this era consisted of disunited semi-nomadic tribes with no central authority to bind them together. In the tribal form of society, the tribe was recognized as the social and political unit and played the role of a state in desert communities. Different tribes had different social traditions and cultural customs.[8] Individual identity was rejected in favor of the collective identity of the tribe who made decisions about individual issues.[9] Decisions made by tribal leaders were binding on all those within the tribe,[10] and women could never undertake the control and management of the tribe.[11] For the individual, this meant the absence of legal protection outside of the tribe, the lack of a developed concept of criminal justice and the reduction of crimes to torts.[12] Affiliation to a tribe meant protection for its members, but also punishment if they violated the value system of the

---

5   Subhi Rajab Mahmasani, *Falsafat Al-Tashri fi Al-Islam, the Philosophy of Jurisprudence in Islam,* trans. Farhat Ziadeh (Leiden: Brill, 1961) p. 15 and Schacht, *An Introduction to Islamic Law,* p. 17.
6   Jeri Altneu Sechzer, "Islam and Women: Where Tradition Meets Modernity: History and Interpretations of Islamic Women's Status", *Sex Roles* Vol. 51, Nos. 5/6 (2004), p. 265.
7   Ahmed El-Ashker and Rodney Wilson, *Islamic Economics: A Short History* (Leiden: Brill, 2002), p. 8; Kim, Sarang, "Reconciliation among the Bedouin", *St Frances Magazine* Vol. 1, No. 5 (2009), p. 4.
8   Some norms retained their validity and importance even in today's Arab societies, see Sarang, "Reconciliation among the Bedouin", pp. 1–14.
9   Berkey, *The Formation of Islam.*
10 Tareq Y. Ismael and Jacqueline S. Ismael, *Government and Politics of the Contemporary Middle East: Continuity and Change* (Abingdon: Routledge, 2011), p. 45.
11 Mehregan, "Islamo-Arabic Culture and Women's Law", p. 412.
12 Since the tribe was considered responsible for the actions of its members, blood feuds were lessened by the institution of blood-money. All these institutions and features, more or less, modified Islam and left their traces in Islamic law. See Schacht, *An Introduction to Islamic Law,* p. 7.

tribe.[13] Disputes between two persons from different tribes often led to conflict between the tribes.[14]

The law of personal status and family, inheritance and criminal law, was dominated by the ancient Arabian tribal system and was different in cities.[15] The customary law of the Bedouins, who constituted the majority of the Arabs, differed from the laws of cities such as Mecca and Medina.[16] Mecca was a trading city, and it is likely that Mecca and other towns such as Medina possessed more sophisticated laws than those of the Bedouins.[17] Muslim scholars maintain that the social structure of Arabia was patriarchal, where women were subordinated to men in the tribe, family, and society. Having sons was profoundly preferred as "many daughters were often viewed as a lack of virility".[18] Female infanticide was common since the pre-Islam Arabs were disgraced with the birth of a girl.[19] Women were generally seen as consumers and as an economic and social burden.[20] The period is usually described by the frequency of divorce and loose unions, since "promiscuity" characterized the relations of sexes in pre-Islamic Arabia.

On the other hand, it is also said that women were strictly controlled, due partly to the endless threat of kidnapping by raiders. The norms in the closed tribal society prevented women from any interaction with male strangers within or outside of the tribe. Women enjoyed no rights whatsoever, or if they did, it was negligible as their status was low.[21] They had no independent identity as they were subjugated to their nearest male relative, who treated them like a commodity, not only by being enslaved but also, since they could be inherited, like a possession.[22] They could be sold in marriage, and because

---

13 Donna Bowen, "Islamic law and the position of women", in *Islam and social policy*, ed. Stephen P. Heyneman (Nashville: Vanderbilt University Press, 2004), p. 50.
14 Sarang, "Reconciliation among the Bedouin", pp. 1–14.
15 Schacht, *An Introduction to Islamic Law*, p. 7. It appears as if polygyny was not practiced in Mecca or Medina. It is suggested that Meccan men might have contracted temporary marriages with tribal women who stayed with their own people, see Gertrude Stern, *Marriage in Early Islam* (London: Royal Asiatic Society, 1939), pp. 62, 66, 70, 73; cited in Mernissi, *Beyond the Veil*, pp. 29–31.
16 Although primitive in character, the customary law of the Bedouins, was by no means simple in its rules or application. For example, penal law was reduced to questions of compensation and payment.
17 Schacht, *An Introduction to Islamic Law*, p. 6.
18 Donald Lee Berry, *Pictures of Islam: A Student's Guide to Islam* (Macron: Mercer University Press, 2007), p. 7.
19 Quran 16:58–59.
20 Mohd Umar, *Bride Burning in India: A Socio Legal Study* (New Delhi: Publishing, 1998), p. 8.
21 Stowasser, "The Status of Women in Early Islam", p. 15.
22 Engineer, *The Rights of Women in Islam*, p. 20.

the tribe's honor was linked to the woman's chastity and fidelity, their behavior was rigorously controlled, as they were considered unreliable and untrustworthy in matters concerning testimony.[23] Marriage usually occurred within the tribe, where the marriage of paternal cousins was preferred, and the male members decided who they could marry.[24]

The predominant form of marriage was contractual, which Islam retained with improvements for women. However, various forms of abusive marriage occurred. The oldest son would be entitled to marry his father's wife after the father had died. If he was willing to marry her, he would throw a cloth over her and inherit her. He could also prevent her from marrying anyone else, and upon her death, he would inherit her wealth.[25] If there was no son, the next male kin of the deceased was granted the same rights.[26] She could only free herself from him by paying a suitable compensation. The mutual exchange of wives also occurred, as well as the exchange of daughters and sisters. Another form of marriage, which was extremely rare among Arabs, but did still occur, involved the husband asking his wife to have sexual intercourse with another man in order to get pregnant. Usually, this only occurred when a man was impotent, and generally, the wives were sent to men who were known for their bravery. Some argue that these marriages were a kind of business, as slave-girls were sent to these men so they could give birth to healthy children which they could employ themselves, or sell in the market. The practice of men who captured women and married them, against their will, also occurred. A man also had the right to marry his female slave, and could choose to free the children that were conceived, keep them as slaves or accept them as his children.[27] While marrying an adoptive son's wife was forbidden in pre-Islamic Arabia, it came to be allowed by the Quran, causing an uproar among the people. Islam did not find anything wrong with such marriages since the Quran maintained that there is no blood relation between the adopted son and the adopter, as the adopter is not the natural father.[28]

---

23   Mernissi, *The Veil and the Male Elite*. See also, Mehregan, "Islamo-Arabic Culture and Women's Law", p. 410.
24   Keddie, *Women in the Middle East*, p. 18.
25   Engineer, *The Rights of Women in Islam*, p. 24.
26   Abdur Rahim, *Muhammadan Jurisprudence* (Lahore: Mansoor Book House, 1995), pp. 7–9 and Rahman, "Status of Women in the Quran", pp. 38–39.
27   A majority of Muslim jurists argue that the prohibition also applies to *zawaj al-badal* marriages, as there is no mahr paid in either case, see Engineer, *The Rights of Women in Islam*, pp. 24–25.
28   Quran 33:37.

The practice of having many wives in order to build relationships with other tribes was common. Men had the right of unrestricted polygyny, whereas women had no right to divorce or inheritance.[29] Men had an absolute right over women in matters of divorce and could take her back for up to three divorces. After the third divorce, he did not have any rights over her. After he had divorced her three times the husband could only remarry his wife if she first freely married and divorced another man. Divorce occurred by declaring, "go back to your parents" or "I separate you" and "your robe is on your shoulder" or "I liberate you". It could also occur that a man might vow to leave his wife for a period of time, during which he would not go near her as a form of punishment.[30]

1.1 The Pre-Islamic Status of Women According to Historical Sources

Despite how the situation for women has been described by some Muslim scholars, it was not quite so bad, at least, not for all women. What can be determined about the status of women before the advancement of Islam is that women had different statuses in different contexts in the same society. Women who lacked the economic or social standing suffered abuse, exploitation, and marginalization. Women were treated differently, not just because of their gender but because of their social and economic status.[31] However, the Muslim claim that women as a group were treated poorly before Islam is a mere religious claim, not confirmed by the few historical accounts of that period. Most of the information pertaining to jahiliyya has come from sources under the censorship of Muslim believers, who wish to disparage everything that preceded Islam.[32] Jahiliyya was and is portrayed as a state of corruption and immorality, the opposite of the Islamic ethos, and basically reduced to a set of morally negative features.[33] Even with the scarce evidence available, it is known that both matriarchal and patriarchal systems existed, which imply fundamental differences in the position of women and their structural relations.[34]

In the matrilineal case, the marriage took place at the home of the woman who also had the right to dismiss her husband. Women stipulated their rights

---

29 Esposito, *Women in Muslim Family Law*, p. 48.
30 There were instances where men divorced their wives as many times as they wanted to and also took her back as many times as they wanted to. See Engineer, *The Rights of Women in Islam*, pp. 26–29.
31 Wiebke Walter, *Women in Islam* (Princeton: Winer, 1993), pp. 90, 115.
32 Ghada Karmi, "Women, Islam and Patriarchalism", in Moghissi, *Women and Islam*, p. 172.
33 Nadia Maria El Cheikh, *Women, Islam and Abbasid Identity* (Cambridge: Harvard University Press, 2015), p. 18.
34 Smith, *Kinship and Marriage in Early Arabia*, pp. 77 ff, 156, 172.

within the marriage, ensuring that they would live with their husbands for as long as they wanted to and could initiate divorce if they wanted to. One method of divorce among Bedouins involved women changing the direction of the entrance to the tent when she wanted to divorce her husband. When the husband saw this, he knew that his wife had divorced him and would not go to her, as the tent was the property of the woman. This was obviously not something ordinary women could do, as the ability to decide the conditions of marriage and the dissolution of the marriage was a consequence of their high status in society.[35]

There was no single fixed institution of marriage: instead, a variety of types of union were practiced by men and women. Even polyandry, where a woman has two or more husbands, was practiced.[36] Women would frequently remarry as soon as they were divorced, and if the woman was pregnant at the time of remarriage, the child would belong to the new husband.[37] A "waiting period" for women before remarriage was not observed.[38] Physical paternity seems to have been unimportant, and any offspring belonged to the mother's kin group, by contrast to what was introduced with Islam.[39]

There were examples of women being landowners, and both publicly and officially registered as owners in legal documents. Their capacity to stand in court on behalf of her party was recognized, as well as having the right to inherit. Women were able to initiate legal documents without the need for a guardian. There are also examples of women who acted in the capacity of a judge in conflict resolution. Queens, goddesses, and female prophets, as well as upper-class women, enjoyed high status and legal rights and privileges. Queens were depicted in coins, draped in long garments girdled at the waist. Public life was typically restricted to specific religious activities such as priestesses or worshippers for women, whereas men dominated other public domains such as legal and political fields.[40] Several female goddesses were held in considerable

---

35 Engineer, *The Rights of Women in Islam*, p. 27.
36 Sechzer, "Islam and Women: Where Tradition Meets Modernity", p. 267.
37 Karmi, "Women, Islam and Patriarchalism", p. 173.
38 Stern, *Marriage in Early Islam*, pp. 61–62 and 172–173.
39 Mernissi, *Beyond the Veil*, p. 27.
40 There were, however, transactions that were restricted to women; women were not allowed to have legitimate heirs to their tombs. Also, while women were known to pass inheritance to their children, it seems as if their daughters were restricted from owning their inheritance by hereditary title, which may be a formula related to male inheritance. Hatoon al-Fassi, *Women in pre-Islamic Arabia: Nabataea* (Oxford: Archaeopress, 2007), pp. 38–65. In Roman Code, the guardian, was known as the tutor, and was usually the father if the woman was unmarried, or the husband if she was married. For widows, the guardianship was transferred to her son, a practice that still occurs in Saudi Arabia.

esteem by the pre-Islamic Arabs. 'Uzza, Manat, and al-Lat, are the best known of these, to whom many shrines existed. These are the same goddesses that are mentioned in the alleged satanic verses.

The existence of such cults, suggests, that society was originally structured on a matriarchal or matrilineal foundation.[41] From such an outlook it becomes evident that the verses relevant to the position of women were meant to maintain a patriarchal family, with a purpose of eliminating or altering some customs that were seen as detrimental to the stability of the family, as perceived by Islam.[42] In those cases, it is apparent that Islam restricted or modified the freedoms, activities, and roles that some of the women in jahiliyya had experienced:[43]

> Jahiliyya women participated actively in society, a habit that necessarily carried over into early Muslim society; after all, these were the people who, by conversion and by conquest, became the first Muslims. Until the latter years of Muhammad's ascendancy, and perhaps later for women other than his wives, women mingled freely with men; even in the last years of Muhammad's life they were not veiled, except his own wives.[44]

Many customs, where women had more rights, were abolished, in favor of a type of marriage which unmistakably favored men in matters of divorce, polygamy and the custody of children. By denouncing all other forms of marriage as fornication,[45] Islam confirmed the transition from a society with matriarchal

---

See Jane F. Gardner, *Women in Roman Law & Society* (London: Croom Helm, 1986), p. 5 and Riet van Bremen, *The Limits of Participation: women and civic life in the Greek East in the Hellenistic and Roman periods* (Amsterdam: Dutch monographs on ancient history and archaeology, J. C. Gieben, 1996), pp. 205–208. Certain Greek and Roman women were not perceived as having legal standing or capacity in public affairs and the Roman court expected a woman to be represented by a guardian. There are instances of women having guardians that were not fathers or husbands, see al-Fassi, *Women in pre-Islamic Arabia*, p. 54.

41   Karmi, "Women, Islam and Patriarchalism", p. 172.
42   Susan Spectorsky, *Themes in Islamic Studies: Women in Classical Islamic Law: A Survey of the Sources* (Boston: Brill, 2009) p. 24.
43   Ahmed, "Women and the Advent of Islam", p. 670.
44   Mernissi, *Women and Gender in Islam*, p. 68.
45   Leila Ahmed argues that "the fact that in prohibiting adultery and sexual misconduct generally Islam was outlawing previously accepted practices is presumably among the reasons for the otherwise surely extraordinary Koranic ruling (4:16) that four witnesses should be produced to convict anyone of these crimes. The ruling suggests both that those engaging in practices being designated by Islam as sexual misconduct were engaging in them with some openness (the openness appropriate to relatively accepted rather

structures to an exclusively patriarchal system.[46] There is no evidence to indicate that the type of polygyny as endorsed by Islam was a practice in Medina, and if there were occurrences of the practice before Muhammad's initiative, it was not common.[47] This was the crucial point in changing the relations between sexes, and Islam confirmed and legitimized the patriarchal structure, through a set of regulations which placed the man as the head of the family and society.[48]

> ... it becomes difficult not to conclude that the absolute empowerment of men in relation to women in all matters relating to sexuality and offspring and the disempowerment of women (and thus the complete transformation of his [Muhammad] society's mores in the areas of the relation between the sexes) was also itself one of Muhammad's prime objectives. In import, and indeed explicitly, Koranic verses do recognize women's rights to equality in marriage for example, 'they [wives] have rights corresponding to those which husbands have, inequitable reciprocity' [2:229], and the Quran's directive to this effect is sufficiently distinct for most schools of Islamic law to grant women the right to be empowered, by marriage contract, to initiate divorce or stipulate their marriage conditions, including monogamy. Nevertheless, the type of marriage Islam was setting up as the norm for that early society evidently was one in which women were disempowered.[49]

Islam replaced the jahilite woman with the Muslim woman, who, with the patriarchal interpretations of the verses in the Quran, is almost the opposite of her predecessor, which eventually led to the seclusion of women.[50]

2 The Wives of Muhammad

To examine the changes that would overtake women in Islamic Arabia, the lives and marriages of two of Prophet Muhammad's wives, Khadija and Aisha,

---

than 'immoral' or prohibited practices) and that Mohamad realized that such practices could not be instantly eradicated." See Ahmed, "Women and the Advent of Islam", p. 670.
46 Karmi, "Women, Islam and Patriarchalism", p. 174.
47 Watt, *Muhammad at Medina*, pp. 277–279: Stern, *Marriage in Early Islam*, p. 62.
48 Smith, *Kinship and Marriage in Early Arabia*; Watt, *Muhammad at Medina*, pp. 272–73.
49 Ahmed, "Women and the Advent of Islam", p. 678.
50 Ahmed, *Women and Gender in Islam*, p. 62.

provide great examples. It was jahiliyya society that shaped the conduct and opportunities of Muhammad's first wife Khadija, whereas Aisha, born to Muslim parents, is part of the transition period and in some aspects her life reflects jahiliyya as well as Islamic practices.[51] During this period, women enjoyed a more independent role, and it is difficult to see how this could have happened unless there had been a tradition of female independence before the introduction of Islam.[52]

2.1   Khadija

Pre-Islamic Arabia was familiar with female entrepreneurs. Muhammad's great-grandfather Hashim met his wife on a trading mission, where she traded on her account through instructions to agents.[53] Muhammad's great-grandmother accepted Hashim's marriage proposal on the pre-nuptial terms that she retained control over her property and had the right to divorce at will.[54] When the Prophet's father married his mother, he remained with her only for three days since she stayed with her tribe. Muhammad's father died while his mother was pregnant with him, but Muhammad was raised and taken care of by her until her death. It was only after her death that Muhammad's father's kin took charge.[55] Muhammad's grandfather had him taken from his mother's clan only with difficulty.[56]

Muhammad, like his great-grandfather, married a businesswoman. Khadija was a wealthy widow who employed Muhammad to oversee her caravan which traded between Mecca and Syria.[57] She belonged to Mecca's social elite and was described as a "woman of honour and power and a hirer of men".[58] She was fifteen years older than Muhammad, and educated to a higher standard as she could read and write, unlike Muhammad, who was illiterate. She had been married twice before she proposed marriage to Muhammad. From her first marriage, she had two sons, and she was entrusted with her second husband's daughter when he died.[59] Khadija is particularly important in the story of

---

[51]   Ibid., pp. 665–691.
[52]   Karmi, "Women, Islam and Patriarchalism", p. 173.
[53]   Benedikt Koehler, "Female Entrepreneurship in Early Islam", *Economic Affairs* Vol. 21, No. 2 (2011), p. 93.
[54]   Muir, *The Life of Mohammad from Original Sources*, p. CXIII.
[55]   Ibn Sa'd, *Kitab al-Tabaqat, Biographien*, 9 vols., ed. E. Sachau (Leiden: Brill, 1904), cited in Mernissi, *Beyond the Veil*, p. 31.
[56]   Watt, *Muhammad at Medina*, p. 375.
[57]   For a brief overview of her life, see Resit Haylamaz, *Khadija – The First Muslim and the Wife of the Prophet Muhammad* (New Jersey: The Light, Inc., 2007).
[58]   Ibn Sa'd, *Kitab al-Tabaqat*, 8:9.
[59]   Haylamaz, *Khadija*, p. 29.

Islam because of her significance to Muhammad: "her wealth freed him from the need to earn a living and enabled him to lead the life of contemplation that was the prelude to his becoming a prophet, and her support and confidence were crucial to him in his venturing to preach Islam".[60] She was the first person to declare her faith to the Prophet and thereby becoming the first Muslim.[61] The Prophet described her as "the best among the women (of this nation)".[62]

While having two wives simultaneously was not an unusual practice in the society that the Prophet lived in, it was a practice that was new to the Prophet following the death of Khadija. This led scholars to speculate that there was a marriage contract between them, specifying that the Prophet would not take another wife during her lifetime.[63]

Khadija's economic independence, her marriage to a man many years younger than herself and her monogamous marriage all reflect the traditions in jahiliyya rather than Islamic practices.[64] The fact that there were wealthy women, such as Khadija, even before the rise of Islam, suggests that women who came from a prominent Arabian family were able to own property and run their affairs, without the interference of men.

2.2 Aisha

After Khadija's death, Muhammad's aunt suggested that Muhammad should take wives.[65] It is soon after these marriages that the Quranic verse permitting polygyny is revealed.[66] Aisha was the six-year-old daughter of Muhammad's

---

60   Ahmed, *Women and Gender in Islam*, p. 42.
61   Even before she married Muhammad, she had dreams and could see signs of his prophet hood. On one occasion, she saw a strong light coming into to her house. She told this to her mentor who told Khadija that he believed it to be the light of the Prophet. See Haylamaz, *Khadija*, p. 50. See also, Muhammad Abduh Yamani, *Umm al-Mu'minin Khadija bint Khuwaylid Sayyidatun fi Qalb al-Mustafa* (Damascus: Mu'assasat al-Ulum al-Quran, 2002), p. 26.
62   "Mary, the daughter of 'Imran, was the best among the women (of the world of her time) and Khadija is the best among the women (of this nation)", Al-Bukhari, *Sahih*, Hadith 3432.
63   Nabia Abbott, *Aishah, the Beloved of Muhammad* (Chicago: University of Chicago, 1942), p. 3; Maxinne Robinson, *Mohamad*, trans. Ann Carter (New York: Penguin Books, 1971), p. 55.
64   Ahmed, *Women and Gender in Islam*, p. 42.
65   Supposedly, when Muhammad had asked whom he should marry, his aunt had suggested "Aisha if he wanted a virgin ... and Sawda if a non-virgin". Muhammad replied that she could speak with both of them. Quote taken from Ahmed, *Women and Gender in Islam*, p. 49. See also, Abbott, *Aishah*, p. 55.
66   The verse was revealed after the battle of Uhud (625 C.E.), where a large number of Muslim men were killed and many women were therefore widowed. Encouraging men to marry more than one woman was beneficial for the Muslim community as it was also

closest supporter, and later on the first caliph, Abu Bakr. When the Prophet asked for permission from Abu Bakr to marry Aisha, Abu Bakr replied: "but you are my brother", the Prophet replied, "you are my brother in the religion of God and the Qur'an, but she is halal to me".[67] There is no suggestion that anyone thought the marriage would be inappropriate because of the age difference. In the early days of Islam, the Khawariji,[68] opposed the practice of concubines and the marriage of young girls, even though the Prophet himself owned a concubine and married Aisha when she was about nine.[69] They argued that God had allowed specific privileges to the Prophet and that those privileges were not permitted for other men.[70] Aisha appears to have had issues on this matter

a way of preventing women to returning to jahiliyya types of relationships, see Ahmed, "Women and the Advent of Islam", p. 680. See also, Quran 4:4.

[67] Nicolas Awde, *Women in Islam: An Anthology from the Qur'an and Hadiths* (Richmond: Curzon Press, 2000), p. 92. See also, Al-Bukhari, *Sahih*, Book, 7, Hadith 12. It is said that Aisha realized that she was married (that is, that the marriage agreement had been concluded) when her mother called her in from her games with her friends and told her she must stay indoors. But she did not ask to whom. When Aisha was no more than nine or ten, Abu Bakr, asked Muhammad why he was delaying consummation of the marriage. When Muhammad replied that he was yet unable to provide the marriage portion, Abu Bakr forthwith provided it himself. The marriage was consummated in Aisha's father's house in Sunh: "my mother came to me and I was swinging on a swing ... She brought me down from the swing, and I had some friends there and she sent them away, and she swiped my face with a little water, and led me till we stopped by the door, and I was breathless [from being on the swing] and we waited till I regained my breath. Then she took me in, and the Prophet was sitting on a bed in our house with men and women of the Ansar [Medinians] and she sat me on his lap, and said, 'These are your people. God bless you in them and they in you'. And then the men and women rose immediately and went out, and the Prophet consummated the marriage in our house." Ahmed, *Women and Gender in Islam*, pp. 49–51.

[68] The Khawariji movements arose in 657 C.E. after the death of Muhammad and the dispute over political leadership that followed. They are considered to be the first and oldest inspiration for the doctrine of political Islam, see Nazih Ayibu, *Political Islam: Religion and Politics in the Arab World* (New York: Routledge, 1993), p. 96. For an overview of the Khawariji, see Crone, *Medieval Political Thought*, chapter 5, and for their theory on the caliphate, see Sir Thomas Arnold, *The Caliphate* (Oxford: Clarendon Press, 1924), pp. 188–189.

[69] Her age at marriage has been widely debated. See Kecia Ali, *The Lives of Muhammad* (Cambridge: Harvard University Press, 2014), pp. 157–158.

[70] In the Khawarij's view, the majority of Muslims were deviating from the straight path. The Khawarij felt that they alone had been entrusted with the true version of Islam and that it was their religious duty to disseminate it. The Khawarij was a short-lived sect in Islamic history, but their position on apostates and their generous interpretation on *tafkir*, declaring Muslims as non-believers and consequently deserving death. Their rhetoric has survived and is the basis for several modern radical movements. Elie A. Salem, *The Political Theory and Institutions of the Khawarij* (Baltimore: John Hopkins University Press, 1956),

when the Prophet announced that he had received a revelation allowing him to enter into marriages not permitted other men. She declared that "it seems to me your Lord hastens to satisfy your desire!"[71] At the end of his life, the Prophet was married to several wives, more than the maximum four as established by the Quran.[72]

Aisha had a special status among Muhammad's wives and became Muhammad's undisputed favorite. When rumors spread that Aisha had committed adultery, Muhammad's dismay prevented him from prophesying. Slandering of her chastity called forth verses in the Quran where she was vindicated in the verses which describe the punishment of adultery, but also the punishment for someone who falsely accuses one of adultery:[73]

> And those who cast it up on women in wedlock, and then bring not four witnesses, scourge them with eighty stripes, and do not accept any testimony of theirs ever; those -- they are the ungodly.[74]

Aisha was often present at battlefields to support those engaged in battle and actively participated in political and public life.[75] Soon after Muhammad's death, the Muslim community began consulting her on Muhammad's ways, and her explanations were used to settle ideas of practices and even points of law.[76] She is one of the renowned and credible narrators of hadiths and is known to have completed and corrected hadiths which were reported

---

p. 86. See also, Al-Misri, Abu Hamza, *The Khawaarij and Jihad* (Birmingham: Makhtabah al-Ansar, 2000); Jeffrey Thomas Kenney, *Heterodoxy and Culture: The Legacy of the Khawarij in Islamic History* (Ann Arbor: U.M.I., 1991); Jeffrey Thomas Kenney, *Muslim Rebels: Kharijites and the Politics of Extremism in Egypt* (Oxford: Oxford University Press, 2006) and Patricia Crone, *God's Rule: Government and Islam* (New York: Columbia University Press, 2006).

71 Ibn Sa'd, *Kitab al-Tabaqat*, 8:112.
72 Annemarie Schimmel, *And Muhammad is His Messenger: The Veneration of the Prophet in Islamic Piety* (Chapel Hills: University of North Carolina Press, 1985), p. 50.
73 Spellberg, *Politics, Gender, and the Islamic Past*, p. 3.
74 Quran 24:4.
75 Sayeh & Morse Jr., "Islam and the Treatment of Women", pp. 322–323 and accompanying footnotes. For an account of the life of Aisha see Abbott, *Aishah* and Spellberg, *Politics, Gender, and the Islamic Past*. It is argued that her status has to do with the fact that it was because of her there were revelations disclosing the punishment for slander and the verse declaring that it was acceptable for Muslims to perform ablution with sand or earth when there was no water. See Haylamaz, *Aisha*, pp. 105–115.
76 Ahmed, *Women and Gender in Islam*, p. 73.

erroneous or insufficient. These corrections often led to the construction of hadiths with different meanings and significance.[77]

Although Aisha lived in a period which is perceived as ideal in the Muslim imagination, her legacy is a source of great controversy. For Sunni, she is a role model for women, but her participation in the first battle between Muslims and her involvement in politics is cause for disagreement.[78] The Shia blame Aisha for opposing Ali's claim to the caliphate and for taking part in the battle against Ali. Some commentators view the conflicts between Aisha and Fatima, the daughter of Muhammad, as an extension of political conflicts outside the house, especially after his death. Aisha was portrayed as prone to jealousy and intrigue, which became the driving force for all her actions and decisions. As part of this hostile environment, Aisha used her knowledge of hadiths as a political tool to give legitimacy to one issue over the other.[79] Other commentators contest a view that Aisha was involved in intrigue and political conflict, arguing that because of her age, it is not likely that she had so much power to influence decision-making. Aisha's participation in the Battle of the Camel is described as a short period of political participation, where she, upon defeat, withdrew herself from the political arena.[80] Another commentator justifies her participation by blaming the companions of the Prophet for drawing Aisha into the conflict.[81]

Because of her position, her attitude toward the troubles of women was considered to be an advantage for women in general. Aisha became a consultant for women; women visited her, confessed their problems, and were given advice by Aisha on how to handle their situation.[82] One woman came to Aisha, telling her that she had been under her husband's control for several years and that he wanted to divorce, but at the same time, he did not want her to marry someone else. Therefore, he would take her back before the waiting period

---

[77] See Hoda Elsadda, "Discourses on Women's Biographies and Cultural Identity: Twentieth-Century Representations of the Life of A'isha Bint Abi Bakr", in *Feminist Studies* Vol. 27, No. 1 (2001), p. 54.

[78] Spellberg, *Politics, Gender, and the Islamic Past*.

[79] For this line of argument, see Abbot, *Aishah*.

[80] The Battle of the Camel, so called after the camel that Aisha sat on while exhorting the soldiers to fight, was one of a series of battles between Ali and various political factions which opposed his accession to the caliphate. For Aisha's part in this battle, as well as in the events leading up to it, see Wilfred Madelung, *The succession to Muḥammad: A study of the early caliphate* (Cambridge: Cambridge University Press, 1997), p. 147 ff.

[81] Abbas Mahmud Al-Aqad, *Fatma Al-Zahra' wa Al-Fatimiyyun*, 2nd ed., (Beirut: Dar Al-Kitab Al-Arabi, 1967), p. 135.

[82] Haylamaz, *Aisha*, p. 25.

finished. Aisha told this to the Prophet, who later received a verse declaring that "divorce is twice; then honourable retention or setting free kindly."[83] The verse made it clear that the second declaration of divorce meant that the husband and wife had separated and therefore, it was forbidden for a man to return to a wife he had divorced three times. The only exception was if the wife was to remarry, divorce, and then marry her former husband again.[84] On another occasion, Aisha was visited by a woman who told her that her husband had divorced her by declaring that she was like his mother's back. Once again, Aisha told the Prophet, who had a revelation which bans the tradition of divorcing women by declaring "be as my mother's back".[85]

3   The Influence of Islam on Women

Although it is argued that the Prophet Muhammad expressed commendable sensitivity in his attitude towards women and how they were treated during his lifetime, religious scriptures, such as the Quran, manifested themselves in cultures of sexual inequality and "male-dominated societies often harnessed even just and egalitarian norms laid down for women in divine scriptures to perpetuate their hold".[86] The ethical aspects of the Quran emphasize equality between men and women and justice, but it is maintained that equality in society would most likely not have been well received, as these aspects would have been too radical for the newly converted Arabs. From that perspective, modest alterations to the status of women as presented by Islam seem logical, if compared to the social and economic roots as described by Muslim theologians. Islam was not able to remove the patriarchal clan or the tribal system, and so, women's status that related to the clan and tribalism was not changed.[87] However, if compared to the contextual factors of a matrilineal society, it is obvious that Islam affirmed a patriarchal structure to the vast disadvantage of women.

Furthermore, the Islamic tradition came to construct the woman in primarily sexual terms and as the source of chaos, *fitna*. The claims about women's

---

83   Quran 2:229.
84   Haylamaz, *Aisha*, p. 26.
85   Quran 58:2.
86   There are several traditions that describe how the Prophet felt about his first wife, see Walther, *Women in Islam*, p. 104; Engineer, *The Rights of Women in Islam*, p. 1 and Tucker, *Women, Family, and Gender in Islamic Law*, p. 3.
87   Mehregan, *Islamo-Arabic Culture and Women's Law*, p. 412.

seductiveness and claims of female temptresses are not literally found in the Quran, but rather, upheld by hadiths: there was no "fitna more harmful to men than women".[88] The tension and conflict regarding the portrayal of women span "the whole spectrum from the saintly to the evil and unclean".[89] Women were the embodiment of seduction and a threat to a healthy, exclusively, male public social order, legitimizing the modesty laws such as gender segregation, the seclusion of women and veiling, implemented in early Muslim societies.[90] The portrayal of women as a "moral hazard, deceiving and tempting decent men" began to emerge.[91] The construction of the female as a seductress went

---

[88] Abdallah Al-Bukhari, *Kitab al-Jami'a al-Sahih*, 4 vols. ed. M. Krehl (Leiden: Brill, n.d.) p. 419.

[89] Stowasser, "The Status of Women in Early Islam", p. 29. During the lifetime of Muhammad, men and women used to perform ablution together, see Al-Bukhari, *Sahih*, Book 4, Hadith 59. Regulations concerning men and women group prayers had its roots in specific notions about the transmission of ritual impurity that originated in the first half of the seventh century. Women were considered as ritually pure in the sense that the water they used remained usable for ritual ablution or ritual bathing and their walking in front of a worshipper did not affect whoever was praying. One approach, most common in Mecca, held that a menstruating woman contaminates water and invalidates the prayers of men and women if she walks in front of them, see Sadeghi, *The Logic of Law Making in Islam*, p. 51. Prayer was considered void if the men and women praying next to each other said the same prayer. However, there was no problem with men and women praying next to each other and no problem if the woman by the man's side was not praying at all, as there was a report of the Prophet praying while Aisha was sleeping at his side, despite the fact that the garment he wore touched her. Aisha narrated that "it is not good that you people have made us (women) equal to dogs and donkeys. No doubt I saw Allah's Messenger praying while I used to lie between him and the Qibla and when he wanted to prostate, he pushed my legs and I withdrew them", see Al-Bukhari, *Sahih*, Book 8, Hadith 166. In Basra, the view was that women contaminate water and invalidate prayers for men, regardless of whether they are menstruating or not, see Marion Katz, *Body of Text* (Albany: State University of New York Press, 2002), pp. 149–150. Women could, however, not contaminate other women, as women could not be further contaminated. This view did disappear, as Basra did not itself give rise to a successful school of law. It did, however, later influence other jurists, see Behnam Sadeghi, "The Traveling Tradition Test: A Method for Dating Muslim Traditions", *Der Islam* Vol. 85, No. 1 (2008), pp. 213–219. See also Quran 2:222–223.

[90] Al-Mawdudi saw the female body as fitna and argued that women should be confined to the home because their entry to the public domain would cause immorality of such proportions as those leading to the decline and fall of the once mighty Greece. See Ahmad I, "Cracks in the 'Mightiest Fortress': Jamaat-e-Islami's changing discourse on women", *Modern Asian Studies* Vol. 42 (2012), p. 556.

[91] Eli Alshech, "Out of sight and therefore out of mind: Early Sunni Islamic modesty regulations and the creation of spheres of privacy", *Journal of Near Eastern Studies* No. 66 (2007), p. 267.

so far in some societies that people avoided using a woman's name or called her by an alternate man's name in public, presumably, as her name was not fit to be disclosed in public. The understanding was also that a woman's voice was a private part that must be concealed.[92]

> The worst characteristics of men constitute the best characteristics of women; namely, stinginess, pride, and cowardice. For if a woman is stingy, she will preserve her own and her husband's possessions; if she is proud, she will refrain from loose and improper words to everyone; and if she is cowardly, she will dread everything and will therefore not go out of her house and will avoid compromising situations for fear of her husband.[93]

Many of the modesty laws that were implemented were a tool for restricting the dangerous sexual powers of women to ensure the sexual morality of men (although Islamic legal theory came to give men extensive sexual privileges), which was necessary to achieve a social order where men could be active parts of society.[94] This was, in turn, connected to the view that the woman's modesty was linked to the social status and honor of the family. Given these presumptions, Muslim scholars created safeguarding mechanisms, such as dress codes, in order to restrict the possibility of the woman putting her or—more importantly—the honor of her family, in question; marriage constituted a common means of cementing social and economic bonds, and imposing a dress code helped to shield the family's social standing.[95] The seclusion of women in society led to an Islamic legal discourse based on legalism and literalism, where the view on women was to confine them in the home.[96] However, the Quran does not advocate the veil or segregation; instead, it focuses on sexual modesty for both sexes,[97] as the "purpose of Islam is chastity, emanating

---

[92] Haifaa G. Khalafallah, "Precedent and Perception: Muslim Records That Contradict Narratives on Women", in *Journal of Women of the Middle East and the Islamic World* Vol. 11 (2013), p. 109.

[93] Abu Hamid Al-Ghazali, *Marriage and Sexuality in Islam*, trans. M. Farah (Kuala Lumpur: Islamic Book Trust, 2012), p. 78.

[94] Adis Duderija, "The Custom ('urf) Based Assumptions Regarding Gender Roles and Norms in the Islamic Tradition: A Critical Examination", *Studies in Religion* Vol. 45, No. 4 (2016), p. 590.

[95] Alshech, "Out of sight and therefore out of mind", pp. 288–289.

[96] Farooq, "Analogical Reasoning (Qiyas)", p. 171.

[97] While the verses in the Quran define a specific code of conduct for Muslim women, the Quran (24:30) also commands men to "cast down their eyes and guard their private parts", suggesting that the principle of modesty is equally applicable to women and men. The difference lies in the fact that women are asked to use an outer garment to cover their

from within men and women, and *not* imposed through closed doors".[98] There was no veil nor segregation of the sexes during the Prophet's lifetime,[99] but the Quran had specific demands for the wives of the Prophet, urging them to "remain in your houses; and display not your finery, as did the pagans of old".[100] Those rules only applied to the wives of the Prophet, because of their special status. The wives of Muhammad are known as the "Mothers of the Believers", and are regarded as favored by God and blessed with rare powers and extraordinary capabilities.[101] The wives did not have the right to re-marry after the death of the Prophet, and they did not inherit either, unlike Muslim women in general.[102]

Segregation and veiling had roots deeper than Quranic injunctions and were most likely strongly linked to class, being a symbol of honor or status.[103] The practice of veiling seemed to have been part of the pre-Islamic society, and by introducing segregation, the already established norms of seclusion in ancient patriarchal cultures of Byzantium and Persia were in some regards borrowed. A contributing factor to the seclusion of women, in a society where owning slaves was common, was that the dress code applied only to free women as a marker of social status.[104] While it is not known how the rules on seclusion and veiling spread to the rest of the community, it is likely that the rules related to the wives of the Prophet, were used as an example to bring about their general adoption.[105]

---

bosom, while men are not to expose the area of their body from the navel to the knee. See Jawad Syed, "A historical perspective on Islamic modesty and its implications for female employment", *Equality, Diversity and Inclusion: An International Journal* Vol. 29, No. 2 (2010), p. 150–166 and Rahman, "Status of Women in the Quran", p. 40.

[98] Taha, *The Second Message of Islam*, p. 141.

[99] It is narrated that: "I came to the Prophet with some other women, to offer our pledge to him. He said to us: '(I accept your pledge) with regard to what you are able to do. But I do not shake hands with women'." See Al-Bukhari, *Sahih*, Vol. 4, Book 24, hadith 2874.

[100] Quran 33:32–33.

[101] Quran 33:6, 33:30–34.

[102] Quran 33:50–53. Azizah Al-Hibri argues correctly that the Quran specifies that the Prophet and his wives are not like other men and women. The wives of the Prophet were not allowed to remarry after his death, while there are no restrictions on Muslim women in general. In fact, widows and divorcees are encouraged to remarry. The justification that the Prophet had several wives, is therefore, according to Al-Hibri, not valid. See "*A Study of Islamic Herstory: Or how did we ever get into this mess?*", p. 216.

[103] Rahman, "Status of Women in the Quran", p. 41.

[104] See Quran 33:50–60.

[105] Ahmed, "Women and the Advent of Islam", p. 684.

Over time, legal, political, and economic developments in the Muslim world merged into an Islamic legal tradition upholding gender inequality.[106] To understand this stance, women's roles, rights, and obligations as articulated in the Muslim world at various critical junctures in the history of Islam, will be described to determine how this position was constructed and developed. Therefore, the Quranic view on women will be presented briefly with a focus on the ethical aspects of the Quran, marriage, sexual relations, fornication and adultery, testimony, compensation for death, inheritance, divorce, public office, and veiling.

3.1 The Ethical Voice

While women came to be seen as the cause of the sins of man, the ethical voice of the Quran makes no distinction between the sexes in the verses describing the creation of man and woman, the spiritual and moral obligations of both sexes, and rewards and punishments.[107] In Islam, there is no human hierarchy, as both genders share the same origin:[108]

> He created you of a single soul, then from it He appointed its mate[109] ... it is He who produced you from one living soul, and then a lodging-place, and then a repository. We have distinguished the signs for a people who understand.[110]

The Bible holds two versions of the creation of humans: one refers to the simultaneous creation of male and female,[111] while the other describes the creation of Adam followed by the creation of a female, from his *tsela'*, usually translated

---

106 Barbara Stowasser argues that concurred territories influenced the interpretations of Islamic law and is an important reason for the decline of women's status, see *Women in the Qur'an: Traditions, and Interpretation* (Oxford: Oxford University Press, 1994), p. 23.
107 See Rahman, "Status of Women in the Quran"; Esposito, *Women in Muslim Family Law*; Al-Hibri, "A Study of Islamic Herstory: Or how did we get into this mess?"; Mernissi, *Women and Islam*; An-Naim, *Toward an Islamic Reformation*; Riffat Hassan, "An Islamic Perspective" in *Women, Religion and Sexuality*, ed. Jeanne Belcher (Geneva: WCC publications, 1990) and Stowasser, "The Status of Women in Early Islam". See also Quran 3:195; 4:125; 4:40; 5:10–11; 5:72; 32:19–20; 33:35; 45:22; 49:11 and 49:13.
108 Azizah Al-Hibri, "Muslim Women's Rights in the Global Village: Challenges and Opportunities", *Journal of Law and Religion* Vol. 15 (2001), p. 46.
109 Quran 39:6.
110 Quran 6:98. See also 4:1; 7:189; 16:72; 30:21; 49:13; 53:45; 75:39; 78:8; 50:7 and 51:49.
111 Genesis 1:26–27.

as a rib.[112] The Quran, on the other hand, describes the creation of the first woman as simultaneous to that of the first man.[113]

Adam and Eve are also held equally responsible for the disobedience and consequent expulsion from paradise:

> Said He, 'Go thou forth from it, despised and banished. Those of them that follow thee -- I shall assuredly fill Gehenna with all of you.' 'O Adam, inherit, thou and thy wife, the Garden, and eat of where you will, but come not nigh this tree, lest you be of the evildoers.' Then Satan whispered to them, to reveal to them that which was hidden from them of their shameful parts. He said, 'Your Lord has only prohibited you from this tree lest you become angels, or lest you become immortals.' And he swore to them, 'Truly, I am for you a sincere adviser.' So he led them on by delusion; and when they tasted the tree, their shameful parts revealed to them, so they took to stitching upon themselves leaves of the Garden. And their Lord called to them, 'Did not I prohibit you from this tree, and say to you, "Verily Satan is for you a manifest foe"?' They said, 'Lord, we have wronged ourselves, and if Thou dost not forgive us, and have mercy upon us, we shall surely be among the lost.' Said He, 'Get you down, each of you an enemy to each. In the earth a sojourn shall be yours, and enjoyment for a time.' Said He, 'Therein you shall live, and therein you shall die, and from there you shall be brought forth.' Children of Adam! We have sent down on you a garment to cover your shameful parts, and feathers; and the garment of god-fearing -- that is better; that is one of God's signs; haply they will remember[114] ... And whosoever does a righteous deed, be it male or female, believing, we shall assuredly give him to live a goodly life; and We shall recompense them their wage, according to the best of what they did.[115]

Unlike the Biblical story of Eve's creation from man's rib, the expulsion from the Garden of Eden because of the woman, and that woman was not created solely from the man,[116] the verse in the Quran describes no such differentiated

---

112   For a feminist discussion of the interpretation of Genesis 2, see Phyllis Trible, who argued that since the word *adam* was ambiguous in the biblical text, the first human was one creature incorporating two sexes, "Depatriarchalizing in Biblical Interpretation", *Journal of the American Academy of Religion* No. 41 (1973), pp. 30–48.
113   Quran 4:1, 7:189, 16:72, 35:11, 30:21, 39:6, 42:11 and 49:13.
114   Quran 7:18–26.
115   Quran 16:97.
116   Bible, Genesis 2:4–3:24.

blame on man and woman.[117] Instead, the verse affirms an account of their equal shares of the responsibility.[118] Despite the differences between the Bible and the Quran, Muslim patriarchal exegeses have interpreted the creation of woman as secondary to a man, reflecting the local tradition in hadiths,[119] even though in the case of conflict between the Quran and the Sunnah, the former prevails.[120] Stripped from patriarchal interpretations, it becomes apparent that the Quran does not differentiate between the man and woman in their creation. Any interpretation upholding such a view should consequently be void.

The Quran further obligates and rewards men and women by affirming that:

> And the believers, the men and the women, are friends one of the other; they bid to honour, and forbid dishonour; they perform the prayer, and pay the alms, and they obey God and His Messenger. Those -- upon them God will have mercy; God is All-mighty, All-wise. God has promised the believers, men and women, gardens underneath which rivers flow, forever therein to dwell, and goodly dwelling-places in the Gardens of Eden; and greater, God's good pleasure; that is the mighty triumph.[121] Men and women who have surrendered, believing men and believing women, obedient men and obedient women, truthful men and truthful women, enduring men and enduring women, humble men and humble women, men and women who give in charity, men who fast and women who fast, men and women who guard their private parts, men and women who remember God oft -- for them God has prepared forgiveness and a mighty wage.[122]

The verse, as such, refers equally to the moral obligation of men and women in the requirement of propagating for what is good and disseminating what is wrong. It also demonstrates that men and women are judged based on the

---

117   See Riffat Hassan, who describes how the Quran does not include a verse stating that Eve was created from Adam's rib, rather it entered the Islamic tradition and its interpretations from the Hebrew Bible, "Made from Adam's Rib: The Woman's creation Question", *Al-Mushir Theological Journal of the Christian Study Center* No. 27 (1985), pp. 124–155.
118   Riffat Hassan, "Challenging the Stereotypes of Fundamentalism: An Islamic Feminist Perspective", *The Muslim World* Vol. 91, No. 1 (2001), pp. 56–57.
119   Jane I. Smith and Yvonne Y. Haddad, "Eve: Islamic Image of Women", *Women's Studies International Forum* Vol. 5 (1982), pp. 135–144.
120   Mohammad H. Kamali, "Law and Society. The Interplay of Revelation and Reason in the Shariah" in Esposito, *Women in Muslim Family Law*, p. 59.
121   Quran 9:71–72.
122   Quran 33:35. See also 40:17; 74:38 and 6:164.

same criteria. The verse was revealed when women asked the Prophet why the Quran addressed only men, when women too were believers.[123] Women felt neglected as the rewards of Paradise are described for male believers, and are rather uncommon for women.[124] It is narrated that women were jealous of men's paradise when Umm 'Umarah Al-Ansariyyah "came to the Prophet and said: 'I do not see but that everything is for the men, and I do not see anything being mentioned for the women.' "[125] So the following verse was revealed:

> and that He may admit the believers, men and women alike, into gardens underneath which rivers flow, therein to dwell forever, and acquit them of their evil deeds; that is in God's sight a mighty triumph; and that He may chastise the hypocrites, men and women alike, and the idolaters men and women alike, and those who think evil thoughts of God; against them shall be the evil turn of fortune. God is wroth with them, and has cursed them, and has prepared for them Gehenna -- an evil homecoming![126]

Instead of providing for differentiation between men and women, the verse provides for differentiation between believers and non-believers. Paradise is promised on equal terms to men and women, as long as they are believers and submit to the will of God.[127]

3.2 Marriage

Many Muslim feminists identify the Islamic marriage as patriarchal,[128] as it transfers the rights to a woman and her sexuality from "her tribe to men".[129] Previous chapters have described how sixth and seventh century Arabian Peninsula customs regarding matrimony, where some tribes practiced matrilineal and matrilocal marriage, where women initiated and ended marriages and were entrusted with the permanent custody of their children. For these tribes, the Quran consolidated a patrilineal marriage practice in which women

---

123   Syed, *The Position of Women in Islam*, p. 14.
124   For verses interpreted to be meant for the male believers see Quran 37:40–49; 44:51–55; 52:17–20; 44:54–59; 55:70–77; 56:37–40 and 78:31–34.
125   Hasan (Darussalam), Vol. 5, Book 44, Hadith 3211.
126   Quran 48:5–6.
127   Quran 33:35.
128   The word most commonly used for marriage in Islam is *nikah*, literally meaning sexual intercourse. As a legal term, it represents the contract which makes sex lawful in relationships. The only other legitimate means of engaging in sexual relations, has been permitted to men who have concubines, or female slaves.
129   Ahmed, *Women and Gender in Islam*, p. 62.

lost their previous status and advantages. At the same time, the Quran did outlaw some abusive marriage practices relatively common at the time of the Prophet, such as the son inheriting the father's wife when he passed away. Joseph Schacht, for example, argues that the legal position of women is not an unfavorable one. While "she is considered inferior to the man and has fewer rights and duties from a religious point of view ... but as regards the law of property and obligations, the woman is equal to the man; the matrimonial regime is even more favorable to her in many respects".[130]

The Quran encourages marriage, which is considered an act of worship, by those who have reached a marriageable age,[131] and includes verses describing suitable marriage partners,[132] proper marriage arrangements[133] and the rights and duties of the husband and wife.[134] Marriage in Islamic law is also considered a legal contract between two parties with the legal capacity to contract.[135] Rules of suitability vary in importance in different schools and function to prevent mismatches between the bride and a groom who is her inferior. Suitability is only an issue for the groom, as no rules prevent a male from marrying an unsuitable bride, as "men are not degraded by cohabitation with women who are their inferiors".[136] While women have the right to

---

130   Joseph Schacht notes that a woman is not executed if she commits apostasy, but forced, by imprisonment and beatings, to return to Islam. She equals half a man when it comes to blood-money, evidence, and inheritance, and her position is less advantageous in matters related to marriage and divorce, and because, on certain grounds, the husband has the right to correction. See *An Introduction to Islamic Law*, pp. 126–127.
131   When a person reaches marriageable age differs for the different schools of thought, the earliest being 9 years for a girl and twelve years for a boy. For a review of the marriage age in Islam, see Asaf Fyzee, *Outlines of Muhammadan Law* (London: Oxford University Press, 1964) and Abdul Hasan Ali ibn Abu Bakr al-Marghinani, *The Hedaya or Guide – A commentary on the Mussulman Laws*, trans. by Charles Hamilton (New Delhi: Islamic Book Trust, 1982). Marriage was also encouraged to men by the Prophet: "O young men! Whoever among you has the ability should marry, for it restrains the eyes and protects chastity", see Ibn Hajar al-'Asqalani, *Fath al-Bari,* cited in El Fadl, *Speaking in God's Name,* p. 206, n. 72.
132   Quran 2:220, 4:22–23.
133   Quran 2:235.
134   Quran 4:34.
135   The contracting parties can only be between a man and a woman, as same sex marriages are not recognized. There is a requirement of religious adherence, in order for the marriage to be valid. Muslim women are only allowed to marry Muslim men, whereas Muslim men could also marry a "woman of the book." For the Sunni, this means Christian and Jewish women, while some Shia jurists also allow for Zoroastrian women to be married to a Muslim man.
136   Quoted from Kecia Ali, "Marriage in Classical Islamic Jurisprudence", in *The Islamic Marriage Contract: Case Studies in Islamic Family Law,* eds., Asifa Quraishi and Frank E. Vogel (Cambridge: Harvard University Press, 2008), p. 16.

enter into marriage, Muslim family law generally upholds that the groom concludes the legal contract with her legal guardian and accepts to pay the dower, *mahr*.[137] Whereas in pre-Islamic times, the father of the bride (or other male relatives) appropriated the dower, Islam makes the woman the sole recipient of the dower.[138]

Although women are permitted to conclude contracts connected to, for example, property,[139] marriage is seen as fundamentally distinct from other transactions, as marriage establishes the sexual lawfulness otherwise forbidden to women. "Those who believed that a woman could not conclude a marriage contract on her behalf or for someone else linked this incapacity to the woman's inability to convey licit sexual access to herself or another woman through marriage."[140] Therefore, a guardian, *wali*, is needed for a marriage contract. Marriage, whether considered a sacrament or a contract, legitimizes sexual intercourse, granting men and women the right to sexual pleasure, where the husband's central right is to derive sexual pleasure from his wife, and to that end, he may control her mobility, since Islamic marriage law links the wife's mobility with the duty to be sexually available at all times to the husband.[141] To obtain his due from her, he may compel her to perform ablution after her menstruation,[142] may take her with him when he travels; and may

---

[137] Schacht, *An Introduction to Islamic Law*, p. 161. There are detailed rules with regard to dowry and when the woman becomes the owner of the full dower. She may refrain from sexual intercourse until she has received the dower. See Sachiko Murata, *Temporary Marriage (Mut'a) in Islamic Law* (London: The Muhammadi Trust, 1987), pp. 14–16.

[138] Ali, *Gender and Human Rights in Islam and International Law*, p. 60. Verse 4:20 also prohibits forcing one's wife to remit the dower in a will entitling the husband the dower.

[139] Once a woman reaches puberty, she has the complete and independent possession of her property. Not her father nor her husband has any right to the ownership, enjoyment or the disposal of her property. She is considered to have full legal capacity as far as her private property is concerned, see Tucker, *Women, Family, and Gender in Islamic Law*, p. 25.

[140] Ali, *Marriage and Slavery in Early Islam*, p. 46.

[141] Duderija, *Maqasid al-Sharia*, p. 197. Hadiths adds far-reaching implications to the obligation of a wife to be available for her husband's sexual desires, describing that the wife should be willing to enact in intercourse on a camel should the husband want to, or if he requests her, to lick her husband's wounds to show her obedience, see El Fadl, *Speaking in God's Name*, pp. 210–218; Tucker, *Women, Family, and Gender in Islamic Law*, p. 40. Penetration is however forbidden during menstruation, see Ibn Qudama, *al-Kafi fi fiqh Ahmad ibn Hanbal* (Beirut: Dar al-Kutub al-'Ilmiyya, 1994), 3:82. See also Ibn al-Naqibi, *Reliance of the Traveler*, p. 526; 'Allama Hilli, *Tahrir al-ihkam (ahkam) al-shariyya 'ala al-mahdab al-imamiyya* (Qom: Maktab al-Tawhid, 1999), 3:482.

[142] Ibn Qudama, *al-Kafi fi fiqh Ahmad ibn Hanbal*, 3:82. See also Ibn al-Naqibi, *Reliance of the Traveler*, p. 526; Hilli, *Tahrir al-ihkam*, 3:482.

forbid her from leaving his home.[143] While the Prophet advocates marriage as commendable and her husband should give the woman her full share of sexual pleasure,[144] the wife is required not to reject the husband's bed. Hadiths add the obligation of a wife to be available for her husband's sexual desires.[145] Marital rape is not recognized, and the husband may enjoy her whenever he wishes "so long as he does not harm her".[146]

The rights and responsibilities of the wife are considered equal to those of the husband, but they are not identical. While the woman has the exclusive right to manage property before, during, and after marriage, and each party retains his or her separate property upon divorce,[147] inequalities emerge as the husband becomes the protector of the wife. The stipulation in the Quran that provides that men are the managers of the affairs of women came to encompass all areas of life.[148] The husband has a financial maintenance obligation during the marriage, such as providing for his wife and a specific period after the divorce.[149] Unlike the payment of mahr, which becomes obligatory as a result of the marriage contract, the payment of support only becomes mandatory as a result of the marriage contract and the obedience of the wife. A husband has no legal obligation to support his wife if she is not obedient.[150] A wife is not required to obey her husband if he demands "un-Islamic" acts from her.[151] Besides housing, wives are entitled to maintenance from the husband, meaning that he is obligated to supply her with food and clothing, although there is no textual evidence to support such a narrow definition of maintenance.[152] It is understood that "when a woman surrenders herself into the custody of her husband, it is incumbent upon him thenceforth to supply her with

---

143 The Maliki's hold that she must be allowed to visit her close kin, see Khalil ibn Ishaq al-Jundi, *Maliki law: Being a Summary from French Translations of the Mikhtasar of Sidi Khalil,* transl. F. X. Ruxton (Westport: Hyperion, 1980), p. 148.
144 The wife's sexual rights are acknowledged, but enforcement mechanisms are uncommon. See al-Marghinani, *Al-Hedaya,* 2nd ed. transl. C. Hamilton (Karachi: n.p., 1989), 1:579.
145 El Fadl, *Speaking in God's Name,* pp. 210–218; Tucker, *Women, Family, and Gender in Islamic Law,* pp. 401–402.
146 Ibn Qudama, *al-Kafi fi fiqh Ahmad ibn Hanbal,* 3:82–83. See also, Ibn al-Naqib, *Reliance of the Traveler,* pp. 525–526; Hilli, *Tahrir al-ihkam,* 3:482 and 3:528; al-Marghinani, *Al-Hedayah,* 1:61.
147 Esposito, *Women in Muslim Family Law,* p. 24.
148 Quran 4:34.
149 Al-Hibri, "Muslim Women's Rights in the Global Village", p. 47; Esposito, *Women in Muslim Family Law,* p. 26.
150 Murata, *Temporary Marriage (Mut'a),* pp. 16–17.
151 Ibid.
152 Al-Haskafi, *Durr-ul-Mikhtar,* transl. B. M. Dayal (New Delhi: Kitab Bhavan, 1992), p. 316.

food, clothing, and lodging, whether she be a Muslim or an infidel, because such is the precept both in the Koran and in the traditions; and also, because maintenance is a recompense for the matrimonial restraint",[153] or that "maintenance is compensation for her confinement".[154] The confinement of the wife also entitles her to an exclusive dwelling just for her enjoyment:

> It is incumbent upon a husband to provide a separate apartment for his wife's habitation, to be solely and exclusively appropriated to her use, so as that none of the husband's family, or others, may enter without her permission and desire, because this is essentially necessary to her, and is, therefore, her due the same as maintenance, the word of God appoints her a dwelling house as well as a subsistence: and as it is incumbent upon a husband to provide a habitation for his wife, so he is not at liberty to admit any person to a share in it, as this would be injurious to her, by endangering her property, and obstructing her enjoyment of his society ...[155]

Women hardly know of the right to have their own space, and Muslim scholars have not directly been in any rush of informing women of or requiring men to uphold this right.[156] However, this privilege is easily circumvented by the husband as the property where they reside is his property. He could withhold any visitors to his property, be that her family or acquaintances.[157]

Although not a unanimous standpoint, a majority of the jurists uphold that the wife does not have a legal obligation to nurse her offspring or to perform household service.[158] The husband has no legal obligation to care for his wife if she should fall sick, although some scholars argue that there is a religious duty to do so.[159] "A sick wife who, on account of her failing health, is unable to discharge her marital duties has no legal right to maintenance by the husband."[160] Marital duties, in this regard is related to her duty to be sexually available.[161]

---

153 Al-Marghinani, *Al-Hedaya*, p. 392.
154 Al-Haskafi, *Durr-ul-Mikhtar*, p. 316.
155 Al-Marghinani, *Al-Hedaya*, p. 392. See also, Al-Haskafi, *Durr-ul-Mikhtar*, p. 322.
156 Farooq, "Analogical Reasoning (Qiyas)", p. 167.
157 Al-Marghinani, *Al-Hedaya*, p. 402.
158 Quote taken from Ali, "Marriage in Classical Islamic Jurisprudence", p. 12.
159 Farooq, "Analogical Reasoning (Qiyas)", p. 169.
160 Hammudah A. Al-Ati, *The Family Structure in Islam* (Indianapolis: American Trust Publications, 1977), p. 151.
161 Hamilton however argues that "If a woman falls sick in her husband's house, she is still entitled to a maintenance. This is upon a principle of benevolence, as *analogy* would suggest that *she is not entitled* to maintenance, where she falls sick so far as to be incapable of

Yet, marriage is described as a source of joy and comfort for both partners. Verses, while directed to men, describe relationships based on love and mercy:

> And of His signs is that He created for you, of yourselves, spouses, that you might repose in them, and He has set between you love and mercy. Surely in that are signs for a people who consider.[162] It is He who created you out of one living soul, and made of him his spouse that he might rest in her. Then, when he covered her, she bore a light burden and passed by with it; but when it became heavy they cried to God their Lord, 'If Thou givest us a righteous son, we indeed shall be of the thankful.'[163] Permitted to you, upon the night of the Fast, is to go in to your wives; -- they are a vestment for you, and you are a vestment for them.[164]

Nevertheless, Islamic marriage laws generally do not consider notions of marriages based on mutual terms between men and women; rather, it focuses on the male role as provider.[165] Commenting on this verse, Fakhr al-Din al-Razi (d. 1210), affirms that the phrase "He created for you" is an indication that God created women for the convenience of men, but also that women, unlike men, were not intended to be considered as subjects of the commands of the law. For al-Razi, women were given moral obligations only to benefit men.[166]

3.2.1   Temporary Marriages

The temporary marriage, *mut'a*, legitimizes sex for a specific period time and was practiced in early Islam and today by Shia Muslims. The Sunni and the Shia agree that temporary marriages were allowed but disagree on the reasons it was permitted. The Shia maintain that since temporary marriages were allowed for by the Prophet, it cannot be forbidden.[167] Sunni Muslims don't deny that this form of marriage was permitted, but argue that it was prohibited by the Prophet after having allowed it during certain battles. The mut'a marriage was generally practiced during long journeys to legalize sexual intercourse to

---

admitting her husband to the conjugal embrace, since in this case she cannot be deemed in custody for the purpose of enjoyment." See Al-Marghinani, *Al-Hedaya*, p. 396.
162   Quran 30:21.
163   Quran 7:189.
164   Quran 2:187.
165   Duderija, *Maqasid al-Sharia*, p. 201.
166   Fakhr al-Din Muḥammad b. ʿUmar al-Razi, *Mafatiḥ al-Ghayb*, 6 vols. (Cairo: al-Maṭbaʿah al-Miṣriyah al-ʿAmiriyah, 1862) 5:185. See also, Fadel, "Is Historicism a Viable Strategy for Islamic Legal Reform?", p. 37.
167   Spectorsky, *Women in Classical Islam*, pp. 93–94.

avoid the offense of *zina,* unlawful sexual intercourse.[168] The Sunni argue that the verse permitting a temporary marriage was abrogated by another verse, "prosperous are the believers ... [who] guard their private parts save from their wives and what their right hands own".[169] As described, a verse which abrogates another verse must be revealed after it. The verse establishing the temporary marriage was revealed after the Prophet had emigrated to Medina and the abrogation as claimed by the Sunni is not correct. However, the practice was also banned by the second caliph 'Umar who declared that he would punish anyone who would practice it. The Shia maintain that 'Umar forbad mut'a with regard to himself, and even if 'Umar's prohibition was based on ijtihad, it is reviewed as baseless, as ijtihad cannot overrule what was is permitted in the Quran.[170]

The Shia schools of law discuss temporary marriages in as great a detail as permanent marriage. Unlike permanent marriages, a man may have as many mut'a wives as he wishes, as there are no numerical restrictions.[171] The mut'a marriage is a contracted marriage valid during a specific period, and although marriages of a day or less are seen as undesirable, they are not prohibited.[172] If the contract does not include a period, most Shia jurists hold the view that the marriage is then regarded as a permanent marriage. Like permanent marriage, there is a marriage contract which can be concluded between the man and the woman, their representatives, or their fathers. The temporary marriage contract must specify mahr, which the woman can request at the beginning of the marriage, and although the woman is not entitled to maintenance, the contract may include such provisions. The contract may also include provisions regulating the number of sexual acts, or if they occur at day or night time. There is no inheritance unless specifically included in the marriage contract. Also, like permanent marriage, marrying someone outside the "people of the book" is not allowed for men, and women are only allowed to marry Muslim men.[173]

Fatima Mernissi describes the mut'a marriage as historically giving women as much freedom as the man and also implied a different set of paternity rules

---

168 Ann Black, Hossein Esmaeili, Nadirsyah Hosen, *Modern Perspectives on Islamic Law* (Cheltenham: Edward Edgar, 2013), p. 122.
169 Quran 23:1–6.
170 Murata, *Temporary Marriage (Mut'a),* pp. 56–59.
171 Ziba Mir-Hosseini, "A Woman's Right to Terminate the Marriage Contract Law", in *The Islamic Marriage Contract,* eds. Asifa Quraishi and Frank E. Vogel (Cambridge: Harvard University Press, 2008), p. 218.
172 Black, Esmaeili, Hosen, *Modern Perspectives on Islamic Law,* p. 122.
173 Murata, *Temporary Marriage (Mut'a),* pp. 30–46.

than those that Sunni Muslim marriages were otherwise based on. She maintains that the children of such marriages belonged to the mother, and had the right to inherit their father's property.[174] The Shia however, uphold that the child belongs to the father, even in a mut'a marriage, however, he does have the possibility of denying the child.[175] While women are given as much freedom as men to engage in temporary marriages, mut'a is also argued to be a form of prostitution, as the sole function of this type of marriage is the sexual enjoyment of the woman, for which the man has to pay a certain amount of money or property.[176] In some works, women who engage in mut'a marriages are referred to as a "rented woman".[177] The definition of rental in Islamic Shia law is "to gain possession of a benefit in exchange for a specified sum".[178] This definition is also applied to temporary marriages.[179]

3.2.2 Polygyny

Polygyny is considered to be legitimized both by the Quran and the Sunnah, as the Prophet engaged in several polygynous marriages after the death of his first wife, Khadija. Because this type of marriage is acceptable in the Quran and endorsed by the Prophet's life, traditionalists uphold the view that polygyny can never be prohibited.[180] Polygyny is permitted under the condition that the husband treats his wives justly. For traditional Sunni jurists, treating wives justly meant that the husband needs to provide residence, food, and clothes to all the wives, and an equal share of his time, which necessarily does not consist of fairness in sexual relations.[181] As long as he can meet these requirements, he is to be considered just and may marry up to four women, whereas strict monogamy is imposed on women:[182]

---

174 Mernissi, *Beyond the Veil*, p. 37 and Engineer, *The Rights of Women in Islam*, p. 24.
175 The waiting period here consists of two menstrual periods. If she were to marry the same man in a new temporary marriage, no waiting period is needed. If the husband should die, the waiting period is instead four months and ten days. The date of expiry is included in the marriage contract, and when the term expires, the marriage ends. It can also be renewed through a new contract, though the woman is still bound by the 'iddah period. See Murata, *Temporary Marriage (Mut'a)*, p. 44–56.
176 Ibid., 28.
177 The term used in Arabic is musta'jara.
178 Ja'far ibn Muhammad ibn Sa'id, *Shara'i al-islam* (Beirut: n.p., 1930), p. 233.
179 Murata, *Temporary Marriage (Mut'a)*, p. 28.
180 Black, Esmaeili, Hosen, *Modern Perspectives on Islamic Law*, p. 122.
181 Khalil ibn Ishaq al-Jundi, *Mukhtasar al-'Allama Khalil fi fiqh al-Imam Malik* (Beirut: Dar ar-Kutub al-'Ilmiyya, 2004), p. 88; al-Jundi, *Maliki law*, p.118; Ibn Qudama, *al-Kafi fi fiqh Ahmad ibn Hanbal*, 3:88; Hilli,*Tahrir al-ihkam*, 3:588 and Ali, "Marriage in Classical Islamic Jurisprudence", chapter 3.
182 Al-Hibri, "A Study of Islamic Herstory: how did we ever get into this mess?", p. 216.

Give the orphans their property, and do not exchange the corrupt for the good; and devour not their property with your property; surely that is a great crime. If you fear that you will not act justly towards the orphans, marry such women as seem good to you, two, three, four; but if you fear you will not be equitable, then only one, or what your right hands own; so it is likelier you will not be partial.[183] You will not be able to be equitable between your wives, be you ever so eager.[184]

The practice of polygyny as such was not introduced by Islam, since it already existed in pre-Islamic societies, where men could have an unlimited number of wives. While Islam did limit the practice of polygyny, it also authorized the practice by allowing it in the first place.[185] It is, however, argued that Islam gradually wanted to change the practice. The restriction of limiting the number of wives to four is seen as the first step, where the final goal was the absolute prohibition of the practice.[186] It is argued that the verses above need to be read in conjunction with each other, where a combined reading of the verses leads to an implied prohibition of polygyny in Islamic law.[187] This view was historically held by the Mu'tazilis, who maintained that a husband could never treat wives equally and that the verse only allowed for polygyny in cases of orphan girls and their widowed mothers.[188] Reading the verses, it is easy to determine that polygyny is allowed

---

183   Quran 4:2–3. When the verse was revealed in the Quran, men who were married to more than four women were advised by the Prophet to keep four and divorce the rest of them, see Engineer, *The Rights of Women in Islam*, p. 22.
184   Quran 4:129.
185   Commentators also uphold that these verses were revealed after the Battle of Uhud, in a time where many men were killed, and women surpassed the number of men, see Jeri Altneu Sechzer, "Islam and Women: Where Tradition Meets Modernity: History and Interpretations of Islamic Women's Status", *Sex Roles* Vol. 51, No. 5/6 (2004), p. 268.
186   Zehra F. Arat, "Women's Rights in Islam: Revisiting Quranic Rights", in *Human Rights: New Perspectives, New Realities*, eds. Adamantia Pollis and Peter Schwab (Boulder: Lynne Rienner Publishers, 2000).
187   See Al-Hibri, "A Study of Islamic Herstory: how did we ever get into this mess?", p. 216 and Rahman, "Status of Women in the Quran", pp. 45–49. The Prophet himself, for example, did not allow his son-in-law Ali to take another wife, until he divorced his daughter Fatima, see Engineer, *The Rights of Women in Islam*, p. 159. See also, Al-Bukhari, *Sahih*, Vol. 7, Book 62, No. 157.
188   On the issue of dealing equally with wives in polygynous marriages, they included love and tenderness as a requirement, which they argued would be impossible to accomplish, see Amira Mashour, "Islamic Law and Gender Equality: Could There be a Common Ground?: A Study of Divorce and Polygamy in Sharia Law and Contemporary Legislation in Tunisia and Egypt", *Human Rights Quarterly* Vol. 27, No. 2 (2005), p. 570. See also, Muhammad Sharif Chaudry, *Human Rights in Islam* (All Pakistan Islamic Education Congress, 1993) and Syed, *The Position of Women in Islam*, p. 43.

under specific circumstances, to help orphans,[189] and the possibility of marrying several women cannot be seen as the rule, but rather as the exception.[190] It is rather interesting that the doctrine of naskh seems not to have been used by the jurists when it comes to the case of polygyny. Especially since the principle of God gradually revealing the way towards how Muslims should behave is upheld in other issues. Had the jurists consistently applied the doctrine of abrogation, then polygyny would have been forbidden as the Quran conditioned the practice by the terms of equal and just treatment of wives, which it affirms is impossible to achieve.[191] Thus, Islamic law, albeit not acknowledged, could be seen, in this aspect, as an arbitrary construction to ensure that the sexual needs of men are satisfied, even though there is nothing in the verse to suggest that the verse permits men to take wives to satisfy sexual urges.

While classical Islamic law allows for polygyny, most Muslim states have, nonetheless, introduced measures to restrict the practice. Tunisia and Turkey have prohibited polygyny, on the basis that the Quran calls for a ban by referring to the phrase that a husband cannot treat wives equally.[192] Other states have allowed for marriage contracts that include a stipulation where the first

---

189 Asma Barlas argues that the verse "serves a very specific purpose: that of securing justice for female orphans", *Believing women in Islam*, p. 190.
190 Engineer, *The Rights of Women in Islam*, pp. 157–158.
191 While traditionalists argued that treating wives just means dividing the number of nights between them, and protecting the sick, older, or barren wife from divorce, reformists advocated for the restriction and even abolition of the practice as the particular social conditions that existed at the time of the Prophet, were no longer prevalent in current societies, see Helmut Gärje, *The Quran and its Exegesis: Selected texts, with Classical and Modern Muslim Interpretations* (London: Routledge, 1976), pp. 252–261. This approach was suggested by Muhammad 'Abduh, who argued that polygyny would lead to greater harm and corruption for society. 'Abduh proposed that the original teachings of the Quran actually encouraged monogamous relationships, based on the verse that declared that the husband must treat wives equally. For 'Abduh, the verse was impossible to achieve, see Esposito, *Women in Muslim Family Law*, p. 248. By the 19th century, several works were introduced by Muslim scholars, challenging the traditional view on polygyny, see Mumtaz 'Ali, *The Rights of Women* (Lahore: n.p., 1898); Tahir al-Haddad, *Our Women in Islamic Law and in Society*, transl. Ronak Husni and Daniel L. Newman (London: Routledge, 2007). Al Haddas' ideas manifested themselves in the 1956 Tunisian Personal Status Law, where polygyny was forbidden. See also, the two works of Qasim Amin, *The Liberation of Women: and, The New Woman, Two Documents in the History of Egyptian Feminism* (Cairo: American University Press, 2000) and *The New Women: Document in the Early Debate on Egyptian Feminism* (Cairo: American University Press, 1996).
192 The gradualist approach has more recently been used to restrict the practice of polygyny. For instance, the 1917 Ottoman Family Law included stipulations to limit polygyny, by requiring the first wife to consent to the husband marrying another wife and by including the right to divorce if the husband takes another wife, see Article 38, 1917 Ottoman Family

wife needs to give her permission for the husband to take another wife, established the requirement for a court to review the financial means of the husband to be able to provide for a new wife (and eventually more children) and by questioning the husband on how he intends to treat his wives equally. Such courts allow for a second wife should the first wife be infertile, incapable of engaging in sexual relations, illness or mentally impaired. The view is that it is fairer and kinder and that the first wife is better off remaining in the marriage with a co-wife, rather than the husband divorcing her and being left on her own.[193] Western countries have also legally recognized polygynist marriages lawfully contracted in countries where the practice has been allowed for.[194]

3.3 *Sexual Relations*

While in pre-Islamic Arabia—where women could engage in multiple sexual relationships—interpretations of the Quran which would allow women, and not men, to assert sexual rights over herself, were rejected by free men.[195] Yet, the Quran prescribes "corrupt women for corrupt men, and corrupt men for corrupt women; good women for good men, and good men for good women".[196] Purity and chastity are seen as a function of conduct and a person's behavior; it is prescribed similarly to both men and women.[197] Purity is not prescribed by the absence of sex; rather, the Quran controls sexual relations by making them lawful during the marriage.[198] On the other hand, Islam only allows for permissible sexual relationships through marriage for women.[199] Men are permitted a sexual license completely forbidden for women; besides the right to marry up to four women, they may also have an unlimited number of concubines.[200]

Code. The right to divorce if the husband takes another wife is now an established notion, however, the schools of law still maintain that a marriage contract cannot include terms that forbid polygyny. For a brief overview of the justifications of states in restricting the practice of polygyny, see Rehman, "The Sharia, Islamic Family Laws and International Human Rights Law", pp. 108–12. There is, however, evidence that the practice still does continue in these countries, where the wives have no rights under the civil law, see Black, Esmaeili, Hosen, *Modern Perspectives on Islamic Law*, p. 123.

193   Ibid., 121–122.
194   These marriages have been recognized in various western countries such as England, Australia and Sweden. Polygynist marriages entered into in the West are not recognized.
195   Ali, *Marriage and Slavery in Early Islam*, p. 14.
196   Quran 24:26.
197   Barlas, *"Believing Women" in Islam*, p. 153.
198   Quran 24:33.
199   Syed, *The Position of Women in Islam*, p. 27.
200   Quran 4:25. See also 4:3; 4:24; 23:5–6; 24:31; 33:50 and 70:29–30. Karmi, *Women, Islam and Patriarchalism*, p. 170.

> O Prophet, We have made lawful for thee thy wives whom thou hast given their wages and what thy right hand owns, spoils of war that God has given thee, and the daughters of thy uncles paternal and aunts paternal, thy uncles maternal and aunts maternal, who have emigrated with thee, and any woman believer, if she give herself to the Prophet and if the Prophet desire to take her in marriage, for thee exclusively, apart from the believers -- We know what We have imposed upon them touching their wives and what their right hands own -- that there may be no fault in thee; God is All-forgiving, All-compassionate.[201]

There was an instance, a few years after the Prophet died, where a Muslim woman took one of her male slaves as a partner. She mentioned this to 'Umar, stating "that ownership by the right hand made lawful to me what it makes lawful to men". 'Umar declared that this was not a correct interpretation and while he did not punish her for illicit sex, he forbade her from ever marrying any free man. The slave was also ordered not to approach her and was sold. Besides the fact that 'Umar restricted this woman's right to marriage (which is encouraged in Islam and seen as part of submitting to the will of God), of relevance is his reasoning; he responds that her position is not of a man. In other words, 'Umar settles that women do not have the same sexual prerogatives as men.

Furthermore, it is argued that there are verses in the Quran that permit a reading suggesting that women are allowed to be treated as the sexual property of men:

> Decked out fair to men is the love of lusts -- women, children, heaped-up heaps of gold and silver, horses of mark, cattle and tillage. That is the enjoyment of the present life; but God -- with Him is the fairest resort.[202]

Asma Barlas maintains that "although women are included among men's 'lust' on earth, this is a list of what men covet, not what God *wants* them to covet, which is nearness to God".[203] Barlas argues that this verse emphasized the primacy of the afterlife over this life; its purpose is not to establish that women are property. It is somewhat difficult to agree with Barlas' interpretation of this verse, as it appears as if the last part of the verse "that is the enjoyment of the present life" is not taken into consideration. While there is nothing in the verse that suggests that women (or any of the other listings) are property or should

---

201   Quran 33:50.
202   Quran 3:14. See also 2:223.
203   Barlas, *"Believing Women" in Islam*, p. 161.

be considered property, it does speak of the lusts of men.[204] The verse does acknowledge that women are an enjoyment, although the forms of it are not described.

With the Quran describing women as objects of enjoyment, hadiths elevated the view of women having a superior sexual desire, one that God counterbalanced with higher levels of modesty. Women as fitna were further exemplified by hadiths warning men of women: "the life of this world is sweet and green, and verily Allah has appointed you as His vice-regents in it so that He may see how you act. So beware of the world and beware of women. For certainly, the first trial (awwal fitna) of Banu Isra'il was through women".[205]

3.4 Fornication and Adultery

We have established that men and women have different rights regarding sexual relations. The Quran also contains verses regarding the punishments of engaging in illegitimate sexual relationships:

> Such of your women as commit indecency, call four of you to witness against them; and if they witness, then detain them in their houses until death takes them or God appoints for them a way. And when two of you commit indecency, punish them both; but if they repent and make amends, then suffer them to be; God turns, and is All-compassionate.[206]

Jurists were not in agreement of what these verses implied; some scholars argued that the first part exclusively applies to women, while the second part includes both genders. Others argued that the first part dealt with fornication, the latter, adultery. The penalty of adultery as prescribed in these verses was considered to be temporary and abrogated for the following verse:[207]

> The fornicatress and the fornicator -- scourge each one of them a hundred stripes, and in the matter of God's religion let no tenderness for them seize you if you believe in God and the Last Day; and let a party of the believers witness their chastisement. The fornicator shall marry none but a fornicatress or an idolatress, and the fornicatress -- none shall marry her but a fornicator or an idolator; that is forbidden to the believers.[208]

---

204   Barlas argues that the Quran does not, in any context, designate a human being (even a slave) as another's property, see *"Believing Women" in Islam*, pp. 161–164.
205   Muhammad Ibn Yacub Al-Kulayni, *Kitab al-Kaf'i* (Beirut: Manshurat al-Fajr, 2007), 5:203.
206   Quran 4:15–16.
207   Burton, *The Sources of Islamic Law*, pp. 124–125.
208   Quran 24:2–3.

The verse carries a fixed penalty, *hadd,* of a hundred lashes for the crime of adultery.[209] There is no difference based on gender affecting the punishment since it is regarded that men and women have the same moral capacity for making decisions. Thus, the same standard for judging them is applied in cases concerning adultery.[210]

Hadiths prescribed stoning as the punishment for adultery. More correctly, however, would be to understand these traditions as describing instances where stoning was prescribed as punishment.[211] The practice was incorporated from the Jewish tradition and applied to the Jews, as stoning was part of the Torah. "Some Jews came to the Messenger of Allah and mentioned to him that a man and women of their number had committed fornication. The Messenger of Allah asked them: What do you find in the Torah about stoning? They replied: We disgrace them and they should be flogged. 'Abd Allah b. Salam said: You lie; it contains (instruction for) stoning. So they brought the Torah and spread it out, and one of them put his hand over the verse of stoning and read what preceded it and what followed it. 'Abd Allah b. Salam said to him: Lift your hand. When he did so, the verse of stoning was seen to be in it. They then said: He has spoken the truth, Muhammad, the verse of stoning is in it. The Messenger of Allah then gave command regarding them, and they were stoned to death."[212] Another tradition describes 'Umar referring to a verse not included in the Quran: "'Umar b. al-Khattab gave an address saying: Allah sent

---

[209] Hadd means limit and in legal terms it meant the mandatory punishments established by the Quran. Islamic criminal law has three broad categories of crimes based on punishments, *hudud* or hadd, *tazir* and *qisas*. Hudud crimes of theft, robbery, apostasy, alcohol consumption, unlawful sexual intercourse and false accusations of unlawful sexual intercourse all carry a fixed penalty, see Baderin, *International Human Rights Law and Islamic Law*, p. 73. Hudud crimes can only be forgiven by God, thus diya is not accepted in these cases, see Mutaz M. Qafisheh, "Restorative Justice in the Islamic Penal Law: A Contribution to the Global System", *International Journal of Criminal Justice Science* Vol. 7, No. 1 (2012), pp. 487–491. Tazir punishments are up to the discretion of the judge, and involves crimes such as embezzlement, perjury, sodomy, usury, breach of trust, abuse, bribery, and other similar transgressions against God, see Susan C. Hascall, "Restorative Justice in Islam: Should Qisas Be Considered a Form of Restorative Justice?", *Berkeley Journal of Middle East & Islamic Law* Vol. 4 (2011), p. 55. Lastly, qisas cover acts of corporal violence, such as murders, non-fatal bodily injuries and unintentional killings, see mad Abd al-Aziz al-Alfi, "Punishment in Islamic Criminal Law", in *The Islamic Criminal Justice System*, ed. M. Cherif Bassiouni (London: Oceana publications, 1982), p. 230.
[210] Barlas, *"Believing Women" in Islam,* p. 140.
[211] For a description of other traditions where stoning was applied and how the jurists incorporated them into the corpus of Islamic law, see Burton, *The Sources of Islamic Law*, pp. 128–158.
[212] Sunan Abi Dawud 4446, Book 40, hadith 96.

Muhammad with truth and sent down the Books of him, and the verse of stoning was included in what He sent down to him. We read it and memorized it. The Messenger of Allah had people stoned to death, and we have done it also since his death. I am afraid the people might say with the passage of time: We do not find the verse of stoning in the Books of Allah, and thus they stray by abandoning a duty which Allah had received. Stoning is a duty laid down (by Allah) for married men and women who commit fornication when the proof is established, or if there is pregnancy or a confession. I swear by Allah, had it not been so that the people might say: 'Umar made an addition to Allah's Book, I would have written it (there)."[213] Stoning is unmentioned in the Quran, nevertheless, some jurists implied that these traditions abrogated the verses in the Quran.[214]

In the instance a husband should accuse his wife of adultery, her oath would be enough to prevent punishment:

> And those who cast it up on their wives having no witnesses except themselves, the testimony of one of them shall be to testify by God four times that he is of the truthful, and a fifth time, that the curse of God shall be upon him, if he should be of the liars. It shall avert from her the chastisement if she testifies by God four times that he is of the liars, and a fifth time, that the wrath of God shall be upon her, if he should be of the truthful.[215]

If there are no witnesses to the adultery, the woman's oath is to be counted as the testimony of four women,[216] which implies that the woman's oath trumps the husband's accusation.[217] However, this is the only instance where a woman's testimony outweighs or is equal to that of a man.

---

213 Ibid.
214 Burton, *The Sources of Islamic Law*, pp. 128–158.
215 Quran 24:6–9.
216 In the unlikely situation of four men testifying that a woman committed fornication, the testimony of four women affirming that the accused woman is still a virgin, is suffice to doubt, and obligates the judge to not prescribe a hadd punishment, see Scott C. Lucas, "Justifying Gender Inequalities in the Shafi'i Law School: Two Case Studies of Muslim Legal Reasoning", *Journal of the American Oriental Society* Vol. 129, No. 2 (2009), p. 256.
217 The couple is then forbidden to each other forever, without divorce. If the man were to repent his allegation, he is liable to the punishment of false accusation. The couple would still be forbidden to each other, but should there be children in the relationship, the child would again be considered legitimate, unlike if the man does not repent, where the child is then considered illegitimate. See Murata, *Temporary Marriage (Mut'a)*, p. 25.

3.5 Testimony

While women have the same financial independence as men and are considered to be able to manage property and wealth on their own, their testimony is not equal to that of a man. The Quran describes the value of the testimony of a woman by requiring it to be corroborated by another woman when testifying about financial transactions. The verse has laid the foundation for the common-held notion that a woman's testimony is worth half that of a man's. Although this incapacity of women to give evidence is only specified in financial transactions, by analogical reasoning, it has been extended so that a woman's corroborating testimony is only allowed in cases regarding financial matters,[218] and completely excluded in an array of cases such as marriage, divorce and hadd cases.[219]

> O believers, when you contract a debt one upon another for a stated term, write it down, and let a writer write it down between you justly, and let not any writer refuse to write it down, as God has taught him; so let him write, and let the debtor dictate, and let him fear God his Lord and not diminish aught of it. And if the debtor be a fool, or weak, or unable to dictate himself, then let his guardian dictate justly. And call in to witness two witnesses, men; or if the two be not men, then one man and two women, such witnesses as you approve of, that if one of the two women errs the other will remind her; and let the witnesses not refuse, whenever they are summoned. And be not loth to write it down, whether it be small or great, with its term; that is more equitable in God's sight, more upright for testimony, and likelier that you will not be in doubt. Unless it be merchandise present that you give and take between you; then it shall be no fault in you if you do not write it down. And take witnesses when you are trafficking one with another. And let not either writer or witness be pressed; or

---

218 For the corroborating verses used to disqualify women from testifying in non-financial cases, see Quran 65:2 and 5:106.

219 Ali, *Gender and Human Rights in Islam and International Law*, p. 72. All those areas involve matters related to the body and its status. The Hanafi accept women's testimony in all cases, even capital cases. Issues dealing solely with the female body, allow for the testimony of two women, without the corroboration of a man's testimony, see Mohammad Fadel, "Two Women, One Man: Knowledge, Power and Gender in Medieval Sunni Legal Thought", *International Journal of Middle East Studies* Vol. 29 (1997), p. 194. The main difference between the Hanafi and the Shafi'i school of law, is that the Hanafi assume that female testimony is allowed, until proven otherwise, while the others assume that female testimony is invalid, unless proven otherwise, see Lucas, "Justifying Gender Inequalities in the Shafi'i Law School", pp. 252, 254.

if you do, that is ungodliness in you. And fear God; God teaches you, and God has knowledge of everything.[220]

The phrase "or if the two be not men, then one man and two women" could easily have been interpreted as meaning women were allowed to testify only if two men were not available, however, on the basis of consensus, it was agreed that women's testimony in financial cases was always permitted, despite the number of men available to testify.[221] While it might not seem like it, in this case, consensus expanded the rights of women. Nevertheless, the verse as such, links the possibility to err to female witnesses, and suggests that women are more prone to error than men. Thus, the need for a second female to corroborate the first woman's testimony. That the Quran appears to imply the testimony of a single woman is less trustworthy than that of a man, was confirmed by various exegetes throughout Islamic history, where it was argued that the reason women were more prone to error than men lay in their nature.[222] A famous and historically significant hadith with a strong chain of transmitters quotes the Prophet Muhammad saying that women were inherently inferior to men, in matters of religion and intelligence.[223] Asked how they were weak in religion, the Prophet declared that " 'because when you menstruate, you are required neither to pray nor fast.' In response to why women are inferior in intelligence, the Prophet declared 'is not your evidence (in a court) half of the value of men's evidence?' The woman replied, 'yes.' The Prophet said, 'this is because of the deficiency of a woman's mind' ".[224]

The established rule of the 2:1 ratio in cases where women have been permitted to testify and if it is generally applicable to all cases tried in court has been called into question.[225] What we can read from the verse is that any relevance to the courtroom is only implicit, as the verse in the Quran is not specifically directed to judges, but parties to a financial transaction.

Islamic procedural law assigns to gender an important role in determining who can participate in the judicial process, to what extent, and in

---

220 Quran 2:282. See also, 2:221; 2:282; 24:30; 4:3; and 4:34.
221 Lucas, "Justifying Gender Inequalities in the Shafi'i Law School", p. 253.
222 Fakhr al-Din al-Razi, *al-Tafsir al-kabir*, 32 vols. (Cairo: Al-Matba'a al-Baha'iyya al-Misriyya, 1938), 7.122; Sayyid Qutb, *Fi zilal al-qur'an*, 6 vols. (Cairo: Dar al-Shuruq, n.d.), 1.336.
223 For a detailed argument that this hadith is forged based upon classical and modern sources, see Khadija al-Bitar, *Fi naqd al-Bukhari ... kana baynahu wa-bayn al-haqq hijab* (Morocco: Dar al-Nashr al-Maghribiyya, 2003), pp. 61–72.
224 Al-Bukhari, *Sahih,* Book 52, hadith 22.
225 Wadud, *Quran and Woman,* pp. 85–86.

what capacity, it also provides a rich site for the exploration of the relationships governing knowledge, power, and gender in medieval Muslim legal thought. Any adequate understanding of the obstacles limiting the admission of female testimony in Islamic law must first come to terms with the manner in which legal discourse attempted to differentiate what I call "political" discourse from "normative" discourse. The former was embodied in those statements which, if admitted, would lead to some immediate, binding consequence, usually in favour of one party and against another. Moreover, the beneficiary of this statement could seek to have it imposed on the losing party in the event of the latter's non-compliance. A witness's testimony and a judge's verdict are both political because the consequences of each are immediate, tangible, and binding, irrespective of the consent of the party who contests either the fact presented by the witnesses or the rule of law applied by the judge. Normative discourse, on the other hand, if admitted, established a universal norm or fact, but only *potentially* affects tangible interests. Muslim jurists used the terms *shahada* (testimony) and *hukm* (verdict) to distinguish discourse that had political consequences from the normative discourse that was described with the terms *riwaya* (narration) and *fatwa* (non-binding legal opinion).[226]

Mohammad Fadel argues that in the political context, witnesses exercise power over the parties of the lawsuit, which bind the third party, in contrast to narration, which binds everyone according to Islamic legal theory. Paradoxically, the nature of women does not affect a woman's credibility when the speech falls within the normative discourse. In the context of narration, or the interpretation of the law, which is also considered to be normative, the statement of one person, regardless of gender, is sufficient, as long as the person is considered credible. This implies that "something other than a woman's general ability to gain, preserve, and communicate knowledge to others must have been behind the decision to reject her uncorroborated statements in the particular context of testimony before a judge. Had there been a natural quality inherent in women rendering their statements more unreliable than those of men, then the law should have consistently discriminated against the statements of women, whether in the normative or in the political domain."[227] In other words, the criteria upon which the truthfulness of speech is evaluated differs

---

226 Fadel, "Two Women, One Man", p. 188.
227 Ibid., 189.

due to context in Islamic law. Speech that falls in the normative category, are not subject to the discriminatory rules of testimony:

> Maleness and freedom are not required of the *mufti*, just as is the case for the narrator ... because the *mufti* is taken to be one reporting the law in a manner non-specific to a person, and in this respect, he is like a narrator, not a witness. Moreover, his *fatwa* is non-binding, in contrast to a judge's [verdict].[228]

Hadiths narrated by women, like Aisha, were considered to have the same authenticity as those narrated by a man. There was no questioning of the validity of the report based on the gender of the narrator. Similarly, because fatwas are considered normative speech, gender is not relevant to the construction of a valid legal opinion. Most interestingly, for the same reason, a woman providing expert testimony before a court, is considered to fall within the normative discourse. The argument is that they are providing objective relevant information, not testifying.[229] Such testimony would not need to be corroborated by another expert, male or female. Maliki jurists did not even allow for a rebuttal of the expert opinions made by men or women.[230]

Shihab al-Din al-Qarafi (d. 1285), argued that in the context of narration, the narrator has little interest in lying as he is affected by the universalness of the tradition. While mistakes or lying could be made when narrating, such mistakes can nevertheless be corrected, unlike during trial where the consequences of false testimony could be so severe, that it could lead to the loss of property, limb or life. As the outcome of the ruling would not affect the witness, it is more likely that the witness would not remember everything correctly, because the witness has no interest in the outcome. The chance to prove that the testimony was false is almost non-existent, according to al-Qarafi. For this reason—the suspicion about the reliability of the witness—gives rise to the requirement of a second witness to corroborate the first witness's testimony, as it was likely that the losing party would hold a grudge against the witness because their testimony would be the reason for their loss. Because the witness exercises authority over them, al-Qarafi argues that the losing party would not respect the court's decision if the witness were a woman. Two women were therefore required by the law, to reduce the blow to the male pride, and

---

[228] Ibid., 190.
[229] Ibn Hisham, *al-Mufid li-l-hukkam fi ma ya'rid lahum min nawail al-ahkam* (Cairo: Arab League Manuscript, n.d.), no. 35, 54a.
[230] Fadel, "Two Women, One Man", p. 196.

increase the chance of the losing party to abide by the court's decision.[231] Al-Qarafi also justifies the appropriateness of using two women to corroborate testimony with the common reference to the deficient minds of women, where he described women as having intellectual powers not far above animals.[232] Al-Qarafi's commentator, Ibn al-Shatt (d. 1323) proves the weakness of such arguments by referring to the fact that women were allowed to narrate hadiths. If women's minds are deficient, they are also deficient when narrating.[233]

'Ali ibn Khalil ibn Al-Tarabulusi (d. 1393), on the other hand, argues that the discriminatory stance on the laws of the testimony of women is a consequence of the social disorder that would arise if a woman were to leave her home to go to court and testify:

> Our opinion is valid because a woman is equal to a man in that [characteristics] upon which the qualifications of testimony are based, and these are the ability to see, to be precise, to memorize, and to rehearse testimony because of the existence of the implement of this power, and it is reason, [that faculty] which distinguishes things and comprehends them and a speaking tongue. Thus, the testimony of women gives rise to overwhelming likelihood [of truth] and to certainty in the heart about the truth of the witnesses. This is in contrast to the testimony of women themselves, which is not accepted. Although their statements result in probability, the law did not take into account as a proof because they are forbidden to go out because that leads to disorder and corruption, and the cause of corruption must be removed. Thus, a male was required as one of two witnesses to prevent decisively the occurrence of corruption to the extent possible.[234]

According to al-Tarabulusi, gender is not a relevant factor when it comes to testimony, as Islamic law justifies the discriminatory rules of testimony as a means to preserve a society where women would not occupy the same space as unknown men.[235] Interestingly, neither al-Qarafi, nor al-Tarabulusi use the

---

231 Ibid., 192. See also, Shihab al-Din al- Qarafi, *al-Furuq*, 4 vols (Beirut: Alam al-Kutub, n.d.), 1.6–1.7.
232 Shihab al-Din Aḥmad b. Idris al-Qarafi, *Nafa'is al-Uṣul fi Sharḥ al-Maḥṣul*, ed. 'Adil Aḥmad 'Abd al-Mawjud and 'Ali Muḥammad Mu'awwaḍ, 9 vols. (Riyad: Maktabat Nizar Muṣṭafa al-Baz, 1997), 9:4051 ("*al-niswan qarib min al-baha'im*").
233 Fadel, "Two Women, One Man", p. 192. Ibn Adb Allah Ibn Muhammad, known as Ibn al-Shatt, *Tahdhib al-furuq* (Beirut: Alam al-Kutub, n.d.), 1:6–7.
234 Fadel, "Two Women, One Man", p. 193.
235 Ibid.

verse in the Quran as the basis for their arguments. Instead, they are focused on describing the difference between the effects the deficient minds of women have on private and public matters and developing a legal doctrine around the existing structure of Islamic law. A structure that had made sure women were not to participate in the public sphere, where women were generally seen as intellectually inferior.

Ahmad Ibn al-Taymiyya (d. 1327) and Ibn Qayyim al-Jawziyya (d. 1350) on the other hand, rejected the division between both political and normative speech and argued that limiting a woman's testimony to financial matters was arbitrary. If a woman was considered reliable, she should be able to testify in all matters. They maintained that the verse in the Quran does not describe the testimony of a woman before a judge, but speaks of recording testimony in a case where there potentially could be a dispute regarding a financial matter in the future. Both of them argue that a judge must accept the testimony of a credible woman in the same manner as the testimony of a credible man. However, these arguments do not mean that Ibn al-Taymiyya and Ibn Qayyim viewed the testimony of men and women alike in all matters. Ibn Qayyim maintains that "the testimony of a man is superior to [that of] a woman because it is usually impossible for women to attend court sessions, and their memory and precision is less than that of males".[236] Although al-Qayyim also upholds the notion that women are more likely to err than men, for him, it did not constitute a complete discrimination of the testimony of women.[237]

Like many other areas of Islamic law, while men are attributed virtues and rights, women must prove to be at the same level as men before they can enjoy the same virtues and rights attributed to men in general. Interestingly, it appears as if commentators have accepted the contradictory stance Islamic law has on women's testimony and tried to validate it by referring to speech and categorizing it differently. Transmission is considered to be gender-neutral while testifying validates discrimination. This is done, not by invoking legal arguments, but by maintaining sociological factors to help preserve a society upholding gender segregation to maintain the sexual modesty of its believers.

---

[236] In his analysis of al-Qayyim, Mohammad Fadel argues that while al-Qayyim maintains that the issue at hand refers to the credibility of the witness and not the gender, and since it is more likely that a female witness will not be able to testify before a court because she lacks the same access to the public sphere than a man, individuals prefer men to testify as it is the most effective means of preserving rights, see "Two Women, One Man", pp. 198. See also, Ibn Qayyim al-Jawziyya, I'lam al-muwaqqi' in bi-rabb al'alamin, 3 vols., ed. Taha 'Abd al-Ra'uf Sa'd (Beirut: Dar al-Jil, n.d.), 1:95.

[237] Fadel, "Two Women, One Man", p. 199.

What is also interesting is the vast difference between the schools of law in the absence of male witnesses. The opinions range from the testimony of the single woman, up to four women and are based on the values the schools of law have assigned women, and not on the merits of the Quran.[238]

3.6 Compensation for Death

Retaliation and financial compensation for death or injury, *diya*, were concepts deeply rooted in pre-Islamic society which also became part of Islamic law.[239] The period before Islam was characterized by hostile relationship between tribes, which often led to personal revenge for homicide. Diya became a nonviolent alternative in seeking revenge. Tribes usually had special funds for making diya payments, and while it was the relatives of the murderer who were obligated to pay the diya, the tribe supported the relatives, especially if they were not able to provide compensation.[240] The concept of diya was integrated into Islam as a means of uniting tribes and making sure that entire tribes were not wiped out due to retaliation. Verses confirm that:

> O believers, prescribed for you is retaliation, touching the slain; freeman for freeman, slave for slave, female for female. But if aught is pardoned a man by his brother, let the pursuing be honourable, and let the payment be with kindliness.[241]
>
> It belongs not to a believer to slay a believer, except it be by error. If any slays a believer by error, then let him set free a believing slave, and bloodwit is to be paid to his family unless they forgo it as a freewill offering. If he belongs to a people at enmity with you and is a believer, let the slayer

---

238 The Hanafi conclude that the testimony of a single woman is sufficient, with the exception of a divorced woman who gives birth. The Hanbali attribute this position to Ibn Hanbal and accept a single woman's testimony in a small number of cases; see Ibn Qudama (d. 1223), *al-Mughni li-Ibn Qudama*, 10 vols. (Cairo: Maktabat al-Qahira, n.d.), 10: 136–37; Ahmad b. 'Abd Allah al-Ba'li (d. 1775), *al-Rawd alnadi sharh Kaf i al-mubtadi* (Cairo: al-Matba'a al-Salafiyya, n.d.), 529. Other opinions are: two women (Malik and Sufyan al-Thawri); two women or one midwife (al-Hasan al-Basri and Ibn 'Abbas); at least three female witnesses (Anas b. Malik and 'Uthman al-Batti); and finally, the requirement of at least four female witnesses (al-Shafi'i and 'Ata' b. Abi Rabah), see Lucas, "Justifying Gender Inequalities in the Shafi'i Law School", p. 254.

239 Lucas, "Justifying Gender Inequalities in the Shafi'i Law School", p. 242.

240 Compensations were usually made in the form of chattel, see Michael J. L. Hardy, *Blood Feuds and the Payment of Blood Money in the Middle East* (Leiden: Brill, 1963), p. 37. See also, Renat I. Bekkin, Islamic Insurance: National Features and Legal Regulations, *Arab Law Quarterly* Vol. 21, No. 3 (2007), p. 13.

241 Quran 2:178.

set free a believing slave. If he belongs to a people joined with you by a compact, then bloodwit is to be paid to his family and the slayer shall set free a believing slave.[242]

And whoso slays a believer willfully, his recompense is Gehenna, therein dwelling forever, and God will be wroth with him and will curse him, and prepare for him a mighty chastisement.[243]

Classical Islamic law allows for the victim's family in homicide cases to kill,[244] or harm the criminal,[245] or receive financial compensation. In cases of unintentional killing or unintentional injury, only compensation is awarded,[246] and in the cases of bodily injury, the victim or the victim's family has the option of pardoning the perpetrator. It is considered to be a compassionate religious act of charity, and according to the Quran, to be the best solution.[247]

The verse in the Quran, however, suggests that a free man cannot be retaliated for a slave and that only a woman can be killed in the retaliation of a woman. It is a hadith, concerning a letter the Prophet sent to the people of Yemen, which endorses that "a man can be killed [in retaliation] for killing a woman,"[248] yet the compensation for a murdered woman is half of that of a

---

242 Quran 4:92.
243 Quran 4:93. A hadith prescribes diya for intentional homicides too: "Whoever kills a believer deliberately for no reason or a crime that he had committed, he should be killed (in retaliation), unless the family of the murdered person agrees to take diyah", see A.A. 'Asqalani, *Bulugh al-Maram*, Vol. I (Riyadh: Dar al-Faraq, 2003), p. 359.
244 See Quran 4.93. The death penalty is carried out by the state, see al-Alfi, "Punishment in Islamic Criminal Law", p. 230.
245 Quran 5:45.
246 Rudolph Peters, *Crime and Punishment in Islamic Law* (Cambridge: Cambridge University Press, 2005), pp. 38–53.
247 Quran 2:178.
248 Abu Ishaq al-Shirazi, *al-Muhadhdhab fi fiqh al-Imam al-Shafi'i*, ed. Muhammad al-Zuhayli, 6 vols. (Damascus: Dar al-Qalam; Beirut: al-Dar al-Shamiyya, 1992–1996), 5:10; Abu Bakr al-Bayhaqi, *al-Sunan al-kubra*, ed. Muhammad 'Atta, 11 vols. (Beirut: Dar al-Kutub al-'Ilmiyya, 1999), 8:51–52; al-Rafi'i, *al-'Aziz*, 10:170–72; Zakariyya al-Ansari, *Asna al-matalib sharh Rawd al-talib*, ed. Muhammad Tamir, 9 vols. (Beirut: Dar al-Kutub al-'Ilmiyya, 2001), 8:36; 'Abd Allah al-Sharqawi, *Hashiyat al-Sharqawi*, 4 vols. (Beirut: Dar al-Kutub al-'Ilmiyya, 1997), 4:175; al-Ghazali, *al-Wasit fi l-madhhab*, ed. Ahmad Mahmud Ibrahim, 7 vols. (al-Ghuriya: Dar al-Salam, 1997), 6:277; 'Abd al-Karim al-Rafi'i, *al-'Aziz sharh al-Wajiz*, ed. 'Ali Mu'awwad and 'Adil 'Abd al-Mawjud, 13 vols. (Beirut: Dar al-Kutub al-'Ilmiyya, 1997), 10:170–72; Ibn al-Farra' [al-Baghawi], *al-Tahdhib fi fiqh al-Imam al-Shafi'i*, ed. 'Ali Mu'awwad and 'Adil 'Abd al-Mawjud, 8 vols. (Beirut: Dar al-Kutub al-'Ilmiyya, 1997), 7:22; al-Khatib al-Shirbini, *al-Iqna' f i hall alfaz Abi Shuja'*, found in Sulayman al-Bujayrimi, *Bujayrimi 'ala l-Khatib*, 4 vols. (Beirut: Dar al-Fikr, 1998), 4:160.

murdered man, according to all schools of Sunni and Shia law.[249] The actual compensation under classical Islamic law is set to "a hundred camels" for a free Muslim man,[250] but the schools vary on the compensation for a non-Muslim.[251] However, there is nothing in the verse to suggest that the life of a woman is financially worth half of a man's; rather, such assumptions can be found in hadiths, and through consensus.[252] The same letter, establishing that a man can be killed in retaliation for killing a woman, is also said to have accepted that "the diya of a woman is half [the diya] of a man".[253] Yet, the hadith is challenged as the chain of transmitters were not considered to be sound in meeting the minimal standards for authenticity. While some jurists argued that the hadith did not contain such a sentence,[254] others meant that there was a consensus reached on the discriminatory legal equation on diya.[255] Through the application of analogical reasoning, it was argued that since women received half of what men receive in financial matters such as inheritance, her diya should also be half that of a man. Scholars who maintained that the diya of a woman should be the same as a man argued that the financial compensation was to serve as a substitute for requiring the killing or harming of the criminal. They compared the question to the diya for a foetus, which was the same, regardless of the gender, and maintained that the diya for women and men should be the same.[256]

There is, however, another verse in the Quran relevant to this discussion, which according to some jurists abrogates the earlier verses:

---

249 Lucas, "Justifying Gender Inequalities in the Shafi'i Law School", p. 243.
250 Daniel Pascoe, "Is Diya a Form of Clemency?", *Boston University International Law Journal* Vol. 34, No. 149 (2016), p. 156.
251 Hanafi and Hanbali hold that the blood money of a non-Muslim should be the same as that of a Muslim, whereas the Maliki hold that a non-Muslim's price is one-half of the blood money for a Muslim. For the Shafi'i it is one-third and the Shia have an even lower threshold, see Pascoe, "Is Diya a Form of Clemency?", p. 156.
252 Lucas, "Justifying Gender Inequalities in the Shafi'i Law School", p. 243. See also, al-Mawardi, *al-Hawi al-kabir*, ed. Mahmud Matraji et al., 24 vols. (Beirut: Dar al-Fikr, 1994), 16:96; Taqi al-Din al-Hisni, *Kifayat al-akhyar f i hall Ghayat al-ikhtisar*, ed. Muhammad Haykal (Cairo: Dar al-Salam, 2005), 567 and Ibn al-Mulaqqin, *'Ujalat al-muhtaj ila tawjih al-Minhaj*, ed. 'Izz al-Din al-Badrani, 4 vols. (Irbid: Dar al-Kitab, 2001), 4:1554.
253 al-Mawardi, *al-Hawi al-kabir*, 16:96; al-Rafi'i, *al-'Aziz*, 10:327; al-Hisni, *Kifayat al-akhyar*, 567.
254 Ibn al-Mulaqqin, *al-Badr al-munir*, 8:442; Ibn Hajar al-'Asqalani, *al-Talkhis al-habir f i takhrij ahadith al-Rafi'i al-kabir*, ed. 'Ali Mu'awwad and 'Adil 'Abd al-Mawjud, 4 vols. (Beirut: Dar al-Kutub al-'Ilmiyya, 1998).
255 Scott C. Lucas argues that the evidence upon which such assumptions are based on is weak, see "Justifying Gender Inequalities in the Shafi'i Law School", p. 246.
256 al-Mawardi, *al-Hawi al-kabir*, 16:96.

And therein We prescribed for them: 'A life for a life, an eye for an eye, a nose for a nose, an ear for an ear, a tooth for a tooth, and for wounds retaliation'; but whosoever forgoes it as a freewill offering, that shall be for him an expiation. Whoso judges not according to what God has sent down -- they are the evildoers.[257]

Verse 5:45 was the last to be revealed, thus abrogating the recourse to social and gender status.[258] "By this approach, it may be argued that during its early stage, Islam tolerated recourse to 'social status', but phased it out subsequently."[259] More interestingly, is that this verse does not even include the concept of diya, but speaks of "retaliation by way of charity", which has been interpreted to mean diya.[260] Other scholars argue that verse 5:45 only prescribes 'life for life' for the people of the Book, that is, Jews and Christians, and does not apply to Muslims.[261] Such an interpretation is based on the opening of the verse, which declares "We prescribed for them". If such a recourse is accepted, the social and gender aspect of retaliation is not abrogated by this verse.[262] The claim that the verse only relates to non-Muslims is, however, contested by reference to hadiths where the Prophet prescribes that no group supersedes other groups:[263]

O People! Your Creator is one, and you are all descendants of the same ancestors. There is no superiority of an Arab over a non-Arab or of the black over the red, except on the basis of righteous conduct.[264]

Other scholars argue that verses are related to different scenarios; where verse 5:45 related to a particular tribe who used to exceed in avenging the death of

---

257   Quran 5:45.
258   I.U. Ibn Kathir, *Tafsir Ibn Kathir*, Vol. I (Cairo: Dar-al-Tayyibah, 1999), p. 489. The abrogation is also confirmed by referring to the practice of the Prophet, who ordered the killing of a Jewish man for killing a woman, see M. Al-Tabari, *Jami' al-Bayan fi Ta'wil al-Quran*, ed. A.M. Shakir, Vol. x (Beirut: Mu'assasat al-Risalah, 2000), p. 360.
259   Musa Usman Abubakar, *Gender Justice in Islamic Law: Homicide and Bodily Injuries* (Oxford: Hart Publishing, 2018), p. 79.
260   M. Bukhari, *Sahih Bukhari*, Vol. 9, Book 83, No. 20.
261   Mohammad Salim El-Awa, *Punishment in Islamic Law: A Comparative Study* (Plainfield: American Trust Publication, 2000), pp. 72–73.
262   Abubakar, *Gender Justice in Islamic Law*, p. 79.
263   M. A. Ibn al-'Arabi, *Ahkam al-Qur'an*, Vol. II (Beirut: Dar al-Kutub al-'Ilmiyyah, 2003), p. 128. See also, Al-Sarakhsi, *Al-Mabsut* (n112), Vol. XXVI, p. 106.
264   Mohammad H. Kamali, *Freedom, Equality and Justice in Islam* (Cambridge: The Islamic Text Society, 2002), p. 52.

one of their own. The verse rather restricted the transgression and dictated equality in retaliation between different tribes.[265]

The Shia adopted another approach based on caliph Ali's opinion on the matter, where killing a woman in retaliation for a man was not considered sufficient:

> Ali said that it is necessary for the close relatives of the deceased woman to pay half of the *diya* [if they execute the male killer in retaliation] in order to make the killing of the man equal to her killing. If a woman kills a man, [Ali] said, it is not sufficient for her to be killed in retaliation—the victim's heirs should receive half of the *diya* in addition to her death.[266]

It becomes apparent that the discriminatory views on the financial aspects of retaliation are not prescribed by the Quran, rather it is by the application of analogy and through the consensus of the jurists, that such a position has been constructed.[267]

3.7 Inheritance

The Quran established the right to inherit, according to fixed shares,[268] to family members that were "totally excluded under the earlier customary tribal tradition".[269] This was a progressive initial step, yet the women's right to inherit property appears to have been an unwelcome pronouncement to the people of Medina. Medina, being a predominantly agricultural community, found the division of land more complex than the commercial Meccans, where it seems that women inheriting property was a custom even before Islam.[270] Nevertheless, the mere existence of verses in the Quran guaranteeing all women and not only those who had high social standing a minimum share was at the time, a great advancement of women's rights:[271]

---

265 al-'Arabi, *Ahkam al-Qur'an*, p. 89.
266 al-Ghazali, *al-Wasit fi l-madhhab*, 6:277. The requirement that the female victim's family pays half the male diya if they opt for retaliation against a male murderer was reactivated in the Islamic Republic of Iran after the revolution, see Haleh Afshar, "Islam and Feminism: An Analysis of Political Strategies," in *Feminism and Islam: Legal and Literary Perspectives*, ed. Mai Yamani (New York: New York University Press, 1996), pp. 201–3; and Shirin Ebadi, *Iran Awakening* (New York: Random House, 2006), pp. 112–18.
267 Lucas, "Justifying Gender Inequalities in the Shafi'i Law School", p. 257.
268 Quran 4:7.
269 Abdulmajeed Hassan Bello, "Islamic Law of Inheritance: Ultimate Solution to Social Inequality against Women", *Arab Law Quarterly* Vol. 29 (2015), p. 261.
270 Ahmed, "Women and the Advent of Islam", p. 680.
271 Ali, *Gender and Human Rights in Islam and International Law*, p. 59.

God charges you, concerning your children: to the male the like of the portion of two females, and if they be women above two, then for them two-thirds of what he leaves, but if she be one then to her a half; and to his parents to each one of the two the sixth of what he leaves, if he has children; but if he has no children, and his heirs are his parents, a third to his mother, or, if he has brothers, to his mother a sixth, after any bequest he may bequeath, or any debt. Your fathers and your sons -- you know not which out of them is nearer in profit to you. So God apportions; surely God is All-knowing, All-wise.[272]

Although the verse clearly affirms that a woman has the right to inherit half a share compared to a man, there are scholars who argue that the verse is not discriminatory towards women. In the historical and social settings of that time, the laws on custody and inheritance reflected the economic realities,[273] which placed the financial responsibility on men. As a consequence of women not being legally required to provide for the household while men are, they are entitled to a greater share as their financial burden is greater.[274] Islamic law does not require women to share her resources in marriage, and she may seek dissolution of the marriage if her husband cannot meet the financial requirement of supporting her and the household. Women are not legally required to provide for anyone, not even themselves, while a husband's financial duties only increase when the family grows, since he is also financially responsible for the children. In some cases, the husband must also care for his parents and siblings.[275] Thus, although a woman is entitled to inherit half a share, it is argued that because she receives her part from three different sources; the father, husband, and son, "this makes her share almost equal to man".[276] But men also inherit from other sources, namely mother, wife, and daughter, which makes their totaling share greater than that of the woman's.[277]

---

[272] Quran 4:11.
[273] Esposito, *Women in Muslim Family Law*, p. 48.
[274] Husband and wife inherit from each other according to set rules, where the only condition is a valid marriage contract. Consummation of the marriage is not required for the parties to inherit from each other, see Murata, *Temporary Marriage (Mut'a)*, p. 26. See also, Karmi, "Women, Islam and Patriarchalism", p. 171.
[275] Bello, "Islamic Law of Inheritance: Ultimate Solution to Social Inequality against Women", pp. 270–272.
[276] Perveen Shaukat Ali, *Human Rights in Islam* (Lahore: Aziz Publishers, 1980), p. 120.
[277] For a detailed description of the Islamic law of inheritance see Muhammad A. Mannan, *Principles of Muhammadan Law* (Lahore: PLD Publishers, 1995), chapters 6–8 and Davis S. Powers, *Studies in the Quran and Hadith: the Formation of the Islamic Law of Inheritance* (Berkeley: University of California Press, 1985).

Nevertheless, it is argued, that while the shares of the man and the woman are not equal, "they are not necessarily unequal in the final analysis, even if they appear mathematically unequal",[278] as the wife, in addition to the woman's inheritance share, also has the right to dower.[279] Such a statement ignores the underlying view of how men and women are perceived which can be exemplified regarding the property they leave behind. Should a wife die without having any relatives, the husband inherits all of her property, whereas if the husband should die without any relatives, the wife is entitled to half of the property. The remaining half goes to the community treasury according to the Sunni schools. The Shia, however, hold that she inherits all the property.[280]

Furthermore, with the selective and arbitrary employment of the doctrine of abrogation, the jurists ensured that many of the financial rights afforded women in the Quran were substantially narrowed. By enforcing fixed shares of inheritance and applying the doctrine of abrogation, verses concerning the treatment of divorced women were connected to the treatment of widows:

> And those of you who die, leaving wives, let them make testament for their wives, provision for a year without expulsion.[281]

The verse establishes a year-long financial support for a widow, but was abrogated for a verse which was revealed later according to the jurists, which substantially reduced the widow's maintenance period:

> And those of you who die, leaving wives, they shall wait by themselves for four months and ten nights.[282]

The jurists viewed these verses in such conflict that they could not be implemented simultaneously. They came to interpret both verses to deal with the waiting period, *iddah,* while the first verse speaks of no such thing. It just concerns the financial provision made in favor of the widow. Furthermore, the assertion that the latter verse was revealed after the first verse is unsupported. When the verse granting women inheritance rights was revealed, it

---

278 Bello, "Islamic Law of Inheritance: Ultimate Solution to Social Inequality against Women", p. 270.
279 Ali, *Gender and Human Rights in Islam and International Law,* p. 73.
280 Murata, *Temporary Marriage (Mut'a),* p. 26. See also, al-Amili, *al-Rawdat al-bahiyya fi sharh al-lum'at al-Dimashqiyya,* p. 367.
281 Quran 2:240.
282 Quran 2:234.

was again assumed that it had replaced earlier verses, and the maintenance of the widow was abandoned, as the verse instead had established that the widow had a specified share of the deceased husband's estate. The rights of widows were tampered with, although the verses regulate specific issues, that could easily be implemented simultaneously. Basically, widows were originally both entitled to maintenance and accommodation for a whole year, only to be abrogated for the inheritance shares established by the Quran, while one right does not cancel out another right. The schools of law, however, came to adopt the procedure granting the same financial rights for divorced women and widowed women.[283]

Over time, the notion of the fixed inheritance share for women became the only share they were entitled to, disregarding any other scenarios.[284] However, there are legal ways of getting around this prescription. The Quranic injunctions do not mean that the possibility of an enhanced share, a share equal to, or more than the share of a man is prohibited. A person may, by executing a valid gift deed, leave his/her entire wealth to a woman and a husband may, under a stipulation in the marriage contract, leave all of his possessions to his wife as part of the dower, since there is no maximum limit to what may be given as dower to a wife.[285] The will also allows for another possibility to increase women's (but also other categories, such as those not legally required to inherit from the estate, such as Christian or Jewish widows) inheritance. Making a will is considered a religious duty in Islam and allows the testator to bequeath one-third of his net estate to whomever he sees fit, unless the other heir's consent to the testator to bequeath more.[286] For the remaining two-thirds, Islamic law imposes the compulsory rules of fixed shares, and the will cannot include a bequest of inheritance to one of the legal heirs unless consented to by the other heirs.[287] Some Muslim countries, however, do allow a bequest in favor of a legal heir, as long as the bequest does not exceed the

---

283 The underlying assumption is that the husband's property rights die with him. The jurists also make the connection that the verses dealt with pregnant women, and that the duty imposed on the property of the dead husband, could only be implemented if the widow did not leave the home. Furthermore, it was later argued that the fixed shares of inheritance, replaced other financial provisions for widows, see Burton, *The Sources of Islamic Law*, pp. 57–74.
284 Rahman, "Status of Women in the Quran", p. 45.
285 Ali, *Gender and Human Rights in Islam and International Law*, p. 59.
286 Bello, "Islamic Law of Inheritance: Ultimate Solution to Social Inequality against Women", p. 265–269.
287 Mohammad H. Kamali, "Islamic Family Law Reform: Problems and Prospects", *Islam and Civilizational Renewal* Vol. 3, No. 1 (2011), p. 47.

bequeathable one-third.[288] The Shia allow for the testator to bequest one-third even without the consent of other heirs. The Islamic principle of selection, takhayyar, would allow for Sunni jurisdictions to adopt the more favorable inheritance laws of Shiite law, although it is not likely, due to the hostile feelings among the groups.[289]

3.8 Divorce

While divorce is allowed in Islamic law, it is highly disapproved of in the Quran which obligates men to treat women kindly or divorce them.[290] Instead, Islam encourages reconciliation between the spouses.[291] While many of the pre-Islamic practices of divorce were abolished by Islam, classical Islamic law still gives the husband the unilateral right to dissolve the marriage, through the unilateral pronouncement of divorce known as *talaq,* without giving any cause and without the interference of the court.[292] The wife, on the other hand, needs to seek dissolution by referring her case to court and convincing the court that there are no ways of working out their differences and that she therefore needs to end the marriage.[293] She must be able to prove her allegations.[294] Legitimate reasons for the wife to end the marriage may be done by claiming fault on the husband's side, such as impotence, failure to consummate the marriage after a certain period of time has elapsed, detention or imprisonment of the husband, failure to provide financial support, insanity, or breach of the terms of the marriage contract, conversion or other rarely used processes, such as the husband taking an oath abstaining from sexual intercourse. The Maliki school also includes abuse, including physical, verbal, and emotional abuse, as a valid ground for the dissolution of the marriage initiated by the wife.[295] In cases

---

288   Bello, "Islamic Law of Inheritance: Ultimate Solution to Social Inequality against Women", p. 266.
289   Kamali, "Islamic Family Law Reform", pp. 47–48.
290   Quran 2:229 and 65:1–2. The four Sunni schools of law have concluded that divorce is disapproved (makruh), when there is hope of reconciliation, see Abdur Rahman I. Doi, *Shariʿah Law: The Islamic Law* (Kuala Lumpur: A. S. Nordeen, 1984), p. 170.
291   Doi, *Shariʿah Law: The Islamic Law*, pp. 168–169. See also Quran 4:35.
292   Many Muslim countries have legislated certain procedural requirements that are needed to be fulfilled for the divorce to be valid.
293   Ali, *Gender and Human Rights in Islam and International Law*, p. 61.
294   Black, Esmaeili, Hosen, *Modern Perspectives on Islamic Law,* pp. 121–135.
295   Any of the spouses may annul the marriage immediately, if a spouse has certain specified physical or mental disabilities, which makes the continuation of the marriage difficult. The schools have different disabilities that allow for annulment to occur, see Murata, *Temporary Marriage (Mutʿa)*, pp. 17–18. For a brief description of the legitimate reasons a wife can invoke in order to obtain a divorce, see Javaid, "The Sharia, Islamic Family Laws and International Human Rights Law", p. 118. See also, Quran 2:226–227.

where the woman initiates the divorce, the right to the dower can be returned to the husband in order to ransom herself from her husband.[296]

> It is not lawful for you to take of what you have given them unless the couple fear they may not maintain God's bounds; if you fear they may not maintain God's bounds, it is no fault in them for her to redeem herself.[297]

In this case, the evidentiary requirements are less demanding as the wife does not need to establish specific grounds for divorce, besides having developed irreconcilable differences with her husband.[298]

After the pronouncement of talaq, a waiting period, iddah, of three months commences, where the husband must abstain from having sexual relations with his wife; before the divorce becomes final.[299] During this period, the husband still needs to provide for his wife and children by allowing them to reside in their marital home.[300]

> Divorced women shall wait by themselves for three periods; and it is not lawful for them to hide what God has created in their wombs; if they believe in God and the Last Day. In such time their mates have better right to restore them, if they desire to set things right. Women have such honourable rights as obligations, but their men have a degree above them; God is All-mighty, All-wise.[301]

Men are given the right to choose to reconcile with his wife during this period. The decision is the husband's alone and does not require the wife's consent.

---

296   This type of divorce is referred to as *khul'*, and Sunni schools allow for a third party to initiate khul'. For example, the third party may offer the husband a sum in exchange for the husband to divorce his wife. The Shia maintain that this is forbidden.
297   Quran 2:229 and 4:128, See also Mashour, "Islamic Law and Gender Equality", p. 574.
298   Javaid, "The Sharia, Islamic Family Laws and International Human Rights Law", p. 118.
299   The waiting period for divorce differs between the schools, where different circumstances are taken in regard to how long the prescribed waiting period is. Marriages that have not been consummated do not initiate a waiting period. The Hanbali and Shia hold that there is no waiting period for a girl younger than 9 years old, while the Maliki and Shafi'i hold that if she was mature enough to participate in sexual intercourse, there is a three-month waiting period. The Hanafi require a three-month waiting period regardless. Sunni schools prescribe a three-month waiting period for a woman who has gone through menopause, while the Shia hold that in such cases it is not necessary. See Murata, *Temporary Marriage (Mut'a)*, p. 23.
300   Esposito, *Women in Muslim Family Law*, p. 36.
301   Quran 2:228.

The pronouncement of divorce is revocable throughout the iddah period and will be irrevocable once the period is over.[302] The period was included as a way of making sure that the woman was not pregnant before the divorce is final. The waiting period need not be considered if the marriage has not been consummated.[303] After the dissolution of the marriage, the husband must pay his wife all her material rights, unless she has returned her dowry as described above. If the man wants to remarry the woman after the iddah period, it will be considered as a first marriage, with a new marriage contract and a new dowry.[304]

3.9 Political Positions

Islamic substantive law generally upholds that only men can hold public office. Thus, positions such as the head of state, or judges of an Islamic court is a realm restricted to women. Except the Hanafi's, all the Sunni schools of law had by the 14th century at the latest, excluded women from public office.[305] Nevertheless, the Muslim world has seen several women in leading positions, such as former Prime Minister of Pakistan Benazir Bhutto, and women serve as judges in various countries.

There are no verses in the Quran that bar women from participating in public and political life. Hadiths, however, declare some professions, such as head of state, out of reach for the realms of women. The most significant hadith, which can be found in various versions, concludes that "those who entrust their affairs to women will never know prosperity".[306] Unlike many other

---

302 The Quran limits the amount of times a husband may pronounce divorce and then take back his wife to two times, thereafter the divorce is considered final and irrevocable, see verse 2:229. The vow a husband could make about leaving his wife was limited to four months, whereas in pre-Islamic times there was no limit to this period. After that period, the husband had to take his vow back or divorce his wife, see Engineer, *The Rights of Women in Islam*, p. 29. The husband is not allowed to abstain from sexual relations with his wife for longer than four months. Should he do so, the wife has a valid divorce reason. The judge has the right to force the husband to stay in the marriage, should he refuse to, then the judge could grant the wife a revocable divorce. The Shia uphold that the judge may, by imprisonment or other means available, compel a husband to return to his wife or divorce her. See Murata, *Temporary Marriage (Mut'a)*, p. 24. The man is not allowed to re-marry the same woman until she is married to another, see Quran 2:230.
303 Quran 2:230 and 33:49.
304 Mashour, "Islamic Law and Gender Equality", p. 573.
305 Fadel, "Is Historicism a Viable Strategy for Islamic Legal Reform?", pp. 28–31. A minority of Muslim jurists allow for women to serve as judges, see Fadel, "Two Women, One Man", p. 196.
306 Al-Bukhari, *Sahih*, Vol. 4, p. 226.

hadiths manifesting misogynist views on women, this hadith is found in the most authoritative collections of the traditions of the Prophet.[307] However, the placement of this hadith in the various collections where it can be found, profoundly effects the interpretation of the hadith and its implications. Al-Bukhari includes the hadith in two different chapters: "The Chapter of [Military] Campaigns, Section: The Prophet's Diplomatic Correspondence with Chosroe and Caesar" and "The Chapter of Civil Strife". Al-Tirmidhi includes it only in his "The Chapter of Civil Strife". For al-Bukhari and al-Tirmidhi, the hadith is connected to a specific incident. They put the hadith in a specific historical context related to diplomatic relations with Persia. The Prophet had given that reply when he was told that the Persian King Khosrow had died and his daughter had taken over the country as queen. Thus, it is argued that the comment from the Prophet should be viewed in the context of this specific woman, who was known to be authoritarian, and not be viewed as an absolute command for Muslims to adhere to at all times and all ages.[308]

Ibn Abi Shayba, on the other hand, places the hadith in the context of Aisha and the losing side of the first civil war.[309] Many Basrans participated in the first civil war, and historical sources agree that the hadith was only narrated by Basrans. This fact allowed for many to view the hadith in relation to Aisha. The preceding hadiths in this collection described how the Prophet had prophesized that there would be a civil war and that the group rebelling would be led by a woman.[310] In this version of the hadith, Abu Bakr declares that he heard "never shall a folk prosper who delegate their affairs to a woman". Abu Bakr recalled the hadith at a moment when Caliph Ali entered Basra after defeating Aisha at the Battle of the Camel, years after the death of the Prophet. Allegedly Abu Bakr, who refused to take sides in the civil war, feared a reprimand from Caliph Ali.[311] The compilation of hadiths from Ibn Abi Shayba falls within

---

307 For a description of the various collections of traditions where this hadith is found, see Fadel, "Is Historicism a Viable Strategy for Islamic Legal Reform?", pp. 10–13. Fadel therefore argues that the validity of the hadith is not a "readily available option." The hadith has, however, been questioned by Fatima Mernissi, see "A Feminist Interpretation of Women's Rights in Islam", in *Liberal Islam: A Sourcebook*, ed. Charles Kurzman (New York: Oxford University Press, 1998), pp. 112–120.

308 Hameed, *Mabadi-e-Nazam ul Hukam Al Islami*, pp. 876–878.

309 'Abd Allah b. Muhammad Ibn Abi Shayba, *Al-Kitab al-Musannaf Fi al-Ahadith wa'l-Athar*, ed. Muhammad 'Abd al-Salam Shahin, 9 vols. (Beirut: Dar al-Kutub al-'Ilmiyyah, 1995), 7:538.

310 Fadel, "Is Historicism a Viable Strategy for Islamic Legal Reform?", p. 27.

311 For further reading regarding this hadith see Rahim, *Muhammadan Jurisprudence*, pp. 58–65.

the category of musannaf, which, as previously described, hadiths that were collected during this era were not necessarily evidenced by a reliable chain of transmitters.[312] Some scholars have questioned its authenticity and argue that Abu Bakr stands disqualified to narrate this hadith since he could not be regarded as a reliable transmitter of hadiths because he was convicted and flogged for false testimony by the second Caliph 'Umar.[313]

Finally, Al-Nasa'i includes the hadith in the chapter entitled "The Chapter of the Rules [Applicable To] Judges". The chapter itself starts with the preface "The Prohibition Against Appointing Women to Rule". The placement of the hadith shows the different perception the compilers had of this hadith. While all of them narrate basically the same version, the implication of their understanding of the hadith and their placement of it in their texts leads to different perceptions of what the hadith suggests. Thus, impacting how the hadith came to be used by others to argue that women should not participate in public and political life.[314]

While schools referred to this hadith to exclude women from holding public office, the Hanafi argued that because women have the right to testify in court, women could also act as judges in all cases where the testimony of women is accepted. They maintained that the hadith does not prohibit women serving in such capacities; it only prohibits the appointment of women. They differentiate between the moral and legal implications of the hadith, arguing that it creates a moral prohibition of the appointment of women to hold public office, but there is nothing that legally disqualifies women from serving in the capacity of a judge. Hanafi jurist Ibn al-Humam, argued that although the

---

312   Fadel, "Is Historicism a Viable Strategy for Islamic Legal Reform?", p. 21.
313   Ibn al-Athir, *Usd al-Gharba*, Vol. 5, p. 38. See also, Mernissi, *Women and Islam*, p. 53. Khaled Abou Fadl also questions the reliability of the report, arguing that Abu Bakr had many reasons for forging it, see *Speaking in God's Name*, pp. 111–114. For a criticism of those questioning the validity of this hadith, see Fadel, "Is Historicism a Viable Strategy for Islamic Legal Reform?", pp. 41–42.
314   Mohammad Fadel argues that "it is almost certain that the increasing formalization of legal education, along with the incorporation of legal debate and the formal study of legal controversy, was the catalyst for the ever-increasing reference to this hadith in legal treaties", see "Is Historicism a Viable Strategy for Islamic Legal Reform?", p. 24–29. He furthermore declares that "Abū Bakra's *ḥadīth* is a good example of how the framing of a text can play an important, even if subtle, role in determining how it is read and understood. Al-Bukhārī's decision to include this *ḥadīth* in the chapter of the Prophet's diplomatic correspondence, for example, or Ibn Abī Shayba's inclusion of it as part of the events of the first civil war, casts the *ḥadīth* in a substantially different light than al-Nasā'ī's decision to include it in the materials dealing with judges, to say nothing of the later *ḥadīth* encyclopaedias in which all (or most) contextual facts were edited out entirely". Ibid., 40.

Quran affirms that women are deficient in comparison to men, the deficiency is not so grave as to strip women of political capacity altogether. Deficiency is a feature attributed to women as a class, not as an absolute individual state. Thus, women's capacity to serve as a judge can be assessed.[315] Again, Islamic law sets conditions on women's capability depending on their capacity. While it incapacitates women as a whole, whereas men do not need to prove their capabilities.

Contradicting such a standpoint are the verses in the Quran describing Bilquis, the Queen of Sheba, and praising her rule. This verse is used by scholars to overturn or dismiss the relevance of Abu Bakr's version of the hadith:[316]

> I found a woman ruling over them, and she has been given of everything, and she possesses a mighty throne ...[317] She said, 'O Council, pronounce to me concerning my affair; I am not used to decide an affair until you bear me witness.' They said, 'We possess force and we possess great might. The affair rests with thee; so consider what thou wilt command.'[318]

The Quran never provides any introductory information about the Queen of Sheba, and since pre-Islamic historical sources refer to her,[319] it is generally held that the audience of the Quran was familiar with her, so she did not need any introduction.[320] The Quran never directly or indirectly condemns

---

[315] Ibid., 33.
[316] For a description of modern Muslim jurists' revisionist treatment of the hadith, see Fadel, "Is Historicism a Viable Strategy for Islamic Legal Reform?", pp. 32–35.
[317] Quran 27:23.
[318] Quran 27:32–33.
[319] The Queen of Sheba, in particular, is claimed by both Yemeni and Ethiopian legend since stories in both regions say that she lived there. Hadith and the Islamic tradition in general, say that Sheba (Saba') was in Yemen.
[320] The Old Testament offers a brief account of her visit to Solomon's kingdom and is a major scriptural source of Queen Sheba (see 1 Kings 10 and 2 Chronicles 9). In this narrative, her visit is described as a diplomatic mission, from one head of state to another. Her immense wealth and gifts to Solomon are described, but unlike in the Quran, Solomon accepts her gifts but does not ask her to accept monotheism. There is no mention about a romantic relationship between the two. The Old Testament describes her as an independent agent and public figure. It is only later that Jewish sources highlight her gender and the perceived threat to the natural order that an independent, powerful woman would present. She is portrayed as symbolically masculine as a result of excessive body hair, who becomes symbolically feminine when—at Solomon's bequest—her body hair is removed. She loses her power and independence when Solomon lies with her, consequently falling under his dominance and restoring the natural order of things. According to some reports, she then bears a child—Nebuchadnezzar—who later destroys the temple in Jerusalem and sends the Jews into exile.

the Queen of Sheba, a woman, for taking on a position of political leadership.[321] Although a powerful monarch, her model of leadership differs as she preferred diplomacy over warfare.[322] The Quran describes how she counsels her chieftains before deciding to engage in war, and that the chieftains submit to her judgment.[323] It is the only Quranic account of a female as the head of a state.[324] If Islamic commands were set against women as heads of state or holding any other political office, then the Queen of Sheba would not have been presented in such a manner in the Quran.[325] However, given the broad understanding and accounts of men's superiority and the deficient minds of women by various scholars, the story of Bilquis "was viewed as anomalous and had to be neutralized by references to male superiority. Abu Bakr's hadith was especially useful in achieving this goal".[326] Some scholars argued that Bilquis was the leader of non-believers. Thus, the verse has no significance for Muslims. Instead, it was upheld that the Islamic rule on the issue can be found in Abu Bakr's hadith.[327]

3.10 Veiling

The institution of veiling and its obligation to women has been widely debated. Quranic injunctions are generally vague and require modesty in behavior from men and women. Veiling and seclusion were practices upheld by Christian upper-class women in 6th century Najran. In some cultures, such as the Greek, only married women wore the veil.[328] There was also a connection between the veil and the goddesses of fertility, like Ishtar and Demeter. Women would veil in the cycle of the seasons, marking their mourning, as a symbolism of hiding during the dead or mourning period, and unveil when they revive in spring following the rhythm of changing seasons and life.[329] Muslim upper-class women also started to veil themselves in public, but exactly when Muslim

---

321   Amina Inloes, "The Queen of Sheba in Shi'a Hadith", *Journal of Shi'a Islamic Studies* Vol. 5, No. 4 (2012), p. 425.
322   Quran 27:34.
323   Quran 27:32–33.
324   The story of the Queen of Sheba and Sulayman is one of the lengthier narratives in the Quran, spanning from Quran 27:15 to 27:44.
325   Ali, *Gender and Human Rights in Islam and International Law*, p. 55.
326   Fadel, "Is Historicism a Viable Strategy for Islamic Legal Reform?", p. 38.
327   Abu Ḥayyan Muḥammad b. Yusuf, *Tafsir al-Baḥr al-Muḥit*, ed. 'Abd al-Razzaq Mahdi, 8 vols. (Beirut: Dar Ihya' al-Turath al-'Arabi, 2002), 7:87.
328   H. Cassimatis, 1985, "Imagerie et Femme", *La Femme dans le Monde Méditerranéen I, Antiquité* (Lyon: CNRS, Maison de l'Orient, No. 10), pp. 19–28.
329   al-Fassi, *Women in pre-Islamic Arabia*, p. 47.

women generally started to veil themselves cannot be pinpointed.[330] Reports describe that society at that time was constructed in such a manner that unveiled women could be assumed to be harassed and would be confronted.[331] Verses in the Quran declare that Muslim women, including women belonging to the Prophet's household, must "draw their veils close to them" when they go out so that they can be recognized as virtuous and not be harassed.[332]

Veiling also symbolized marriage with the Prophet,[333] and his wives were asked to remain behind a curtain, *hijab*, when believers visit them at home.[334] Many of the verses referring to the practice of seclusion or veiling for Muhammad's wives occurred after his wedding to Zeinab bint Djahsh. Some of the wedding guests stayed in Zeinab's room conversing, and some of the hands of men touched the hands of Muhammad's wives, more specifically, Aisha's hand touched 'Umar's.[335] According to Aisha, 'Umar had urged Muhammad to seclude his wives, to guard them against the insults of "hypocrites".[336] Another account describes 'Umar maintaining the necessity of the seclusion of Muhammad's wives as Muhammad's success was bringing different kinds of visitors to the mosque,[337] and many would try to approach his wives to enlist their assistance in receiving a favor from the Prophet.[338] It is narrated that "the wives of the Prophet used to go to Al-Manasi, a vast open place (near Baqi' at Medina) to answer the call of nature at night. 'Umar used to say to the Prophet 'Let your wives be veiled,' but Allah's Apostle did not do so. One night, Sauda bint Zam' a wife of the Prophet went out at 'Isha' time, and she was a tall lady. 'Umar addressed her and said, 'I have recognized you, O Sauda.'

---

330 Eleanor, A. Doumato, "Hearing Other Voices: Christian Women and the Coming of Islam", *International Journal of Middle East Studies* Vol. 23, No. 2 (1991), pp. 177–199.

331 Barbara Stowasser, *Women in the Quran, Traditions and Interpretations* (Oxford: Oxford University Press, 1994), pp. 91–92.

332 Quran 33:59–60.

333 "During the Prophet's and Safiyya's wedding feast, some of the Muslims asked: 'Will she be one of the Mothers of the Faithful – or just a concubine of his?' Others replied: 'If he veils her, then she is one of the Mothers of the Faithful, but if he does not then she has become a concubine for him.' When it was time to saddle up and depart, the Prophet made a place for Safiyya to ride behind him, and he spread the veil." Quote taken from Awde, *Women in Islam: An Anthology from the Qur'an and Hadiths*, pp. 88–89. See also, Al-Bukhari, *Sahih*, Book 5, hadith 370.

334 Quran 33:53.

335 Quran 33:54. Ibn Sa'd, *Kitab al-Tabaqat*, 8:126; see also, Abbot, *Aishah*, pp. 20–24.

336 Ibn Sa'd, *Kitab al-Tabaqat*, 8:125–127; Ibn Hanbal, *Musnad*, 6 vols. (Beirut: al-Maktab al Islami lil Tiba'a wa'l nashr, 1969), 6:271.

337 Abbot, *Aishah*, p. 25.

338 Watt, *Muhammad at Medina*, p. 285.

He said so, as he desired eagerly that the verses of Al-Hijab may be revealed. So Allah revealed the verses of 'Al-Hijab' ".[339] Another hadith describes 'Umar declaring that: "And as regards the (verse of) the veiling of the women, I said, 'O Allah's Apostle! I wish you ordered your wives to cover themselves from the men because good and bad ones talk to them.' So the verse of the veiling of the women was revealed. Once the wives of the Prophet made a united front against the Prophet and I said to them, 'It may be if he (the Prophet) divorced you, (all) that his Lord (Allah) will give him instead of you wives better than you.' So this verse (the same as I had said) was revealed". [340] Based on this hadith, it has been suggested that the Prophet gave the option of divorce for his wives once the new behavioral rules were established.[341]

The Quran advocates "they cast down their eyes and guard their private parts".[342] Barbara Stowasser argues that the difference between the commentaries of the traditionalists—Abu Ja'far Muhammad ibn Jarir al-Tabari (d. 923), Abdallah ibn Umar al-Baydawi (d. 1286) and Ahmad ibn al-Khafaji (d. 1659)—on this verse indicate how Muslim women were forced to disappear behind the veil, "not only physically but as a symbol of their invisibility from public life".[343] While Tabari argued that veiling does not include the face, half of the forearm, eye makeup, rings, bracelets and dyes, Baydawi interprets the verse as *"let them lower their gaze* before the men at whom it is not lawful to look, and *let them guard their private parts* by veiling them, or by bearing of (or guarding against) fornication. The lowering of the glances is presented because the glance is the messenger of fornication. And let them not display of their adornment such as jewellery, dress, make-up – let alone the parts where they are worn or applied – to those to whom such display is not lawful ... what is meant by adornment is the place where adornment is put (or worn) ..."[344] Furthermore, Baydawi argues that the prohibition of display does not include the face and hands as "this applies to prayer only, not appearance, because the whole body of a free woman is pudendal, and it is illicit for anyone (except the husband or the dhawu mahram)[345] to look at any part of her except by necessity such

---

339   Al-Bukhari, *Sahih*, Book 8, hadith 53.
340   Al-Bukhari, *Sahih*, Book 44, hadith 3318.
341   Stern, *Marriage in Early Islam*, pp. 114–115. See also, Quran 33:28–29.
342   Quran 24:30.
343   Stowasser, "The Status of Women in Early Islam", p. 27.
344   Stowasser, "The Status of Women in Early Islam", pp. 26–27.
345   A man and woman cannot lawfully enter into a contract of marriage including a father, brother, son, uncle (whether paternal or maternal), grandfather (whether paternal or maternal). Her husband is *mahram*.

as (medical) treatment, or the bearing of witness".[346] Al-Khajafi further reinforces this restrictive interpretation by justifying the complete "disappearance" of women behind the veil declaring that "the whole body of the women is pudendal, even face and hand, without exception". Al-Khajafi argues that interpreting this verse is "command of exception from the established rule, which applies to such exceptional circumstances as the giving of evidence in law courts and medical treatment only".[347] One of the most conservative contemporary Muslim scholars, Abu al-A'la al-Mawdudi, argues that segregation will prevent "loose western morals" from slowly becoming a part of Islamic society, and will be a method of keeping the family intact. Mawdudi claims that Islam detests women leaving home unless it is absolutely necessary to earn a living.[348]

Arguably, Quranic injunctions show that there was a need for some ground rules for male-female interaction, as the statements on modesty imply that there was no segregation between the sexes and that veiling did not occur. If segregation of sexes existed, there would have been no need for a rule on how sexes should be behaving. While originally, hijab referred to the curtain that separated the Prophet's wives from inappropriate male visitors in their homes; it later became associated with the concealment outside the home and became the word for the covering garment worn by women outside of the home. As his wives were targeted by disbelievers and mistreated, the wives started wearing the veil as a means of protection.[349] Ultimately, the wives of Muhammad were the first women whose lives would begin to be constrained.[350] One can question why the Quran imposed on women this responsibility, and why women had to suffer the consequences of men not behaving, but that is an issue that has not been discussed in the Islamic tradition.

---

346 Stowasser, "The Status of Women in Early Islam", pp. 26–27.
347 Quotes taken from Ali, *Gender and Human Rights in Islam and International Law*, pp. 76–77.
348 Abdul A. Mawdudi, *Purdah* (Lahore: Islamic Publications, 1997), pp. 235–239.
349 Bruce Lawrence, *The Quran: A Biography* (London: Atlantic Books, 2006), chapter 3. They were instructed to "draw their cloaks close around them. That will be better, so that they may be recognized and not annoyed". See Quran 33:59.
350 Many nomadic women maintained their traditional freedom of movement and less restrictive dress codes even after conversion to Islam, see Karen Armstrong, *The Gospel According to Women: Christianity's Creation of the Sex War in the West* (London: Tree Books, 1986); Amr Abdalla, "Principles of Islamic Interpersonal Conflict Intervention: A Search Within Islam and Western Literature", *Journal of Law and Religion* Vol. 15, No. 1–2 (2000), pp. 151–184; Bernard Lewis, *Islam from the Prophet Muhammad to the Capture of Constantinople* (London: Macmillan, 1976).

3.11 The Consequences of the Death of the Prophet on the Status of Women

It is after the death of the Prophet, and under the rule of the third caliph 'Umar, that many of the rules on segregation and the veiling of the Prophet's wives were expanded to include all Muslim women. Many religious, civil and penal ordinances were initiated,[351] including the punishment of stoning for adultery.[352] 'Umar apparently complained about the different customs of marriage and attitudes towards polygyny in cities such as Medina and Mecca. He stated that before coming to Medina "we the people of Quraysh [Mecca] used to have the upper hand over our wives, but when we came among the Ansar [Medinians], we found that their women had the upper hand over their men, so our women also started learning the ways of the Ansari women. One day I became angry with my wife, so when she started talking back to me, I rebuked her, and she said: 'What bothers you about that? By Allah! The wives of the Prophet talk back to him, and one of them may stay away from him a whole day until the night?' "[353] The women of Medina were supposedly more assertive, and one Medinian woman offered herself in marriage to Muhammad, only to withdraw the accepted offer when her disapproving family pointed out that she could never put up with co-wives.[354] At the time of Muhammad's arrival in Medina, it is said that the Meccans were accustomed to beating women, who supposedly "did not complain of it" and "did not consider it an attack on their dignity".[355] The Medinians did not beat their women, which resulted in a clash of cultures, as Meccan women started to feel that they should not be beaten.[356]

Several traditions describe 'Umar as a harsh man, both in public and private and who physically assaulted his wives:

> Once 'Umar asked the leave to see Allah's Messenger in whose company some Quraishi women were talking to him and asking him for more

---

351 In the field of penal law, 'Umar even went beyond the scope of the Quran and imposed sanctions, such as punishing authors of satirical poems directed against rival tribes with flogging. The punishment of having the hands of a thief cut off was mostly replaced with flogging, as it was difficult to enforce a punishment unknown to the ancient Arabs, see Schacht, *An Introduction to Islamic Law*, p. 18. See also, Vago, *Law and Society*, pp. 184–186.
352 Ahmed, "Women and the Advent of Islam", p. 689.
353 Al-Bukhari, *The Translation of the Meaning of Sahih*, 7:88.
354 Ibn Sa'd, *Kitab al-Tabaqat*, 8:107–108.
355 Muhammad Al-Talbi, *Ummat Al-Wasat: Al-Islam Wa Tahaddiyat Al-Mu'asira* (Tunis: Ceres Edition, 1996), p. 119.
356 Rachel M. Scott, "A Contextual Approach to Women's Rights in the Qur'an: Readings of 4:34", *The Muslim World* Vol. 99, No. 1 (2009), p. 70.

financial support raising their voices. When 'Umar asked permission to enter the women got up (quickly) hurrying to screen themselves. When Allah's Messenger admitted 'Umar, Allah's Messenger was smiling, 'Umar asked, 'O Allah's Messenger! May Allah keep you in happiness always.' Allah's Messenger said, 'I am astonished at these women who were with me. As soon as they heard your voice, they hastened to screen themselves.' 'Umar said, 'O Allah's Apostle! You have more right to be feared by them.' Then he addressed (those women) saying, 'O enemies of your souls! Do you fear me and not Allah's Messenger?' They replied. 'Yes, for you are a fearful and fierce man as compared with Allah's Messenger.' On that Allah's Messenger said (to 'Umar), 'By Him in Whose Hands my life is, whenever Satan sees you taking a path, he follows a path other than yours.'[357]

Conditions for women began to deteriorate under the rule of 'Umar and continued with his successors. He encouraged and supported the movement to exclude women from partaking in different aspects of public life. 'Umar sought to confine women to the home and prevent them from attending mosques and prohibited men to enter through the door reserved for women in the mosque.[358] As he was unsuccessful in deterring women from the mosque, he instituted segregated prayers instead, appointing separate imams for each sex.[359] Unlike Muhammad, who had appointed a woman to act as imam for her household, which included men and women,'Umar appointed a male imam for women.[360] He also prohibited Muhammad's wives from going on pilgrimage. There are no

---

[357] Al-Bukhari, *Sahih*, 3294, Book 59, hadith 103.
[358] Abbott, *Aishah*, p. 88. See also Daif (Al-Albani), *Sunan Abi Dawud*, Book 2, hadith 74. It is reported that 'Umar heard the Prophet saying "if we left this door for women (it would have been better) ... 'Umar did not enter (the door) until his death", see (Al-Albani), *Sunan Abi Dawud*, 2146, Book 12, hadith 101. It was also narrated that the Prophet said, "if your women ask permission to go to the mosque at night, allow them", see Al-Bukhari, *Sahih*, Book 10, hadith 256. Another tradition declares that "One of the wives of 'Umar (bin Al-Khattab) used to offer the Fajr and the 'Isha' prayer in congregation in the Mosque. She was asked why she had come out for the prayer as she knew that 'Umar disliked it, and he has great *ghaira* (self-respect). She replied, 'What prevents him from stopping me from this act?' The other replied, 'the statement of Allah's Apostle: 'do not stop Allah's women-slaves from going to Allah's Mosques' prevents him'", see Al-Bukhari, *Sahih* 900, Book 11, hadith 24.
[359] On the issue of women praying with men, see Sadeghi, *The Logic of Law Making in Islam*, pp. 50–75.
[360] Ibn Sa'd, *Kitab al-Tabawat*, 8:335: Gertrude Stern, "The First Women Converts in Early Islam", *Islamic Culture* Vol. 12, No. 3 (1939), p. 299.

records of the opinions of the wives regarding these rules, but, 'Uthman, the fourth caliph, revoked them, allowing Muhammad's wives to go on pilgrimage and revoked the arrangement of separate imams. Men and women were again allowed to be in the mosque; however, women were to be held back while men left the mosque.[361] 'Uthman's restoration of some liberties was a brief exception to the religious, political, and societal changes moving inevitably in the contrary direction.[362]

Essentially, the process for the improvement of the status of women, as established to some extent by the Quran and in the practice of Muhammad, was curtailed as soon as the Prophet died. Starting from the period of the Caliphs, and thereafter with the different schools of law, female participation in public life was severely restricted. Interpretations of Islamic law came to be based on the premises of protecting the chastity of women, which for these jurists, gradually became tantamount to segregation of the genders and the veil itself. Seclusion of women became the norm to maintain female morality, as women came to be portrayed as temptresses.[363]

361 Ibn Sa'd, *Kitab al-Tabawat,* 5:17.
362 Ahmed, "Women and the Advent of Islam", p. 690.
363 Sayeh & Morse Jr. "Islam and the Treatment of Women", p. 324.

CHAPTER 4

Guardianship of Women

Guardianship or *wilaya*, means the legal authority to manage the affairs of another person who lacks the required capacity, that is, to act without a guardian requires full legal capacity.[1] This legal authority recognized in a person who is fully qualified and competent to safeguard the rights and interests of the person incapable of doing so on their own.[2] Legal capacity is the capability of a person to enter into obligation and to be bound by it. Generally, a guardianship may be of persons or property and is essentially a mandatory duty on a person, on the grounds of relationship, testament or by court order, declaring a person of nil legal capacity. Guardianship of any form indicates the state of the inadequacy of the ward, being of partial or nil legal capacity to care for their person or manage their property. The appointed guardian is to act in the best interest of the ward and can be described as "the carrying through of a decision affecting a third person whether the latter wishes or not".[3]

Legal capacity progresses with the development of the person and is essentially regarded as the capacity to consent. A minor has as such no legal personality; it is the age of maturity, which makes legal capacity applicable. In Islamic law, legal capacity has two aspects, the first is eligibility for duty, which arises for every person by the mere fact that they are born. Birth makes this aspect of legal capacity applicable, where that person is deemed fit to be bound by the dispositions undertaken by a financial guardian. This aspect of legal capacity progresses as the person ages, and when he is a rational man, he acquires full legal capacity. The second aspect of legal capacity is the capacity to act on another's behalf. The basis for this is reason; a minor does not have full executive capacity as he is not fully rational. A person's life in terms of executive capacity is divided into three parts. In the first stage, from birth until the age of reason (no less than seven years), the person has no executive capacity as he is not rational. From the age of reason, until the age of maturity, the person has partial executive capacity. This means that the minor may accept gifts and legacy, and is allowed to perform specific actions that are beneficial for him.

---

1 Nasir, *The Islamic Law of Personal Status*, p. 190 and Imran Nyazee, *Outlines of Islamic Jurisprudence* (Lahore: Advanced Legal Studies Institute, 2000), p. 205.
2 Dawoud S. El Alami, "Legal Capacity with Specific Reference to the Marriage Contract", *Arab Law Quarterly* No. 6 (1991), p. 192.
3 Nasir, *The Islamic Law of Personal Status*, p. 186.

However, giving gifts is not allowed, and other actions not included in these categories are up to the discretion of the guardian to decide upon. In the third stage, when the person has reached the age of maturity, it is considered that the person has full executive capacity:[4]

> The highest degree of legal capacity is that of the free Muslim man who is sane and of age; he is fully responsible (*mukallaf*). The majority is determined by physical indications, by the declaration of youth in question, or, failing this, by reaching the age of fifteen lunar years. The *mukallaf* can contract and to dispose of, he is bound to fulfill religious duties, and he is fully subject to criminal law, being capable of deliberate intent.[5]

Certain conditions may, however, affect this capacity. Besides minority, madness or dementia may also limit executive capacity and subject the person to compulsory guardianship regarding all their actions. While determining guardianship for minors is less problematic, as it is easy to conclude who is a minor, difficulties arise in determining the case of the insane and the incompetent. Like a child, those with continuous insanity have no legal capacity.[6] Other conditions, such as incompetence, restricts a person's right to deal with financial affairs and the person is subject to financial guardianship.[7]

1   Guardianship of Minors

In most legal systems, appointing a guardian is a legal proceeding, stemming from the best interests of the child. Guardians are, in such a sense, substitute parents during the period of incapacity.[8] Guardianship of the child in Islamic law, however, does not become an issue unless the parents separate, upon which it is the father, or in the event of the father's incapacity, male paternal relatives, who retain guardianship of the child.[9] Sunni schools list guardians in the order of descendants (the son and the son's son and lower), ascendants

---

4   El Alami, "Legal Capacity with Specific Reference to the Marriage Contract", p. 191.
5   Quote taken from Michael W. Dols, Historical Perspective: Insanity in Islamic Law, *Journal of Muslim Mental Health* No. 2 (2007), p. 81.
6   Ibid.
7   El Alami, "Legal Capacity with Specific Reference to the Marriage Contract", p. 192.
8   Scott J. Shackelford and Lawrence M. Friedman, "Legally Incompetent: A Research Note", *The American Journal of Legal History* Vol. 49, No. 3 (2007), p. 321.
9   Judith E. Tucker, *In the House of The Law: Gender and Islamic Law in Ottoman Syria and Palestine* (Berkeley: University of California Press, 1998), pp. 138–41: Mahdi Zahraa and

(the father and the grandfather and higher), full brothers and their male descendants and finally, uncles and their sons. In the absence of any male relatives to axel the role of guardian, it shall be vested in the head of the state and his representative, particularly the judge. The Shia also appoints the father as the guardian, and after that, it passes to the grandfather, and in the absence of male relatives, the judge.[10] Guardianship constitutes the legal representation of the child, which includes both full financial authority and far-reaching powers when it comes to the child's personal affairs,[11] most noticeably, the right to marry off a minor against his or her will.[12] While the woman's capacity of managing money and property independently and without the interference of the husband is acknowledged and protected in Islamic law, she is not viewed to have the same capability to do so with her children's assets, as that right is entitled to the father.[13]

Child custody is distinguished between legal custody and physical custody in most western states, while the father always retains the legal custody of the child in Islamic law.[14] A father's authority or status as a guardian is founded on the underlying assumption that he knows what is best for his child and is acting in the child's best interest. The mother is considered the natural custodian of her infant child. Her custody of the children is only temporary, as the child is the father's possession, and once the child has reached a certain

---

Normi A. Malek, "The Concept of Custody in Islamic Law", *Arab Law Quarterly* Vol. 13 (1998), pp. 155, 157.

[10] Nasir, *The Islamic Law of Personal Status*, p. 53.

[11] Lena-Maria Moller, "An Enduring Relic: Family Law Reform and the Inflexibility of Wilaya", *American Journal of Comparative Law* No. 63 (2015), p. 894.

[12] Fadel, "Reinterpreting the Guardian's Role in the Islamic Contract of Marriage", p. 4. The right for the father to contract marriage stems from the pre-Islamic practices, where the marriage was considered a tribal obligation, rather than an agreement between two individuals. The father's right was based on precepts that the father would protect the honour of the family or of the tribe. The power of the father in pre-Islamic times even allowed for the father to pawn his children, and, although rarely exercised, to kill them. See Muhammad Khalid Masud, "Gender Equality and the Doctrine of Wilaya", in *Gender and Equality in Muslim Family Law: Justice and Ethics in the Islamic Legal Tradition*, eds. Ziba Mir-Hosseini, Kari Vogt, Lena Larsen and Christian Moe (London: I. B. Tauris, 2013), p. 129.

[13] Moller, "An Enduring Relic: Family Law Reform and the Inflexibility of Wilaya", p. 918.

[14] Legal custody involves the right to make decisions about the child's life such as health, education, and welfare. This also includes decisions about religious upbringing. Physical custody is connected to where the child will live and the responsibility for the daily care and provision of the child, see Kristine Uhlman & Elise Kisselburg, "Islamic Shariʻa Contracts: Pre-Nuptial and Custody Protections", *Journal of Child Custody* Vol. 10, No. 3–4 (2013), p. 365.

age, the custody is vested in the father.[15] The mother has physical, not legal, custody until the child reaches the age of custodial transfer, which usually is seven years, sometimes twelve years for girls. However, the right to physical custody is not absolute as the father can challenge a mother's ability to provide an appropriate upbringing. Legitimate reasons to do so are if the father asserts that the mother has dishonored the family or has been disobedient. Any attempts by the mother to not raise the child as a Muslim could jeopardize the mother's physical custody.[16] The lifelong attachment of a mother to her child has no legal recognition in Islamic law as she does not have any claim to guardianship unless such guardianship is awarded her by either the guardian or by a court. It is known that men have given testamentary guardianship of their minor children to the mother. Such appointed guardianships included the right to marry off daughters.[17]

The child is not recognized with the capacity to decide on marriage until reaching puberty, as consent is assigned to adults. Principally, "the importance of the guardian's role is exclusively a function of the majority, or lack thereof, of the ward, not the gender of the ward. Thus, the guardian of a minor, assuming he is the biological father, has almost absolute powers to compel the marriage of both his minor sons and daughters. At the other extreme, the biological father has no power to compel the marriage of either his adult son or daughter".[18] As such, the guardian can give a minor in marriage, without their consent, until they reach the age of puberty.[19] The Maliki school compares the power of the father to conclude the marriage to the power of a master, "no one may compel anyone to marry except the father in the case of his virgin daughter and his minor son, and [the master] in the case of his female slave and his male slave and the marriage guardian in the case of fatherlessness, *yatimihi*".[20] The Shafi'i school too, conjoins the power of the father to

---

15 For an overview of the different legal schools thought on child custody, see Nasir, *The Islamic Law of Personal Status*, pp. 181–189 and David Pearl, *A Textbook on Muslim Law* (London: Croom Helm, 1979), pp. 83–87.
16 Uhlman & Kisselburg "Islamic Shari'a Contracts: Pre-Nuptial and Custody Protections", pp. 356–366.
17 Moller, "An Enduring Relic: Family Law Reform and the Inflexibility of Wilaya", p. 902. In those cases, it appears as if there was no significant unequal treatment of the mother-guardian by the courts; see Tucker, *In the House of The Law*, p. 141–147 and Margaret L. Meriwether, "The Rights of Children and the Responsibilities of Women. Women as Wasis in Ottoman Aleppo, 1770–1840", in *Women, the Family and Divorce Laws in Islamic History*, ed. Amira E. Sonbol (Syracuse: Syracuse University Press, 1996), p. 219.
18 Fadel, "Reinterpreting the Guardian's Role in the Islamic Contract of Marriage", p. 4.
19 Syed, *The Position of Women in Islam: A Progressive View*, p. 41.
20 Quote taken from Ali, *Marriage and Slavery in Early Islam*, p. 38.

that of the master. There are, however, several traditions that contradict such a coercive right.[21] The guardian also loses his authority to compel his wards to marry if he loses his sanity, is absent for a long period of time, or exercises his authority without legal justification. The guardian can also withdraw his authority.[22]

A specific minimum age for marriage was not laid down in the Quran, which allowed for the jurists to develop the position that one becomes an adult at puberty.[23] A marriage contract can be concluded for a girl or boy at any age, implying that a considerable amount of time can pass between the contract and the consummation of the marriage.[24] Upon reaching puberty, the female child has the opportunity to dissolve the marriage.[25] There are schools of law that held that the right to rescission does not exist if it was her father or grandfather who gave her in marriage. However, most countries have banned child marriages and others have restricted the marriage of minors by including a minimum marriageable age in national laws, which ranges from 17 to 20 years for males, and 12 to 18 for females.[26]

While a young man is presumptively emancipated from the control of the father upon reaching the age of majority, discriminatory standards were developed for women in Sunni Islam. In contrast, an adult woman must prove that she is capable of managing her affairs to be emancipated. Until such a time, she remains subject to the control of the father and treated as a minor, until her first marriage. An adult woman can be emancipated if her father, or a guardian designated by the father, declares her to be mature in front of a court. But the

---

21 "The *ayyim* (a woman who has been married) has more right to herself than her wali, and the *bikr* (virgin) is consulted about herself. In the case of the *bikr*, her silence is tantamount to her consent", see Shaybani, *Mutawwa'*, 220; Sunan an-Nasa'i, book 26, hadith 71. In another instance, "a virgin girl came to the Prophet and said that her father had married her against her wishes and the Prophet gave her right to repudiate her marriage", see Ibn Abbas, 12:25. Another tradition declares that "the father or any other guardian cannot give in marriage a virgin or one who has been married before without her consent", see Bukhari, *Sahih*, 67:42. Quotes taken from Syed, *The Position of Women in Islam*, p. 39. A female who has the right to accept or withhold consent to a wedding proposal is said to be "*ahaqqu bi nafsiha*," meaning having more right to herself, or to have "*malakat amraha*," meaning taking control of her affairs, see Ali, *Marriage and Slavery in Early Islam*, p. 37.
22 Masud, "Gender Equality and the Doctrine of Wilaya", p. 130.
23 Black, Esmaeili, Hosen, *Modern Perspectives on Islamic Law*, p. 116.
24 Spectorsky, *Women in Classical Islamic Law*, p. 64.
25 The right of *khiyar al-bulugh*, means the opportunity to repudiate the marriage contract. This also applies to the boy child, see Syed, *The Position of Women in Islam*, p. 41; Schacht, *An Introduction to Islamic Law*, p. 161.
26 Masud, "Gender Equality and the Doctrine of Wilaya", p. 144.

fact remains: an adult woman can only be emancipated by legal proceedings or marriage, unlike an adult man.[27] For the Shia, a father does not hold guardianship over an adult woman.[28]

2   Legally Incompetent but Financially Independent

> Mankind, fear your Lord, who created you of a single soul, and from it created its mate, and from the pair of them scattered abroad many men and women; and fear God by whom you demand one of another, and the wombs; surely God ever watches over you.[29]

The passage opens the chapter in the Quran entitled *An-Nisa*, the women. The passage as such is a general address with an ethical voice that is non-discriminatory and stipulates equality between the sexes.[30] The non-discriminatory notion is, however, not reflected in how the rest of the chapter has been interpreted. Instead, Muslims have made a "selective and scarce use of the ethical dimension of regulatory norms favoring equality and non-discrimination for women",[31] where the notion of equal human worth is suspended in matters relating to the rights and responsibilities of males and females.[32] However, such conclusions are not ideally backed by the textual sources, as they include many conflicting guidelines. The Quran outlines the relationship between men and women as one where they are "friends one of the other" and are equally responsible for their actions and fulfilment of

---

27   Fadel, "Reinterpreting the Guardian's Role in the Islamic Contract of Marriage", pp. 4, 9.
28   Sedigheh Vasmaghi, *Women, Jurisprudence, Islam* (Harrassowitz Verlag, 2014), p. 86. See also Beatrix Immenkamp, *Marriage and Celibacy in Mediaval Islam : A Study of Ghazal's Kitab Arab Al-Nikah* (Ph.D. dissertation, Cambridge: King's College, 1994), pp. 67-68 and Abu Talib Muhammad Ibn al-Hasan Ibn Yusuf Ibn a1-Mutahhar al-Hilli, *Idah al-fawaid* (Mu'assasa Isma'iliyan, 1969- 70), Vol. 3, p. 14.
29   Quran 4:1.
30   See Rahman, "Status of Women in the Quran"; Esposito, *Women in Muslim Family Law*; Al-Hibri, "A Study of Islamic Herstory"; Utas, *Women in Islamic Societies*; Mernissi, *Women and Islam*; An-Naim, *Toward an Islamic Reformation*; Hassan, "An Islamic Perspective" and Stowasser, "The Status of Women in Early Islam".
31   Ali, *Gender and Human Rights in Islamic and International Law*, p. 47. See also, Ann Elizabeth Meyer, *Islam and Human Rights Traditions and Politics* (Boulder: Westview Press, 1996), p. 79; Mahmassani, "Adaptation of Islamic Jurisprudence to Modern Social Needs", pp. 181–187.
32   Ziba Mir-Hosseini, "Muslim Women's Quest for Equality: Between Islamic Law and Feminism", *Critical Inquiry* Vol. 32 (Summer 2006), p. 629.

religious duties.[33] The rewards promised believers, or the punishment given if the divine path is not followed, is a system based on individual deeds of righteousness and piety; it is not based on gender, class, color, ethnicity or wealth.[34] When the Quran speaks of socio-economic differences, it describes the superiority of some people over others due to these differences:

> What, is it they who divide the mercy of the Lord? We have divided between them their livelihood in the present life, and raised some of them above others in rank, that some of them may take others in servitude; and the mercy of thy Lord is better than that they amass.[35]
>
> And God has preferred some of you over others in provision; but those that were preferred shall not give over their provision to that their right hands possess, so that they may be equal therein. What, and do they deny God's blessing?[36]
>
> Behold, how We prefer some of them over others! And surely the world to come is greater in ranks, greater in preferment.[37]

The question then is, are these socio-economic differences, the basis for unequal rights among human beings?[38] Within the category of men (and women), the answer is, "no" according to the jurists. But between the different groups of men and women, the answer becomes, "definitely" as Islamic law allows for guardianship for those that are under *"the state of being female"*.[39]

Legal differentiation is a common feature of the law, a *sine qua non* of justice. The fact that Islamic law differentiates its subjects is therefore not necessarily controversial or unjust. There are instances where people need to be treated differently, because some characteristics require different treatment, so that the equal treatment of that group, does not cause a disadvantage.[40] The

---

33 Quran 9:71. See also, Zainab Alwani, "The Qur'anic model on Social Change: Family Structure as a Method of Social Reform", *Islam and Civilizational Renewal* Vol. 3, No. 1 (2011), p. 56.
34 Alwani, "The Qur'anic model on Social Change", p. 56.
35 Quran 43:32.
36 Quran 16:71.
37 Quran 17:21.
38 Mohsen Kadivar, "Revisiting Women's Rights in Islam: 'Egalitarian Justice' in Lieu of 'Desert-based Justice' ", in *Gender and Equality in Muslim Family Law: Justice and Ethics in the Islamic Legal Tradition*, eds. Ziba Mir-Hosseini, Kari Vogt, Lena Larsen and Christian Moe (London: I. B. Tauris, 2013), p. 229.
39 Nasir, *The Islamic Law of Personal Status*, p. 186.
40 Anver M. Emon, "The Paradox of Equality and the Politics of Difference: Gender Equality, Islamic Law and the Modern Muslim State", in *Gender and Equality in Muslim Family*

issue that remains, is what characteristics should justify different laws? And under what conditions do such laws become discriminatory?

2.1   *Men Are the Managers of Women*

Islamic law entitles individuals to justice according to their status, abilities and potential, upon which free adult men naturally possess all requirements to be included in the concept of justice. The underlying principle in the case of men and women's capabilities, is that they are entitled to the same rights, as long as their capabilities are the same. When their capabilities differ, they are also entrusted with different rights. The notion of women being deficient in faith, reason, and wealth, has allowed for the jurists to constructs laws, where women's rights under those categories differ, for "it is the essence of injustice if women who lack certain abilities and capacities, though they may possess others, are given the same rights and duties as men".[41]

> Men are the managers [*qawwamuna*] of the affairs of women for that God has preferred in bounty one of them over another, and for that they have expended of their property. Righteous women are therefore obedient [*qanitatuun*], guarding the secret for God's guarding. And those you fear may be rebellious [*nushuz*] admonish; banish them to their couches, and beat [*daraba*] them. If they then obey you, look not for any way against them; God is All-high, All-great.[42]

The verse is frequently invoked as the main textual evidence for mandating men's authority over women, as it is regarded that the verse confirms the different capabilities of men and women.[43] The notion of men managing women, rationalizes other legal inequalities; such as polygyny, the lesser inheritance or women serving as judges or political leaders. The full verse deals with various gender issues and is extremely problematic from a gender

---

Law: Justice and Ethics in the Islamic Legal Tradition, eds. Ziba Mir-Hosseini, Kari Vogt, Lena Larsen and Christian Moe (London: I. B. Tauris, 2013), p. 238. See also, Joan W. Scott, "The conundrum of equality", *Institute of Advanced Studies, Occasional Paper Series* (March 1999), available at http://www.sss.ias.edu/files/papers/papertwo.pdf (accessed 10 October 2019).

41   Kadivar, "Revisiting Women's Rights in Islam", p. 222.
42   Quran 4:34.
43   Ziba Mir-Hosseini, "Justice, Equality and Muslim Family Laws: New Ideas, New Prospects", in *Gender and Equality in Muslim Family Law: Justice and Ethics in the Islamic Legal Tradition*, eds. Ziba Mir-Hosseini, Kari Vogt, Lena Larsen and Christian Moe (London: I. B. Tauris, 2013), p. 7.

equality perspective. Discussing the ethical aspects of the Quran or that women are considered equal to men in human dignity, is not a sufficient argument when analyzing what this verse implies. One aspect of the verse to regard is whether it applies to men and women generally, or if the verse relates to the relationship of the husband and wife. The first part defines men as the managers of women, which has been interpreted to reducing the legal status of a woman to a minor, or a person who has been deemed incompetent or insane—unless it involves financial transactions. Generally, the term *qawwamun* means protector or maintainer and refers to a person who takes the responsibility of safeguarding the interests of another.[44] Qawwamun in verse 4:34, however, was understood as mandating men's authority over women.[45] The second part of the verse describes the treatment of a disobedient wife. The implications have validated restrictive measures to keep women under control, which involves beating. These aspects will be considered separately, where the corrective measures will only be presented briefly.

2.1.1   Marriage Based on Cooperation or Supervision?

Al-Tahir al-Haddad (1899–1935) criticized the classical fiqh positions and argued that the Quran in verse 2:228 encourages cooperation and mutual affection as the basis of marriage:[46]

---

44   Ragaʿ el-Nimr, "Women in Islamic Law", in *Feminism and Islam, Legal and Literary Perspectives*, ed. Yamani May (Berkshire: Garnet Publishing Limited, 1996), p. 97. Syed describes the term as "one who stands firm in another's business, protects his interests and looks after his affairs or standing firm in his own business". In certain aspects, it is regarded that men have dominance over women. For example, if a woman would convert to Islam, but her husband remains faithful to a non-Islamic religion, "a continuation of the marriage when the husband is an infidel would imply the supremacy and primacy of an infidel over a Muslim woman; because 'Men are the Managers of Women.'" Such a marriage is not acknowledged in Islamic law and would be dissolved. See Syed, *The Position of Women in Islam*, p. 51. See also, the following verses in the Quran; "O believers, be you securers [*qawwameena*] of justice, witnesses for God, even though it be against yourselves, or your parents and kinsmen, whether the man be rich or poor; God stands closest to either. Then follow not caprice, so as to swerve; for if you twist or turn, God is aware of the things you do." (4:135) And "O believers, be you securers [*qawwameena*] of justice, witnesses for God. Let not detestation for a people move you not to be equitable; be equitable -- that is nearer to god-fearing. And fear God; surely God is aware of the things you do." (5:8) See also, verse 5:11.
45   Ziba Mir-Hosseini, "Justice, Equality and Muslim Family Laws", p. 7.
46   See also, Quran 2:187.

> And of His signs is that He created for you, of yourselves, spouses, that you might repose in them, and He has set between you love and mercy. Surely in that are signs for a people who consider.[47]

He further meant that the only duty prescribed, was that the man is required to financially support his wife and children, "on the grounds that they are not able to do so themselves. With the exception of this, no duty is specified, for either the husband or the wife, to dictate how they behave within the marriage or toward each other. Whatever duties the man has towards his wife, they are equal to the duties she has towards him".[48] He argues that both verses [4:34 and 2:228] must be read in the context of their revelations, and furthermore, that verse 4:35 needs to be included in order to understand the implications of verse 4:34. Verse 4:35 declares that "And if you fear a breach between the two, bring forth an arbiter from his people and from her people an arbiter, if they desire to set things right; God will compose their differences; surely God is All-knowing, All-aware." Essentially, al-Haddad means that the Quran's objective was to restrain the power the husband had to divorce, by encouraging reconciliation. Likewise, he means that if verse 2:228 is read in conjunction with the preceding and following verses, it would be made clear that they all are related to marital separation and the protection of women. For al-Haddad, the problem was not with Islam, but with patriarchy, and the reason why women are reduced to sex objects is "due to the fact that we regard them as vessels for our penises".[49]

As described in the beginning of this chapter, guardianship or wilaya, means the legal authority to manage the affairs of another person who lacks the required capacity.[50] The terms *wali* and *wala'*,[51] derived from the term wilaya, are often referenced in the Quran and Sunnah. Wali, is often attributed to God and used in reference to human beings with various meanings.[52] The

---

47   Quran 30:21.
48   Quran 2:228. Ronak Husni and Daniel Newman, *Muslim Women in Law and Society: Annotated Translation of al-Tahir al-Haddad's* Imra'tuna fi 'l-shari'a wa 'l-mujtama', *with an introduction* (Routledge: London, 2007), p. 59.
49   Husni, and Newman, *Muslim Women in Law and Society*, p. 60.
50   Nasir, *The Islamic Law of Personal Status*, p. 190 and Imran Nyazee, *Outlines of Islamic Jurisprudence* (Lahore: Advanced Legal Studies Institute, 2000), p. 205.
51   When referencing God, synonyms to wali are also used in the Quran, see, for example, *nasir* (helper, 4:45, 4:89, 4:123, 9:116, 29:22, 33:17 and 42:13), *shafi'* (one who intercedes, see 34:4), *waq* (shield, 13.37) and *murshid* (guide, 18:17).
52   See Quran 2:282; 4:144; 5:51; 5:81; 7:30; 9:71 and 17:33. In the Arabic language, wali is used in two instances; *wali al-yatim*, with reference to the orphan where the wali has the right to manage his ward's affairs, and *wali al-mar'a*, with reference to a woman and the wali's

term wala' is used in hadith literature, where the term was closely associated with slavery; wala' and wilaya were the legal rights of the master.[53] Classical jurists developed the theory of guardianship in the tribal structural framework, where the view was that a marriage guardian is an absolute requirement for the marriage to be valid. In later periods, as the social structures changed, we see that the schools of law reconstruct the requirement of guardianship, to be necessary in order to ensure that the woman marries someone who is equal.

> That is because marriage is a contract for the whole life and is founded on aims and objectives like companionship, familiarity, living together, and building relationships. That can be accomplished only between equals. The principle of ownership of a woman is a kind of slavery. Marriage is slavery. One must, therefore, be careful where one places one's noble ward because humiliating oneself is forbidden. No believer is allowed to humiliate oneself.[54]

The historical overview of the development of the status of women, prove how scholars reached their conclusions based on specific assumptions with a specific understanding of religious and sociological arguments.[55] Interpretations of the verse 4:34 became more and more restrictive of women's rights over time. For some commentators, the expression "one of them over another" implied that God bestowed upon men unrestricted authority over women,[56] by correlating to the hadiths describing the deficiency of the minds of women.[57] One of the earliest Muslim traditionalist commentators on the Quran, Abu Jafar Mohammad ibn Jarir al-Tabari's (d. 923) makes a very literal commentary on the verse:

---

authority to conclude and consent to her marriage contract, see Ibn Manzur, *Lisan al-'Arab* (Beirut: Dar Sadir, 1882), p. 408.

53 Masud, "Gender Equality and the Doctrine of Wilaya", p. 133. The connection between the term and the practice of slavery is also affirmed by Imam Ali, who declared that "wala' is a branch of slavery". See Ibn Qudama, *Al-Mughni* (Cairo: Hajr, 1992), Vol. 9, p. 27. Several traditions narrated by Aisha also describe how a slave, after freedom, owed his or her wala' to the leader of the tribe. The right of wala' was also inherited like property, see Malik, *Al-Muwatta'* (Cairo: 'Isa al-Babi, 1951), Vol. 2, p. 781.

54 Abu Bakr Al-Sarakhsi, *Al-Mabsut* (Beirut: Dar al-Kutub al-'Ilmiyyah, 2001), Vol. 5, p. 23.

55 Kadivar, "Revisiting Women's Rights in Islam", p. 227.

56 Similar to the expression "one of them to excel the other" is found in a verse related to divorce. See Quran 2:228.

57 Sachedina, *Islam and the Challenge of Human Rights*, p. 143.

> Men are in charge of their women with respect to disciplining (or chastising) them, and to providing them with restrictive guidance concerning their duties toward God and themselves (i.e., the men); by virtue of that which God has given excellence (or preference) to the men over their wives: i.e., payment of their dowers to them, spending of their wealth on them, and providing for them in full. This is how God has given excellence to (the men) over (the women), and hence (the men) have come to be in charge (of women) and hold authority over them in those of their matters with which God has entrusted them.[58]

Al-Tabari argued that the most suitable interpretation of the term qawwamun was that men were "responsible for … caring for their needs" and "supporting them". To al-Tabari, this verse was primarily concerned with the spousal relationship, legitimizing men's authority over their wives,[59] including the right for a man to discipline his wife as long as it is deserved, to ensure obedience, not only to himself but also to God. Rebellion is described as "female appropriation of superiority over the husband, undue freedom of movement, objection to sexual contact when desired by the husband and other acts of defiance".[60] While al-Tabari upheld that men were superior to women, he limited the advantage to the economic aspects described in the Quran.[61] His comments, like other interpreters of the verse, were not only influenced by his personal opinions, but also by the social environment.[62]

By the Middle Ages, Muslim commentators had developed extremely patriarchal interpretations of qawwamun and the verse as a whole, influencing not only the understanding of the position of women, but also remaining relevant for centuries. Imam Abu Al-Qasim Mahmood Bin 'Omar Al-Zamakhshari (d. 1144), who belonged to a medieval rationalist school, explained that men rule women just as rulers govern their flock of subjects, with kindness. He provided a list of the qualities and privileges that men had, and consequently, women lacked:

---

58   Stowasser, "The Status of Women in Early Islam", p. 26.
59   Abu Ja'far Muhammad ibn Jarir al-Tabari, *Jami' al-Bayan 'am Ta'wil 'ay al-Qur'an*, ed. Mahmud M. Shakir and Ahmad M. Shakir, Vol. 8 (Cairo: Dar al-Ma'arif, 1972), pp. 290–317.
60   Stowasser, "Gender Issues and Contemporary Quran Interpretation", p. 33.
61   Ruth Roded, "Jewish and Islamic Religious Feminist Exegesis of the Sacred Books: Adam, Woman and Gender", *Nashim: A Journal of Jewish Women's Studies & Gender Issues* No. 29 (2016), pp. 56–80.
62   Karen A. Bauer, *Room for Interpretation: Quranic Exegesis and Gender* (Ph.D. dissertation, Princeton University, 2008), p. 184.

Reason, discretion, determination, strength, *kitaba* (literacy), horsemanship, spear/throwing, the emergence of prophets and scholars from among them, the greater imamate (leading the Muslim community), and the lesser imamate (leading the communal prayer), *jihad*, the call to prayer, the Friday sermon, the *I'tikaf* (pious retreats), reciting "Allah is the greatest" (*takbir*, after compulsory prayer during the month of Dhu al-Hijja), testimony in *hudud* (penal offenses) and *qisas* (retribution), a greater share in inheritance, privileging male agnates in inheritance, taken the burden of bloodwit (a fine paid as compensation for shedding of blood), performing a collective oath, guardianship in marriage, divorce and repeal of divorce, the number of spouses, patrilineal descent (from the agnatic line), and having beards and wearing turbans. And (the men are *qawwamun*) because they spend of their wealth on dowers and support of their wives.[63]

His ideas seem to echo ideas common in Islamic literature from an earlier time. Along this line of thought, Nasir al-Din Abu al-Khayr 'Abd Allah ibn Umar al-Baydawi (d.1286) describes women's limitations even more strongly and likens it to that of rulers over their subjects:

> Men are in charge of women, i.e., men are in charge of women as rulers are in charge of their subjects ... God has preferred the one (sex) over the other, i.e. because God has preferred men over women in the completeness of mental ability, good counsel, complete power in the performance of duties and the carrying out of (divine) commands. Hence to men have been confined prophecy, religious leadership (*'imama*), saintship (wilaya), the performance of religious rites, the giving of evidence in law courts, the duties of Holy War, and worship (in the mosque) on Friday, etc., the privilege of electing chiefs, the larger share of inheritance, and discretion in matters of divorce, by virtue of that which they spend of their wealth, in marrying (the women) such as their dowers and cost of their maintenance.[64]

---

[63] Quote taken from Roded, "Jewish and Islamic Religious Feminist Exegesis of the Sacred Books", p. 64.

[64] Stowasser, "The Status of Women in Early Islam", p. 26. See also, Abd Allah ibn Umar al-Baydawi, *Anwar al-Tanzil wa-Asrar al-Ta'wil*, Vol. 1 of *Reproductio Phototypica Editionis 1846–1848* (Osnabrück: Biblio, 1968), pp. 290–317.

The commentary is more detailed and restrictive as al-Baydawi sanctions the view of women as unfit for public duties and bars women from religious rituals such as the call to prayer, the second call to prayer, the Friday sermon and Friday worship in the mosque. Ismail Ibn Kathir (d. 1373) argues that men have custody over women and that a man has the right to exercise authority over a woman to the extent that he can even reprimand her if she misbehaves. According to Ibn Kathir men are superior to women, "and it is for this reason that the prophethood was limited to men just as the great kingship was". He holds that "men are more virtuous than women, and a man is better than a woman".[65] He cites the tradition where the Prophet warns his community that those who entrust their affairs to women will never know prosperity, for justifying his standpoint.[66] The restrictive view of the personhood of women is further developed by Ahmad ibn Mohammad al-Khafaji (d. 1659), who argues that wilaya is "assuming of responsibility for the women in matters of marriage, which means the power to make decisions". By the 17th century, women had come to be completely excluded from all spheres of public life.[67]

A more modern commentary on the Quran upholds these traditional views on women, although Shaykh Muhammad Abduh (1849–1905) and his student Rashid Rida (1865–1935), who are seen as Islamic modernism's early important representatives, understood qawwamun as the right for men to rule over women as heads of family, with the requirement of treating women kindly, and not using their hands:[68]

> Know that the men who try to be masters in their houses by oppressing women beget but slaves for others.[69]

Abduh separated the *ibadat*, (laws on religious duties) from the *muamalat*, (laws on social transactions), and argued that while ibadat was not subject to change because of its nature, muamalat by its nature requires interpretation and adaptation to the needs of each generation of Muslims.[70] He also argued

---

65 Isma'il b. Umar b. Kathir, *Tafsir Ibn Kathir*, ed. Sami b. Muḥammad al-Salama, 8 vols. (Riyadh: Dar Tiba, 1997), 2:292.
66 Ibid., 2:275.
67 Stowasser, "The Status of Women in Early Islam", pp. 25–26.
68 Quote taken from Roded, "Jewish and Islamic Religious Feminist Exegesis of the Sacred Books", p. 65.
69 Muhammad Abduh, *al-Islam wa-al-Mar'ah fi Ra'y al-Imam Muhammad Abduh*, ed. Muhammad 'Imara (Cairo, n.d.), p. 69.
70 Barbara Stowasser, "Women's Issues in Modern Islamic Thought", in *Arab Women*, ed. Judith E. Tucker (Bloomington: Indiana University Press, 1993), pp. 8–9.

that while polygamy was a practice by the early believers, it had developed into a corrupted practice and that women should have greater rights in initiating divorce. For Abduh, women's status was connected to the well-being or decay of social life as a whole.[71]

Sayyid Abu A'la Mawdudi (1903–1979), the father of modern Islamism, ascribes men the privilege of managing the affairs of women as men are superior to women in "natural qualities" but not in honor.[72] According to Mawdudi, God has bestowed upon men with knowledge, religious faith, intellect, and authority over women, because of their physical strength and capacity for strenuous work. Because of this, God sees men as superior to women and have been appointed the managers of women's affairs.[73] Sayyid Qutb (1905–1966), leader of the Muslim Brotherhood, claimed that "women prefer for the man to assume authority and responsibility for the family … many women worry, feel dissatisfied, and are unhappy when they live with men who relinquish their role for any reason".[74] According to Qutb, God both favored and bestowed the man with the necessary qualities and skills for the guardianship, and restricts the meaning to the relationship between the husband and the wife.[75]

Aisha Abd al-Rahman (1918–1998), one of the modern Muslim women to undertake Quranic exegesis, argues that women want to be dominated by men, but specifies that men's guardianship is conditional:

> Guardianship, according to Islam, is a right for manhood, and we, as liberated Muslim women, would like nothing better than to willingly and gladly admit this guardianship to our men. It is about time for our men to understand that their legitimate right of guardianship is neither absolute, nor is it for all men in general over all women. It is a conditional right, "because *Allah* has given the one more (strength) than the other, and because they support them from their means" (4:34), and if a man could not meet this condition, he loses his right to guardianship.[76]

---

71 Abduh, *al-Islam wa-al-Mar'ah fi Ra'y al-Imam Muhammad Abduh*, pp. 83–157.
72 Roded, "Jewish and Islamic Religious Feminist Exegesis of the Sacred Books", p. 65.
73 Maulana Abul Alla Maudoodi, "Tahfimul Quran – *A translation and tafsir of the Quran in Urdu*", trans. by Mohammad Abdul Rahim (Dhaka: Kausar Publications, 1958).
74 Roded, "Jewish and Islamic Religious Feminist Exegesis of the Sacred Books", p. 66.
75 Sayyid Qutb, *Fi Zilal al-Qur'an*, Vol. 2 (Beirut: Dar al-Shuruq, 1982), pp. 648–657.
76 'Aysha Abd al-Rahman, "The Islamic Conception of Women's Liberation", transl. Nazih Khater, *al-Raida*, 125 (2009), p. 41: see also, 'Aysha Abd al-Rahman, *al-Mafhum al-Islami li Tahrir al-Mar'a* (Islamic understanding of women's liberation: Cairo: Matba'at Mukhaymir, 1967).

Scholars that have challenged the male superiority as understood in verse 4:34, maintain that it is by the cultural deficiency as practiced by the tribal norms of seventh century Arabia that recognized a husband acting as his wife's custodian. The harsh social conditions of that time made her vulnerable and in need of protection.[77] They maintain that the verse only applies to matters related to moral guidance and caring, and only in extreme cases, such as insanity, do women lose their right to self-determination.[78]

Other scholars uphold that the word *qawwam* in verse 4:34 declares that the husband is the breadwinner of the family.[79] As the providers of the family, men are appointed to spend their economic resources on their wives.[80] Riffat Hassan reasons that:

> while Muslims through the centuries have interpreted the verse as giving them (men) unequivocal mastery over women, a linguistically, and philosophically/theologically accurate interpretation of this passage would lead to radically different conclusions. In simple words what this passage is saying is that since only women bear children (which is not to say either that all women should bear children or that women's sole function is to bear children) – a function whose importance in the survival of any community cannot be questioned – they should not have the additional obligation of being breadwinners whilst they perform this function. Thus during the period of a woman's child-bearing, the function must be performed by men (not just husbands) in the Muslim *"ummah"* ... It enjoins men, in general, to assume responsibility for women in general when they are performing the vitally important function of child-bearing.[81]

For Hassan, just because the Quran determines that the husband is financially responsible for the wife, it does not mean that "women cannot or should not provide for themselves".[82]

Azizah al-Hibri, argues that verse 4:34 does not make any reference to a male's physical or intellectual superiority. Instead:

---

77   Sachedina, *Islam and the Challenge of Human Rights*, p. 143.
78   Al-Hibri, "A Study of Islamic history: Or how did we ever get into this mess?", p. 218.
79   Syed, *The Position of Women in Islam*, pp. 51–52.
80   Zainab Alwani argues that "without this divine law, some men may not fulfil their financial responsibility towards their family", see "The Qur'anic model on Social Change: Family Structure as a Method of Social Reform", *Islam and Civilizational Renewal*, p. 65.
81   Quote taken from Ali, *Gender and Human Rights in Islam and International Law*, p. 65.
82   Hassan, "An Islamic Perspective", p. 354.

men are *qawwamun* over women in matters where God gave *some* of the men more than *some* of the women, *and* in what the men spend of their money, then clearly men *as a class* are not *qawwamun* over women *as a class*.[83]

For Al-Hibri, two conditions must be met for being a qawwamun; first, the man must be someone who God gave more than the woman and second, that the man must be the women's provider. If both conditions are met, it entitles the man to provide her "with moral guidance". It is only under extreme conditions, for example, insanity, that the woman loses her right to self-determination, including entering into any business contracts without permission from her husband. According to Al-Hibri, "no one has the right to counsel a self-supporting woman".[84] Al-Hibri also relies on another verse in the Quran, which determines that "the believers, men, and women, are *awliya*, of one another".[85] Awliya, like qawwamun, may be translated as protectors, in charge or guides.[86]

Similarly, Fazlur Rahman argues that the male's superiority is reduced if a woman earns an income and contributes to the household:[87]

> what the Quran appears to be saying is that since men are the primary socially operative factors and bread-winners, they have been wholly charged with the responsibility of defraying household expenditure and upkeep of their womenfolk. For their duties and economic struggles and experiences they have become entitled to manage women's affairs and, in case of recalcitrance on the part of women, to admonish them, leave them alone in their beds and as a last resort, beat them.[88]

For Rahman, men's superiority in the verse is purely functional; if a woman is self-sufficient and contributes to the household, "the male's superiority would to that extent be reduced since as a human, he has no superiority over his wife".[89] Along this line of thought, Muhammad Shahrur argues that verse

---

83   Al-Hibri, "A Study of Islamic herstory: Or how did we ever get into this mess?", p. 218.
84   Ibid.
85   Quran 9:71.
86   Arberry translates these words as "friends".
87   Frederick Mathewson Denny, "Fazlur Rahman: Muslim Intellectual", *Muslim World* No. 79 (1989), pp. 91–101. See also, Fazlur Rahman, *Major Themes of the Quran* (Minneapolis: Bibliotheca Islamica, 1980).
88   Rahman, "Status of Women in the Quran", p. 44.
89   Rahman, *Major Themes of the Qur'an*, p. 49.

4:34 applies to both men and women; whoever is stronger is responsible for guardianship.[90]

John Esposito adds that the priority attributed to men over women originated within the socio-economic context of the Arabs during the lifetime of the Prophet. Esposito contends, that verse 4:34 argues for economic superiority only for those men who fulfil the task of responsibility for the household. By analyzing relevant verses in the Quran through a system of "hierarchization of Quranic notions", it will lead to different interpretations regarding the status of women. This method is indicative of the process by which Quranic principles were first applied. In the formative period of Islam, socio-economic and ethnic-religious categories in Quranic legislation were differentiated. By applying such a method to the rights of women, it would mean that women are regarded as inferior to men within the socio-economic category, but full equals in the ethnic-religious category when considering their spiritual and moral obligations imposed upon them, their relation to God and how they are compensated in the hereafter. Social relations, which are subject to change, contain the values that differentiate women and men in a socio-economic context, while the religious duties towards God are immutable. By arguing that the religious duties towards God are immutable and not relative to the context of space and time, and since Islam does not differentiate between its believers in spiritual duties, Esposito argues that it constitutes the most important aspect of the Quranic paradigm on the issue.[91]

Abdulaziz Sachedina claims that because these injunctions were part of divine revelation, jurists treated them as immutable, demanding a wife's absolute obedience to her husband, even if she was the breadwinner. The jurists took biological differences in men and women as displays of social and functional inequality. Functional differences leading to different social responsibilities were generalized by the jurists, to argue for the superiority of man over woman, as was the case in seventh century Arab tribes.[92]

Ustadh Mahmood Mohammed Taha argues similarly, stating that the inferior status of women and practices such as wearing the veil, polygyny, and gender segregation, are not original teachings of Islam. The discriminatory practices were imposed for a transitory period after the period of jahiliyya as adopting complete equality was too drastic for the seventh

---

90   Mohammad Shahrur, *Al-Kitab wa al-Qur'an: Qira'a Mu'asira* (Beirut: Sharikat al-Matbu'a li al-Tawzi' wa al-Nashr, 1992), p. 620. See also, Andreas Christmann, *The Qur'an, Morality, and Critical Reason: The Essential Muhammad Shahrur* (Leiden: Brill, 2009), pp. 279–292.
91   Esposito, *Women in Muslim Family Law*, p. 108.
92   Sachedina, *Islam and the Challenge of Human Rights*, p. 126.

century Arabian society.[93] Taha bases his position on the Quran, which declares that:

> It was by some mercy of God that thou wast gentle to them; hadst thou been harsh and hard of heart, they would have scattered from about thee.[94]

The message of Islam, according to Taha, is of complete equality. He suggests that the Quran and early Sunnah of life in Mecca establish the fundamental message of Islam and that its implementations were simply postponed until such time it was possible to sanction them in law.[95]

From a Shia perspective, 'Allama Tabatabi argues:

> A woman is independent in her personal affairs and work. A man does not have the right to hinder her if she engages in any approved or blameless act she likes. A man's guardianship over his wife does not mean that she is not free in the management of her own property, that she is not independent in protecting and defending her personal and social rights, or may not take action to attain those rights. This verse, in fact, specifies men's status vis-à-vis women in marriage and society, not the absolute power of men's guardianship over women, or women's incapacity or lack of independence.[96]

The fact that there are so many readings of this verse proves that the legal status of women in Islamic law amounts to "matters merely of emphasis and interpretation about the same acts" and that "texts are capable of yielding what is in effect, for women, fundamentally different Islams".[97] Separating the ethical voice of the Quran, which is eternal, from the verses that were revealed to clarify a socioeconomic situation prevalent at the time, should no longer be the basis for the rules of Sharia. The eternal message establishes equality between men and women. As the dependency of women on men for economic and security reasons no longer exists, such an approach would mean that the verse would be repealed, thus ending the right for men to maintain women and their affairs. As Abdullahi An-Naim argues, "men and women should now

---

93 Taha, *The Second Message of Islam*, pp. 139–145.
94 Quran 3:159.
95 Taha, *The Second Message of Islam*, p. 23.
96 Quote take from Vasmaghi, *Women, Jurisprudence, Islam*, p. 89.
97 Ahmed, *Women and Gender in Islam*, p. 71.

2.2 Correcting Women

The second part of verse 4:34 describes good women as obedient and specifies corrective measures that can be taken towards the disobedient wife if deemed necessary: "Righteous women are therefore obedient (qanitatuun), guarding the secret for God's guarding. And those you fear may be rebellious (nushuz) admonish; banish them to their couches, and beat (daraba) them. If they then obey you, look not for any way against them".

Qanitatuun has been translated as "dutiful" or "devoutly obedient"[99] and "obedient"[100] and it has been understood that the good wife should be obedient to the husband and in his absence guard his reputation.[101] Some commentators argue that the verse only demands obedience to God,[102] as the Quran "never orders a woman to obey her husband. It never states that obedience to their husband is a characteristic of the 'better women' ".[103] Men are urged to treat the obedient wife well:

> O believers, it is not lawful for you to inherit women against their will; neither debar them, that you may go off with part of what you have given them, except when they commit a flagrant indecency Consort with them honourably; or if you are averse to them, it is possible you may be averse to a thing, and God set in it much good.[104]

If a wife is rebellious, the Quran allows for the use of physical violence to correct women.[105] Most commentators agree that the prescription of nushuz should be applied only in extreme circumstances as a last resort when all other

---

98 An-Naim, *Toward an Islamic Reformation*, p. 180.
99 Yusuf Ali, *The Holy Quran – Text, translation and commentary*, 4th ed. (Lahore: Ahmadiyyah Anjuman Ishaat Islam, 1946).
100 Muhammad Marmaduke Pickthall, *The glorious Quran – Text and explanatory translation* (New York: Muslim World League, 1977).
101 Zamakshari, *Al-Kashaf* (Beirut: Dar al-Maʿarif, Beirut, 1977); Ali, *The Holy Quran*.
102 Mir Ahmed Ali, *The Holy Quran with English translation of the Arabic text and commentary according to the version of the Holy Ahlul-Bait* (New York: Tahrike Tarsile Quran, 1988).
103 Wadud, *Qur'an and Women*, p. 70.
104 Quran 4:19.
105 The concept of *nashiza*, or the disobedient wife, forfeits her rights to marital support and is also subject to corporal punishment (according to some jurists), see Tucker, *Women, Family, and Gender in Islamic Law*, p. 25.

remedies have failed.[106] Historically, it has been accepted that men have a right to beat a disobedient wife, under certain circumstances: the wife's rise against her husband, resisting and deserting the husband, leaving the husband to live somewhere else, and breaching sexual conduct.

The beating measure has been met with resistance by many authorities both past and present.[107] Most measures have focused on limiting the severity of the implications of the permission, rather than questioning it *per se*.[108] Some interpreters argue that the beating should not cause injury,[109] as the corrective measure did not allow for abuse,[110] referring to the last part of the verse which states, "then if they obey you, seek not a way against them".[111] Amina Wadud argues that the verse is actually "prohibiting unchecked violence against females. Thus, this is not permission, but a severe restriction of existing practices".[112] Fatima Mernissi upholds that view; in the newly formed Islamic community, it was feared that, by prohibiting violence against women, the Prophet would encourage "female rebellion". The verse reinstated male superiority to quell those fears.[113] Similarly, Asma Barlas states that "in a time

---

106 Syed, *The Position of Women in Islam*, p. 55.
107 Mohamed Mahmoud, "To Beat or Not to Beat: On the Exegetical Dilemmas over Qur'an, 4:34", *Journal of the American Oriental Society* Vol. 126, No. 4 (2006), p. 537.
108 al-Tabari (838–923) argued that the beating should not be "severe" or "violent", see Muhammad al-Talbi, *Ummat Al-Wasat: Al-Islam Wa Tahaddiyat Al-Mu'asira* (Tunisia: Ceres Edition, 1996), pp. 128–129: al-Tabari, *Tafsir Al-Tabari*, Vol. 8 (Cairo: Dar al-Ma'arif, n.d.), pp. 313–316; Ismail Ibn Umar Ibn Kathir, *Tafsir Ibn Kathir* (Abridged), trans. Shaykh Safiur-Rahman al-Mubarakpuri, 10 vols., Vol. 2 (Riyadh: Darussalam, 2000), p. 446: Hadia Mubarak, "Breaking the Interpretive Monopoly: A Re-Examination of Verse 4:34", *Hawwa* 2/3 (2004), pp. 261–262. Muhammad 'Abduh (1849–1905) and Rashid Rida (1865–1935), defended the hitting of women as long as it was done without severe harm. 'Abduh also argues that the Prophet had placed an absolute prohibition on the beating of wives, citing the tradition in which the Prophet said "the best of you would not beat their wives", see al-Talbi, *Ummat Al-Wasat: Al-Islam Wa Tahaddiyat Al-Mu'asira*, p. 129; Mahmoud, "To Beat or Not to Beat", p. 545. Sayyid Qutb (1906–1966), defended the measure as preventative "in an unhealthy situation in order to protect the family against collapse". See Sayyid Qutb, *Fi Zilal Al-Quran* (In the Shade of the Qur'an), 6 vols., Vol. 4 (Beirut: Dar al-Shuruq, 1982), p. 137. Yusuf al-Qaradawi argued that the husband has the right to "beat her lightly with his hand, avoiding her face and other sensitive areas" if he does not receive obedience and cooperation from his wife, see Yusuf al-Qaradawi, *The Lawful and the Prohibited in Islam*, trans. M. Siddiqi K. al-Hilbawi, and S. Shukri (Cairo: al-Falah, 2001), p. 200.
109 Hadiths stipulate that the beating is allowed "in a way that is not agonizing" by hitting women with a toothpick or something similar, see Spectorsky, *Women in Classical Islamic Law – A Survey of the Sources*, p. 57.
110 al-Ghazali, *Qadaya al-Mar'ah Byna al-Taqalid al-Rakidah wa al-Wafidah*, pp. 174–177.
111 Quran 4:34.
112 Wadud, *Qur'an and Women*, p. 76.
113 Mernissi, *Women and Islam*.

when men did not need permission to abuse women, this Ayah simply could not have functioned as a license; in such a context, it could only have been a restriction insofar as the Quran made daraba the measure of last, not the first, or even the second, resort".[114] According to Sedigheh Vasighi, "men sometimes killed their wives because they had committed adultery or because they suspected that this had happened. They considered this to be their right. Under these circumstances, the Quran deterred men from violence toward women and killing them".[115]

The interpretation of the word daraba to mean striking has also been questioned. Some commentators maintain that it means "to prevent" and does not entail violence or force.[116] They read the verse to mean that the husband should not go to bed with their wife, and that the verse only permits the husband to prevent the wife from going outside of the house.[117] It is also suggested that the treatment prescribed by the verse depends on the status of the woman: "punish them 'refers to unmarried' and 'confine them to houses' refers to the women who are married".[118]

The Prophets view on the punishment of beating a wife has been recorded in several hadiths, where he condemned and warned against beating a wife and commended those who did not beat their wives.[119] After

---

114   Barlas, *"Believing Women" in Islam*, p. 188.
115   Vasmaghi, *Women, Jurisprudence, Islam*, p. 89. She refers to verses 24:6–10, where the Quran advise cursing the spouse in case of suspicion of adultery, and verse 4:15.
116   Syed, *The Position of Women in Islam*, p. 54.
117   Rafi Ullah Shahab, *Muslim Women in Political Power* (Lahore: Maqbool Academy, 1993), p. 231. Shahab also uses verse 4:15 in the Quran for his interpretation of this verse.
118   Sunan Abu Dawud 4414, Book 40, hadith 64.
119   Abu Dawud, hadith 1830. It is also narrated that "the best of you is he who is the best to his wife", "you have a right in the matter of your wives that they do not allow anyone who you don't like to come to your houses. If they do this, chastise them in such a manner that it should not leave an impression". Quote taken from Syed, *The Position of Women in Islam*, p. 54. In another tradition it was narrated that, "my father told me that he was present at the Farewell Pilgrimage with the Messenger of Allah. He praised and glorified Allah, and reminded and exhorted (the people). Then he said: 'I enjoin good treatment of women, for they are prisoners with you, and you have no right to treat them otherwise unless they commit clear indecency. If they do that, then forsake them in their beds and hit them, but without causing injury or leaving a mark. If they obey you, then do not seek means of annoyance against them. You have rights over your women, and your women have rights over you. Your rights over your women are that they are not to allow anyone whom you dislike to tread on your bedding (furniture), nor allow anyone whom you dislike to enter your houses. And their right over you is that you should treat them kindly about their clothing and food.'" see Al-Bukhari, *Sahih*, Vol. 3, Book 9, hadith 1851. In another hadith, the Prophet declared: "Do not beat Allah's handmaidens." The term slaves are used in another version of this hadith; it was narrated that Iyas bin 'Abdullah bin Abu Dhubab

women complained of their husband's ill-treatment of them,[120] he declared that "you will not find these men as the best among you".[121] One interesting hadith describes a situation where the wife initially was allowed by the Prophet to take revenge against the husband who beat her but was later overruled by verse 4:34. The hadith describes an incident where one of the chiefs of the Ansar disobeyed her husband, and he slapped her. When her father came to the Prophet to complain about that, the Prophet declared that she could take revenge on her husband.[122] It is after 'Umar, complained about emboldened women to the Prophet, that the Prophet permitted the beating of wives.[123]

Conversely, the Quran declares the remedy for a husband's nushuz quite differently:

> If a woman fear rebelliousness or aversion in her husband, there is no fault in them if the couple set things right between them; right settlement is better; and souls are very prone to avarice. If you do good and are god-fearing, surely God is aware of the things you do.[124]

A women's duty of correcting the husband is different from the husband's in relation to his wife's, as it is argued that the wife is capable of preventing the

---

said: "The Prophet said: 'Do not beat the female slaves of Allah.' Then 'Umar came to the Prophet and said: 'O Messenger of Allah, the women have become bold towards their husbands? So order the beating of them,' and they were beaten. Then many women went around to the family of Muhammad. The next day he said: 'Last night seventy women came to the family of Muhammad, each woman complaining about her husband. You will not find that those are the best of you.'" See Al-Bukhari, *Sahih*, 900.

Al-Bukhari, *Sahih*, 3294; Sunan Abu Dawud 2145, Book 12, hadith 101.

120 Another hadith conveys that the Prophet supposedly said: "not one of you should beat your wife as hard as you beat your slave, for you might have sex with her at the end of the day", see Awde, *Women in Islam: An Anthology from the Qur'an and Hadiths*, p. 92. See also Al-Bukhari, *Sahih*, 7:98, 100.

121 Quote taken from Syed, *The Position of Women in Islam*, p. 54.

122 Quote taken from Spectorsky, *Women in Classical Islamic Law – A Survey of the Sources*, p. 32.

123 It is narrated that "the Prophet declared: 'Do not beat Allah's handmaidens', but when 'Umar came to the Messenger of Allah (saws) and said: 'Women have become emboldened towards their husbands', he (the Prophet) gave permission to beat them. Then many women came round the family of the Messenger of Allah (saws) complaining against their husbands. So the Messenger of Allah (saws) said: 'Many women have gone round Muhammad's family complaining against their husbands. They are not the best among you'", see Al-Bukhari, *Sahih*, 3294; Sunan Abi Dawud 2145, Book 12, hadith 101.

124 Quran 4:128.

husband from committing an immoral act, with words only. Besides, they do not have the physical strength to force them to abstain from specific acts.[125]

3   The Marriage Contract

Marriage, according to fiqh, is a contract that renders the female vagina the property of a male. The Qur'an's view, however, is that marriage is one of the divine signs. 'And of His signs is that He created for you, of yourselves, spouses, that you might repose in them, and He has set between you love and mercy. Surely in that are signs for a people who consider.'[126]

Statistics show that Muslim women are waiting longer to get married, and in some Muslim countries, they are even participating in the Western trend of declining child-birth.[127] Such a shift is detrimental to the traditional view of Islam, where marriage is commended and encouraged. As of today, women in most Muslim societies have not only restricted access to divorce; they also have fewer rights when it comes to child custody and guardianship. Muslim women opposing a traditional view of their rights are resorting to finding loopholes within the system, to gain greater rights. The marriage contract has proven to be such a loophole. This contract brings focus to many complex issues of Muslim marriage and divorce and practically illuminates the status of contemporary Muslim women.[128] In the vast majority of marriages, for example, in the Maghreb, the written contract rarely includes additional conditions. A majority of the contracts only include provisions with the names and signatures of the parties and their witnesses, the amount of the dowry and the date of the marriage.[129] Most modern marriage contracts are standardized, which

---

125   Vasmaghi, *Women, Jurisprudence, Islam*, p. 88.
126   Abu-Zayd, "The Status of Women Between the Qur'an and Fiqh", p. 153. See Quran 30:21.
127   Priscilla Offenhauer, "Women in Islamic Societies: A Selected Review of Social Scientific Literature, A Report Prepared by the Federal Research Division", Library of Congress under an Interagency Agreement with the Office of the Director of National Intelligence/National Intelligence Council (ODNI/ADDNIA/NIC) and Central Intelligence Agency/Directorate of Science and Technology, November 2005, p. 3.
128   Asifa Quraishi and Frank E. Vogel, eds., *The Islamic Marriage Contract, Case Studies in Islamic Family Law* (Cambridge: Harvard University Press, 2008), p. 1.
129   Stephanie Willman Bordat with Saida Kouzzi, "The Marriage Contract in Maghreb, Challenges and Opportunities for Women's Rights", in *Self-determination and Women's Rights in Muslim Societies*, eds. Chitra Raghavan and James P. Levine (Lebanon: Brandeis University Press, 2012), p. 158.

arguably can, not only limit the parties in making their stipulations, but generally, also weaken the woman's position to bargain.[130] Illiterate women are not aware of the content of their contracts, or nobody reads to them the terms of the contract at the time of the marriage. Most importantly, many Muslim women are not aware of the fact that they have the right to stipulate the terms of the marriage contract. The fear that the family of the future husband, or the future husband himself, would not agree to the terms of the marriage if the woman includes clauses to her benefit, which might mean that the woman would never marry, discourages many from even discussing such conditions. There are also women who are against the whole idea of stipulating the terms of the marriage contract. Some because they believe that they will have no problems in the marriage, others because they have sons who are to be married, and thus, do not want to disadvantage them with a contract that could be in favor of the future wife.[131]

While the standard Islamic marriage contract favors the husband, it does allow for both the man and woman to include stipulations. The inequality imposed on women can be addressed, at least in part, where power relations between spouses can be balanced by including rights-based protective clauses in detailed marriage contracts.[132] Not all contract terms will be upheld, as they cannot violate the Sharia and should be intended to further the object of the marriage. Nevertheless, the marriage contract can be a powerful tool for women to establish advantageous or beneficial clauses. This chapter examines the potential of the strategic use of the marriage contract in Islamic law as an initiative for individual Muslim women to advance their legal status, although the contract is "based on a strong patriarchal ethos imbued with religious ideas and ethics",[133] where the husband undertakes power over those supposed to be vulnerable—namely, women and children. The marriage contract is also of importance for non-Muslim women who marry Muslim men, especially if living in countries where Islamic law is influencing the laws or traveling to countries where the husband has prior citizenship. Being able to travel back home with the children or being awarded custody might prove to be difficult for the

---

130   Nik Norriani Nik Badli Shah, "The Islamic Marriage Contract in Malaysia", in Asifah Quarishi and Frank E. Vogel, eds., *The Islamic Marriage Contract* (Cambridge: Harvard University Press, 2008), p. 208.
131   Bordat with Kouzzi, "The Marriage Contract in Maghreb", pp. 160–164.
132   Ibid., 158.
133   Ziba Mir-Hosseini, "Tamkin: Stories from a Family Court in Iran", in Donna Bowen and Evelyn Early, eds., *Everyday Life in the Muslim Middle East* (Bloomington: Indiana University Press, 2002), p. 137.

woman in some Muslim countries. For any woman, the clearer the terms of the marriage contract are, and how it should be interpreted, is of utmost importance for her status during and after the marriage. Although conditions in the marriage contract are included to preserve or guarantee specific rights for women, their enforceability in Islamic courts may vary.[134] At times, it is simply stipulated that the contract is "governed by Islamic law", but this is a vague phrase, particularly because the various schools of law differ on key aspects of interpreting marriage contracts.[135] There are numerous methods of limiting the uncertainty of interpretation. If the couple is married in a country where the marriage was conducted under local Islamic law, the (foreign) court could consider the country's law for the interpretation of the marriage contract.[136] It could also be stipulated which school of Islamic law that is to oversee the interpretation.

As previously described, from a legal perspective, Muslim marriage is a civil contract.[137] The marital relationship is a consequence of a valid marriage contract, meaning that it is the actual marriage contract which creates the state of marriage.[138] The contract does not have to be in writing, but most of the marriage contracts concluded today *are* in writing.[139] The contract must be settled in the presence of free witnesses, either two men or one man and two women. The Shia do not require witnesses for the marriage contract to be considered valid but do for a divorce.[140] The requirement of having witnesses when the marriage contract is concluded has the aim of providing proof of marriage as well as ensuring chastity. However, the jurists differ over whether

---

134 Black, Hossein Esmaeli, Nadirsyah Hosen, *Modern Perspectives on Islamic Law* (Cheltenham: Edward Elgar, 2013), p. 120.

135 See generally, Dawoud S. El Alami, *The Marriage Contract in Islamic Law in the Shariah and Personal Status Laws of Egypt and Morocco* (London: Graham and Trotman, 1992), pp. 138–141; Quraishi and Vogel, *The Islamic Marriage Contract: Case Studies in Islamic Family Law* and Esposito, *Women in Muslim Family Law*.

136 Emily C. Sharpe, "Islamic Marriage Contracts as Simple Contracts Governed by Islamic Law: A Roadmap for U.S. Courts", *Georgetown Journal of Gender and the Law* Vol. 14, No. 1 (2013), p. 192.

137 Quran 4:21. See e.g. Azizah Al-Hibri, The nature of the Islamic marriage: sacramental, covenantal, or contractual? In *Covenant Marriage in Comparative Perspective,* eds. John Witte and Eliza Ellisson (Grand Rapids: William B. Eerdmans Publishing, 2005).

138 Sharpe, "Islamic Marriage Contracts as Simple Contracts Governed by Islamic Law", p. 200.

139 Asifa Quraishi and Najeeba Syeed-Miller, "No Altars: A Survey of Islamic Family Law in the United States", in *Women's Rights and Islamic Family Law: Perspectives on Reform* (Bloomsbury: Zed Books, 2004), p. 189.

140 Divorce must be performed in front of two witnesses, see Murata, *Temporary Marriage (Mut'a)*, pp. 14, 18.

the witnesses must observe the contracting event and what qualifications they must have. There is also no consensus on whether the consent of one or both spouses is required, or if a female can contract her marriage or must have a guardian to do so on her behalf, or what the impact of a valid dower has on the contract.[141] The schools that do require the consent of a guardian in marriage contracts, generally do not discuss the requirement per se; rather, the requirement is taken for granted.[142] In the Maliki school, while the requirement of the guardian to consent to the marriage is a necessity, the woman is free to ignore the wishes of her male relatives, and instead ask for permission from the public authority. Such a marriage would be considered valid, as long as she consented.[143] The schools also differ in their view on the role of the guardian and the woman's choice of marriage partner.[144] A woman must marry a man who is her equal. For the Shia, this means that he must be Muslim. The Sunni schools understand equality in terms of various social considerations, restricting a woman from marrying someone who is below her rank in society, although a man may do so.[145]

3.1 The Guardians Right to Conclude the Marriage Contract

So marry them, with their people's leave ...[146]

Women who have full legal capacity should be asked to give consent to marriage, as the Sharia forbids a woman to be married off against her will.[147]

---

141 Ali, "Marriage in Classical Islamic Jurisprudence", p. 13.
142 Fadel, "Reinterpreting the Guardian's Role in the Islamic Contract of Marriage", p. 5.
143 Ibid., 4, 12.
144 Alami, "Legal Capacity with Specific Reference to the Marriage Contract", p. 196.
145 The social considerations vary between the Sunni schools. The Hanafi's maintain religion, lineage, profession and that he must be a free man (meaning that a Muslim woman may not marry a slave), piety and property. The Shafi'i and Hanbalis also specify religion, lineage and profession and only differ in the usage of the words used to describe the social considerations. The Malikis require piety and no physical defects detrimental to the marriage. Murata, *Temporary Marriage (Mut'a)*, p. 9. See also, 'Abd al-Rahman al-Jaziri, *al-Fiqh 'ala al-màhdahib al-arba'a* (Cairo, 1969), p. 24.
146 Quran 4:25.
147 Fadel correctly points out: "there is a fundamental mistake of law in the Maliki treatment of a guardian's powers over a female ward who has attained physical maturity. Since the preferred reason for her continued legal incapacity is an inability to manage her affairs independently, she is a profligate (*safiha*), and therefore should no longer be subject to the guardian's power to compel her marriage. Thus, even within the strict parameters of the Maliki school, a physically mature woman's marriage cannot be compelled. The fact that Maliki's allowed such a woman to be married against her will, insofar as they

Despite a woman's right to reject marriage, the validity of the marriage is conditioned on the approval of the guardian.[148] The issue of consent from the guardian is a legal requirement for the woman, in contrast to the man, who may marry without the consent of his father or any other relative.[149] Islamic law consider the marriage guardian, no matter if it is a right or a duty, an authority that cannot be cancelled unilaterally as long as the conditions requiring the guardian to be in charge exist. However, although the law describes this person as a guardian, his role is more akin to a legal representative, *wakil*. The distinction with an ordinary legal representative, wakil, nevertheless, is that the wakil has accepted through a private agreement, to represent another party. Such representation could include the authority to conclude marriage contracts, but the representation itself is subject to the consent of the guardian.[150]

When discussing the requirement of a marriage guardian for a woman, the jurists refer to different verses in the Quran. However, none of the verses in the Quran, like the abovementioned verse, use the term wali or wilaya,[151] understood as marriage guardian. Ibn Rush (d. 1198), is of the view that the requirement of guardianship is not even derived from the hadiths, instead it originates from social practice[152]:

> Jurists differ because there is no verse of the Quran or the Sunnah of the Prophet that clearly stipulates guardianship as a condition for the marriage contract, let alone any explicit text on the point. Rather, the verses and the Sunnah cited by the proponents of guardianship and their opponents are equally ambiguous and probable. The authenticity of the cited hadiths is also debatable.[153]

---

considered her to lack complete legal capacity, can only be described *as a major error in legal reasoning".* See "Reinterpreting the Guardian's Role in the Islamic Contract of Marriage", p. 11.

148 Ibid., 12.
149 The Maliki, Hanbali and Shafi'i schools maintain that the guardian may only give a virgin in marriage without her consent. Her age is not relevant. The Hanafi and Shia hold that only a girl who has not reached puberty may be married off against her will. This also applies for boys not of age and mentally incompetent men. Murata, *Temporary Marriage (Mut'a)*, pp. 13–14. See also, al-Jaziri, *al-Fiqh 'ala al-madhahib al-arba'a*, p. 51.
150 El Alami, "Legal Capacity with Specific Reference to the Marriage Contract", p. 192.
151 Quran 2:221, 2:232, 2:234, 4:2–3, 4:6, 4:25, 24:32, 60:10 and 65:4.
152 The practice of not consulting virgins occurred in Medina, see Malik, *Al-Muwatta'*, p. 525.
153 Ibn Rush, *Bidayat al-Mujtahid,* trans. M. K. Masud (Cairo: Maktaba al-Kulliyyat al-Azhariyya, 1969), Vol. 2, pp. 10–13.

One hadith declares that "no marriage (is valid) without a guardian",[154] and another prescribes that "any woman who is married (or marries herself) without the permission of her guardian, her marriage is void."[155] Yet, as upheld by Ibn Rush, the chain of transmission for these hadiths are contested.[156] Another hadith cited declares that "a single woman (*ayyim*) who has been previously married is entitled regarding herself more than her guardian.[157] The virgin's consent regarding herself must be sought, her silence is her consent".[158] The hadith has been interpreted differently by jurists from the various schools of law; Hanafi and Maliki understand the term ayyim to include all unmarried women,[159] Shafi'i argue that the guardian should only consult unmarried women, but consultation is not mandatory.[160] Shafi'i and Maliki both maintain that the hadith only distinguishes between virgins and those previously married; it does not remove the requirement of a marriage guardian.[161] Maliki understand the phrase "having more right", as the guardian has the right to conclude the marriage contract, instead the woman has more rights when it comes to other aspects.[162] The Shafi'i, Maliki, and Hanafi hold that the guardianship continues if the female is a virgin even after reaching the age of majority. If the female ceases to be a virgin before the age of majority, the guardianship also

---

154 Abu Da'ud, *Sunan Abi Da'ud* (Riyadh: Dar al-Salam, 2000), Hadith Aisha no. 2083, p. 1376; Tirmidhi, Abu 'Isa, *Jami' al-Tirmidhi* (Riyadh: Dar al-Salam, 2000), Hadith Aisha no. 1102, p. 1757.

155 Ibn Majah, *Sunan ibn Majah* (Riyadh: Dar al-Salam, 2000), Hadith ibn 'Abbas no. 1880, p. 2589; Tirmidhi, Abu 'Isa, *Jami' al-Tirmidhi* (Riyadh: Dar al-Salam, 2000), Hadith ibn 'Abbas no. 1108, p. 1757. The Maliki, Shafi'i and Hanbali schools insist that a female must always be married off by a guardian or *wali*, citing a tradition where "the Prophet said: There can be no marriage without a wali, and the sultan is the wali of the one who has no other". See Ibn Abi Shayba, *Musannaf*, 3:272, no. 15. Sultan in this context means "political authority". See also, Hanbal, *Musnad*, 6:47. In another report, the Prophet said, "if a woman has not been given in marriage by one of her walis, her marriage is void". Ibn Abi Shayba, *Musannaf*, 3:272, no. 1.

156 Masud, "Gender Equality and the Doctrine of Wilaya", p. 135.

157 It is also narrated that "the widow or the divorced woman has greater right to dispose of herself in marriage than her guardian" and "the guardian has no business in the matter of the divorced woman or the widow", see Syed, *The Position of Women in Islam*, p. 39.

158 Muslim b. Hajjaj, *Sahih Muslim* (Riyadh: Dar al-Salam, 2000), Hadith ibn Abbas no. 3467, p. 914; Abu Da'ud, *Sunan Abi Da'ud*, Hadith ibn 'Abbas 2098, p. 1377; Tirmidhi, *Jami' al-Tirmidhi*, Hadith ibn 'Abbas 1108, p. 1759.

159 Ibn Humam, *Sharh Fath al-Qadir* (Quetta: Maktaba Rashidiyya, n.d.), Vol. 3, p. 159, Al-Zurqani, *Sharh Muwatta' Imam Malik* (Cairo: Matba'a al-Istiqama, 1954), Vol. 3, p. 126.

160 Al-Shafi'i, *Al-Umm* (Beirut: Dar al-Kutub al-'Ilmiyya, 1993), Vol. 5, p. 22.

161 Syed, *The Position of Women in Islam: A Progressive View*, p. 39.

162 Masud, "Gender Equality and the Doctrine of Wilaya", p. 136.

ceases.[163] However, the Hanafi's allows the wali to dissolve the marriage, with the judge's intervention if the bride marries an unsuitable groom. The Ja'fari uphold that a female does not need a wali, to contract her marriage, even if she has not been married before, as long as she has attained majority. They do, however, require a guardian for concluding the marriage contract of minors, or an incompetent or insane woman.[164]

The requirement for a woman to conduct a marriage contract exclusively through an agent has been legitimized for various reasons. A bride's wali must be a legally responsible adult Muslim, where the right to be a guardian is restricted if used for anything other than intended. That is, if a guardian should harm the interests of the woman or use the guardianship for his own interests, it could be considered unjustified prevention of marriage. The jurists differ on whether the guardianship is then passed to the nearest male relative or a judge.[165] While the Malikis, Shafi'is, and Hanbalis hold that he must be a male, the Hanafis allow for female guardianship, under certain circumstances. A woman is allowed to conclude a marriage contract for another, or someone under her guardianship if she acts as a proxy by the Hanafis.[166] Jafaris do not allow for female guardianship, but if a mother marries off her child, the marriage is still considered valid if the child approves.[167] While the guardian is to act in the best interest of the woman and to take her wishes into consideration, it is considered that the guardian will be able to negotiate a better deal for the woman, than if she were to bargain the terms of the marriage contract directly with the prospective groom. It also "gives the impression that his role is exclusive to 'protect' the woman's interests".[168] A women also needs a guardian as it is improper for a woman to mix in a male society outside of her immediate family; "there is no sphere in which a woman may associate with men, and she could be courted by a man who is not her equal and marry him unwittingly, which would be harmful to her and a disgrace to her family. It is, therefore, valid to restrain her in the contract of marriage, although not in any other contract".[169] Although a woman has the right to conclude other contracts, the schools do not acknowledge in her the capacity to conclude her

---

163   El Alami, "Legal Capacity with Specific Reference to the Marriage Contract", p. 193.
164   Murata, *Temporary Marriage (Mut'a)*, p. 13.
165   El Alami, "Legal Capacity with Specific Reference to the Marriage Contract", pp. 194–195.
166   For more on the issue of women as proxies, see El Alami, "Legal Capacity with Specific Reference to the Marriage Contract", p. 197.
167   Hilli, 1999, 3:438.
168   Fadel, "Reinterpreting the Guardian's Role in the Islamic Contract of Marriage", p. 16.
169   El Alami, "Legal Capacity with Specific Reference to the Marriage Contract", p. 193.

marriage contract, or to conclude another woman's marriage contract,[170] citing a tradition where the Prophet declared "no woman can give another in marriage. Nor can she give herself in marriage. Only an adulteress gives herself in marriage".[171]

3.2 Mahr

The only component of marriage consistently agreed to be unquestionably essential to conclude a valid marriage is an offer, *ijab*, acceptance, *qabul*, and the payment of the dower, mahr, "a sum of money given by the husband to the wife in consideration of marriage".[172] The mahr belongs to the bride, and cannot be claimed or appropriated by any guardian, including parents.[173] Mahr can be divided into two portions: prompt mahr, due at the time of the signing of the contract, and deferred mahr, which is usually due upon divorce or death of the husband and is often more substantial than prompt mahr.[174] In the latter situation, any remaining mahr will be in addition to her share of her husband's estate. The mahr, or financial obligation of the husband to the wife, is taken seriously by Muslim women, as it represents financial security in the event of divorce or the death of the husband.[175] While the provision of mahr is required, no maximum or minimum has been set, nor has it been specified in its form.[176] Yet, the word mahr, which usually connotes commercialization of marriage, as such, does not exist in the Quran.[177] Instead, the Quran institutes *sadoqat*, or gifts:[178]

---

170 Ali, "Marriage in Classical Islamic Jurisprudence", p. 14.
171 Ibn Maja, *Sunan*, 1:605, no. 1881.
172 For more on the standard practice of offer and acceptance see Ali, "Marriage in Classical Islamic Jurisprudence", pp. 13–14.
173 H. A. Al-Ati, *The Family Structure in Islam* (Indianapolis: American Trust Publications, 1977), pp. 68–69.
174 Esposito, *Women in Muslim Family Law*, pp. 24–26.
175 Sharpe, "Islamic Marriage Contracts as Simple Contracts Governed by Islamic Law", p. 198.
176 Al-Alti, *The Family Structure in Islam*, p. 67.
177 Mahr seems to have been incorporated into the Islamic vocabulary by the comments of Ibn 'Abbas when he explained the nihla to be mahr, see Nimat Hafex Barazangi, *Woman's Identity and Rethinking the Hadith* (Surrey: Ashgate Publishing Limited, 2015), p. 97.
178 It is questioned whether a gift can be obligatory or not, see Hassan Yousefi Eshkevari, "Rethinking Men's Authority over Women: Qiwama, Wilaya and their Underlying Assumptions", in *Gender and Equality in Muslim Family Law: Justice and Ethics in the Islamic Legal Tradition*, eds. Ziba Mir-Hosseini, Kari Vogt, Lena Larsen and Christian Moe (London: I. B. Tauris, 2013), p. 205.

> And give the women their dowries as a gift [*sadogat*] spontaneous; but if they are pleased to offer you any of it, consume it with wholesome appetite.[179]

Mahr occurs very infrequently in hadiths; when it does, it is usually accompanied by other terms such as *faridah* (God-given right), or *sadaq* (which is connected with a root word meaning marriage-gift, charity, friendship, fidelity, truth, and so on). The jurists have used these terms interchangeably as denoting the God-given right to dowry. But it is not certain whether, in these interchangeable usages, the traditional connotations of the term mahr were sublimated to the moral and charitable denotations of terms like sadaq, faridah, and so on; or whether these terms themselves took on the traditional connotations of mahr. A review of the classical legal texts would seem to indicate that where it occurs, the term mahr is used in a sublime moral sense indistinguishable from the meaning of sadaq, faridah, and similar terms. But the law books and usages of subsequent centuries seem to use mahr and other alternate terms in a sense very much akin to the traditional meaning of bride-price. Muslim jurists of later centuries have held the technical view that:

> Dowry is enjoyed in return for the man's right, at least potentially, to have legitimate access to cohabitation with the woman in question. She is entitled to dowry because she has consented to marriage and made herself accessible. Much discussion among the jurists has centered on this issue. But the exponents of this view appear to assume or to infer that women have no sexual desires or need of their own, that gratification is not reciprocal, that sex is a cheap commodity in view of the permissibility of nominal dowries, and that marriage is a little more than a *commercial transaction*. That list of assumptions and interferences may be extended. Yet, these seem contrary to the bio-psychological facts and to the very idea of marriage which is depicted in the Qur'an (e.g., 30:21) as a shelter of peace and comfort, and as a means of mutual love and mercy.[180]

As the mahr is given "in return for the sexual gratification" the husband is to receive, the wife may refrain from sexual intercourse until she has received the dower unless specified in the marriage contract that the mahr will be paid at some later date. Should she have intercourse before receiving the mahr, she

---

179 Quran 4:4.
180 Farooq, "Analogical Reasoning (Qiyas)", p. 163 quoting Mir-Hosseini, "Tamkin: Stories from a Family Court in Iran", p. 68.

may no longer refuse her husband, unless it is proven that he is not able to pay the mahr. Contrary to the other schools of law, the Hanbali allows the woman to annul the marriage even after consummation if the husband is unable to pay the mahr.[181] The Shia maintain that once the marriage has been consummated, the wife may not refrain from sexual intercourse as a consequence of the husband's inability to pay the mahr.[182]

Mahr agreements establish economic rights for the woman, but the marriage contract as such does not establish equality in rights or obligations between spouses.[183] Although, the wife has every opportunity to do so by including such clauses to the marriage contract.[184] As the contract is a negotiated agreement between two consenting parties, the clauses in the marriage contract are legally enforceable. As with any other contract, parties are free to define the terms of the contract, or in the case of the marriage contract, their rights and duties in detailed clauses.[185] The principle of *pacta sunt servanda* is paramount in Islamic law since it requires contracting parties to uphold their commitments,[186] and the Quran instructs believers "to fulfil the contracts which ye have made".[187] Every contract entered into by the faithful must include a forthright intention to remain loyal to performing the obligations specified by the terms of the contract.[188] The fulfilment of contracts ranks among the highest achievements and noblest of virtues in the Quran. Failing to respect the terms

---

181   The Hanafi and Shia uphold that a woman may not annul the marriage, but she may refuse intercourse. al-Jaziri, *al-Fiqh 'ala al-madhahib al-arba'a*, pp. 109–110.
182   Murata, *Temporary Marriage (Mut'a)*, p. 16.
183   Farooq, "Analogical Reasoning (Qiyas)", p. 162 quoting Mir-Hosseini, "Tamkin: Stories from a Family Court in Iran", p. 137.
184   Most frequently, the contract will stipulate that the above legal marriage has been concluded in accordance with Almighty God's Holy Book and the Rules of His Prophet to whom all God's prayers and blessings be, by legal offer and acceptance from the two contracting parties, see generally, Alami, *The Marriage Contract in Islamic Law*, pp. 138–141; Quraishi and Vogel, *The Islamic Marriage Contract: Case Studies in Islamic Family Law* and Esposito, *Women in Muslim Family Law*.
185   Bordat with Kouzzi, "The Marriage Contract in Maghreb", p. 156.
186   See Sara M. Mitchell and Emilia J. Powell, *Domestic Law Goes Global: Legal Traditions and International Courts* (Cambridge: Cambridge University Press, 2011), p. 43; Rayner, S. E., *The Theory of Contracts in Islamic Law: a comparative analysis with particular reference to the modern legislation in Kuwait, Bahrain and the United Arab Emirates* (London: Graham & Trotman, 1991), p. 100; Hossein Askari, Zamir Iqbal and Abbas Mirakhor, *Globalization and Islamic Finance: Convergence, Prospects and Challenges* (Singapore: John Wiley & Sons, 2010), p. 65.
187   Quran 2:177.
188   Saba Habachy, "Property, Right and Contract in Muslim Law", *The International Executive* Vol. 4, No. 3 (1962), pp. 11–12.

of the contract is considered a breach of the contract, which in this case allows for the wronged spouse to seek damages or initiate divorce. Most schools of Sunni Islam uphold the view that stipulations in marriage contracts are not permitted if they alter core marital rights, such as stipulations preventing the husband of taking more than one wife, taking concubines or moving his wife away from her town. In such cases, the marriage is binding, but the specific stipulations are void.[189] For the Shafi'i, an invalid marriage condition invalidates the whole marriage contract.[190] As such, a wife cannot force her husband to remain monogamous, but it does give her the opportunity of leaving the marriage, rather than tolerating a co-wife.[191]

3.3 The Analogy to a Sales Contract

No general theory of contracts or explicit definition of a contract exists in Islamic law;[192] instead Islamic contract law is one of particular contracts, where different types are defined in terms of their ends.[193] While each contract had its own distinctive rules, there were plenty of overlaps between the sales-contract model and other forms such as the marriage contract. It is still argued that the classical jurists, with their case-related approach to treating legal problems that could arise from contractual obligations, drew "clear lines of demarcation between commercial exchange and, for example, the sphere of those social relations that are mediated through kinship, marriage, sexual relations ..."[194] Yet the jurists never considered the need to establish a separate theory or framework for the marriage contract.[195]

> It is said that in the market, the master buys his slave, whereas, in marriage, the husband purchases his wife's productive part.[196]

---

189 It is reported that "a man married a woman in the era of 'Umar b. al-Khattab and stipulated to her that he would not take her away from her hometown. 'Umar set aside that stipulation for him and said, a woman [goes] with her husband". Quote taken from Ali, *Marriage and Slavery in Early Islam*, p. 72–73.
190 Black, Esmaeli, Hosen, *Modern Perspectives on Islamic Law*, p. 120.
191 Ali, *Marriage and Slavery in Early Islam*, p. 75.
192 The Quran allows for property to be exchanged through trade and mutual consent, see Quran 4:29. See also 9:71 on fulfilling all contracts and 2:219 and 5:93–94 on the prohibition of *gharar*, speculative uncertainty.
193 Hussein Hassan, "Contracts in Islamic Law: The Principles of Commutative Justice and Liberty," *Journal of Islamic Studies* Vol. 13, No. 3 (2002), 257–97, esp. 282–3.
194 Hassan, "Contracts in Islamic Law," 260.
195 Farooq, "Analogical Reasoning (Qiyas) and the Commodification of Women," 171.
196 John Ralph Willis, "The Ideology of Enslavement in Islam", *Slaves and Slavery in Muslim Africa*, Vol. 1 (London: Cass, 1985), p. 1.

Classical Islamic law on marriage is based on an assumption that likens women to slaves, or marriage to purchase of the bride.[197] The view was that the husband paid the wife to be in control of her, much like the master's power over his female slave. However, unlike the slave owners right to sell his slave, the husband is not free to do so with his wife.[198]

The concept of guardianship of women as embedded in the laws of marriage stems from the view that marriage is a contract containing an element of ownership, which gives rise to different rights and duties based on gender.[199] It is patterned after the contract of sale and developed out of the purchase of the bride, where the groom generally concludes the contract with the guardian of the bride and undertakes to pay the nuptial gift, mahr, to the bride and not the wali as was custom in the pre-Islamic period.[200] The position that marriage is viewed as a commercial transaction is supported by the standpoint of Hanafi sources, and upheld by other schools of law:

> A woman may refuse to admit her husband to a carnal connection until she has received her dower of him, so as that her right may be maintained to the return, in the same manner as that of her husband to the object for which the return is giver, *as in sale*. What is here advanced proceeds upon a supposition of the whole dower, or a certain portion of it, being *Moajil*, or prompt; but if the whole be *Mowjil*, or deferred, the woman is not at liberty to refuse the embraces of her husband, as she has dropped her right by agreeing to make her dower Mowjil, – *the same as in the case of sale*, where, if the price of the article sold be made deferrable, the seller is not at liberty to detain the article sold on account of the price. It is proper to observe, that where the woman refuses to admit the husband to a repetition of the carnal act, as above stated, yet she has, nevertheless,

---

197 Duderija, "Maqasid al-Sharia", p. 201.
198 Ali, *Marriage and Slavery in Early Islam*, p. 168. Al-Alti argues that it would be more correct to describe the Muslim marriage as a lease contract; "tenants are not responsible for the repairs and improvements to the premises. They must pay only the rent; the rest is the owner's charge. As a tenant, a husband is not responsible for the cost of any treatment his wife may undergo to restore or improve her health", see *The Family Structure in Islam*, p. 154–155. As described, Islamic law does not stipulate that the husband is to take care of his wife if she falls sick, mainly because she cannot fulfil her end of the marriage contract, to sexually satisfy her husband, even though the Quran and the Sunnah call for kindness to the wife, see Farooq, "Analogical Reasoning (Qiyas)", p. 168; Al-Marghinani, *Al-Hedaya*, p. 392.
199 Duderija, "Maqasid al-Sharia", p. 196 and Ali, *Marriage and Islam in Early Islam*.
200 Schacht, *The Origin of Muhammadan Jurisprudence*, p. 160.

(according to Haneefa) a claim to her subsistence, as her refusal does not, in any case, proceed from any stubbornness or disobedience, since it is not exerted in resistance to a right, but rather in maintenance of one. – The two disciples hold that she is not entitled to any subsistence; – and their argument on this occasion is, that the sole object of the contract has been duly delivered to the husband, either by the single carnal act, or by the single complete retirement, as aforesaid; on which account it is that her right to her whole dower is confirmed and established, and consequently no right of further detention of her person remains with her; *as in a case of sale*, where the seller has delivered the article sold to the purchaser, before receiving the price, has no further right over it.[201]

Shafi fiqh describes the integrals of a marriage contract similarly:

> The first integral is the explicitly stated form: comprising a spoken offer by the guardian and its acceptance by the groom, like other, non-marital transactions. *Its necessary conditions are the same as those of valid sale.*[202]

The Hanbali discuss the marriage contract in the context of a transaction:

> Al-Khiraqi's three principles on *khulʿ* are repeated verbatim in the post-classical Sunni corpus of the erudite Hanbali legist, Muwaffaq al-Din Ibn Qudama (d. 1223), with the further specification that 'separation (*khulʿ*) does not require action by a judge: this is the position of Ahmad [b. Hanbal, school founder, d. 840] ... and also that of Malik, Al-Shafiʿi and the party of opinion (*ahl al-ray*: the Hanafis) ... Since *it is a transaction* (*exchange; muʿawada*), *similar to a sale or a marriage contract*, it does not require a judge, and also because it is dissolution of contract by mutual consent (*qat ʿaqd bil taradi*).[203]

It is through qiyas that the jurists applied the analogy linking marriage and commercial transactions.[204] Obviously, it is problematic invoking a sale analogy, as it is invariably assigning the notion of women as a commodity in

---

201 Farooq, "Analogical Reasoning (Qiyas)", p. 163 quoting Al-Marghinani, *Al-Hedaya*, p. 150.
202 Farooq, "Analogical Reasoning (Qiyas)", p. 164 quoting Ibn Al-Naqib, *Reliance of the Traveller*, m. 3.2.
203 Ibid. See also Oussama Arabi, *Studies in Modern Islamic Law and Jurisprudence* (Leiden: Brill, 2001), p. 181.
204 Ibid., 165.

the context of a marital relationship. The notion of a commodity is usually described as "a substance or product that can be traded, bought, or sold".[205] The related notion of property, meaning something that is "owned or possessed",[206] makes the concept of marriage and commercial transactions even more problematic. "By applying sales contracts as the basis for qiyas to marriage contracts, essentially the women are commodified, that is, reduced to commodities that can be owned and traded."[207] Yet, the understanding of the woman as a commodity is not inconceivable in a society where Muslim scholars did not reject or abandon the idea of human beings as a commodity, or as slaves, and where many of them were slave-owners. It is even argued that "their own status as slaveholders cannot help but have influenced the jurists' rulings".[208] The acceptance and allowance for slavery and the application of sale contracts on slaves allows for the view that women are a commodity and deriving their rights from sales contracts.[209]

---

205 See the Cambridge Dictionary, meaning of the word commodity: https://dictionary.cambridge.org/dictionary/english/commodity (accessed 10 October 2019).
206 See the Cambridge Dictionary, meaning of the word property: https://dictionary.cambridge.org/dictionary/english/property (accessed 10 October 2019).
207 Farooq, "Analogical Reasoning (Qiyas)", p. 173.
208 Ali, *Marriage and Slavery in Early Islam*, pp. 12–16.
209 Farooq, "Analogical Reasoning (Qiyas)", p. 173.

CHAPTER 5

Advancing the Legal Status of Women in Islamic law

> Patriarchy is taken for granted in the classical milieu: a change to this has had to wait until the paradigm change in our modern era of gender equality and feminism.[1]

One of the greatest challenges facing the Islamic feminist movement is not only the struggle to challenge patriarchy, but to show that equal standing is afforded women in the Quran. Such attempts essentially involve female emancipation at the cost of rights and privileges traditionally afforded men. Muslim men would be stripped of the interpretation that entails a God-given right to guard women and their sexuality for women to have the legal capacity as independent adults, and not as minors who are bound by the supervision of their father or other male relatives—or in need of protection and maintenance from their husbands. Not surprisingly, the opposition against feminist readings of Islam has been strong; those who engage and call for interpretations which include gender equality are accused of being disloyal to Islam. However, Muslim women and men have every right to question the authoritarian claims made by jurists concerning their interpretations of women's status in Islamic law. As has been described in previous chapters, interpretations of the Quran, but also other sources of law, is the product of the male interpretive elite, who have granted themselves the right to speak authoritatively for Islam,[2] even though the Quran does not acknowledge such a privilege.[3]

> Many Muslims, however, are of two views about the role of subjectivity. On the one hand, they hold that modern readings of the Qur'an, especially by women, are tainted by biases, while on the other hand, they embrace the religious knowledge produced by a small number of male

---

1 Nasr Abu-Zayd, "The Status of Women Between the Qur'an and Fiqh", p. 163.
2 Suha Taji-Farouki, ed., *Modern Muslim Intellectuals and the Qur'an* (Oxford: Oxford University Press, 2004), p. 12.
3 Quran 3:7.

scholars in the classical period as the only objective and authentic knowledge of Islam.[4]

The belief in the "theoretically infallibility"[5] of these male scholars is unjustified and leads to the notion that the knowledge they produced transcends its historical context.[6] There is no questioning that when the jurists formulated the Sharia, they were influenced by their understanding of the Quran and the Sunnah. Their subjective understandings set the bar against which the development of the rights of women have developed in Islam. Traditional scholarship has, either consciously or unconsciously, excluded relevant concepts when constructing the legal status of women.[7] Many jurists indisputably accepted the notion of the deficient mind of the woman—much like they accepted the institution of slavery—where the perceived male superiority came to be the basis for how the commands of the Quran were interpreted, and where they regarded women as a tool for the pleasure of men, incapable of taking care of themselves. As time passed, the jurists even resorted to formulations which reduced the rights given to women in the Quran, and further advanced the privileged status men had been granted.[8] In some instances, revealed principles in the Quran were set aside for certain traditions, giving precedence to the Sunnah over the Quran, even though the Quran technically exceeds the Sunnah. In a sense, we are still in a period of ignorance, where the development of human reasoning is portrayed as not being compatible with Islam, although it has been an integral part of Islamic law from its commencement. Despite what traditionalists maintain, there are no legal injunctions in the Quran that prescribe that a development subject to the social conditions of time would not be consistent with the main purpose of the Islamic faith and tradition; to achieve justice for the believers in this life. The temporality of the Sharia is recognized in other fields of Islamic law as well as claims that the principles of the Quran were not eternal but subject to historical contingency.[9]

---

4   Barlas, *"Believing Women" in Islam*, p. 24.
5   Fazlur Rahman, *Islamic Methodology in History* (Karachi: Central Institute of Islamic Research, 1965), p 77.
6   Barlas, *"Believing Women" in Islam*, p. 24.
7   Duderija, "Maqasid al-Sharia", p. 200.
8   Engineer, *The Rights of Women in Islam*, p. 13.
9   Norma Salem, "Islam and the Status of Women in Tunisia" in *Muslim Women*, ed. Freda Hussain (New York: St. Martin's Press, 1984), p. 144.

1 Gradual Changes

While the notion of male superiority is a sociological concept, the issue that arises is why a sociological concept should become a legal one?[10] Principally, there is nothing in verse 4:34 that suggests that the perception of men being the guardians of women, should be a legal matter. While it might have been a requirement of the circumstances of historical times and in some instances justified by the conditions of the Arabs, there has been significant advancements in society, especially when it comes to the issue of economy and men and women's economic opportunities, thus allowing for the construction of laws related to the legal status of women, that include the realities of modern societies.

> Shari'a accorded lower status to women than men in certain situations ... [and] make us believe that in essence [Islam] favoured men ... If we look into their aims [the Quran and the Sunnah], we realize that they want to make women equal to man in every respect of life.[11]

As previously described, the Quran and the Sunnah are both normative and contextual. If the Prophet's behavior was to have any relevance for those who believed in him, it needed to be rooted in their history, culture, and tradition; and as such, the Quran contains elements which were significant for the Arabs to whom it was revealed.[12] While the Prophet led by an example and acted (in most aspects) according to the teachings revealed in the Quran;[13] he also acted as a political leader and his actions and deeds were based on the conditions and needs of that society. As such, Sharia is in many aspects a situational, and not a transcendental law. There is a need to distinguish between the normative

---

10   Engineer, *The Rights of Women in Islam*, p. 6.
11   Husni and Newman, *Muslim Women in Law and Society*, p. 104. Al-Haddad criticized how Tunisian women were treated in his book *Our Women in the Shari'a and Society*, causing an outrage, where he was declared an apostate. See Salem, "Islam and the status of women in Tunisia", pp. 141–168. Yet, Al-Haddad is also criticized for reinforcing patriarchal notions of women's traditional roles as wives, mothers and guardians, see Lamia Ben Youssef Zayzafoon, *The Production of the Muslim woman: Negotiating Text, History, and Ideology* (New York: Lexington Books, 2005), chapter 4.
12   Engineer, *The Rights of Women in Islam*, p. 12.
13   Take for instance, the fact that he had several wives at the time of his death, more than the four the Quran supposedly allows for. See Schimmel, *And Muhammad is His Messenger*, p. 50.

actions of the Prophet from the behavior, which was contextual. If its situational character is recognized, Sharia could very well be capable of responding to various challenges and problems that may arise during the continuation of time and must be viewed as such.[14] The Quran restricts immutability solely to the order of nature, calling it God's tradition, which is unchangeable. That does not mean that immutability was extended or was intended to be extended to include social laws, especially since human conditions governed social laws and continue to do so today.

> In twenty-three years the condition that called forth some judgments changed, then as the condition changed some of the judgments changed. Indeed, a question might require a (positive) command, then the circumstances would change, and it would require a prohibition ... So if this happened in twenty-three years in the life of the Prophet, what do you think when times have changed and more than a thousand years have passed ...? Does the observer not think that if the Prophet was alive and faced these circumstances, many verses of abrogation would descend upon him and God the Generous and Merciful would not leave the Islamic nation without flexible legislation confronting this new life with absolute ijtihad?[15]

Although Muslims believe that the verses in the Quran were revealed for all times, there is nothing that suggests that the changes in society which occurred during the lifetime of the Prophet "was the hoped-for final stage".[16] Many cultural practices and socio-economic realities of the Arabs were accepted, and instead, through a gradual revelation of verses, it is argued that Islam aimed at changing society. The elementary tendency of the Quran supports a gradualist approach to change the societal norms into the social order Islam wanted to establish, and consequently, its teachings are linked with its historical reality. The example of alcohol proves the use of gradualism as a method in the Quran. Arabs were accustomed to drinking alcohol and gambling, and initially, the Quran only issued a recommendation to the believers that in wine and gambling, "their sin is greater than their benefit".[17] Later, a verse was revealed which

---

14   Engineer, *The Rights of Women in Islam*, p. 9.
15   Ahmad Amin, *Duha al-Islam*, Vol. III (Cairo, 1961), pp. 325–326; cf. William Shephard, *The Faith of a Modern Muslim Intellectual* (Delhi: Indian Institute of Islamic Studies, 1982).
16   Salem, "Islam and the Status of Women in Tunisia", p. 144.
17   Quran 2:219.

urged followers not to drink during the hour of prayer,[18] and in a final verse, intoxicants and gambling are attributed to Satan and believers are urged to avoid it.[19] The example shows how alcohol came to be forbidden, by the revelation of a series of verses, which gradually changed over a number of years, so the newly-converted Muslims could get used to the new demands. It is also argued that this method was used to change pre-Islamic practices towards women. The dower was the bride-price paid to male members of the woman's family, whereas in the Islamic tradition it was modified to become a sum of money or property paid directly to the woman. The practice of polygyny was restricted to up to four women, unlike previous customs which allowed men to marry an unlimited number of wives.

One of the obstacles towards the gradualist approach in the case of the guardianship of women is the fact that, in the case of gambling and alcohol, there are strict verses in the Quran that forbid the occurrence of such practices. The same clarity does not exist to support an absolute prohibition of guardianship. Nonetheless, this was not an aspect that discouraged the call for the abolition of slavery. Muslims considered slavery quite justifiable throughout the middle ages, by quoting the Quran. Just like owning property, owning slaves was considered a right in Muslim societies and there were elaborate rules of behavior for slaves and their masters when it came to their ownership, possession, and even removal. But it is also maintained that slavery was tolerated because of the socio-economic realities of the time of revelation, where the proper treatment and liberation was encouraged, until society was ready for its full abolition.[20] Now that slavery is regarded intolerable, very few would invoke the holy texts to justify it and argue that it is a divine right. Similarly, few would uphold the right of Muslim men to have sexual intercourse with their slave girls, a practice which used to be common and compatible with historical readings and regarded as divinely ordained. What we see here is that the theory of divine law is no longer used to justify the institution of slavery.[21] Why should it be for the treatment of women?

---

18   Quran 4:43.
19   Quran 5:90–92.
20   Husni and Newman, *Muslim Women in Law and Society*, p. 48.
21   Engineer, *The Rights of Women in Islam*, p. 2.

2 Could the Abolition of Slavery Be a Model for Advancing the Rights of Women?

The Islamic law of slavery is patriarchal and belongs more to the law of family than to the law of property.[22]

Slavery was widespread in pre-Islamic times and continued after Islam was introduced in society. The Prophet himself gave, received, and owned slaves, and there is considerable material demonstrating the Prophet's preference for the emancipation of slaves.[23] The emancipation of Bilal ibn Rabah, an Ethiopian slave rescued by a pagan Meccan owner, is often used as proof both of Islam's emancipatory ethic concerning slavery and its intolerance of racial discrimination.[24] The emancipatory ethic in the Quran asserts that "[by] the freeing of a slave ... those are the companions of the right hand".[25] Bilal became a devoted Muslim, and his role in early Islamic history is noteworthy as it is said that he was the first prayer caller in Islam. The Quran later recognized the call to prayer as an important part of maintaining communal public worship.[26] Later, the Prophet Muhammad appointed Bilal as interim governor of Medina, entrusting him with important duties in the new Islamic state.[27]

While the Prophet's ways inspired his companions to liberate thousands of slaves,[28] there was never any substantial native incentive for the abolition of slavery and slave trading in the Muslim world. With that in mind, there is also no verse in the Quran that specifically sanctions the institution of slavery. Instead, the Quran contains quite a few verses describing the proper relationship to slaves, which explicitly suggest the legality of slavery under certain conditions.[29] The verses are mostly concerned with the issues that might arise

---

22   Schacht, *An Introduction to Islamic Law*, p. 130.
23   Robert K. Freamon, "ISIS, Boko Haram, and the Human Right to Freedom from Slavery under Islamic Law", *Fordham International Law Journal* Vol. 39, No. 245 (2015–2016), p. 290.
24   Khalid Muhammad Khalid, *Men around the Messenger*, trans. Sheik Muhammad Mustafa Gemeiah (Cairo: Al-Azhar Al-Sharif Islamic Research Academy, 1997), p. 71.
25   Quran, 90:1–20.
26   Quran 62:9.
27   Kamali, *Freedom, Equality, and Justice in Islam*, p. 58.
28   Abdul Ali, *Insights Into Islamic Humanism: A Comprehensive Approach* (New Delhi: MD Publications Pvt Ltd., 2007), p. 79; Shibli Numani, *Umar: Makers of Islamic Civilization* (London: I. B. Tauris, 2004), pp. 125–127.
29   See Quran, 2:177, 2:178, 2:221, 4:3, 4:24, 4:25, 4:36, 4:92, 5:89, 9:60, 23:6, 24:31, 24:32, 24:33, 24:58, 30:28, 33:50, 33:52, 33:55, 70:30. See also, Bernard K. Freamon, "Definitions and Conceptions of Slave Ownership in Islamic law", in *The Legal Understanding of*

concerning the treatment of slaves, the relationship of slaves to free persons and conditions leading to their emancipation.[30] However, the verses are "situated in a context that overwhelmingly encourages emancipation" and not the capture of slaves. Islamic law acknowledges that the only way a person who was born free could be enslaved was through military defeat in war sanctioned by Sharia.[31] Once a slave, or if born to slave parents, the person remains a slave until emancipated.[32]

The many verses about slavery and slave trade in the Quran is contradictory to the egalitarian message of Islam,[33] which unfortunately made little contribution to the closing of the slave trades and the eventual elimination of chattel slavery in most Muslim communities.[34] In places where slavery was eliminated, it was, by and large, the resulting pressure from Western governments, through naval anti-slaving patrols, diplomatic coercion, treaties, financial reward schemes for local sheikhs, colonial sanctions, and the shaming exhortations of abolitionist movements.[35] Some have even suggested, now that colonialist legacy has receded, slavery might appear again in the Muslim world. In some communities in the Sahel and parts of sub-Saharan Africa, the Persian Gulf, and the Arabian Peninsula, it is still very much a problem. Nevertheless, while the various initiatives of Western governments and antislavery activists were contributory factors to ending slavery, Islamic law did play an important part in the efforts to abolish chattel slavery and slave trades. Some Muslims

---

Slavery: From the Historical to the Contemporary, ed. Jean Allain (Oxford: Oxford University Press, 2012), pp. 49–52.

30   Freamon, "ISIS, Boko Haram and the Human Right to Freedom from Slavery under Islamic Law", p. 282.

31   The Shafi'i school, in dealing with prisoners of war, allowed for their immediate execution, enslavement or release with or without ransom. The Maliki school restricted the options to execution, enslavement or release with ransom, whereas the Hanafi school went the furthest and only allowed execution or enslavement. See Khadduri and Liebesny, *Law in the Middle East*, pp. 355–356 and Majid Khadduri, *War and Peace in the Law of Islam* (Baltimore: John Hopkins Press, 1955), pp. 126–130.

32   See, for example, Quran 9:60; 2:177; 4:92; 5:83; 90:11–13; and 24:33.

33   Kamali, *Freedom, Equality, and Justice in Islam*, p. 58.

34   Ennaji, *Slavery, the State and Islam*; Ronald Segal, *Islam's Black Slaves: The Other Black Diaspora* (New York: Farrar, Straus and Giroux, 2001).

35   Bernard Lewis, *Race and Slavery in the Middle East* (New York: Oxford University Press, 1990), p. 79; Murray Gordon, *Slavery in the Arab World* (New York: New Amsterdam, 1989), pp. 191–229; Keith Hamilton and Patrick Salmon, eds., *Slavery, Diplomacy, and Empire: Britain and the Suppression of the Slave Trade, 1807–1975* (Brighton: Sussex Academic Press, 2009); see also, Suzanne Miers, *Britain and the Ending of the Slave Trade* (New York: Africana, 1975).

opposed slavery from within, which later turned into a crucial program to abolish the institution.[36]

2.1   The Status of Slaves

A slave is defined as a human being who is owned by another human being, subject to the status of personal property by the owner or owners.[37] This means that a slave can be bought, sold, given away as a gift, mortgaged, rented, borrowed, used or even "destroyed", just like any other piece of owned personal property. In classical legal texts, rules regarding ownership and disposal of slaves frequently reference ownership and disposal of livestock.[38] The slave is subject to the absolute will and control of the slaveholder, although it is maintained that the owner of a slave must not overwork his slave and allow enough time to rest and the right to receive maintenance from his owner. The slave is less protected in criminal law than a free man, as only *taʿzir*, discretionary punishment, is carried out against a person guilty of causing bodily harm to a slave.[39] The bodily harm caused to a free man would automatically lead to a hadd punishment. However, retaliation for the intentional killing of a slave takes places even against a free man. The slave has no protection against his owner, and since retaliation and blood-money are vested in the owner himself, the slave cannot sue. The slave is also liable for less than a free man if he should commit a crime. For example, the slave is not stoned to death for unlawful intercourse, and he is punished by half of the number of lashes applicable for drinking wine. Financial liability for torts caused by the slave is borne by the owner, but the owner can surrender the slave as an alternative. The slave cannot be a witness.[40]

---

36   Robert Harms, Bernard F. Freamon, and David W. Blight, *Indian Ocean Slavery in the Age of Abolition*, ed. Robert Harms (New Haven: Yale University Press, 2013), p. 63–81. For a more detailed overview of the literature, see William Gervase Clarence-Smith, *Islam and the Abolition of Slavery* (London: Hurst, 2006), pp. 16–19.

37   Brunschvig, "'Abd". See also, Freamon, *Definitions and Conceptions of Slave Ownership in Islamic Law*, pp. 40–60.

38   Ibn Rushd, *The Distinguished Jurist's Primer*, pp. 208–211.

39   This is because the slave is not regarded *muhsan*. Muhsan is a legal concept describing the personal status of an individual who is free (not a slave) and who either has never committed an act of illicit sexual intercourse or has consummated a lawful marriage to a free partner. In the latter case, the person is subject to the sentence of death by stoning if he or she commits adultery, see Oxford Islamic Studies Online, Muhsan.

40   Schacht, *An Introduction to Islamic Law*, p. 128.

Many of the rules on slaves, also reflect the views on women. The connection between the status of women and slaves can be seen in the statement made by Ibn Qayyim al-Jawziyya:

> The wife is her husband's prisoner, a prisoner being akin to a slave. The Prophet directed men to support their wives by feeding them with their own food and clothing them with their own clothes; he said the same about maintaining a slave.[41]

The slave is not completely without protection, as it is acknowledged that they do have rights as a person; in particular, he or she can get married. The male slave may have two female slaves and marry a free woman who is not his owner whereas the female slave may marry a free man who is not her owner. The owner needs to permit the slave to enter into marriage, but the owner can also give the slave in marriage against his or her will. Minor slaves are not to be separated from their parents or near relatives in the sale. The children of a female slave retain the status of the mother, unlike, the children of the concubine, whom the owner has recognized as his own, are considered free. All rights of children from a marriage with a free woman are applied to the child of the concubine, a rule which had profound influence on the development of Islamic society.[42]

2.2 Female Slaves

While female slaves were not common and were concentrated in urban centers, the need for slaves became greater and continued to swell as Islamic conquests continued to expand.[43] In particular, there was a growing need for female slaves, as Islamic law had authorized the slave master who possessed female slaves to have sexual relations with any one of them.[44]

---

41 Ibn Qayyim Al-Jawziyya, *I'lam al-Muwaqqi' in äan Rabb al-'Alamin* (Beirut: Dar al-Fikr al-'Arabi, 1995), Vol. 3, p. 1. Quote taken from Yossef Rapoport, Marriage, *Money and Divorce in Medieval Islamic Society* (Cambridge: Cambridge University Press, 2005), p. 52.
42 Schacht, *An Introduction to Islamic Law*, p. 127.
43 Khalil 'Athamina, "How did Islam Contribute to Change the Legal Status of Women: The Case of the Jawari, or the Female Slaves", *Al-Qantara* Vol. XXVIII, No. 2 (2007), p. 384.
44 See Quran, 4:3; 4:24–25; 23:5–6; 24:31: 33:50 and 70:29–30. For Sunna showing the free practice of slavery during the Prophet's time, see Khadduri, *Islamic Law of Nations*, p. 80 ff. For a critical review of these verses and the argument that Islam does not allow sexual relations with female slaves, or that a sexual relationship with a female slave actually constitutes marriage, see Syed, *The Position of Women in Islam*, pp. 33–36.

Female slaves filled a void in the sexual life of the Muslim man, since the Arab woman, or the Oriental one, bound as she was by conservative traditions and a complicated system of values of dignity and rules of modesty, could not give her husband what the female slaves could.[45] When marriage to a free Arab woman was weighed in the balance against marriage to a slave woman, the scales tipped in favour of the latter, who was preferred because she could be obtained at a lower cost, provided better service to her husband, and did not incur numerous daily expenses.[46]

The whole construction of the Muslim marriage was to make sex lawful for men and women, yet classical Islamic law also entitles a man to sex from his ownership of an unmarried female slave.[47] While the unmarried female slave can be used as a concubine by the male owner, a similar provision does not apply between a male slave and his female owner. The slave women also have the right to rescission when she becomes free, if her master has given her in marriage against her will, much like the guardian can give a minor in marriage, without their consent, until they reach the age of puberty.[48]

A child born to a female slave, *jawari*, was not legally recognized and was not entitled to inherit from his father. A concubine's child could always be recognized by the father, but sons of slave women were at first the target of contempt and ridicule.[49] It was only after the increasing number of jawari, resulting from an increasing number of births among the Arab aristocracy, that the derogatory attitudes began to change. For example, only three of thirty-eight Abbasid caliphs were born to Arab mothers, while the rest were born to freed slave women. The grandchildren of Abu Bakr, 'Umar and Ali were all born from freed slave women, which led to the improving status of the slave son.[50]

The legal status of the slave mother was not changed, but attempts were made to increase her status.[51] 'Umar, the second caliph, declared that a slave master could not sell or trade a female slave who bore him a son, but had to keep her, and upon his death, she would become a free woman. Ali, the fourth caliph, allowed slave women to be included in her son's portion of inheritance

---

45 'Athamina, "How did Islam Contribute to Change the Legal Status of Women", p. 384.
46 Ibid., 397.
47 See Ali, *Money, Sex, and Power* and *Sexual Ethics and Islam,* pp. 39–47.
48 Syed, *The Position of Women in Islam,* p. 41.
49 Ignaz Goldziher, *Muslim Studies* 1, eds. S. M. Stern and Hamid Dabashi (London: Aldine Transaction, 2006), pp. 115–116.
50 'Athamina, "How did Islam Contribute to Change the Legal Status of Women", p. 395–397.
51 Schacht, *The Origins of Muhammadan Jurisprudence*, p. 245 ff.

"after her fiscal value had been established".[52] As time passed, slave women did not only serve to handle the needs of the slave-owner's family but became a symbol of the purchasers social standing; the more slaves he had, the more prestigious and higher social status he was considered to have. Wives of caliphs would give their husbands slaves as a gift to prove her loyalty to him. Slaves came to be highly sought-after merchandise, and the slave trade developed into a profitable branch of commerce, not only in Islamic countries but also internationally. Educated female slaves were worth more as there was a demand for educated slave women from the ruling elite, which contributed to the prevalence of education among women, a privilege formerly monopolized by men.[53] As more and more places were conquered by Muslims and became part of the Islamic territory, slavery became the norm in the new empires and the use of a successful system of slave trading and transporting became established and continued for over one thousand years.[54]

2.3 Abolishing Slavery

Historically, jurists' opinions do assume and support the institution of slavery in a great variety of circumstances, without questioning its morality. While no

---

52 'Athamina, "How did Islam Contribute to Change the Legal Status of Women", p. 387.
53 Ibid., 393–403.
54 See generally, Reginal Coupland, *East Africa and Its Invaders From Its Earliest Times to the Death of Sayyid Said in 1856* (London: Oxford University Press, 1961); Reginal Coupland, *The Exploitation of East Africa 1856–1890: The Slave Trade and The Scramble* (Evanston: Northwestern University Press, 1967); Segal, *Islam's Black Slaves: The Other Black Diaspora*; John Wright, *The Trans-Saharan Slave Trade* (London: Routledge, 2007); Lewis, *Race and Slavery in the Middle East: An Historical Enquiry*; Gordon, *Slavery in the Arab World*; James Francis Warren, "The Sulu Zone: The World Capitalist Economy and the Historical Imagination", *Southeast Asian Studies* Vol. 35, No. 2 (1997); Paul E. Lovejoy, *Transformations in Slavery: A History of Slavery in Africa* (Cambridge: Cambridge University Press, 2012); Gwyn Campbell, "Slavery and the Trans-Indian Ocean World Slave Trade: A Historical Outline", in *Cross Current and Community Networks: The History of the Indian Ocean World, eds.* Himanshu Prahba Ray and Edward A. Alpers (Oxford: Oxford University Press, 2007); Mohammed Ennaji, *Slavery, The State and Islam* (Cambridge: Cambridge University Press, 2013); Eve Troutt-Powell, *Tell this In My Memory: Stories of Enslavement from Egypt, Sudan, and the Ottoman Empire* (Stanford: Stanford University Press, 2012); Terenze Walz and Kenneth M. Cuno, eds., *Race and Slavery in the Middle East: Histories of Trans-Saharan Africans in Nineteenth Century Egypt, Sudan, and the Ottoman Empire* (Cairo: American University in Cairo Press, 2010); Gwyn Campbell, Suzanne Miers and Joseph C. Miller, eds., *Women and Slavery: Africa, The Indian Ocean and the Medieval North Atlantic*, Vol. 1 (Ohio: Ohio University Press, 2007); Ehud R. Toledano, *As If Silent But Absent: Bonds of Enslavement in the Islamic Middle East* (New Haven: Yale University Press, 2007); Elizabeth Savage, ed., *The Human Commodity: Perspectives on the Trans-Saharan Slave Trade* (London: Routledge, 1992).

verses advise that the practice of slavery should remain, there is no single verse explicitly proclaiming the end of the practice either.[55]

> Should the legal condition for the enslavement of anyone be proven (because he had been taken prisoner fighting against Islam with a view to its extirpation and persisted in invincible ignorance in his sacrilegious and infidel convictions, or because there did exist legal proof that all his ancestors without exception had been slaves descended from a person taken prisoner concluding a warfare of such invincible ignorance) Islam would be bound to recognize such slavery as legal, even though recommending the freeing of the person and if possible his conversion, in this modern age.[56]

This would mean that slavery is lawful in Islamic law, simply because it is permitted in the Quran and "just as one may not permit what God forbids, so one may not forbid what God permits".[57] Nevertheless, there would be very few Muslim commentators who would agree that Islam allows for slavery today. Modern Muslim scholars frequently maintain that Islam supports an absolute abolition of slavery and slave trading.[58] They mean that while Islam initially allowed for slavery, it was only because the Prophet had been forced to comply with the centrality of slavery in the social order of society, postponing the implementation of a complete abolition of the institution until modern times.[59] Contrary to the perception of modern Muslim scholars and jurists, most Muslims and Muslim jurists, scholars and government officials, did not embrace the demands of the abolition of the institution from European

---

55 Freamon, "ISIS, Boko Haram and the Human Right to Freedom from Slavery under Islamic Law", pp. 279–282.
56 Sultanhussein Tabandeh, *Muslim Commentary on the Universal Declaration of Human Rights* (London: F. T. Goulding and Co., 1970), p. 27.
57 Lewis, *Race and Slavery in the Middle East: An Historical Enquiry*, p. 78.
58 Farhad Malekian, *Principles of Islamic International Criminal Law: A Comparative Search*, 2nd ed., (Leiden: Brill, 2011), p. 229. Malekian declares that "according to the legal, social, economic and political philosophy of Islamic international criminal law mankind is equal in all social phenomena. Islamic jurisdiction therefore prohibits any type of action degrading a person to the statue of slavery".
59 Taha, *The Second Message of Islam*, pp. 2–23, 31, 47, 137–138, 161–164; 'Abdullahi An-Na'im, "Shari'a and Basic Human Rights Concerns", in *Liberal Islam: A Sourcebook*, ed. Charles Kurzman (New York: Oxford University Press, 1998), pp. 228–231, 231–234, 237; Mohamed I. Khalil, "Human Rights and Islamization of the Sudan Legal System", in *Religion and Conflict in Sudan*, ed. Yusuf Fadl Hassan and Richard Gray (Nairobi: Paulines Publications Africa, 2002), pp. 58–71.

colonial powers.[60] There was, in fact, strong resistance against the elimination of the practice.[61] Abolition of slavery in Muslim communities varied in each location, depending on the nature of the institution, economic conditions, the attitudes of the elite, including the religious elite, and the local approach to the empire.[62] At first, the ulama behind the Islamic abolitionist movement focused on the Quran itself, affirming that it did not sanction the enslavement of non-combatants or the procurement of infidels by purchase or tribute. Enslavement was only permitted through the capture of infidels who refused to convert to Islam, in properly constituted holy wars, or through the birth from such captives. By 1870, Muslim reformers began advocating an absolute prohibition of the institution. They offered the theory that slavery had been unlawful since the time of the Prophet, but ending the institution had merely become conceivable in modern times.[63] The differing cultures in which Islamic law found itself was a decisive factor for why some Muslim societies were able to abolish slavery successfully, and others were not.

2.3.1 Egypt

Initially, the Egyptian ulama condemned the enslavement of free Muslims but remained restrained concerning slavery as an institution.[64] Methods of enslaving infidels were gradually questioned and by the early 1880s,[65] a majority of

---

60 Freamon, "ISIS, Boko Haram, and the Human Right to Freedom from Slavery under Islamic Law", p. 279.
61 William Gervase Clarence-Smith, "Islamic Abolitionism in the Western Indian Ocean from c. 1800", in Harms, Freamon, and Blight, *Indian Ocean Slavery in the Age of Abolition*, pp. 140–142; Amal Ghazal, "Debating Slavery in Arab Middle East: Abolition Between Muslim Reformers and Conservatives", in Behnaz Mirzai, Ismael Musah Montana and Paul E. Lovejoy, *Islam, Slavery and Diaspora* (Lawrenceville: Africa World Press, 2009), pp. 139–153.
62 Harms, Freamon, and Blight, *Indian Ocean Slavery in the Age of Abolition*, p. 69.
63 Clarence-Smith, *Islam and Abolition*, chapters 10–11; John Hunwick, "Islamic Law and Polemics over Race and Slavery in North and West Africa, Sixteenth to Nineteenth Century", *Princeton Papers: Interdisciplinary Journal of Middle Eastern Studies* No. 7 (1999), pp. 43–68.
64 Gilbert Delanoue, *Moralists et politiques musulmans dans l'Égypte du XIXe siècle* (Cairo: Institut Français d'Archéologie Orientale, 1982), p. 57; Jay Spaulding, "Slavery, Land Tenure, and Social Class in the Northern Turkish Sudan", *International Journal of African Historical Studies* Vol. 15, No. 1 (1981), pp. 4, 10.12; Terence Walz, "Black Slavery in Egypt during the Nineteenth Century, as Reflected in the Mahkama Archives of Cairo", in *Slaves and Slavery in Muslim Africa*, ed. John R. Willis II (London: Frank Cass, 1985), pp. 147–149, 158.
65 Mohammad ibn-Omar el-Tousy, *Voyage au Darfour* (Paris: Benjamin Duprat, 1845), pp. viii–xi, 269–270; Mohammad ibn-Omar el-Tousy, *Voyage au Ouadây* (Paris: Benjamin Duprat, 1851), pp. 404–405, 467–490; John Hunwick and Eve Troutt Powell, *The African Diaspora in*

the ulama in Cairo declared that enslavement was only permissible for non-Muslim captives taken in holy war.[66] Sayyid Muhammad Rashid Rida, the follower of Muhammad 'Abduh, the leading figure of Egyptian modernism, maintained that taking slaves in holy wars was permissible, as long as they were not Muslim, Arabs or close relatives. There needed to be a caliph who could declare a defensive holy war and affirm that taking captives as slaves was in the public interest.[67]

The establishment of the Manumission Bureaus in 1877, was only supported by some of the ulama.[68] Some defended the institution of slavery with the view that women freed by the bureaus had to obtain the consent of their owner to marry, which allegedly was a contributing factor to why many of those women turned to prostitution.[69] Others argued that the same civil rights that a free person held should be obtained by those slaves liberated by the bureaus, but it was deemed that it "would be overriding the [holy] law in decreeing the abolition of slavery".[70] By 1881, the ulama told the British occupiers that they could not prohibit slavery as the Prophet had not banned it himself, but by 1886 slavery was eventually abolished by British-sponsored legislation,[71] which did not cause

---

the *Mediterranean Lands of Islam* (Princeton: Markus Wiener, 2002), pp. 53–54; Y. Hakan Erdem, *Slavery in the Ottoman Empire and Its Demise, 1800–1909* (London: Macmillan, 1996), pp. 89–90.

[66] Gabriel Baer, "Slavery and Its Abolition", in *Studies in the Social History of Modern Egypt*, ed. Gabriel Baer (Chicago: University of Chicago Press, 1969), pp. 163–166; Wilfrid Blunt, *Secret History of the English Occupation of Egypt* (London: Fisher Unwin, 1907), pp. 253–254.

[67] Clarence-Smith, "Islamic Abolitionism in the Western Indian Ocean from c. 1800", p. 86; Ghazal, "Debating Slavery in the Arab Middle East: Abolition between Muslim Reformers and Conservatives", pp. 139–154; Mazheruddin Siddiqi, *Modernist Reformist Thought in the Muslim World* (Islamabad: Islamic Research Institute, 1982), p. 182; A. Chris Eccel, *Egypt, Islam and Social Change: Al-Azhar in Conflict and Accommodation* (Berlin: Klaus Schwarz, 1982), pp. 416–417; M. A. Zaki Badawi, *The Reformers of Egypt* (London: Croom Helm, 1978), p. 114.

[68] Ray W. Beachey, *A Collection of Documents on the Slave Trade of Eastern Africa* (London: Rex Collings, 1976), p. 33.

[69] Judith E. Tucker, *Women in Nineteenth-Century Egypt* (Cambridge: Cambridge University Press, 1985), pp. 177–178, 187–188; Baer, "Slavery and Its Abolition", pp. 183–185.

[70] Erdem, *Slavery in the Ottoman Empire*, pp. 89–90.

[71] Abolition, in the strict juridical sense, did actually not occur in Egypt until the adoption of the Egyptian Constitution of 1923, see Lord Cromer, *Modern Egypt* (New York: Macmillan, 1908), 2:503; Article 4, Constitution of Egypt (Royal Rescript No. 42 of April 30, 1923), in Amos J. Peaslee, *Constitutions of Nations* (Rumford: Concord, N. H; 1950), 1:722; Gabriel Baer, "Social Change in Egypt, 1800–1914" in *Political and Social Change in Modern Egypt: Historical Studies from the Ottoman Conquest to the United Arab Republic*, ed. P. M. Holt (London: Oxford University Press, 1968), pp. 187–189.

much controversy for most of the ulama,[72] although the traditionalists maintained that no law could forbid what the Quran permitted.[73] A trial in 1894, where several high-ranking Egyptians were prosecuted for buying slaves, revealed considerable support for the action, although selling slaves was not encouraged in the same way.[74] Hasan al-Banna, the founder of the Muslim Brotherhood, stated that "Islam replaced the historical sentence for a captive from capital punishment (death) to life imprisonment through enslavement. However, Islam has made it very easy for the slaves to regain their freedom".[75] Consequently, other members of the Muslim Brotherhood offered similar comments regarding the matter.[76]

2.3.2   India

In India, the East India Company asked the muftis for a fatwa on slavery in 1808. The fatwa declared that only "infidels fighting against the faith" were legitimate to enslave and that their descendants inherited the status of being a slave, and were transferable by sale, gift or inheritance. The sale of oneself or children was rejected by the muftis, although it was at that time a relatively common practice in India at times of famine or for debt.[77] By 1830, the civil court in Calcutta used the fatwa, instead of the Hidaya code, which was a commentary on the law from the twelfth-century, adding that it was compulsory for the owners to substantiate slave status.[78] The fatwa was confirmed by the muftis of the Madras court in 1841, three years before the colonial government implemented the abolition of slavery in directly ruled British India.[79] Reactions from conservative Muslims followed, where one fatwa justified slavery and another declared the conflict with the British to be a holy war.[80] The

---

72   Baer, *Slavery and Its Abolition*, p. 188. See also Demetrius A. Zambaco, *Les eunuques d'aujourd'hui et ceux de jadis* (Paris: Masson, 1911), pp. 36–38.
73   Eccel, *Egypt, Islam and Social Change*, p. 417.
74   Eve M. Troutt Powell, *A Different Shade of Colonialism: Egypt, Great Britain and the Mastery of the Sudan* (Berkeley: University of California Press, 2003), pp. 147, 150–155.
75   Hasan al-Banna, "Peace in Islam" (1948), available at: https://www.scribd.com/document/97406376/Peace-in-Islam-Hassan-Al-Banna (accessed 3 October 2019).
76   Sayyid Qutb, *Social Justice in Islam*, trans. John B. Hardie (New York: Octagon, 1970), pp. 44, 47–49, 112–113, 136, 156–159, 214.
77   Amal K. Chattopadhyay, *Slavery in the Bengal Presidency, 1772–1843* (London: Golden Eagle, 1977), pp. 158, 170–177.
78   Dady R. Banaji, *Slavery in British India* (Bombay: Taraporevala Sons, 1933), p. 43.
79   Indrani Chatterjee, *Gender, Slavery and Law in Colonial India* (New Delhi: Oxford University Press, 1999), p. 213.
80   Avril Powell, "Indian Muslim Modernists and the Issues of Slavery in Islam", in *Slavery and South Asian History*, ed. Indrani Chatterje and Richard Eaton (Bloomington: Indiana University Press, 2006), pp. 271–272.

defeat of those engaged in a holy war for slavery became an opportunity for modernist Muslim intellectuals to oppose slavery.

In 1873, Sayyid Amir 'Ali, a Shia Muslim, declared that Muslims "should try to efface that dark page from their history ... by proclaiming in explicit terms that slavery is reprobated by their faith and discountenanced by their code".[81] Amir 'Ali argued that, while the Quran did not abolish slavery, it disapproved of the institution and instead improved the status and treatment of slaves, as abolishing the institution would cause people to turn against Islam. Amir 'Ali argued that the Prophet trusted that slavery would die out and hoped that "a synod of Moslem doctors will authoritatively declare that polygamy, like slavery, is abhorrent to the laws of Islam".[82] Sunni Muslim Sayyid Ahmad Khan went further, stating that slavery was contrary to the will of God and should have disappeared from the beginning of Islamic history. He cited verses in the Quran, arguing that enslavement was forbidden and only ransom or immediate release of war captives was permissible.[83] Khan maintained that these verses could not be abrogated by verses revealed later.[84] At the same time, traditionalists kept defending the institution of slavery,[85] stressing the need to observe traditional rules on slavery,[86] arguing that the Prophet only ordered an improvement of the status of slaves, not the abolition of slavery.[87] Their argument was that if slavery were to be abolished, it would "deny future generations the opportunity to commit the virtuous deed of freeing slaves".[88]

---

81   Amir 'Ali, *A Critical Examination of the Life and Teachings of Mohammad*, later reprinted under the title *The Spirit of Islam* (London: W. H. Allen, 1891), pp. 330–331.
82   'Ali, *The Spirit of Islam*, pp. 360–388.
83   Quran 47:4–5.
84   Powell, "Indian Muslim Modernists", pp. 269–274; Ahmad Khan Bahador, *Life of Mohammed and Subjects Subsidiary Thereto* (Lahore: Sh. Mubarak Ali, 1870), pp. 422–427; M. S. Baljon, *The Reforms of Religious Ideas of Sir Ahmad Khan* (Lahore: Sh. Muhammad Ashraf, 1970), pp. 43–44, 143; Bashir A. Dar, *Religious Thought of Sayyid Ahmad Khan* (Lahore: Dr. Khalifa Abdul Hakim, 1957), pp. 236–239; 258–260; Shan Muhammad, *Sir Syed Ahmad Khan, A Political Biography* (Meerut: Meenakshi Prakashan, 1969), pp 214–217.
85   Barbara D. Metcalf, *Islamic Revival in British India: Deoband, 1860–1900* (Princeton: Princeton University Press, 1982), pp. 268–69, 278–280.
86   Achille Sékaly, *Le congrès du khalifat (Le Claie 13–19 mai 1926) et le congrès du monde musulman (La Mekka 7 juin–5 juillet 1926)* (Paris: Leroux, 1926), p. 201.
87   Aziz Ahmad, *Islamic Modernism in India and Pakistan, 1857–1964* (London: Oxford University Press, 1967), pp. 254–255; M. Mujeb, *The Indian Muslims* (London: Allen and Unwin, 1967), p. 450.
88   Jamal J. Elias, *Islam* (London: Routledge, 1999), p. 108.

2.3.3 Persia

In Persia, formal legislation had little impact, as those engaging in the slave trade believed that it was religiously lawful. The ulama was divided, some relying on a hadith where the prophet declared that "the seller of men are the worst of men" to oppose the practice,[89] while others maintained that it was permissible for infidels taken in war to become slaves.[90] Slavery was abolished in Persia's constitution of 1907,[91] and later affirmed by a fatwa from Sufi leader Ni'matullahi 'Ali Shah in 1912. The fatwa confirmed that "the purchase and sale of human beings is contrary to the dictates of religion and the practice of civilization; and therefore in our eyes any persons, men or women alike, who are claimed as slaves, are in legal fact completely free, and the equals of all other Muslims of their community".[92]

Nevertheless, the question of the legality of slavery in Islamic law continued. In 1970, the grandson of 'Ali Shah, Sultanhussein Tabandeh, questioned the validity of his grandfather's fatwa and upheld the view that anybody "taken prisoner fighting against Islam to its extirpation, and [who] persisted in his sacrilegious and infidel convictions" would be a slave. He further concluded that anyone for whom there was "legal proof that all his ancestors without expectation had been slaves descended from a person taken as a prisoner" was still a slave.[93] Ali Shari'ati, ideologue of the Iranian revolution, criticized slavery, asserting that true Islam would overthrow this "evil of class society" which he regarded slavery to be.[94] Sayyid Mahmud Taleqani, condemned enslavement even if it occurred during jihad. He argued that reducing fellow Muslims to slavery was a Sunni abuse and that modern Muslims should reject the institution.[95]

89　Quote taken from Clarence-Smith, "Islamic Abolitionism in the Western Indian Ocean from c. 1800", p. 88.

90　John B. Kelly, *Britain and the Persian Gulf, 1795–1880* (Oxford: Clarendon Press, 1968), pp. 495, 594–604; Behnaz A. Mirzai, "The 1848 Abolitionist Farman: A Step Towards Ending the Slave Trade in Iran", in *Abolition and Its Aftermath in Indian Ocean, Africa and Asia*, ed. Gwyn Campbell (London: Routledge, 2005), pp. 94–102.

91　For the laws, see Eugène Aubin, *La Perse d'aujourd'hui Iran, Mesopotamie* (Paris: Librairie Armand Collin, 1908), pp. 210–212; Vanessa Martin, *The Qajar Pact: Bargaining, Protest and the State in Nineteenth Century Persia* (London: Tauris, 2005), pp. 160–164.

92　Quote taken from William Gervase Clarence-Smith, "Islamic Abolitionism in the Western Indian Ocean from c. 1800", p. 89.

93　Sultanhussein Tabandeh, *A Muslim Commentary on the Universal Declaration of Human Rights* (London: Goulding, 1979), pp. vii–viii, 27.

94　Ali Shari'ati, *On the Sociology of Islam* (Berkeley: Mizan, 1979), pp. 103–109.

95　Seyyed Mahmoud Taleqani, *Islam and Ownership* (Lexington: Mazda, 1983), pp. xii–xiii, 186–200.

2.4 Is There an Ijma on Slavery?

It is hard to pinpoint exactly when the majority of Muslims accepted the abolition of slavery as religiously legitimate, as "Muslims from previous generations reached the awareness that slavery is immoral and unlawful, as a matter of conscience".[96] Most likely, it was during the 1960s that an Islamic religious consensus against slavery became dominant.[97]

> The *ijma'* that would articulate the abolition of slavery is probably an *ijma'* that would take into account the views of the community as a whole and not just the view of the *mujtahidun*. This kind of *ijma'* is one that was contemplated by Imam Shafi'i and recently confirmed as viable in the writing of scholars like Wael Hallaq. All of these views make it clear that the Islamic doctrine of consensus or *ijma'*, in the hands of the modern-day 'ulema', could effectively authorize an Islamic declaration that slavery is now forbidden by the *Shari'a*.[98]

Only a minority of conservative Muslims dispute this consensus.[99] As previously described, while the scope and operation of ijma is difficult to define, ijma can be definite and binding when there is clear textual support; whereas it is seen speculative when it addresses an issue for which there is no clear or ambiguous textual support. Technically, ijma is only considered binding when it does not contradict the primary sources.[100] In the case of slavery, it is argued that there is consensus on its abolition, although the primary sources do not provide clear support for that perspective.

Although Islam is often regarded as a doctrine which rigorously demands governments to adapt to a religious and legal ideology, slavery is probably the best example of exceptions to such demands. Although conservative clerics objected, many Muslim jurists acknowledged that the abolition of the

---

96 El Fadl, *Speaking in God's Name: Islamic Law, Authority, and Women*, p. 269.
97 Clarence-Smith, "Islamic Abolitionism in the Western Indian Ocean from c. 1800", p. 92.
98 Bernard K. Freamon, "Slavery, Freedom, and the Doctrine of Consensus in Islamic Jurisprudence", *Harvard Human Rights Journal* Vol. 11 (1998), pp. 63–64. Freamon also contests much of the existing historiography on the abolition of slavery as largely inspired by outside European efforts. He argues that specifically Islamic arguments to abolish slavery emerged in the latter half of the nineteenth and early twentieth centuries, see pp. 56–63.
99 Clarence-Smith, *Islam and the Abolition of Slavery*, pp. 219–221.
100 Musa Usman Abubakar, *Gender Justice in Islamic Law: Homicide and Bodily Injuries* (Oxford: Hart Publishing, 2018), pp. 17–19.

institution was in the best interest of their community,[101] stressing the Islamic principle of maslahah.[102] The concept of tawhid also offered a jurisprudential foundation for affirming the abolition of slavery—mostly for Shia jurists such as Muhammad Baqir al-Sadr, a powerful Iraqi jurist, and Ayatollah Murtaza Mutahhari, an Iranian disciple of Ayatollah Khomeini. Baqir al-Sadr claimed that "man's submission to God in Islam ... is the toll whereby man breaks all other chains of submission or slavery ... Therefore no power on earth has the right to fare with his destiny".[103] Mutahhari maintained that the Quran only recognized the authority of God over a human being, not a human being over another as the verse proclaims "we serve none but God, and that we associate not aught with Him".[104] Submission to any other being than God would constitute *shirk* (association of other beings or things with Allah) and would be destructive to one's freedom. According to Mutahhari, true freedom in the Islamic sense, cannot include slavery.[105]

Now, considering that whole parts of the Quran are argued by the ulama not to be the true intention of God, and accepted by Muslims out of moral convictions, why should verse 4:34 have a special status to justify the legal basis for male-female relationships?

3   Does the Principle of Justice Include Female Autonomy?

There can be no interpretation of the verses about women in general—and more specifically on the guardianship of women—without considering justice and the Islamic concept of it. While it is true that justice is a relative concept, which may vary depending on circumstances, nevertheless, for a claim to be

---

101 Freaman argues that the evolution of Muslim jurists on slavery is similar to American jurists' reasoning regarding the decision in *Dred Scott v. Sandford*, 60 U. S. 393 (1857). The decision held that Congress did not have the right to deprive the property of slave owners, even if that property, the slave, would travel to a free territory. Also, descendants of African slaves could never be citizens of the United States. See "ISIS, Boko Haram, and the Human Right to Freedom from Slavery under Islamic Law", p. 290, n. 129. Mark A. Graber argued, that the decision was right at that time and it is only because of the development of American law that slavery came to be intolerable. See *Dred Scott and the Problem of Constitutional Evil* (Cambridge: Cambridge University Press, 2006), pp. 8–14.
102 See Kamali, *Principles of Islamic Jurisprudence*, pp. 351–168.
103 Kamali, *Freedom, Equality and Justice in Islam*, p. 10, n. 39, citing Muhammad Baqir al-Sadr, *Contemporary Man and the Social Problem* (Tehran: Yasin T. A. al-Jibouri, 1980), p. 141.
104 Quran 3:64.
105 Kamali, *Freedom, Equality and Justice in Islam*, p. 10, n. 39, citing Ayatullah Murtaza Mutahhari, *Spiritual Discourses* (Alauddin Pazargardy, 1986), p. 28.

just and valid, "it must be relevant to an established public order under which a certain scale of justice is acknowledged".[106]

> "Islam is not opposed to equal rights for men and women, but it is opposed to identical rights ... Since men and women are different by nature, then different rights for them are not only more concordant with both justice and natural rights but provide more happiness in the family and progress in society. Justice and the natural and human rights of men and women require a certain disparity in rights ... Any innate aptitude is in itself the basis of, and evidence for, a natural right."[107]

Gender equality has generally not been relevant to Islamic notions of justice, as equality between men and women is a modern ideal. As such, it is an issue Muslim scholars have not needed to address, that is, until the last century. The contemporary ideals of human rights which uphold gender equality and personal autonomy is not surprisingly in contrast to the Islamic legal discourses that sanction discrimination based on gender. However, a growing number of scholars and jurists maintain that gender equality is a basic principle upheld by Islam and that "there is an acute need to work for greater gender equality before the law."[108] They argue that gender hierarchy was tolerated until the necessary conditions in society allowed for complete justice and fairness, which is the essential aim of Islam.[109]

3.1　The Concept of Justice

The Quran's primary concern is with values and objectives, such as justice, mercy, compassion, the promotion of good and the prevention of evil and helping the poor and the needy,[110] that are rooted in tawhid, oneness of God. The relationship between believers is based and defined on a scale of justice, where principles such as freedom, equality, brotherhood and tolerance are included. While justice is described many times as being of moral character, it also includes social values as several verses describe and encourage greater

---

106　Majid Khadduri, *The Islamic Concept of Justice* (Baltimore: The John Hopkins University Press, 1984), p. 1.
107　Morteza Motahhari, *Nezam-e Huquq-e Zan dar Islam* (Tehran: Sadra, 1990), pp. 144, 155 and 180.
108　Mir-Hosseini, Vogt, Larsen and Moe, "Introduction: Muslim Family Law and the Question of Equality", pp. 1–2, 4.
109　Husni and Newman, *Muslim Women in Law and Society,* p. 48.
110　Mohammad Hashim Kamali, "Issues in the Legal Theory of Usul and Prospects for Reform", *Islamic Studies* Vol. 40 (2001), p. 13.

social and economic justice, such as *al-Zakah*, a charge to purify wealth, for the welfare of the poor.[111] Another example is *Awqaf*, an institution that endows schools, hospitals, travelers, and the poor.[112]

Despite the many references to justice in the Quran—how to measure justice, or distinguish just acts from unjust acts— is not found in the Quran or the traditions of the Prophet. Scholars had difficulty describing the abstract concept of justice as a practical tool for the Islamic community. Jurists came instead to focus on what is permissible, *halal*, and what is prohibited, *haram*, to determine the underlying principles governing the difference between just and unjust acts.[113] Additionally, two subsidiary terms were developed to define justice as a concept; *al nasf*, meaning dividing something into equal portions, and *al wasat*, meaning middle course.[114] Basically, whatever is developed, should be developed with a sense of fairness, a middle ground.[115] It is from these principles that maqasid al-shariah, the ultimate goal of Islamic law is determined.[116]

While Ibn Qayyim al-Jawziyya accepted slavery and argued that wives should be viewed the same way as slaves, he upholds the ideals of justice in the following manner:

> The fundamentals of the Shariʻa are rooted in wisdom and promotion of welfare of human beings in this life and the Hereafter. Shariʻa embraces Justice, Kindness, the Common Good and Wisdom. Any rule that departs from justice to injustice, from kindness to harshness, from the common good to harm, or from rationality to absurdity cannot be part of Shariʻa.[117]

Abu Nasr Al-Farabi (d. 950) held that justice meant that goods in society had to be distributed, and protective laws should ensure that everyone could enjoy their share:

---

111 Rahman, "Islam's Origins and Ideas", p. 15.
112 The lasting example is a huge hospital built in the twelfth century in Cairo, still treating the blind today. The hospital's policy declares: "in this hospital patients shall be treated – locals and foreigners; men and women irrespective of race, religion, and color; old and young. Everyone will be treated". See Rahman, "Islam's Origins and Ideas", pp. 15–16.
113 Khadduri, *The Islamic Concept of Justice*, p. 136.
114 Quran 2:143.
115 See Mahmoud Ayoub, "The Islamic Concept of Justice", in *Islamic Identity and the Struggle for Justice*, eds. Nimat Hafez Barazangi, M. Raquibuz Zaman and Omar Afzal (Gainseville: University Press of Florida, 1996), p. 20.
116 Khadduri, *The Islamic Concept of Justice*, p. 137.
117 Quote taken from Rapoport, *Marriage, Money and Divorce in Medieval Islamic Society*, p. 52.

Justice, initially, is in [demarcating] the portion of the shared goods that are for all in the city. Thereafter, [justice] has to do with preserving the distribution among them. Those goods consist of security, property, dignity, rank, and all the goods that are possible for all to share in. Each person among the people of the city has an equal share of these goods *based on his worth*. To diminish or exceed his portion is unjust. Any diminishment is unjust toward the individual. Any increase is unjust to the people of the city. Perhaps any diminishment is also unjust to the people of the city.[118]

This notion is very close to Aristotle's notion of "distributive justice".[119] Much like the Athenian concept of democracy, which only included adult male citizens,[120] the same restrictive and contradictory stance can be seen in Islamic law. What the traditional Muslim jurists are essentially saying is that equal persons must be treated equal. Equality, however, does not mean that everyone is treated the same; only those in the same category are to be treated equally. The categories are based on abilities. So, various groups in society have rights in proportion to their abilities.[121] Thus, women (as well as slaves) came to be exempted from the principle of justice, or rather, it was considered that women are to be treated equally within their category, which is not the same or equal to the category in which men fall into. Consequently, any real concept of justice, kindness and the common good, were attributed only to adult Muslim men.

3.2 An Unjust God?

Traditional Muslim thinkers assumed that all or most laws legislated in early Islam were fixed and eternal. If this were so, then these laws should still be producing justice and ethics that are superior to other methods, and contemporary human wisdom would not reject them. But this is not the case. This is strong evidence that these laws are not of the fixed kind.

---

118 Abu Nasr Al-Farabi, *Fusul Muntaza'a*, ed. Fawzi Najjar (Beirut: Dar al-Mashraq, 1971), p. 71.
119 Aristotle wrote "since an unjust man is one who is unfair, and the unjust is the unequal, it is clear that corresponding to the unequal there is a mean, namely which is equal; for every action admitting of more and less admits of the equal also. If then the unjust is the unequal, the just is the equal – a view that commends itself to all without proof." See *The Nicomachean Ethics*, trans. Harris Rackham (Hertfordshire: Wordsworth, 1971), p. 118.
120 For an overview of Athenian democracy, see A. H. M., Jones, *Athenian Democracy* (New York: Praeger, 1958).
121 Kadivar, Revisiting Women's Rights in Islam, p. 222.

A fixed and immutable ruling is always just, ethical, superior and reasonable. However, men's privilege and qiwama over women, corporal punishment of a disobedient wife, permitting the marriage of an underage girl, men's right to unilateral divorce, two women's testimony being equal to one man's, a woman's blood money being equal to half of a man's, a son's inheritance being twice that of a daughter, men's obligation to pay maintenance and dower – these rulings are debatable.[122]

The principle of justice takes on different shapes in the Quran and although the term is not specific,[123] it is regarded as perfect, universal and valid for eternity,[124] ingrained in the concept of tawhid. Tawhid rests in the premise that the greatest injustice one can do to oneself is to deny God, whilst at the same time, tawhid protects against humanity's own excesses, which is considered to be injustice or oppression, *zulm*.[125] In its ideal form, Islamic justice is an

---

122   Ibid., 227.
123   The standards of justice that were provided for by jurists indicated the right (and wrong) path for believers, and came to be associated with the just person, characterized by *'adl*. 'Adl means justice, equity or fair play, and can be found extensively in the Quran. See, for example, Quran 6:152. See also, Rahman, "Islam's Origins and Ideas", p. 15. A. John Simmons, argues that the Islamic legal thought on justice, where justice is fundamentally contextual—based on an economic context of individuals and networks of social relationships and obligations—seems to be in discord with the commands of the Quran, where the hadd punishments are the sole measure of justice. Islamic legal thought came to discuss hadd and contextual justice as distinct categories of law. "Justice in relation to hadd punishments is rather seen as something fixed and invariable, invariable of any requirement of consulting the context of social relationships and obligations … what may seem odd about the hadd-type wrongs is the combination for the specific wrongs these comprise … On the one hand, these wrongs include adultery, defamation, treason, alcoholism, and theft, but not killing. On the other hand, the rationale for the hadd prescribed for each of these wrongs is that it intrudes on God's domain, which is taken to be a 'world of premonitory chaos.' The oddity, of course, lies in the fact that potential for causing social chaos attaches equally to many of the ta'zir-type wrongs. Consistency would seem to demand either that these wrongs also be treated as matters for objective, non-contextual justice or that God's reasons for the hadd be accepted as inscrutable". See "Fault, Objectivity, and Classical Islamic Justice", in *Perspectives on Islamic Law, Justice, and Society*, ed. R. S. Khare (Lanham: Rowman & Littlefield Publishers, Inc., 1999), pp. 58–60.
124   See, for example, Quran 5:96 where 'adl means example or alike; 49:10 stipulates that "the believers are indeed brothers" which has been interpreted to provide the basis for equality in law of having equal rights; 2:137 and 8:11, in these verses the notion of the middle path is expressed as believers are called to be "a nation in the middle". See Khadduri, *The Islamic Concept of Justice*, pp. 6–7.
125   Alwani, "The Qur'anic model on Social Change", p. 53.

expression of the *jus divinum*,[126] with the underlying assumption that "God never does zulm to anyone"; in other words, God cannot oppress.[127] The Quran repeatedly assures its believers that God cannot be unjust and that the believers who act according to the divine path, with the right intentions, will be rewarded in the hereafter. As God only provides the basis for the good acts, believers are responsible for their actions, be they good or bad. As such, all obligatory acts were considered to be just, since God would not demand any unjust actions from his believers.[128]

Although zulm is often interpreted as oppression, "the primary meaning of Z[U]LM is, in the opinion of many of the authoritative lexicographers, that of 'putting in a wrong place.' In the sphere of ethics, it seems to primarily mean 'to act in such a way as to transgress the proper limit and encroach upon the right of some other person.' Briefly and generally, zulm, is to do injustice in the sense of going beyond one's bounds and doing what one has no right to do".[129] As such, zulm goes beyond merely oppression and is related to the notion of sharing; "zulm is to get a bigger share than your fellow human being, which creates opacity, darkness, and confusion".[130]

Now, if the Quran suggests that the main objective of the scripture is the establishment and maintenance of justice but does not provide a specific definition of the term, one must understand the term as relative to time and space. While it might be difficult to pinpoint what zulm constitutes, the verses on slavery show that one cannot assume that God, in its teachings, is not upholding zulm, even though at the same time it can be argued that God never does zulm to anybody. This rather demonstrates that the Quran is a direct response to the times in which it was revealed. The verses on slavery constitute a mere reflection of the times and not universal standards to be implemented at all times. The same can be said of the notion of justice in the form of retaliation and the payment of blood-money which was constructed as a consequence of being under attack.[131] Thus, justice in the Islamic tradition needs to be separated between the norms of justice that the Prophet established as a Prophet, and the decrees that were issued as a reaction to the norms and conditions of the society in which he lived in. The latter was a method to cope

---

126 Khadduri, *The Islamic Concept of Justice*, p. 192.
127 Ayoub, "The Islamic Concept of Justice", p. 21.
128 Quran 8:53.
129 Toshihiko Izutsu, *Ethico-Religious Concepts in the Qur'an* (Montreal: McGill University Press, 1966), pp. 164–165.
130 Ayoub, "The Islamic Concept of Justice", p. 22.
131 Khadduri, *The Islamic Concept of Justice*, p. 9.

with the circumstances of that time to achieve justice. In a sense, the Islamic tradition needs a separation of religion from the state—but not equivalent to the history of the Church in the West. Separation of powers in the Islamic sense would instead mean a separation of the interpretations of Islamic law founded on norms based on a political state that no longer exists, in order to revise sources of law for interpretations that are feasible for the standards of societies today.

> While the principles and maxims of justice, as derived from the textual sources of law, were seen as infallible and designed for all time, the public order, composed of the Law as well as state acts and the rulings and opinions of the scholars on all matters arrived at through human reasoning, are by necessity subject to adaptation and refinement to meet changing conditions and the growing needs of the community.[132]

Essentially, there can be no justice in a modern legal system that does not see all its subjects as equals. There can be no divine or higher justice if women are treated less than the ethical norms upheld in the Quran. Values such as human dignity, fairness, and justice, as laid down in the Quran, need to be the basis for any laws affecting women.

4   Political Reform

Throughout the 1950s–1970s, scholars argued that Islam would play no role in the social, political and cultural development of the countries in the Middle East. The process of economic and social development would eliminate traditional social, political and cultural structures and would lead to the secularization of society, and consequently, religion would play a lesser role in society.[133] Against expectations, religion has not diminished from society.[134] Since the 1960s, the Muslim world especially, has witnessed religion re-emerging as a powerful socio-political force. With more constitutions in

---

132   Ibid., 3.
133   See, for example, Walter Z. Laquer, *The Middle East in Transition* (New York: Praeger, 1958); Daniel Lerner, *The Passing of Traditional Society: Modernizing the Middle East* (Glencoe: Free Press, 1958) and Hunter, *Reformist Voices of Islam,* pp. 16–17.
134   See generally, Peter Berger, *The Desecularization of the World* (Grand Rapids, Michigan: William B. Eerdmans Publishing Company, 1999), and Gilles Kepel, *The Revenge of God* (Pennsylvania: Penn State University Press, 1994).

the Muslim world including clauses requiring national laws to be compatible with Sharia,[135] this direction is completely the opposite of what occurred with the role of Islamic law at the beginning of the twentieth century. By the time of the First World War, as the pessimistic view against the fuqaha had grown,[136] no major Muslim country had a clause in their constitution requiring state law to be compatible with Sharia.[137] This disappearance was, however, only temporary, as pressure from various traditional Muslim groups led many Muslim states to include the requirement of Sharia compliance in their constitutions.[138] Essentially, what this means, is that even if a law is constitutionally enacted correctly, the law must be treated as void if it is not in adherence with Sharia.[139]

This modern legal codification of Islamic law in Muslim states challenged the way in which Islamic law was traditionally interpreted and applied. Notably during the last century, nation-states have obtained a greater role in how Islam is to be constructed and integrated within the state. The codification of Islamic law deprived Muslims jurists of their authority in the law-finding process and transferred it to secular administrations.[140] The fall of the Ottoman Empire after World War I, and the establishment of nation-states in Muslim countries, where the adopted legal codes were either based on Western law or to a great extent inspired by Western law, was a contributing factor leading to the continual marginalization of Islamic law. At the same time, there has been a call for democratization, which has led a number of Muslim states, even before

---

135   Said Amir Arjomand, Introduction, in *Constitutional Politics in the Middle East: With Special Reference to Turkey, Iraq, Iran and Afghanistan*, ed. Said Amir Arjomand (Oxford: Hart Publishing, 2008).
136   In some pre-modern states, the ruler institutionalized a process of consultation with the fuqaha, to legitimize their rule, where opposition from the fuqaha could affect a ruler's legitimacy, see Carl L. Brown, *Religion and State: the Muslim Approach to Politics* (New York: Columbia University Press, 2000), p. 37. The Ottomans, for example, justified their reforms in part by cooperating with the fuqaha, see Clark Lombardi, *State Law as Islamic Law in Modern Egypt: The Incorporation of the Shari'a into Egyptian Constitutional Law* (Leiden: Brill, 2006), pp. 57–58.
137   Nathan Brown, *Constitutions in a Nonconstitutional World: Arab Basic Laws and the Prospects for Accountable Government* (New York: State University of New York Press, 2001), pp. 91–94.
138   Clark Lombardi, "Constitutional Provisions Making Sharia "a" or "the" Chief Source of Legislation: Where Did They Come from? What Do they Mean? Do They Matter?", *American University International Law Review* Vol. 28, No. 733 (2013).
139   Clark Lombardi, "Designing Islamic constitutions: Past trends and options for a democratic future", *International Journal of Constitutional Law* Vol. 11, No. 3 (2013), p. 613.
140   Aharon Lawish, "The Transformation of the *Shari'a* from Jurists' Law to Statutory Law in the Contemporary Muslim World", *Die Welt des Islams* Vol. 44 (2004), pp. 85–113.

the Arab spring events, to draft constitutions that require the state to respect principles of liberal democracies and the inherent principles of Sharia.[141] The process is ongoing and the outcome is uncertain, but the strong trend is that Muslim polities are demanding a more participatory form of politics. In turn, the question for the state has been what interpretation of the sSharia it must abide to—and which one will be accepted by different Muslim groups. Interestingly, the modern era shows that qualifying credentials of interpretations are not enough for the public to accept the interpretation. The Guardian Council in Iran have repeatedly failed to deliver widely accepted opinions. Instead, interpretations of less qualified interpreters from an Islamic law perspective, made by the Supreme Constitutional Court in Egypt, seem to have been respected by the majority, at times.[142]

This book has described how a majority of Muslim reformers are focusing on the potential reinterpretation (through various methods) can have on the advancement of the legal status of women, however, few recourse to the rules of *siyasa*, the positive law of the state, promulgated by those in power.[143] Can states pave the way for legal reforms of Islamic law?

4.1   *State Law*

The common perception is that only rules of fiqh are considered truly Islamic, whereas the positive law of the state, that is, the rules derived from siyasa, are considered secular.[144] However, we do know that Muslims adopted many non-Islamic laws and "Islamized" them in the first one hundred and fifty years of Islamic history.[145] Muslim scholars also referred to positive law, *qanun*, as necessary for political and moral reform of Islamic law.[146] In this respect, it is relevant to describe how the legitimacy of the caliph, became a question of justice, which influenced the construction of new laws within the Islamic legal tradition.

---

141   Ran Hirschl, *Constitutional Theocracy* (Cambridge: Harvard University Press, 2011), p. 13.
142   Lombardi, "Designing Islamic constitutions", pp. 637, 641.
143   Mohammad Fadel describes the relationship between Islamic law and the Muslim state in "State and *Sharī'a*" in *The Ashgate Research Companion to Islamic Law*, ed. Peri Bearman and Rudolph Peters (Surrey: Ashgate, 2014), pp. 29–42.
144   Fadel, *Islamic Law Reform: Between Reinterpretation and Democracy*, p. 46.
145   Joseph Schacht, "Problems of Modern Islamic Legislation", *Studia Islamica* Vol. 12 (1960), pp. 99–129.
146   For an overview of scholars' views on political reform by positive law, see Mohammad Fadel, "Modernist Islamic Political Thought and the Egyptian and Tunisian Revolutions of 2011", *Middle East Law and Governance* Vol. 3 (2011), pp. 94–104.

The egalitarian theological assumptions of Sunnism posed a problem for political ordering. If all persons were morally equal (or substantially so) insofar as each of them was in principle capable of understanding God's law, and each of them would be individually accountable to God for his or her adherence to divine teachings, and none of them could claim a special knowledge of that law that was inaccessible to anyone else, religious doctrine could not provide an obvious answer to the question of who should assume the mantle of political leadership.[147]

The debate on justice in Islam began with the debate on the legitimacy of the caliphate, since the Prophet died without providing rules on succession. It was taken for granted that political justice was an expression of God's will through the words and actions of the Prophet. It was only after his death that questions arose whether a successor's actions should also be considered as being part of God's will. It was assumed that if the successor lacked in legitimacy, his decisions would be based on their own will, and would be unjust.[148] It is also linked to the fact that the Quran declares that no one can interpret the words of God, thus acknowledging that no interpretation is better than the other, implying the equality of all believers. Nevertheless, the Islamic political theory of the leader, the caliph, came to provide an exception to this notion. The question of how to rule, given the assumption that no one could exercise power over the another, laid the ground for a theory of political power in Islam, based on the principle of representation through agency, that is, the belief that the caliph is the ideal public agent, wakil, acting on behalf of the community. The same ideals were also applied to public officials, who, through a delegation of power from the caliph, were authorized to act on behalf of the caliph. This agency principle, which is central in the concept of Sunni public law, renders the agent's acts as binding on the community, as long as the acts don't contravene the Sharia, validating the exercise of authorized actions of the agent, and not only by virtue of acts based on interpretation from an agent who is a mujtahid.[149] Sunni scholars between the eleventh and fourteenth centuries began to argue that the ruler should have considerable discretion to impose a statute body of law, even if such statute would restrict Muslims from following their preferred version of Islamic law, even though it is considered to be a fundamental principle of Islamic law to allow Muslims the choice of which

---

147   Fadel, *Islamic Law Reform: Between Reinterpretation and Democracy*, pp. 51–52.
148   Majid Khadduri, *The Islamic Concept of Justice* (Baltimore: The John Hopkins University Press, 1984), p. 194.
149   Fadel, *Islamic Law Reform: Between Reinterpretation and Democracy*, pp. 48–67.

school of law to follow.¹⁵⁰ It was conditioned that, in order for the statute to be legitimate, it could never compel someone to act in a way that would violate the commands of the Quran, and, that the state could not harm the welfare, maslaha, of the public. Welfare in this aspect referred to the material benefits not implicitly disapproved of by the material sources.¹⁵¹ The Shia concept of leadership and authority is also based on the perception that God's justice includes being guided in implementing the divine words of the Quran.¹⁵²

More interestingly, are cases where the caliph established laws that did contravene well-established rules. Jurists from the Ottoman era, came to the conclusion that such commands could be morally binding as it was in the best interest of the community, despite not being acknowledged from the perspective of the jurist's law. The Sunni jurists essentially viewed the Muslim community as an entity entitled to rights, equivalent to a natural person. Public authority, *wilaya*, was understood by pre-nineteenth century Sunni law, to "include a special instance of the fiduciary duties of the general law of agency, *wikala*".¹⁵³ Essentially, commands from the caliph were valid and morally binding, when they entailed the administrative power of the public, as they were seen as an expression of the public will. In other words, the caliph issued commands based on the perceived public good of the community, without resorting to interpretations for his commands.

Many of the terms used to describe the authority of the caliph and the delegated authority of public officials, are also used when describing the authority men have over women, or fathers have over their children. The term "wilaya", which is also used to describe the authority granted to the guardian over the ward, is in this respect used to describe the jurisdiction of public officials.¹⁵⁴

> Regarding the difference between the actions of public officials which are given effect in the law and those which are not ... the first category [of actions that are invalid] are those actions which were not included in their original jurisdiction. You should know that whoever exercises authority over another, from the caliph down to the guardian of an

---

150   Frank Vogel, *Siyasa*, pt. III (In the Sense of Siyasa Shari'a), in 9 *Encyclopaedia of Islam* 695 (2d ed. 1997); Lombardi, *State Law as Islamic Law in Modern Egypt*, pp. 49–58; Erwin J. Rosenthal, *Political Thought in Medieval Islam* (Cambridge: Cambridge University Press, 1958), pp. 43–61.
151   Ibid. See also, Lombardi, "Designing Islamic constitutions", p. 618.
152   Ayoub, "The Islamic Concept of Justice", p. 21.
153   Fadel, *Islamic Law Reform: Between Reinterpretation and Democracy*, p. 49.
154   Fadel, *Islamic Law Reform: Between Reinterpretation and Democracy*, pp. 59, 80, 86.

orphan, is not authorized to act except to attain a good or to ward off a harm in accordance with God most High's statement "Do not approach the property of the orphan except in the fairest manner ..."[155] and because of the statement of the Prophet Muhammad, may God's peace and blessings be upon him, "Any person who is given authority over any of my community's affairs, and fails to exercise that authority in good faith for their benefit, is forbidden entry to Paradise." Accordingly, caliphs and governors have no jurisdiction to act except in accordance with the requirements of good faith judgment. Decisions that reduce well-being are never "in the fairest manner," but rather are their opposite. ... The authority conferred by virtue of holding public office therefore is limited to acts that produce either an absolute increase in well-being or a net gain in overall well-being, or to acts that prevent an absolute loss of well-being or prevent a net loss in overall well-being.[156]

The underlying premise is that in any case where authority is exercised by a public official, rationality is a requirement, either from the perspective of the specific person, where the judge is to act in the best interest of the person, and act according to the legal requirements that may be in place, as determined from the perspective of the public.[157] From this perspective, the positive law of the State, is not distinct from fiqh, instead it is "the result of the deliberations of an idealized agent acting to further the rational good of his principal, the Muslim community".[158] Essentially, rules that developed through practical reasoning—like rules developed through interpretation—were historically considered legitimate parts of Sharia, as "the principles of the Shari'a could not be made effective without their proper specification in accordance with the variable demands of time and place". In other words, rules provided by the views of the community, could potentially be just as Islamic as rules derived from interpretation. This means that the Sunni tradition has historically acknowledged "positive law as expressions of the public will that meet Islamic conditions of validity and not as interpretations of divine will."[159] Thus, according to Mohammad Fadel, effective reform of Islamic law is not a reinterpretative reform formulated by the mujtahids, but rather, a political one,

---

155 Quran 17:34.
156 Quote taken from Fadel, *Islamic Law Reform: Between Reinterpretation and Democracy*, pp. 70–71.
157 Ibid.
158 Ibid., 49.
159 Ibid., 47, 88.

through legitimate representative politics, where "substantive reforms which are rightly demanded could be accomplished in a morally compelling fashion if promulgated through the positive law of a properly constituted representative state,[160] without any need to advance implausible claims about the meaning of revelation".[161] Such states could even have the right to formulate morally binding positive law, which goes beyond the law developed by the jurists. Fadel concludes that "if the role of the government is to act as an agent for a properly constituted public will, legitimacy comes from adequately representing that public will, not from the law-finding skill of legislators through interpretation".[162] However, even if public will or opinion were considered authoritative, it does not necessarily mean that women's rights would improve. If popular opinion continues embracing a tradition of patriarchy, the advancement of women's rights in Islamic law will continue to face great hurdles.

[160] There is however an ongoing debate whether an Islamic constitution can be truly democratic. For a brief overview of this debate, see Lombardi, "Designing Islamic constitutions".
[161] Fadel, *Islamic Law Reform: Between Reinterpretation and Democracy*, p. 50.
[162] Ibid., 89.

CHAPTER 6

Concluding Remarks

How we deal with the status of women in Islamic law as outlined in the Quran, depends significantly on how we understand the Quran. For instance, one important question to consider is whether the Quran is descriptive, or prescriptive?[1] This book argues that it is both. What I have described in this book, is that what Sharia entails is very much a question of who is rightfully allowed to interpret the sources and decide on what Sharia requires. And this has been the case throughout Islamic history. The range of opinions show how interpretations are based on the subjective arguments of the jurists, that rely on accounts of behavior, semantics, methods of arguments, but also, what verses are selected as part of the interpretations, that are later considered to be Islamic law. The arbitrary use of hadiths also proves that we are not discussing divine law, but rather, what we are seeing is the construction of law, based on sociological concepts,[2] which are created by fallible human beings.

This book does not claim to offer the right interpretation of verse 4:34, nor does it want or even try to present and describe God's intended meaning of "men are the managers of the affairs of women". However, what *is* questioned, is the idea that the guardianship of women is an inseparable part of Islamic law. The fact is that the verse does not bring forward a prescribed penalty (that is, a penalty for men who do not assume the role as the managers of the affairs of women), and it does not fall within the category of what should be prohibited (nothing in the verse declares a prohibition against women managing their own affairs). More importantly, traditional scholarship neglects to consider that if both genders are created from the same essence, how can one be superior to the other?[3] While many of the laws that govern the legal status of individuals in Islamic law are formed from the idea of status-based rights; modern concepts of equality before the law and justice, rightfully undermine such status-based concepts. Today's society has brought forward various legal issues, which cannot be dealt with through adherence to explanations or understanding of historical interpretations made by jurists living in a society

---

1 See Hassan Yousefi Eshkevari, "Rethinking Men's Authority over Women: Qiwama, Wilaya and their Underlying Assumptions", in Mir-Hosseini, Vogt, Larsen and Moe, *Gender and Equality in Muslim Family Law*, p. 206.
2 Masud, "Gender Equality and the Doctrine of Wilaya", p. 134.
3 Kadivar, "Revisiting Women's Rights in Islam", p. 215.

with significantly different issues. Muslim women increasingly participate in different aspects of public life all over the world, but this is not reflected in the legal interpretations of the rights of women, as made by the schools of law. Essentially, it is not about denying "the moral integrity of the traditional interpretations ... rather, *we instead deny their moral relevance to us at this time*."[4]

The Islamic legal thoughts on justice—where justice is fundamentally contextual, based on an economic context of individuals and networks of social relationships and obligations—need to be replaced by a concept of justice that does not include economic interests. If equality before the law—which is a necessary outcome of the developmental changes occurring within the Islamic legal tradition—is to be achieved, it will require that women give up the specific rights they have been granted by traditional scholarship, such as mahr and maintenance during the marriage.[5] At the same time, evaluating the rules of inheritance, (as was done by Tunisia), and by examining the consequences that unequal shares of inheritance cause—which basically is receiving a bigger share than a fellow human being—clearly demonstrates the unfair outcome. The same applies to the guardianship of women. Essentially, any interpretation that reduces half its population to incompetence, or renders them incapable of making their own decisions, must be considered unjust in today's societies, even by Islamic standards. In the end, if the ulama refuse to agree upon changes of certain laws regarding women, such as, guardianship, polygyny, evidence, divorce and so forth, it is not because it contradicts the Quran and the Sunnah—it is because societies are still male-dominated and there is a resistance towards accepting change.[6]

---

4 Fadel, "Is Historicism a Viable Strategy for Islamic Legal Reform?", p. 44.
5 Mir-Hosseini, Vogt, Larsen and Moe, "Introduction: Muslim Family Law and the Question of Equality", p. 3.
6 Engineer, *The Rights of Women in Islam*, p. 11.

Bibliography

Books

'Abd al-Mawjud, 'Adil, 4 Vols. (Beirut: Dar al-Kutub al-'Ilmiyya, 1998).

'Ali, Amir, *A Critical Examination of the Life and Teachings of Mohammad*, later reprinted under the title *The Spirit of Islam* (London: W. H. Allen, 1891).

'Asqalani, Al-Hafiz Ibn Hajar, *Bulugh al-Maram*, Vol. 1 (Riyadh: Dar al-Faraq, 2003).

Abbott, Nabia, *Aishah, the Beloved of Muhammad* (Chicago: University of Chicago, 1942).

Abd al-Rahman, 'Aysha, *al-Mafhum al-Islami li Tahrir al-Mar'a* (Cairo: Matba'at Mukhaymir, 1967).

Abduh, Muhammad, *al-Islam wa-al-Mar'ah fi Ra'y al-Imam Muhammad Abduh*, ed. Muhammad 'Imara (Cairo: n.d.).

Abou El-Fadl, Khaled, *A Search for Beauty in Islam: The Conference of the Books* (Lanham: University of America Press, 2001).

Abu Da'ud, *Sunan Abi Da'ud* (Riyadh: Dar al-Salam, 2000).

Abu Ḥayyan Muḥammad b. Yusuf, *Tafsir al-Baḥr al-Muḥit*, ed. 'Abd al-Razzaq Mahdi, 8 vols. (Beirut: Dar Ihya' al-Turath al-'Arabi, 2002).

Abu Ishaq al-Shirazi, *al-Muhadhdhab fi fiqh al-Imam al-Shafi'i*, ed. Muhammad al-Zuhayli, 6 vols. (Damascus: Dar al-Qalam; Beirut: al-Dar al-Shamiyya, 1992–1996).

Abu Ja'far Muhammad ibn Jarir al-Tabari, *Jami' al-Bayan 'am Ta'wil 'ay al-Qur'an*, ed. Mahmud M. Shakir and Ahmad M. Shakir, Vol. 8 (Cairo: Dar al-Ma'arif, 1972).

Abu Sulayman, Abdul Hamid A., *Islam: Source and Purpose of Knowledge* (Herndon, VA: The International Institute of Islamic Thought, 1988).

Abul Alla Maudoodi, Maulana, "Tahfimul Quran – *A translation and tafsir of the Quran in Urdu*", trans. by Mohammad Abdul Rahim (Dhaka: Kausar Publications, 1958).

Ahmad, Aziz, *Islamic Modernism in India and Pakistan, 1857–1964* (London: Oxford University Press, 1967).

Ahmed, Leila, *Women and Gender in Islam: The Historical Roots of a Modern Debate* (New Haven: Yale University Press, 1992).

Ahmed, Leila, *A Border Passage: From Cairo to America - A Woman's Journey* (New York: Penguin Books, 1999).

Ali, Abdul, *Insights into Islamic Humanism: A Comprehensive Approach* (New Delhi: MD Publications Pvt Ltd., 2007).

Ali, Kecia, *Sexual Ethics and Islam: Feminist Reflections on Qur'an, Hadith, and Jurisprudence* (Oxford: Oneworld, 2006).

Ali, Kecia, *Marriage and Slavery in Early Islam* (Cambridge: Harvard University Press, 2010).

Ali, Kecia, *The Lives of Muhammad* (London: Harvard University Press, 2014).

Ali, Khan L., and Hisham M. Ramadan, *Contemporary Ijtihad: Limits and Controversies* (Edinburgh: Edinburgh University Press, 2011).

Ali, Mir Ahmed, *The Holy Quran with English translation of the Arabic text and commentary according to the version of the Holy Ahlul-Bait* (New York: Tahrike Tarsile Quran, 1988).

Ali, Shaheen Sardar, *Gender and Human Rights in Islamic and International Law* (The Hague: Kluwer Law International, 2000).

Ali, Yusuf, *The Holy Quran – Text, translation and commentary*, 4th ed. (Lahore: Ahmadiyyah Anjuman Ishaat Islam, 1946).

Allain, Jean, ed., *The Legal Understanding of Slavery: From the Historical to the Contemporary* (Oxford: Oxford University Press, 2012).

al-Alwani, Taha, *Issues in Contemporary Islamic Thought* (London: International Institute of Islamic Thought, 2005).

Amin, Qasim, *The New Women: Document in the Early Debate on Egyptian Feminism* (Cairo: American University Press, 1996).

Amin, Qasim, *The Liberation of Women: and, The New Woman, Two Documents in the History of Egyptian Feminism* (Cairo: American University Press, 2000).

An-Naim, Abdullahi Ahmed, *Toward an Islamic Reformation* (Syracuse: Syracuse University Press, 1987).

Anderson, Norman, *Law Reform in the Muslim World* (London: Athlone, 1976).

al-Ansari, Zakariyya, *Asna al-matalib sharh Rawd al-talib*, ed. Muhammad Tamir, 9 Vols. (Beirut: Dar al-Kutub al-'Ilmiyya, 2001).

al-Aqad, Abbas Mahmud, *Fatma Al-Zahra' wa Al-Fatimiyyun*, 2nd ed. (Beirut: Dar Al-Kitab Al-Arabi, 1967).

Aristotle, *The Nicomachean Ethics*, trans. Harris Rackham (Hertfordshire: Wordsworth, 1971).

Arjomand, Said Amir, *Constitutional Politics in the Middle East: With Special Reference to Turkey, Iraq, Iran and Afghanistan* (Oxford: Hart Publishing, Oxford, 2008).

Arkoun, Mohammed, *Rethinking Islam: Common Questions, Uncommon Answers*, trans. Robert D. Lee Boulder (Colorado: Westview Press, 1994).

Armstrong, Karen, *The Gospel According to Women: Christianity's Creation of the Sex War in the West* (London: Tree Books, 1986).

el-Ashker, Ahmed, and Rodney Wilson, *Islamic Economics: A Short History* (Leiden: Brill, 2002).

Askari, Hossein, Zamir Iqbal, and Abbas Mirakhor, *Globalization and Islamic Finance: Convergence, Prospects and Challenges* (Singapore: John Wiley & Sons, 2010).

al-Ati, Hammudah Abt, *The Family Structure in Islam* (Indianapolis: American Trust Publications, 1977).

Aubin, Eugène, *La Perse d'aujourd'hui Iran, Mésopotamie* (Paris: Librairie Armand Collin, 1908).

Auda, Jasser, *Maqasid al-Shari'ah as Philosophy of Islamic Law: A Systems Approach* (London: The International Institute of Islamic Thought, 2008).

el-Awa, Mohammad Salim, *Punishment in Islamic Law: A Comparative Study* (Plainfield: American Trust Publication, 2000).

Baderin, Mashood A., *International Human Rights and Islamic Law* (Oxford: Oxford University Press, 2005).

Baer, Gabriel, ed., *Studies in the Social History of Modern Egypt* (Chicago: University of Chicago Press, 1969).

Bahador, Ahmad Khan, *Life of Mohammed and Subjects Subsidiary Thereto* (Lahore: Sh. Mubarak Ali, 1870).

Baljon, Johannes, M. S., *The Reforms of Religious Ideas of Sir Ahmad Khan* (Lahore: Sh. Muhammad Ashraf, 1970).

Banaji, Dady R., *Slavery in British India* (Bombay: Taraporevala Sons, 1933).

Barazangi, Nimat Hafez, M. Raquibuz Zaman, and Omar Afzal, eds., *Islamic Identity and the Struggle for Justice* (Gainseville: University Press of Florida, 1996).

Barazangi, Nimat Hafex, *Woman's Identity and Rethinking the Hadith* (Surrey: Ashgate Publishing Limited, 2015).

Barlas, Asma, *"Believing Women" in Islam: Unreading Patriarchal Interpretations of the Quran* (Austin: University of Texas Press, 2002).

Bauer, Karen A., *Room for Interpretation: Quranic Exegesis and Gender* (Ph.D. dissertation, Princeton University, 2008).

al-Bayhaqi, Abu Bakr, *al-Sunan al-kubra*, ed. Muhammad 'Atta, 11 vols. (Beirut: Dar al-Kutub al-Ilmiyya, 1999).

Beachey, Ray W., *A Collection of Documents on the Slave Trade of Eastern Africa* (London: Rex Collings, 1976).

Bearman, Peri, and Rudolph Peters, eds., *The Ashgate Research Companion to Islamic Law* (Surrey: Ashgate, 2014).

Belcher, Jeanne, ed., *Women, Religion and Sexuality* (Geneva: WCC Publications, 1990).

Berger, Peter, *The Desecularization of the World* (Grand Rapids, Michigan: William B. Eerdmans Publishing Company, 1999).

Berkey, Jonathan, *The Formation of Islam: Religion and Society in the Near East, 600–1800* (New York: Cambridge University Press, 2003).

Berry, Donald Lee, *Pictures of Islam: A Student's Guide to Islam* (Macron: Mercer University Press, 2007).

Bilal Philips, Abu Ameena, *The Evolution of Fiqh: Islamic Law and the Madh-dabs* (Riyadh: International Islamic Publishing House, 1988).

Black, Ann, Hossein Esmaeili, and Nadirsyah Hosen, *Modern Perspectives on Islamic Law* (Cheltenham: Edward Edgar, 2013).

Blunt, Wilfrid, *Secret History of the English Occupation of Egypt* (London: Fisher Unwin, 1907).

Bonner, Michael, *Jihad in Islamic History: Doctrines and Practice* (Princeton: Princeton University Press, 2008).

Bowen, Donna, and Evelyn Early, eds., *Everyday Life in the Muslim Middle East* (Bloomington: Indiana University Press, 2002).

Breiner, Bert, ed., *Two papers on Shari'ah* (Birmingham: Centre of Islam & Christian Relations, 1992).

Brown, Carl L., *Religion and State: the Muslim Approach to Politics* (New York: Columbia University Press, 2000).

Brown, Jonathan, *Hadith: Muhammad's Legacy in the Medieval and Modern World* (Oxford: One World, 2009).

Brown, Nathan, *Constitutions in a Nonconstitutional World: Arab Basic Laws and the Prospects for Accountable Government* (New York: State University of New York Press, 2001).

al-Bujayrimi, Sulayman, *Bujayrimi 'ala l-Khatib*, 4 vols. (Beirut: Dar al-Fikr, 1998).

al-Bukhari, Abdallah, *Kitab al-Jami'a al-Sahih*, ed. M. Krehl, 4 vols. (Leiden: Brill, n.d.).

Burton, John, *The Sources of Islamic Law: Islamic Theories of Abrogation* (Edinburgh: Edinburgh University Press, 2007).

Campbell, Gwyn, ed., *Abolition and Its Aftermath in Indian Ocean, Africa and Asia* (London: Routledge, 2005).

Campbell, Gwyn, Suzanne Miers, and Joseph C. Miller, eds., *Women and Slavery: Africa, The Indian Ocean and the Medieval North Atlantic*, Vol. 1 (Ohio: Ohio University Press, 2007).

Chatterjee, Indrani, *Gender, Slavery and Law in Colonial India* (New Delhi: Oxford University Press, 1999).

Chatterjee, Indrani, and Richard Eaton, eds., *Slavery and South Asian History* (Bloomington: Indiana University Press, 2006).

Chattopadhyay, Amal K., *Slavery in the Bengal Presidency*, 1772–1843 (London: Golden Eagle, 1977).

el-Cheikh, Nadia Maria, *Women, Islam and Abbasid Identity* (Cambridge: Harvard University Press, 2015).

Cherif Bassiouni, M., ed., *The Islamic Criminal Justice System* (London: Oceana Publications, 1982).

Christmann, Andreas, *The Qur'an, Morality, and Critical Reason: The Essential Muhammad Shahrur* (Leiden: Brill, 2009).

Clarence-Smith, William Gervase, *Islam and the Abolition of Slavery* (London: Hurst, 2006).

Coulson, Noel J., *History of Islamic Law* (Edinburgh: Edinburgh University Press, 1964).

Calder, Norman, and M. B. Hooker, *Sharia. Encyclopaedia of Islam* (Leiden: Brill, 2003).

Coupland, Reginal, *East Africa and Its Invaders from Its Earliest Times to the Death of Sayyid Said in 1856* (London: Oxford University Press, 1961).

Coupland, Reginal, *The Exploitation of East Africa 1856–1890: The Slave Trade and The Scramble* (Evanston: Northwestern University Press, 1967).

Crone, Patricia, *Medieval Political Thought* (Edinburgh: Edinburgh University Press, 2005).

Crone, Patricia, *God's Rule: Government and Islam* (New York: Columbia University Press, 2006).

Curtiss, Samuel Ives, *Primitive Semitic Religion Today: A Record of Researchers, Discoveries and Studies in Syria, Palestine and the Sinaitic Peninsula* (Oregon: Wipf and Stock Publishers, 2004).

Dar, Bashir A., *Religious Thought of Sayyid Ahmad Khan* (Lahore: Dr. Khalifa Abdul Hakim, 1957).

Delanoue, Gilbert, *Moralistes et politiques musulmans dans l'Égypte du XIXe siècle* (Cairo: Institut Français d'Archéologie Orientale, 1982).

Doi, Abdur Rahman I., *Shari'ah Law: The Islamic Law* (Kuala Lumpur: A. S. Nordeen, 1984).

Duderija, Adis, ed., *Maqasid al-Shari'a and Contemporary Reformist Muslim Thought* (New York: Palgrave Macmillan, 2014).

Ebadi, Shirin, *Iran Awakening* (New York: Random House, 2006).

Eccel, A. Chris, *Egypt, Islam and Social Change: Al-Azhar in Conflict and Accommodation* (Berlin: Klaus Schwarz, 1982).

Ennaji, Mohammed, *Slavery, the State and Islam* (Cambridge: Cambridge University Press, 2013).

Erdem, Y. Hakan, *Slavery in the Ottoman Empire and Its Demise, 1800–1909* (London: Macmillan, 1996).

Esposito, John L., *Women in Muslim Family Law* (Syracuse: Syracuse University Press, 1982).

Esposito, John L., and John O. Voll, *Makers of Contemporary Islam* (Oxford: Oxford University Press, 2001).

Fadel, Mohammad, *Islamic Law Reform: Between Reinterpretation and Democracy* (Leiden: Brill, 2017).

el-Fadl, Khaled, *Speaking in God's Name: Islamic Law, Authority and Women* (London: Oneworld, 2014).

Fakhr al-Din al-Razi, *al-Tafsir al-kabir*, 32 vols. (Cairo: Al-Matba'a al-Baha'iyya al-Misriyya, 1938).

al-Farabi, Abu Nasr, *Fusul Muntaza'a*, ed. Fawzi Najjar (Beirut: Dar al-Mashraq, 1971).

Farooq, Mohammad Omar, *Toward Our Reformation: From Legalism to Value-Oriented Islamic Law and Jurisprudence* (Herndon: International Institute of Islamic Thought, 2011).

Feener, R. Michael, *Muslim Legal Thought in Modern Indonesia* (Cambridge: Cambridge University Press, 2007).

Feldman, Noah, *The Fall and Rise of the Islamic State* (Princeton: Princeton University Press, 2008).
Gärje, Helmut, *The Quran and its Exegesis: Selected texts, with Classical and Modern Muslim Interpretations* (London: Routledge, 1976).
al-Ghazali, *al-Wasit fi l-madhhab*, ed. Ahmad Mahmud Ibrahim, 7 vols. (al-Ghuriya: Dar al-Salam, 1997).
al-Ghazali, Abu Hamid, *Marriage and Sexuality in Islam*, trans. M. Farah (Kuala Lumpur: Islamic Book Trust, 2012).
Ghobadzadeh, Naser, *Religious Secularity, a Theological Challenge to the Islamic State* (New York: Oxford University Press, 2015).
Gordon, Murray, *Slavery in the Arab World* (New York: New Amsterdam, 1989).
Gurnah, Abdulrazak, ed., *The Cambridge Companion to Salman Rushdie* (Cambridge: Cambridge University Press, 1997).
Haddad, Yvonne Yazbeck, and John L. Esposito, eds., *Islam, Gender and Social Change* (Oxford: Oxford University Press, 1998).
Haddad, Yvonne Yazbeck, and Barbara F. Stowasser, eds., *Islamic Law and Challenges of Modernity* (Walnut Creek: Altamira Press, 2004).
Haikal, Muhammad H., *The Life of Muhammad* (American Trust Publications, 2005).
Hallaq, Wael B., *Law and Legal Theory in Classical and Medieval Islam* (Aldershot: Ashgate, 1994).
Hallaq, Wael B., *Authority, Continuity, and Change in Islamic Law* (Cambridge: Cambridge University Press, 2001).
Hallaq, Wael B., *The Origins and Evolution of Islamic Law* (Cambridge: Cambridge University Press, 2005).
Hallaq, Wael B., *An Introduction to Islamic Law* (Cambridge: Cambridge University Press, 2009).
Hallaq, Wael B., *Sharīʿa: Theory, Practice, Transformations* (Cambridge: Cambridge University Press, 2009).
Hamilton, Keith, and Patrick Salmon, eds., *Slavery, Diplomacy, and Empire: Britain and the Suppression of the Slave Trade, 1807–1975* (Brighton: Sussex Academic Press, 2009).
Hardy, Michael J. L., *Blood Feuds and the Payment of Blood Money in the Middle East* (Leiden: Brill, 1963).
Hashemi, Kamran, *Religious Legal Traditions, International Human Rights and Muslim States* (Leiden: Martinus Nijhoff, 2008).
Hassan, Yusuf Fadl, and Richard Gray, eds., *Religion and Conflict in Sudan* (Nairobi: Paulines Publications Africa, 2002).
Haylamaz, Resit, *Khadija – The First Muslim and the Wife of the Prophet Muhammad* (New Jersey: The Light, Inc., Somerset, 2007).

Hefner, Robert W., *Shar'ia Politics: Islamic Law and Society in the Modern World* (Bloomington: Indiana University Press, 2011).

Hefner, Robert W., ed., *The New Cambridge History of Islam: Muslims and Modernity: Culture and Society since 1800* (Cambridge: Cambridge University Press, 2010).

Heyneman, Stephen P., ed., *Islam and Social Policy* (Nashville: Vanderbilt University Press, 2004).

Hirschl, Ran, *Constitutional Theocracy* (Cambridge: Harvard University Press, 2011).

Holt, P. M., ed., *Political and Social Change in Modern Egypt: Historical Studies from the Ottoman Conquest to the United Arab Republic* (London: Oxford University Press, 1968).

Howland, Courtney W., ed., *Religious Fundamentalisms and the Human Rights of Women* (London: Palgrave Macmillan, 1999).

Hunt, Janin, and Andre Kahlmeyer, *Islamic Law. The Sharia from Muhammad's Time to the Present* (Jefferson: McFarland & Company, Inc. Publishers, 2007).

Hunter, Shireen T., *Reformist Voices of Islam: Mediating Islam and Modernity* (New York: M. E. Sharpe, Inc., 2009).

Hunwick, John, and Eve Troutt Powell, *The African Diaspora in the Mediterranean Lands of Islam* (Princeton: Markus Wiener, 2002).

Husni, Ronak, and Daniel Newman, *Muslim Women in Law and Society: Annotated Translation of al-Tahir al-Haddad's* Imra'tuna fi 'l-shari'a wa 'l-mujtama', *with an introduction* (Routledge, London, 2007).

Ibn al-'Arabī, Muḥammad b. 'Abd Allah, *Aḥkam Al-Qur'an*, ed. Muḥammad Bakr Isma'il, 4 vols. (Cairo: Dar al-Manar, 2002).

Ibn al-Farra' [al-Baghawi], *al-Tahdhib fi fiqh al-Imam al-Shafi'i*, ed. 'Ali Mu'awwad and 'Adil 'Abd al-Mawjud, 8 vols. (Beirut: Dar al-Kutub al-'Ilmiyya, 1997).

Ibn Hajjaj, Muslim, *Sahih Muslim* (Dar al-Salam, Riyadh, 2000).

Ibn Ishaq, Muhammad, *The Life of Muhammad: A translation of Ishaq's Sirat rasul Allah*, ed. 'Abdu'l-Malik Ibn Isham, transl. Alfred Guillaume (Karachi: Oxford University Press, 1990).

Ibn Ishaq al-Jundi, Khalil, *Maliki law: Being a Summary from French Translations of the Mikhtasar of Sidi Khalil,* transl. F. X. Ruxton (Westport: Hyperion, 1980).

Ibn Ishaq al-Jundi, Khalil, *Mukhtasar al-'Allama Khalil fi fiqh al-Imam Malik* (Beirut: Dar ar-Kutub al-'Ilmiyya, 2004).

Ibn Kathir, Ismail Ibn Umar, *Tafsir Ibn Kathir*, trans. Shaykh Safiur-Rahman al-Mubarakpuri, 10 vols., (Riyadh: Darussalam, 2000).

Ibn Majah, Muhammad ibn Yazid, *Sunan ibn Majah* (Riyadh: Dar al-Salam, 2000).

Ibn Muhammad Ibn Abi Shayba, 'Abd Allah, *Al-Kitab al-Musannaf Fi al-Ahadith wa'l-Athar*, ed. Muhammad 'Abd al-Salam Shahin, 9 vols. (Beirut: Dar al-Kutub al-'Ilmiyyah, 1995).

Ibn Qayyim al-Jawziyya, *I'lam al-Muwaqqi' in 'an Rabb al-'Alamin* (Beirut: Dar al-Fikr al-'Arabi, 1995).

Iqbal, Mohammad, *Reconstruction of Religious Thought in Islam* (Delhi: Kitab Publishing House, 1974).

Ismael, Tareq Y., and Jacqueline S. Ismael, *Government and Politics of the Contemporary Middle East: Continuity and Change* (Abingdon: Routledge, 2011).

Izutsu, Toshihiko, *Ethico-Religious Concepts in the Qur'an* (Montreal: McGill University Press, 1966).

Izzi Dien, M., *Islamic Law from Historical Foundations to Contemporary Practice* (Indiana: University of Notre Dame, 2004).

Ja'far Ibn Muhammad Ibn Sa'id, *Shara'i al-islam* (Beirut: n.p., 1930).

Jones, A. H. M., *Athenian Democracy* (New York: Praeger, 1958).

Junyboll, G. H. A., *The Authenticity of the Tradition Literature: Discussion in Modern Egypt* (Leiden: Brill, 1969).

Kamali, Hashim, *Shari'ah Law: An Introduction* (Oxford: Oneworld, 2008).

Kamali, Mohammad H., *Freedom, Equality and Justice in Islam* (Cambridge: The Islamic Texts Society, 2002).

Kamali, Mohammad H., *Principles of Islamic Jurisprudence* (Cambridge: Islamic Texts Society, 2003).

Kamali, Mohammad H., *A Textbook of Hadith Studies, Authenticity, Compilation, Classification and Criticism of Hadith* (Leicestershire: The Islamic Foundation, 2005).

Kassam, Zayn R., ed., *Women and Islam* (Santa Barbara: Praeger, 2010).

Kelly, John B., *Britain and the Persian Gulf, 1795–1880* (Oxford: Clarendon Press, 1968).

Kenney, Jeffrey Thomas, *Heterodoxy and Culture: The Legacy of the Khawarij in Islamic History* (Ann Arbor: U.M.I., 1991).

Kenney, Jeffrey Thomas, *Muslim Rebels: Kharijites and the Politics of Extremism in Egypt* (Oxford: Oxford University Press, 2006).

Kepel, Gilles, *The Revenge of God* (Pennsylvania: Penn State University Press, 1994).

Khadduri, Majid, *War and Peace in the Law of Islam* (Baltimore: John Hopkins Press, 1955).

Khadduri, Majid, and Herbert J. Liebesny, eds., *Law in the Middle East* (Washington DC: The Middle East Institute, 1955).

Khadduri, Majid, *The Islamic Concept of Justice* (Baltimore: The John Hopkins University Press, 1984).

Khare, R. S., ed., *Perspectives on Islamic Law, Justice, and Society* (Lanham: Rowman & Littlefield Publishers, 1999).

Kokot, Waltrud, Khachig Tölölyan, and Carolin Alfonso, eds., *Diaspora, Identity and Religion: New Directions in Theory and Research* (London: Routledge, 2004).

Kuru, Ahmet T., *Islam, Authoritarianism, and Underdevelopment: A Global and Historical Comparison* (Cambridge: Cambridge University Press, 2019).

Kurzman, Charles, ed., *Liberal Islam: A Sourcebook* (New York: Oxford University Press, 1998).
Laquer, Walter Z., *The Middle East in Transition* (New York: Praeger, 1958).
Lawrence, Bruce, *The Quran: A Biography* (London: Atlantic Books, 2006).
Lerner, Daniel, *The Passing of Traditional Society: Modernizing the Middle East* (Glencoe: Free Press, 1958).
Lewis, Bernard, *Race and Slavery in the Middle East* (New York: Oxford University Press, 1990).
Liebesny, Herbert J., *The Law of the Near and Middle East* (Albany: State University of New York Press, 1975).
Lombardi, Clark, *State Law as Islamic Law in Modern Egypt: The Incorporation of the Shari'a into Egyptian Constitutional Law* (Leiden: Brill, 2006).
Lord Cromer, Evelyn Baring, *Modern Egypt* (New York: Macmillan, 1908).
Lovejoy, Paul E., *Transformations in Slavery: A History of Slavery in Africa* (Cambridge: Cambridge University Press, 2012).
Mahmasani, Subhi Rajab, *Falsafat Al-Tashri fi Al-Islam, the Philosophy of Jurisprudence in Islam,* trans. Farhat Ziadeh (Leiden: Brill, 1961).
Mahmood, Tahir, *Personal Law in Islamic Countries* (New Delhi: Academy of Law and Religions, 1987).
Makdisi, George, *Religion, Law and Learning in Classical Islam* (Aldershot: Ashgate, 1991).
Malekian, Farhad, *Principles of Islamic International Criminal Law: A Comparative Search,* 2nd ed. (Leiden: Brill, 2011).
Marmaduke Pickthall, Muhammad, *The glorious Quran – Text and explanatory translation* (New York: Muslim World League, 1977).
Martin, Vanessa, *The Qajar Pact: Bargaining, Protest and the State in Nineteenth Century Persia* (London: Tauris, 2005).
al-Mawardi, 'Ali ibn Muhammad, *al-Hawi al-kabir,* ed. Mahmud Matraji et al., 24 vols. (Beirut: Dar al-Fikr, 1994).
Mawdudi, Abdul A., *Purdah* (Lahore: Islamic Publications, 1997).
May, Yamani, ed., *Feminism and Islam, Legal and Literary Perspectives* (Berkshire: Garnet Publishing Limited, 1996).
Maydell, Natalie, and Sep Riahi, *Extraordinary women from the Muslim World* (Lancaster: Global Content Ventures, 2007).
Mayer, Ann Elizabeth, *Islam and Human Rights: Tradition and Politics* (Boulder: Westview Press, 2007).
Melchert, Christopher, *The Formation of the Sunni Schools of Law, 9th–10th Centuries CE* (Leiden: Brill, 1996).
Mernissi, Fatima, *Beyond the Veil: Male-Female Dynamics in Modern Muslim Society* (Bloomington: Indiana University Press, 1987).

Mernissi, Fatima, *Women and Islam: An Historical and Theological Enquiry*, transl. Mary Jo Lakeland (Oxford: Blackwell, 1991).

Mernissi, Fatima, *Veil and the Male Elite: A Feminist Interpretation of Women's Rights in Islam*, trans. Mary Jo Lakeland (Reading: Addison-Wesley, 1991).

Mernissi, Fatima, *Dreams of Trespass: Tales of a Harem Girlhood* (New York: Addison-Wesley, 1994).

Metcalf, Barbara D., *Islamic Revival in British India: Deoband, 1860–1900* (Princeton: Princeton University Press, 1982).

Miers, Suzanne, *Britain and the Ending of the Slave Trade* (New York: Africana, 1975).

Mir-Hosseini, Ziba, ed., *Men in Charge? Rethinking Authority in Muslim Legal Tradition* (London: Oneworld, 2015).

Mir-Hosseini, Ziba, Kari Vogt, Lena Larsen, and Christian Moe, eds., *Gender and Equality in Muslim Family Law: Justice and Ethics in the Islamic Legal Tradition* (London: I. B. Tauris, 2013).

Mirzai, Behnaz, Ismael Musah Montana and Paul E. Lovejoy, *Islam, Slavery and Diaspora* (Lawrenceville: Africa World Press, 2009).

al-Misri, Abu Hamza, *The Khawaarij and Jihad* (Birmingham: Makhtabah al-Ansar, 2000).

Mitchell, Sara M., and Emilia J. Powell, *Domestic Law Goes Global: Legal Traditions and International Courts* (Cambridge: Cambridge University Press, 2011).

Moghissi, Haideh, *Feminism and Islamic Fundamentalism: The Limits of Postmodern Analysis* (Oxford: Oxford University Press, 1999).

Moghissi, Haideh, ed., *Women and Islam, Critical Concepts in Sociology* (New York: Routledge, 2005).

Motahhari, Morteza, *Nezam-e Huquq-e Zan dar Islam* (Tehran: Sadra, 1990).

Moussa, Jasmine, *Competing Fundamentalisms and Egyptian Women's Family Rights: International Law and Reforms of Shari'a-Derived Legislation* (Leiden: Brill, 2011).

Muhammad, Shan, *Sir Syed Ahmad Khan, A Political Biography* (Meerut: Meenakshi Prakashan, 1969).

Muhammad Khalid, Khalid, *Men around the Messenger*, trans. Sheik Muhammad Mustafa Gemeiah (Cairo: Al-Azhar Al-Sharif Islamic Research Academy, 1997).

Muir, William, *The Life of Muhammad* (Oxford: Oxford University Press, 2002).

Mujeb, Mohammad, *The Indian Muslims* (London: Allen and Unwin, 1967).

Mujtahed Shabestari, Muhammad, *Hermeneutic, the Scripture and the Tradition* (Tehran: Tarh-e No Publisher, 2000).

Murata, Sachiko, *Temporary Marriage (Mut'a) in Islamic Law* (London: The Muhammadi Trust, 1987).

Musa Usman, Abubakar, *Gender Justice in Islamic Law: Homicide and Bodily Injuries* (Oxford: Hart Publishing, 2018).

Muslehuddin, Mohammad, *Philosophy of Islamic Law and the Orientalists* (New Delhi: Taj Company, 1986).

Nashat, Guity, ed., *Women and Revolution in Iran* (Boulder: Westview Press, 1983).
Nasir, Jamal J., *The Islamic Law of Personal Status*, 3rd ed. (Leiden: Brill, 2009).
Numani, Shibli, *Umar: Makers of Islamic Civilization* (London: I. B. Tauris, 2004).
Nyazee, Imran, *Outlines of Islamic Jurisprudence* (Lahore: Advanced Legal Studies Institute, 2000).
Pearl, David, and Paul Menski, *Muslim Family Law* (London: Sweet and Maxwell, 1998).
Peaslee, Amos J., *Constitutions of Nations* (Concord, N. H; Rumford, 1950).
Peters, Rudolph, *Crime and Punishment in Islamic Law* (Cambridge: Cambridge University Press, 2005).
al-Qaradawi, Yusuf, *The Lawful and the Prohibited in Islam,* trans. M. Siddiqi K. al-Hilbawi, and S. Shukri (Cairo: al-Falah, 2001).
Quraishi, Asifa and Frank E. Vogel, eds., *The Islamic Marriage Contract: Case Studies in Islamic Family Law* (Cambridge: Harvard University Press, 2008).
Qutb, Sayyid, *Social Justice in Islam*, trans. John B. Hardie (New York: Octagon, 1970).
Qutb, Sayyid, *Fi Zilal al-Qur'an* (Beirut: Dar al-Shuruq, 1982).
al-Rafi'i, 'Abd al-Karim, *al-'Aziz sharh al-Wajiz*, ed. 'Ali Mu'awwad and 'Adil 'Abd al-Mawjud, 13 vols. (Beirut: Dar al-Kutub al-'Ilmiyya, 1997).
Raghavan, Chitra, and James P. Levine, eds., *Self-determination and Women's Rights in Muslim Societies* (Lebanon: Brandeis University Press, 2012).
Rahim, Abdur, *Muhammadan Jurisprudence* (Lahore: Mansoor Book House, 1995).
Rahman, Fazlur, *Islam and Modernity: Transformation of an Intellectual Tradition* (Chicago: University of Chicago Press, 1965).
Rahman, Fazlur, *Islamic Methodology in History* (Karachi: Central Institute of Islamic Research, 1965).
Rahman, Fazlur, *Islam* (Chicago: Chicago University Press, 1979).
Ramadan, Said, *Islamic Law: Its Scope and Equity* (London: Macmillan, 1970).
Rapoport, Yossef, *Marriage, Money and Divorce in Medieval Islamic Society* (Cambridge: Cambridge University Press, 2005).
Ray, Himanshu Prahba, and Edward A. Alpers, eds. *Cross Current and Community Networks: The History of the Indian Ocean World* (Oxford: Oxford University Press, 2007).
Rayner, Susan E., *The Theory of Contracts in Islamic Law: A Comparative Analysis with Particular Reference to the Modern Legislation in Kuwait, Bahrain and the United Arab Emirates* (London: Graham & Trotman, 1991).
Robertson Smith, W., *Kinship and Marriage in Early Arabia* (Cambridge: Cambridge University Press, 1985).
Rosenthal, Erwin J., *Political Thought in Medieval Islam* (Cambridge: Cambridge University Press, 1958).
Rushd, Idb, *The Distinguished Jurist's Primer, Bidâyat al-Mujtahid wa Nihâyat al-Mugtasid,* trans. Imran A. K. Nyazee (Doha: Center for Muslim Contribution to Civilization, 2000).

Sachedina, Abdulaziz, *Islam and the Challenge of Human Rights* (Oxford: Oxford University Press, 2009).
Sadeghi, Behnam, *The Logic of Making Law in Islam: Women and Prayer in the Legal Tradition* (Cambridge: Cambridge University Press, 2013).
Salem, Elie A., *The Political Theory and Institutions of the Khawarij* (Baltimore: John Hopkins University Press, 1956).
al-Sarakhsi, Abu Bakr, *Al-Mabsut* (Beirut: Dar al-Kutub al-'Ilmiyyah, 2001).
Savage, Elizabeth, ed., *The Human Commodity: Perspectives on the Trans-Saharan Slave Trade* (London: Routledge, 1992).
Schacht, Joseph, *An Introduction to Islamic Law* (Oxford: Clarendon Press, 1964).
Schacht, Joseph, *Origins of Muhammadan Jurisprudence* (Oxford: Clarendon Press, 1976).
Schimmel, Annemarie, *And Muhammad is His Messenger: The Veneration of the Prophet in Islamic Piety* (Chapel Hills: University of North Carolina Press, 1985).
Segal, Ronald, *Islam's Black Slaves: The Other Black Diaspora* (New York: Farrar, Straus and Giroux, 2001).
Sékaly, Achille, *Le congrès du khalifat (Le Caire 13–19 mai 1926) et le congrès du monde musulman (La Mekke 7 juin–5 juillet 1926)* (Paris: Leroux, 1926).
Shabana, Ayman, *Custom in Islamic Law and Legal Theory: The Development of the Concepts of 'Urf and 'Adah in the Islamic Legal Tradition* (New York: Palgrave Macmillan, 2010).
al-Shafi'i, Abu 'Abdillah, *Kitab Al-Umm* (Beirut: Dar al-Kutub al-'Ilmiyya, 1993).
Shahab, Rafi Ullah, *Muslim Women in Political Power* (Lahore: Maqbool Academy, 1993).
Shahrur, Mohammad, *Al-Kitab wa al-Qur'an: Qira'a Mu'asira* (Beirut: Sharikat al-Matbu'a li al-Tawzi' wa al-Nashr, 1992).
Shari'ati, Ali, *On the Sociology of Islam* (Berkeley: Mizan, 1979).
al-Sharqawi, 'Abd Allah, *Hashiyat al-Sharqawi*, 4 vols. (Beirut: Dar al-Kutub al-'Ilmiyya, 1997).
Shephard, William, *The Faith of a Modern Muslim Intellectual* (Delhi: Indian Institute of Islamic Studies, 1982).
Siddique, Kaukab, *Liberation of Women Through Islam* (Kingsville Md: American Society for Education and Religion Inc., 1990).
Sonbol, Amira, ed., *Gulf Women* (Syracuse: Syracuse University Press, 2012).
Souaiaia, Ahmed E., *Contesting Justice: Women, Islam, Law and Society* (New York: State University of New York Press, 2008).
Spectorsky, Susan, *Themes in Islamic Studies: Women in Classical Islamic Law: A Survey of the Sources* (Boston: Brill, 2009).
Spellberg, Denise A., *Politics, Gender, and the Islamic Past: The Legacy of 'A'isha bint Abi Bakr* (New York: Columbia University Press, 1994).

Stetkevych, Suzanne, *Abū Tammam and the Poetics of the 'Abbasid Age* (New York: Brill, 1991).
Stowasser, Barbara, *Women in the Quran, Traditions and Interpretations* (Oxford: Oxford University Press, 1994).
Syed, Mohammad Ali, *The Position of Women in Islam: A Progressive View* (Albany: State University of New York, 2004).
Tabandeh, Sultanhussein, *A Muslim Commentary on the Universal Declaration of Human Rights* (London: Goulding, 1979).
al-Tabari, M., *Jami' al-Bayan fi Ta'wil al-Quran*, ed. A.M. Shakir, Vol. 10 (Beirut: Mu'assasat al-Risalah, 2000).
Taha, Mahmoud Mohamed, *Second Message of Islam*, transl. Abdullahi A. An-Naim (Syracuse: Syracuse University Press, 1996).
al-Talbi, Muhammad, *Ummat Al-Wasat: Al-Islam Wa Tahaddiyat Al-Mu'asira* (Tunis: Ceres Edition, 1996).
Taleqani, Seyyed Mahmoud, *Islam and Ownership* (Lexington: Mazda, 1983).
Taqi al-Din, al-Hisni, *Kifayat al-akhyar f i hall Ghayat al-ikhtisar*, ed. Muhammad Haykal (Cairo: Dar al-Salam, 2005).
Tirmidhi, Abu 'Isa, *Jami' al-Tirmidhi* (Riyadh: Dar al-Salam, 2000).
el-Tousy, Mohammad ibn Omar, *Voyage au Darfour* (Paris: Benjamin Duprat, 1845).
Tucker, Judith E., *Women in Nineteenth-Century Egypt* (Cambridge: Cambridge University Press, 1985).
Tucker, Judith E., ed., *Arab Women* (Bloomington: Indiana University Press, 1993).
Tucker, Judith E., *In the House of The Law: Gender and Islamic Law in Ottoman Syria and Palestine* (Berkeley: University of California Press, 1998).
Tucker, Judith E., *Women, Family, and Gender in Islamic Law* (Cambridge: Cambridge University Press, 2008).
Toledano, Ehud R., *As If Silent but Absent: Bonds of Enslavement in the Islamic Middle East* (New Haven: Yale University Press, 2007).
Troutt Powell, Eve M., *A Different Shade of Colonialism: Egypt, Great Britain and the Mastery of the Sudan* (Berkeley: University of California Press, 2003).
Umar, Mohd, *Bride Burning in India: A Socio Legal Study* (New Delhi: Publishing, 1998).
Vago, Stephen, *Law and Society* (New Jersey: Pearson, Prentice Hall, 2006).
Voorhoeve, Maaike, *Gender and Divorce Law in North Africa: Sharia, Custom and the Personal Status Code in Tunisia* (London: I. B. Tauris, 2014).
Wadud, Amina, *Quran and Women: Rereading the Sacred Text from a Woman's Perspective* (Oxford: Oxford University Press, 1999).
Wadud, Amina, *Inside the Gender Jihad: Women's Reform in Islam* (Oxford: Oneworld, 2006).
Walther, Wiebke, *Women in Islam* (Princeton: Wiener, 1993).

Walz, Terenze, and Kenneth M. Cuno, eds., *Race and Slavery in the Middle East: Histories of Trans-Saharan Africans in Nineteenth Century Egypt, Sudan, and the Ottoman Empire* (Cairo: American University in Cairo Press, 2010).

Watt, W. Montgomery, *Muhammad at Mecca* (Oxford: Clarendon Press, 1956).

Watt, W. Montgomery, *Muhammad at Medina* (Oxford: Clarendon Press, 1956).

Weiss, Bernard G., ed., *Studies in Islamic Legal Theory* (Leiden: Brill, 2002).

Witte, John, and Eliza Ellisson, eds., *Covenant Marriage in Comparative Perspective* (Grand Rapids: William B. Eerdmans Publishing, 2005).

Willis II, John R., ed., *Slaves and Slavery in Muslim Africa* (London: Frank Cass, 1985).

Yamani, Mai, ed., *Feminism and Islam: Legal and Literary Perspectives* (New York: New York University Press, 1996).

Yassari, Nadjma, ed., *Changing God's Law: The Dynamics of Middle Eastern Family Law* (London: Routledge, 2016).

Zaki Badawi, M. A., *The Reformers of Egypt* (London: Croom Helm, 1978).

Zamakshari, Abu al-Qasim, *Al-Kashaf* (Beirut: Dar al-Ma'arif, 1977).

Zambaco, Demetrius A., *Les eunuques d'aujourd'hui et ceux de jadis* (Paris: Masson, 1911).

Zayzafoon, Lamia Ben Youssef, *The Production of the Muslim woman: Negotiating Text, History, and Ideology* (New York: Lexington Books, 2005).

Zysow, Aron, *The Economy of Certainty: Introduction to the Typology of Islamic Legal Theory* (Cambridge: Harvard University Press, 1984).

Articles

'Athamina, Khalil, "How did Islam Contribute to Change the Legal Status of Women: The Case of the Jawari, or the Female Slaves", *Al-Qantara* Vol. 28, No. 2 (2007), pp. 383–408.

Abbott, Nadia, "Women and the State in Early Islam", *Journal of Near Eastern Studies* Vol. 1 (1942), pp. 106–126.

Abdalla, Amr, "Principles of Islamic Interpersonal Conflict Intervention: A Search Within Islam and Western Literature", *Journal of Law and Religion* Vol. 15, No. 1–2 (2000), 151–184.

Afshari, Reza, "Egalitarian Islam and Misogynist Islamic Tradition: A Critique of the Feminist Interpretation of Islamic History and Heritage", *Critique: Journal of Critical Studies of Iran and Middle East* (1994), pp. 13–34.

Ahangar, Mohd Altaf Hussain, "Crime and Punishment in a Modern Muslim State: A Pragmatic Approach", *The American Journal of Islamic Social Sciences* Vol. 3, No. 1 (2014), pp. 51–69.

Ahmad, Irfan, "Cracks in the 'Mightiest Fortress': Jamaat-e-Islami's changing discourse on women", *Modern Asian Studies* Vol. 42 (2012), pp. 549–575.

Ahmed, Leila, "Women and the Advent of Islam", *Signs* Vol. 11, No. 4 (1986), pp. 665–691.

el-Alami, Dawoud S., "Legal Capacity with Specific Reference to the Marriage Contract", *Arab Law Quarterly* No. 6 (1991), pp. 190–204.

Alshech, Eli, "Out of sight and therefore out of mind: Early Sunni Islamic modesty regulations and the creation of spheres of privacy", *Journal of Near Eastern Studies* No. 66 (2007), pp. 267–290.

Alwani, Zainab, "The Qur'anic model on Social Change: Family Structure as a Method of Social Reform", *Islam and Civilizational Renewal* Vol. 3, No. 1 (2011), pp. 53–74.

Bauer, Karen, "The Gender Hierarchy and the Question of Women as Judges and Witnesses in Pre-Modern Islamic Law", *The Journal of the American Oriental Society* Vol. 130, No.1 (2010), pp. 1–2.

Bekkin, Renat I., "Islamic Insurance: National Features and Legal Regulations", *Arab Law Quarterly* Vol. 21, No. 3 (2007), pp. 3–34.

Bielefeldt, Heiner, " 'Western' Versus 'Islamic' Human Rights Conceptions? A Critique of Cultural Essentialism in the Discussion of Human Rights", *Political Theory* Vol. 28, No. 90 (2000), pp. 90–121.

Cassimatis, Helene, "Imagerie et Femme", *La Femme dans le Monde Méditerranéen I, Antiquité*, CNRS, Maison de l'Orient, No. 10 (1985), pp. 19–28.

Dallal, Ahmad, "Appropriating the Past: Twentieth Century Reconstruction of Pre-Modern Islamic Thought", *Islamic Law and Society* Vol. 7 (1999), pp. 333–342.

Denny, Frederick Mathewson, "Fazlur Rahman: Muslim Intellectual", *Muslim World* No. 79 (1989), pp. 91–101.

Dols, Michael W., "Historical Perspective: Insanity in Islamic Law", *Journal of Muslim Mental Health* No. 2 (2007), pp. 81–99.

Doumato, Eleanor A., "Hearing Other Voices: Christian Women and the Coming of Islam", *International Journal of Middle East Studies* Vol. 23, No. 2 (1991), pp. 177–199.

Duderija, Adis, "The Custom ('urf) Based Assumptions Regarding Gender Roles and Norms in the Islamic Tradition: A Critical Examination", *Studies in Religion* Vol. 45, No. 4 (2016), pp. 581–599.

Eliash, Joseph, "Ithna 'ashari Shi'i Juristic Theory of Political and Legal Authority", *Studia Islamica* Vol. 29 (1969), pp. 2–30.

Elsadda, Hoda, "Discourses on Women's Biographies and Cultural Identity: Twentieth-Century Representations of the Life of A'isha Bint Abi Bakr", *Feminist Studies* Vol. 27, No. 1 (2001), pp. 37–64.

Fadel, Mohammad, "Two Women, One Man: Knowledge, Power and Gender in Medieval Sunni Legal Thought", *International Journal of Middle East Studies* Vol. 29 (1997), pp. 185–204.

Fadel, Mohammad, "Reinterpreting the Guardian's Role in the Islamic Contract of Marriage: The Case of the Maliki School", *The Journal of Islamic Law* Vol. 3, No. 1 (1998), pp. 1–26.

Fadel, Mohammad, "Modernist Islamic Political Thought and the Egyptian and Tunisian Revolutions of 2011", *Middle East Law and Governance* Vol. 3 (2011), pp. 94–104.

Fadel, Mohammad, "Is Historicism a Viable Strategy for Islamic Legal Reform? The Case of 'Never Shall a Folk Prosper Who Have Appointed a Woman to rule Them' ", *Islamic Law & Society* Vol. 18, No. 2 (2011), pp. 131–176.

Freamon, Bernard K., "Slavery, Freedom, and the Doctrine of Consensus in Islamic Jurisprudence", *Harvard Human Rights Journal* Vol. 11 (1998), pp. 1–64.

Freamon, Bernard K., "ISIS, Boko Haram, and the Human Right to Freedom from Slavery under Islamic Law", *Fordham International Law Journal* Vol. 39, No. 245 (2015–2016), pp. 245–306.

Gibreel, G., "The Ulama: Middle Eastern Powers Broken", *The Middle East Quarterly* Vol. 8, No. 4 (2001), pp. 15–23.

Habachy, Saba, "Property, Right and Contract in Muslim Law", *The International Executive* Vol. 4, No. 3 (1962), pp. 11–12.

Hallaq, Wael B., "Was the Gate of Ijtihad Closed?", *International Journal of Middle East Studies* (1984), pp. 3–41.

Hasan, Ahmed, "The Classical Definition of 'Ijma': The Nature of Consensus", *Islamic Studies* Vol. 14 (1975), pp. 261–270.

Hascall, Susan C., "Restorative Justice in Islam: Should Qisas Be Considered a Form of Restorative Justice?", *Berkeley Journal of Middle East & Islamic Law* Vol. 4 (2011), pp. 35–55.

Hassan Bello, Abdulmajeed, "Islamic Law of Inheritance: Ultimate Solution to Social Inequality against Women", *Arab Law Quarterly* Vol. 29 (2015), pp. 261–273.

Hassan, Hussein, "Contracts in Islamic Law: The Principles of Commutative Justice and Liberty,"*Journal of Islamic Studies* Vol. 13, No. 3 (2002), pp. 257–97.

Hassan, Riffat, "Made from Adam's Rib: The Woman's creation Question", *Al-Mushir Theological Journal of the Christian Study Center* No. 27 (1985), pp. 124–155.

Hassan, Riffat, "Challenging the Stereotypes of Fundamentalism: An Islamic Feminist Perspective", *The Muslim World* Vol. 91, No. 1 (2001), pp. 56–57.

al-Hibri, Azizah, "Muslim Women's Rights in the Global Village: Challenges and Opportunities", *Journal of Law and Religion* Vol. 15 (2001), pp. 37–66.

Hunwick, John, "Islamic Law and Polemics over Race and Slavery in North and West Africa, Sixteenth to Nineteenth Century", *Princeton Papers: Interdisciplinary Journal of Middle Eastern Studies* No. 7 (1999), pp. 43–68.

Inloes, Amina, "The Queen of Sheba in Shi'a Hadith", *Journal of Shi'a Islamic Studies* Vol. 5, No. 4 (2012), pp. 423–440.

Javaid, Rehman, "The Sharia, Islamic Family Laws and International Human Rights Law: Examining the Theory and Practice of Polygamy and Talaq", *International Journal of Law, Policy and the Family* Vol. 21 (2007), pp. 108–127.

Kamali, Mohammad H., "Issues in the Legal Theory of Usul and Prospects for Reform", *Islamic Studies* Vol. 40 (2001).

Kamali, Mohammad H., "Islamic Family Law Reform: Problems and Prospects", *Islam and Civilizational Renewal* Vol. 3, No. 1 (2011), pp. 37–52.

Khadduri, Majid, "Nature and Sources of Islamic Law", *George Washington Law Review* Vol. 3, No. 22 (1953–1954), pp. 3–23.

Khalafallah, Haifaa G., "Precedent and Perception: Muslim Records That Contradict Narratives on Women", *Journal of Women of the Middle East and the Islamic World* Vol. 11 (2013), pp. 108–132.

Khan, Ali, "The Reopening of the Islamic Code: The Second Era of Ijtihad", *University of St Thomas Law Journal* Vol. 1, No. 1 (2003), pp. 341–385.

Kim, Sarang, "Reconciliation among the Bedouin", *St Frances Magazine* Vol. 1, No. 5 (2009), pp. 1–14.

Koehler, Benedikt, "Female Entrepreneurship in Early Islam", *Economic Affairs* Vol. 21, No. 2 (2011), pp. 93–95.

Lawish, Aharon, "The Transformation of the *Shari'a* from Jurists' Law to Statutory Law in the Contemporary Muslim World", *Die Welt des Islams* Vol. 44 (2004), pp. 85–113.

Libson, Gideon, "On the Development of Custom as a Source of Law in Islamic Law: Al-rujū'u ilā al-'urfi ahadu al-qawā'idi al-khamsi allatī yatabannā 'alayhā al-fiqhu", *Islamic Law and Society* Vol. 4, No. 2 (1997), pp. 131–155.

Lombardi, Clark, "Constitutional Provisions Making Sharia "a" or "the" Chief Source of Legislation: Where Did They Come from? What Do they Mean? Do They Matter?", *American University International Law Review* Vol. 28, No. 733 (2013), pp. 733–774.

Lombardi, Clark, "Designing Islamic constitutions: Past trends and options for a democratic future", *International Journal of Constitutional Law* Vol. 11, No. 3 (2013), pp. 615–645.

Lowry, Joseph E., "The First Islamic Legal Theory: Ibn al-Muqaffa' on Interpretation, Authority, and the Structure of the Law", *Journal of the American Oriental Society* Vol. 128, No. 1 (2008), pp. 25–40.

Lucas, Scott C., "Justifying Gender Inequalities in the Shafi'i Law School: Two Case Studies of Muslim Legal Reasoning", *Journal of the American Oriental Society* Vol. 129, No. 2 (2009), pp. 237–258.

Mahmoud, Mohamed, "To Beat or Not to Beat: On the Exegetical Dilemmas over Qur'an, 4:34", *Journal of the American Oriental Society* Vol. 126, No. 4 (2006).

Marcinkowski, Muhammad Ismail, "Some Reflections on Alleged Twelver Shi'ite Attitudes Toward the Integrity of the Qur'an", *The Muslim World* Vol. 91 (2001), pp. 137–153.

Mashour, Amira, "Islamic Law and Gender Equality: Could There be a Common Ground? A Study of Divorce and Polygamy in Sharia Law and Contemporary Legislation in Tunisia and Egypt", *Human Rights Quarterly* Vol. 27, No. 2 (2005), pp. 562–596.

Mehregan, Abbas, "Islamo-Arabic Culture and Women's Law: An Introduction to the Sociology of Women's Law in Islam", *International Journal for the Semiotics of Law* Vol. 29 (2016), pp. 405–242.

Mir-Hosseini, Ziba, "Muslim Women's Quest for Equality: Between Islamic Law and Feminism", *Critical Inquiry* Vol. 32, No. 4 (2006), pp. 629–645.

Moller, Lena-Maria, "An Enduring Relic: Family Law Reform and the Inflexibility of Wilaya", *American Journal of Comparative Law* No. 63 (2015), pp. 893–925.

Nahal Behrouz, Andra, "Transforming Islamic Family Law: State Responsibility and the Role of Internal Initiative", *Columbia Law Review* Vol. 103, No. 5 (2003), pp. 1136–1162.

O'Connor, June, "Rereading, Reconceiving and Reconstructing Traditions: Feminism Research in Religion", *Women's Studies* Vol. 17 (1989), pp. 102–104.

Opwis, Felicitas, "Maslaha in Contemporary Islamic Legal Theory", *Islamic Law and Society* Vol. 12, No. 2 (2005), pp. 182–223.

Peters, Rudolph, "Ijtihad and Taqlid in 18th and 19th Century Islam", *Die Welt des Islams* Vol. 20 (1980), pp. 131–144.

Qafisheh, Mutaz M., "Restorative Justice in the Islamic Penal Law: A Contribution to the Global System", *International Journal of Criminal Justice Science* Vol. 7, No. 1 (2012), pp. 487–491.

Rehman, Javaid, "The Sharia, Islamic Family Laws and International Human Rights Law: Examining the Theory and Practice of Polygamy and Talaq", *International Journal of Law, Policy and the Family* No. 21 (2007), pp. 108–112.

Roded, Ruth, "Jewish and Islamic Religious Feminist Exegesis of the Sacred Books: Adam, Woman and Gender", *Nashim: A Journal of Jewish Women's Studies & Gender Issues* No. 29 (2016), pp. 56–80.

Sadeghi, Behnam, "The Traveling Tradition Test: A Method for Dating Muslim Traditions", *Der Islam* Vol. 85, No. 1 (2008), pp. 213–219.

Samei, Mohammad, "Between Traditional Law and the Exigencies of Modern Life, Shia Responses to Contemporary Challenges in Islamic Law", *Journal of Shi'a Studies* Vol. 2, No. 3 (2009), pp. 255–271.

Sanday, Peggy R., "Toward a Theory of the Status of Women", *American Anthropologist* Vol. 75, No. 4 (1973), pp. 1168–1170.

Sayeh, Leila P., and Adriaen M. Morse Jr., "Islam and the Treatment of Women: An Incomplete Understanding of Gradualism", *Texas International Law Journal* (1995), pp. 311–334.

Schacht, Joseph, "Problems of Modern Islamic Legislation", *Studia Islamica* Vol. 12 (1960), pp. 99–129.

Scott, Rachel M., "A Contextual Approach to Women's Rights in the Qur'an: Readings of 4:34", *The Muslim World* Vol. 99, No. 1 (2009), pp. 60–85.

Seaman, Bryant W., "Islamic Law and Modern Government: Saudi Arabia Supplements the Shari'a to Regulate Development", *Columbia Journal of Transnational Law* Vol. 18, No. 3 (1980), pp. 413–481.

Sechzer, Jeri Altneu, "Islam and Women: Where Tradition Meets Modernity: History and Interpretations of Islamic Women's Status", *Sex Roles* Vol. 51, No. 5/6 (2004), pp. 263–272.

Shackelford, Scott J., and Lawrence M. Friedman, "Legally Incompetent: A Research Note", *The American Journal of Legal History* Vol. 49, No. 3 (2007), pp. 321–342.

Sharpe, Emily C., "Islamic Marriage Contracts as Simple Contracts Governed by Islamic Law: A Roadmap for U.S. Courts", *Georgetown Journal of Gender and the Law* Vol. 14, No. 1 (2013), pp. 189–[ix].

Smith, Jane I., and Yvonne Y. Haddad, "Eve: Islamic Image of Women", *Women's Studies International Forum* Vol. 5 (1982), pp. 135–144.

Spaulding, Jay, "Slavery, Land Tenure, and Social Class in the Northern Turkish Sudan", *International Journal of African Historical Studies* Vol. 15, No. 1 (1981), pp. 1–20.

Stern, Gertrude, "The First Women Converts in Early Islam", *Islamic Culture* Vol. 12, No. 3 (1939), pp. 291–305.

Syed, Jawad, "A historical perspective on Islamic modesty and its implications for female employment", *Equality, Diversity and Inclusion: An International Journal* Vol. 29, No. 2 (2010), pp. 150–166.

Teipen, Alfons, "Jahilite and Muslim Women: Questions of Continuity and Communal Identity", *The Muslim World* Vol. 92 (2002), pp. 437–459.

Tibi, Bassam, "The Return of The Sacred to Politics as Constitutional Law: The Case of Shari'atization of Politics in Islamic Civilization", *Theoria: A Journal of Social and Political Theory* No. 115 (2008), pp. 91–119.

Trible, Phyllis, "Depatriarchalizing in Biblical Interpretation", *Journal of the American Academy of Religion* No. 41 (1973), pp. 30–48.

Uhlman, Kristine, and Elise Kisselburg, "Islamic Shari'a Contracts: Pre-Nuptial and Custody Protections", *Journal of Child Custody* Vol. 10, No. 3–4 (2013), pp. 359–370.

Warren, James Francis, "The Sulu Zone: The World Capitalist Economy and the Historical Imagination", *Southeast Asian Studies* Vol. 35, No. 2 (1997), pp. 177–222.

Weaver, Katherine M., "Women's Rights and Sharia Law: A Workable Reality? An Examination of Possible International Human Rights Approaches through the Continuing Reform of the Pakistani Hudood Ordinance", *Duke Journal of Comparative and International Law* Vol. 17 (2007), pp. 483–506.

Zahraa, Mahdi, and Normi A. Malek, "The Concept of Custody in Islamic Law", *Arab Law Quarterly* Vol. 13, No. 2 (1998), pp. 155–177.

Reports

Priscilla Offenhauer, "Women in Islamic Societies: A Selected Review of Social Scientific Literature, A Report Prepared by the Federal Research Division", Library of Congress under an Interagency Agreement with the Office of the Director of National Intelligence/National Intelligence Council (ODNI/ADDNIA/NIC) and Central Intelligence Agency/Directorate of Science and Technology, November 2005.

Conventions

See the Cairo Declaration of Human Rights in Islam, Aug. 5, 1990, U.N. GAOR, World Conf. on Hum. Rts., 4th Sess., Agenda Item 5, U.N. Doc. A/CONF.157/PC/62/Add.18 (1993).

Websites

http://english.ahram.org.eg/NewsContent/1/64/275762/Egypt/Politics-/AlAzhars-grand-imam-says-Islamic-inheritance-law-i.aspx.
http://www.egyptindependent.com/calls-gender-equality-inheritance-islamic-teachings-al-azhar/.
http://www.usislam.org/pdf/Lawful&Prohibited.pdf.
https://dictionary.cambridge.org/dictionary/english/commodity.
https://dictionary.cambridge.org/dictionary/english/property.
https://www.scribd.com/document/97406376/Peace-in-Islam-Hassan-Al-Banna.

Index

a degree above 20, 63, 113
Abbasids 31, 31n2
Abdallah ibn Umar al-Baydawi 120
Abu Al-Qasim Mahmood Bin 'Omar Al-Zamakhshari 136
Abu al-A'la al-Mawdudi 121
Abu Bakr 24n3, 39, 42, 42n99, 73, 73n67, 84n131, 105n248, 115, 116n313, 116–118, 135n54, 171, 197, 206
Abu Hanifa 25, 40n89
Abu Ja'far Muhammad ibn Jarir al-Tabari 120, 136n59, 195
Abu Nasr Al-Farabi 182, 183n118
adat 6
adultery xi, xii, 47, 69n45, 74, 80, 95–97, 122, 146, 146n115, 169n39, 184n123
advancement 21, 37, 55, 67, 108, 188, 192
aqd
  agreement x
age of majority 13n58, 129, 153
Ahmad Hanbal 25
Ahmad ibn al-Khafaji 120
Ahmad Ibn al-Taymiyya 103
Ahmad ibn Mohammad al-Khafaji 138
Aisha 70, 72, 72n65, 73n67, 74n75, 73–75, 75n80, 75n82, 76n84, 77n89, 101, 115, 119, 135n53, 139, 153n154
Aisha Abd al-Rahman 139, 139n76, 195
al nasf 182
al wasat 182
Al-Ahwaal Ash-Shakhsiya
  personal status 27
al-Azhar 12, 60, 167n24, 175n67, 199, 204
al-Bukhari 20n82, 43n102, 72n62, 73n67, 77n88, 77n89, 79n99, 91n187, 99n224, 114n306, 114–115, 119n333, 120n339, 120n340, 122n353, 123n357, 123n358, 146n119, 147n119, 147n120, 147n123
Ali xii, 1n1, 5n21, 16n69, 20n82, 24n3, 24–25, 30n27, 35, 35n62, 36n65, 42, 42n100, 45n112, 52n151, 73n69, 75, 75n80, 84n131, 84n136, 85n138, 85n140, 87n158, 90n181, 91n187, 93n195, 98n219, 108, 108n271, 109n276, 110n279, 111n285, 112n293, 115, 118n325, 121n347, 128n20, 129n21, 130n31, 135n53, 140n81, 144n101, 144n102, 144n99, 151n141, 155n170, 155n172, 158n189, 158n191, 159n198, 159n199, 161n208, 167n28, 171, 171n47, 177n84, 177–178, 178n94, 195–197, 203, 206–207, 211
'Ali ibn Khalil ibn Al-Tarabulusi 102
al-Lat 43n101
al-Mamoun 41
al-Manat 43n101
al-Mutasim 41
al-Nasa'i 116
al-Tahir al-Haddad 133
al-Tirmidhi 115
analogy xi, 33, 42, 52, 87n161, 108, 160
Ansar 73n67, 74n70, 122, 147, 204
apostasy 14n64, 30n24, 84n130, 96n209
aql
  reason x
Arab 2, 5–6, 9n43, 11, 17, 27, 27n12, 35n62, 38, 42, 64n8, 73n68, 101n229, 104n240, 107, 108n269, 125n2, 127n9, 138n70, 142, 157n186, 168n35, 171, 172n54, 174n61, 175n67, 175n71, 187n137, 187–188, 198, 200–201, 205, 207, 209–210, 213
Aristotle 183, 183n119, 196
authentic traditions 31, 44
authoritative 7, 14n61, 35–36, 50n140, 61, 115, 185, 192
authority xii, 1n3, 1–2, 2n4, 7, 11, 19, 21–22, 25n7, 27, 31, 33n41, 38, 39n82, 45, 45n112, 56, 59, 61, 64, 101, 125, 127, 129, 132, 135n52, 134–136, 138–139, 151–152, 153n155, 180, 187, 190–191
autonomy 11, 19, 62, 181
awliya 141
'awra 28n17
ayah x, 146
Ayatollah x, 56n172, 180

Basrans 115
Battle of Camel 75

Battle of Uhud   72n66
Bedouins   65, 65n16, 68
bequest   109, 111, 117n320
Bible   20n84, 21n87, 80, 81n116, 81–82, 82n117
bid'ah   x
Bilal ibn Rabah   167
blood-money   63, 64n12, 84n130, 169, 185
bounty   13, 63, 132
by the right hand   94
Byzantines   15
    Byzantium   79

Canon law   29n18, 42
capabilities   3, 21, 79, 117, 132
chain of transmitters   43n102, 43–44, 99, 106, 116
character   xi, 3, 14n61, 30n25, 32, 35, 65n16, 165, 181
charity   27n11, 82, 105, 107, 156
chastity   66, 74, 78, 84n131, 93, 124, 150
Christian   14n62, 30n23, 36n67, 54n160, 60, 82n117, 84n135, 111, 118, 119n330, 127n12, 131n38, 132n40, 132n43, 155n178, 198, 204, 209–210
civil war   25, 42n100, 115, 116n314
clans   4n14
closing the gate of ijtihad   x
codification   3, 11, 187
commentators   16, 20, 22–23, 43n101, 75, 103, 135–136, 144, 146, 173
    commentaries   3, 20n84, 21n87, 120
commodity   65, 156, 160, 161n205, 214
Companions of the Prophet   24, 50n137
compatibility   12
compensation   9, 65n16, 65–66, 80, 87, 104–105, 137
competence   2, 52
complementary   2, 9
concubines   73, 83n128, 93, 158
confinement   19, 87
consent   x, 22n93, 92n192, 100, 111, 113, 125, 128, 129n21, 135n52, 151, 152n149, 152–153, 158n192, 160, 171, 175
conservative   16, 61, 121, 171, 176, 179
constitution   11, 27, 59n188, 178, 187, 192n160
consummation   109n274

contracts   3, 9n40, 22, 22n93, 27n11, 85, 92, 141, 148–150, 152, 154, 157–158, 158n192, 161
contradictions   26, 37, 46
controversy   12, 49, 75, 116n314, 176
corrective measures   133, 144
criminal law   65, 96n209, 126, 169, 173n58
culture   3, 11, 17, 29, 164
custody   26n8, 53n158, 69, 83, 86, 88n161, 109, 127, 127n14, 128n15, 138, 148–149

daraba   132, 144, 146
darurah
    principle of necessity   x
daruriyyat   x
deficiency   20n84, 99, 117, 135, 140
deficient mind   20n84, 163
democracy   183, 183n120
    democratization   7, 187
discrimination   7, 62, 103, 130, 167, 181
    discriminatory   4, 13, 13n58, 15, 29, 56, 101–102, 106, 108–109, 129–130, 132, 142
divine   x, 1n2, 3, 14n61, 25n7, 27, 29–30, 30n25, 34, 34n52, 36, 38, 42, 43n101, 45, 48, 52, 59, 61, 76, 131, 137, 140n80, 142, 148, 166, 185–186, 189–191, 193
divorce   xi, xii, 2, 4, 9, 9n43, 14n64, 20, 22, 26n8, 33n47, 53n158, 65, 67–71, 75, 80, 84n130, 86, 91n183, 92n191, 92n192, 97n217, 97–98, 112n290, 112n292, 112n295, 113n296, 113n299, 112–114, 114n302, 120, 134, 135n56, 137, 139, 148, 150, 155, 158, 184, 194
diya   96n209, 104, 105n243, 105–108, 108n266
doctrine   xi, 7, 9n40, 18, 18n75, 26, 37n73, 36–38, 50, 50n137, 50n140, 54, 57–58, 60, 73n68, 92, 103, 110, 179, 189
dower   2, 22, 85, 85n137, 85n138, 110–111, 113, 151, 155–156, 159, 166, 184

economic transactions   2, 4
education   42, 61, 116n314, 127n14, 172
egalitarian   9, 15, 15n68, 22, 76, 168, 189
Egypt   9n43, 12, 12n54, 14n64, 25n4, 27n11, 30n24, 46n115, 59n188, 74n70, 91n188, 150n135, 172n54, 174, 174n64, 175n66, 175n67, 175n69, 175n71, 176n73, 176n74,

INDEX

187n136, 187–188, 190n150, 197, 199, 201–203, 207–208, 212, 214
emancipation 162, 167–168
enforcement 3, 86n144
epistemology 10, 17n72
equality 2, 4, 12, 12n54, 17n71, 17–18, 22, 46, 70, 76, 108, 130, 132n40, 132–133, 142–143, 151, 157, 162, 181, 184n124, 189, 193–194, 214
 gender equality 4, 12, 181
ethical 15n68, 17, 29, 76, 80, 130, 133, 143, 184, 186
exegesis xii, 17n71, 36, 139

family x, 2, 4n14, 4–5, 9, 12, 17, 21, 27n11, 37, 46, 58n183, 63, 65, 69–70, 72, 78, 85, 87, 104–105, 105n243, 108n266, 108–109, 121–122, 127n12, 127–128, 138–140, 140n80, 145n108, 147n119, 147n123, 149, 154, 166–167, 172, 181
faqih x
faridah 156
Fatimah 25
fatwa x, 100–101, 176, 178
female participation 124
female slaves 83n128, 147n119, 170n44, 170–172
feminism 11, 14n64, 16n68, 16n69, 162
 feminist 12, 14, 15n66, 16n68, 16n69, 75n77, 82n118, 115n307, 136n61, 137n63, 138n68, 139n72, 139n74, 195, 204, 208–210, 212
fidelity 66, 156
financial obligations 3
financial support 110, 112, 123
financial transactions 98, 133
fiqh
 Islamic jurisprudence x, 14n62, 29n20, 30n28, 29–32, 34n53, 39n83, 39n84, 51, 54n160, 55n170, 148n126, 151n145, 152n149, 157n181, 162n1, 197
fitna x, 46, 76, 77n90, 95
fixed shares 108, 110–111, 111n283
fornication xi, xii, 69, 80, 95–96, 97n216, 120
fundamentalism 15n64, 30n24
 fundamentalists 12
fuqaha x, 40n89, 51n142, 59, 187, 187n136

gender 1, 3–5, 12, 12n54, 17n71, 19, 19n81, 21, 28, 67, 77, 80, 96, 99–103, 103n236, 106–107, 117n320, 128, 131–132, 142, 159, 162, 181, 214
gradual 38, 165
 gradualism 165
guardian 3, 27, 56, 68, 68n40, 85, 98, 128n17, 125–129, 129n21, 135, 151n147, 152n149, 153n155, 153n157, 151–155, 159–160, 171, 190
guardianship 3–4, 9, 13n58, 19–20, 22, 63, 68n40, 125–126, 128, 130–131, 134, 137, 139, 142–143, 148, 152–154, 159, 166, 180, 193–194

hadd x, 96, 96n209, 97n216, 97–98, 169, 184n123
hadith
 traditions of the Prophet x, 16n69, 38n79, 39n81, 39n82, 40n84, 43n102, 43–44, 44n105, 44n108, 44n109, 45n110, 50n138, 51n145, 72n62, 73n67, 77n89, 83n125, 109n277, 117n319, 118n321, 153n154, 153n155, 153n158, 153n158, 155n177, 195, 197–198, 202, 210
halal x, 73, 182
Hanafi 9n40, 25, 25n4, 40, 40n87, 40n88, 49n135, 57n176, 57n177, 98n219, 104n238, 106n251, 113n299, 113–114, 116, 151n145, 152n149, 152–153, 157n181, 159, 168n31
Hanbali 9n40, 25, 25n4, 104n238, 106n251, 113n299, 152n149, 153n155, 157, 160
haqq
 rights x, 99n223
haram x, 33n48, 167n23, 168n30, 173n55, 174n60, 180n101, 182, 210
head of state 114, 117n320
heirs 54, 68n40, 108–109, 111
heresy 30, 30n24, 51
hermeneutic 10, 14n64, 30n24
hijab 15n66, 99n223, 119, 121
homicide 104–105
hudud x, 96n209
hukm x
human rights 7, 181
huquq x, 181n107, 204

ibadat   xi, 26n8, 53n158, 59n183, 138
Ibn Abi Shayba   44n108, 115, 115n309, 153n155, 201
Ibn al-Shatt   102, 102n233
Ibn Qayyim al-Jawziyya   103, 103n236, 170, 182
Ibn Rush   152n153, 152–153
iddah
    waiting period   xi
ignorance   xi, 5, 5n19, 64, 163, 173
ijab
    offer   155
ijma
    consensus   xi, 30n25, 33, 50n140, 50–52, 179, 210
ijtihad   x, xi, 8, 8n37, 12, 13, 13n57, 13n59, 13n60, 14n63, 18n74, 23, 25, 30n27, 32–33, 36n65, 50n137, 52, 52n151, 53n159, 54n161, 53–55, 55n166, 55n171, 61–62, 89, 165, 196, 210–212
illah
    ratio legis   xi
imam   xi, 25, 25n7, 40n84, 90n181, 105n248, 135n53, 135–136, 138n69, 139n71, 153n159, 179, 195, 201
immutable   26, 29, 142, 184
    immutability   29, 165
inclusion   17, 116n314
incompetent   3, 126, 133, 152n149, 154
independence   19, 71–72, 98, 117n320, 143
    independent   xi, 2, 6n26, 6–8, 25, 31–33, 52–55, 65, 71, 85n139, 117n320, 143, 162
India   19n81, 25n4, 65n20, 176, 176n78, 176n79, 177n85, 177n87, 195, 197–198, 204, 207
inequality   6, 11–12, 76, 80, 142, 149
infanticide   5, 65
inheritance   4–5, 12, 12n54, 15, 20n84, 25, 26n8, 53n158, 56, 63, 65, 67, 68n40, 80, 84n130, 89, 106, 109n277, 109–111, 111n283, 132, 137, 172, 176, 184, 194, 214
insanity   3, 27n11, 112, 126, 140–141
interpretation   9, 10n49, 12–13, 14n61, 15n66, 18, 21, 23–24, 26–28, 28n17, 30, 32, 32n39, 35–36, 36n65, 49, 50n140, 52, 54–55, 57, 58n181, 58–61, 73n70, 81n112, 81–82, 94, 100, 107, 115, 121, 136, 138, 140, 143, 146, 146n117, 150, 162, 180, 188–189, 191, 193–194

interpretations   xi, xii, 3, 7–8, 12–14, 14n61, 15n66, 17, 19, 19n79, 20n83, 20n84, 21n87, 20–22, 24, 26, 26n8, 28, 36, 52, 53n158, 55–56, 59, 59n183, 61–63, 70, 80n106, 82, 82n117, 93, 136, 142, 162, 186, 188, 190–191, 193
Iran   10, 15n65, 16n68, 16–17, 25n4, 27, 108n266, 149n133, 156n180, 157n183, 178n90, 178n91, 187n135, 187–188, 196, 199, 205, 208
Islamic sources   x, 19
Isma'ili   25, 25n4
istishab   xi, 42, 57
istishan   xi, 58n183
istislah   42, 52, 58, 58n181, 59n184
Itna 'Ashari   25

Ja'fari   25, 154
jahiliyyah   xi
jawari   171–172
Jewish law   29n18, 42
Jews   30n23, 96, 107, 117n320
jihad   xi, 14n64, 16n69, 38n73, 38n75, 74n70, 198, 204, 207
judges   8n36, 16, 36, 42n97, 99, 107, 114, 114n305, 116, 116n314, 132
jurists   x, 8n38, 9n40, 8–11, 13n59, 17n72, 16–18, 21, 27, 28n17, 30n25, 30–31, 36–37, 37n73, 39, 40n89, 45, 47, 49, 50n140, 50–51, 53–55, 60, 66n27, 77n89, 84n135, 87, 89–90, 92, 96n211, 96–97, 100–101, 106, 108, 110, 111n283, 114n305, 117n316, 124, 129, 131–132, 135, 142, 144n105, 150, 152–154, 156, 158, 160, 162–163, 172–173, 179, 180n101, 180–181, 183, 184n123, 187, 190, 192–193
justice   12, 15, 18, 28, 34, 41n92, 58, 64, 76, 92n189, 131–132, 133n44, 163, 184n123, 180–186, 188–189, 193–194

Kabah   xi
Khadija   2, 2n5, 71n57, 71n59, 70–72, 72n61, 72n62, 90, 99n223, 200
Kharijites   25n6, 74n70, 202
Khawariji   73, 73n68
Kufa   40n88, 40n89

legal capacity   1, 27n11, 125–126
legal custody   127

legal pluralism 36
legitimacy xi, 10, 28, 39n84, 45, 59, 75, 187n136, 187–189, 192
liability 169

mahdhab xi
Mahdi xi, 25, 25n7, 118n327, 126n9, 195, 213
Mahmoud Mohamed Taha 14n64, 18n76, 30n24
maintainer 133
maintenance 58n181, 86–87, 87n161, 89, 110–111, 137, 160, 162, 169, 184–185, 194
makruk xi
Malak ibn Anas 25
Maliki 13n58, 25, 25n4, 40, 40n88, 48, 49n135, 58n181, 86n143, 90n181, 101, 106n251, 112, 113n299, 128, 151, 151n147, 152n149, 152–153, 153n155, 168n31, 201, 209
managers 13, 23, 63, 86, 132–133, 139, 193
mandub xi
Manumission Bureaus 175
maqasid al-shariah xi, 52, 182
marginalization 11, 67, 187
marital rights 158
marja' 56
marriage contract 3n11, 9, 22, 56, 70, 72, 85–86, 89, 90n175, 93n192, 109n274, 111–112, 114, 129, 129n25, 135n52, 148–150, 152–154, 156–158, 159n198, 159–160
maslahah
  welfare, benefit xi, 42, 52, 58, 58n181, 58n183, 180
matrilineal
  matrilocal 5, 67, 69, 76, 83
Mecca xi, 2, 5, 6n27, 18, 20n84, 34, 43n101, 65, 65n15, 71, 77n89, 122, 143, 208
Medina 2n3, 6n27, 18, 20n84, 31, 34, 40n88, 40n89, 50n140, 65, 65n15, 70, 70n47, 70n48, 71n56, 89, 108, 119, 119n338, 122, 152n152, 167, 208
methodology 32, 32n37, 53
minimum age 129
minority 1, 3, 25n6, 27n11, 50n140, 114n305, 126, 179
misogyny 3, 11, 21
  misogynist 14, 21, 46, 115
monogamy 70, 90
  monogamous 72, 92n191, 158

moral xii, 4, 10n49, 15n65, 23, 29, 31–32, 35, 41, 64, 77, 80, 82, 88, 96, 116, 140–142, 156, 180–181, 188, 194
Mothers of the Believers 79
mu'amalat 26n8
mubah xi
mufti x, xi, 101
Muhammad 'Abduh 92n191, 145n108, 175
Muhammad Baqir al-Sadr 180, 180n103
Muhammad ibn Idris al-Shafi'i 25
muhsan xi, 169n39
mujtahid x, xi, 55, 14n63, 152n153, 189, 205
Murtaza Mutahhari 180, 180n105
musannaf 44, 116
Muslim Brotherhood 10, 139, 176
musnad 44
mut'a
  temporary marriage 88–90
Mu'tazila 25n6
  Mu'tazilis 41, 41n91, 91

Nasir al-Din Abu al-Khayr 'Abd Allah ibn Umar al-Baydawi 137
naskh
  abrogation xi, 18, 18n74, 18n75, 37n73, 38n73, 47–48, 92
Nasr Hamid Abu Zayd 14n64, 30n24
Ni'matullahi 'Ali Shah 178
non-Muslim 1, 14n64, 43n101, 106, 106n251, 149, 175
normative 38, 52, 100–101, 103, 164

opinion prudentium 42
oppression x, 7, 19, 184–185
Ottoman Empire 11, 172n54, 175n65, 175n70, 187, 199, 208
ownership 2, 85n139, 94, 135, 159, 166, 169, 171

pacta sunt servanda 157
parental 9
patriarchal
  patriarchy 11, 17n71, 21, 134, 162, 192
  patrilocal 5, 7, 9, 11, 14, 15n64, 17, 17n71, 20n83, 20n84, 20–21, 28, 30n24, 65, 67, 69–70, 76, 79, 82–83, 136, 149, 164n11, 167
people of the Book 107
persecution x, 18, 41

Persia   79, 115, 178, 178n91, 203
   Persians   15
personal status   8, 8n36, 10–11, 27, 27n11, 65, 169n39
physical custody   127
polygyny   4–5, 28, 65n15, 67, 70, 72, 90–92, 92n192, 122, 132
positive law   10, 10n49, 58, 61, 188, 188n146, 191
possession   2, 65, 85n139, 90, 127, 166
power   1, 1n3, 4, 6n26, 6–7, 16, 28, 31, 42n100, 45, 49, 55n171, 60, 63, 71, 75, 100, 102, 117n320, 127n12, 127–128, 134, 137–138, 143, 149, 151n147, 159, 180, 188–190
pregnancy   97
pre-Islamic   1, 5–6, 6n29, 15n66, 20, 37, 49, 63, 65–66, 68n40, 68–69, 79, 85, 91, 93, 104, 112, 114n302, 117, 118n329, 127n12, 159, 166–167
pre-nuptial   71
principles   x, xi, 15, 18n75, 25, 27, 32, 37, 57n174, 58n183, 142, 160, 163, 181–182, 186, 188, 191
private law   31
property   x, 2, 2n4, 3n11, 8n38, 22n93, 27n11, 54, 58n181, 58n183, 63, 68, 71–72, 85n139, 84–87, 90–91, 94, 95n204, 98, 101, 108, 110, 111n283, 125, 127, 132, 135n53, 143, 148, 151n145, 158n192, 161, 161n206, 166–167, 169, 180n101, 183, 191, 214
protector   86, 133
public interest   42, 58n183, 175
public law   18n75, 31, 189
public office   80, 114, 116, 191
public order   181, 186
public sphere   6n26, 12, 19, 28, 103, 103n236

qabul
   acceptance   155
qadfh   xi
qadi
   judge   xi, 31, 42n97
qanun   188
qawwamun   13n59, 133, 136–138, 141
qiyas
   analogy   xi, 30n25, 52–53, 53n153, 53n157, 78n96, 87n156, 87n159, 156n180, 157n183, 158n195, 159n198, 160n201, 160n202, 160n203, 160n204, 161n207, 161n209
Queen Sheba   117n320
Quraysh   122

Rashid Rida   138, 145n108, 175
ratio legis   xi, 52
ra'y   xi, 138n69, 139n71, 195
rebellion   136
reform   15, 19, 25n7, 54, 61, 188, 188n146, 191
   reformism   15n68
   reformists   26, 92n191
   reforms   7, 10, 19, 187n136, 187–188, 192
reinterpretation   16, 18n74, 188
representation   17, 27, 60, 127, 152, 189
retaliation   104–105, 105n243, 107–108, 108n266, 169, 185
revelation   x, 3, 10, 17n71, 26, 38–39, 47, 74, 76, 142, 165–166, 192
riddah   110, 113–114
right to rescission   129, 171
rights   iv, x, 3–5, 7, 9, 11, 13, 15, 17–19, 22, 26, 29, 32, 35, 37, 55, 58n183, 63, 65–70, 80, 83–84, 86, 86n144, 93, 93n192, 95, 99, 103, 103n236, 110, 111n283, 113–114, 125, 130–132, 135, 139, 142–143, 144n105, 146n119, 148–149, 153, 157, 159, 161–163, 170, 175, 181, 183, 184n124, 190, 192–194

sacred   xii, 8, 16, 29n18, 31, 45, 57, 60
sadaq   156
sadoqat   155
sahih
   authentic   xii, 20n82, 43n102, 44, 46, 72n62, 73n67, 77n88, 77n89, 79n99, 91n187, 99n224, 107n260, 114n306, 119n333, 120n339, 120n340, 122n353, 123n357, 123n358, 129n21, 146n119, 147n119, 147n120, 147n123, 153n158, 198, 201
sale   159–160, 170, 176, 178
Sassanian law   42, 42n97
satanic verses   69
Sauda bint Zamʿ   119
Saudi Arabia   8n38, 25n4, 27, 27n12, 31n34, 68n40, 213
Sayyid Abu Aʿla Mawdudi   139

INDEX

Sayyid Ahmad Khan   18n75, 177, 177n84, 199
Sayyid Amir 'Ali   177
Sayyid Mahmud Taleqani   178
Sayyid Qutb   99n222, 139, 139n75, 145n108, 176n76
schools of law   9, 12, 24, 26, 29, 33n41, 35, 37–38, 45, 49n135, 55, 89, 93n192, 104, 111, 112n290, 114, 124, 129, 135, 150, 153, 157, 159, 194
seclusion   70, 77–79, 118–119
secular   10–11, 16n68, 61, 187–188
    secularization   7, 186
segregation   4, 19, 19n81, 28, 28n17, 77–79, 103, 121–122, 124, 142
self-defense   18
semi-divine   31
sexist   15n66
sexual relationships   93, 95
Shafi'i   24n1, 24–25, 25n4, 27n10, 47n120, 47n124, 47–48, 49n135, 97n216, 98n219, 99n221, 104n238, 104n239, 105n248, 106n249, 106n251, 106n252, 106n255, 108n267, 113n299, 128, 151n145, 152n149, 152–153, 153n155, 153n160, 158, 160, 168n31, 179, 195, 201, 206, 211
Shaykh Muhammad Abduh   138
Shia   x, xi, xii, 8n38, 13, 13n58, 17, 24–25, 25n4, 25n6, 29, 33n41, 35, 35n62, 42, 48, 56, 57n173, 59n188, 59–60, 75, 84n135, 88–90, 106, 106n251, 108, 110, 112, 113n296, 113n299, 114n302, 127, 130, 143, 150, 152n149, 157, 157n181, 177, 180, 190, 212
Shihab al-Din al-Qarafi   101
shirk   51n142, 180
shura
    consultation   xii, 51n142
siyasat   26n8, 53n158
slavery   1, 5, 23, 135, 135n53, 161, 163, 166–168, 170n44, 173n58, 172–179, 179n98, 180n101, 182, 185
socio-economic   26, 36, 131, 142, 165–166
sociological   17, 103, 135, 164, 193
sources of law   13, 22–24, 26, 33, 35, 59, 162, 186
sovereignty   60
spousal   9, 136

state of being female   3, 131
stoning   96, 96n211, 122, 169n39
subjugation   15
submission   39n80, 180
succession   75n80, 189
Sudan   27n12, 30n24, 172n54, 173n59, 174n64, 176n74, 200, 207–208, 213
Sufi   178
Sultanhussein Tabandeh   173n56, 178, 178n93
Sunnah   x, xii, 9, 13, 13n60, 15, 24, 30n25, 33n41, 30–34, 38, 40n87, 40–42, 42n99, 43n102, 45n112, 49n135, 45–50, 50n140, 51n142, 51–53, 53n159, 55, 56n171, 58, 62, 82, 90, 134, 143, 152, 159n198, 163–164, 194
Sunni   xii, 8, 12, 13n57, 13n58, 21n88, 24n2, 24–25, 25n4, 25n6, 29, 30n25, 35, 40n90, 42, 43n102, 48, 54–55, 56n172, 60, 62, 75, 77n91, 84n135, 88, 90, 98n219, 106, 110, 112, 112n290, 113n296, 113n299, 113–114, 126, 129, 151, 151n145, 158, 160, 177–178, 189–191, 203, 209
superiority   2n4, 14, 20, 27, 63, 107, 118, 131, 136, 140–142, 145, 163–164
supervision   9, 162
surah   xii

tafsir
    exegesis   xii, 18n75, 36, 73n70, 99n222, 107n258, 118n327, 138n65, 138n66, 145n108, 195, 199, 201
takhayyar   9, 9n40, 112
talaq   xii, 9n40, 35n59, 112–113, 210, 212
taqlid
    legal conformism   xii, 8n37, 54, 56n172, 212
tarjih   36
tawhid   xii, 85n141, 184
tazir   xii, 96n209, 169
testimony   xii, 8n38, 20n84, 28, 66, 74, 80, 97n216, 98n219, 97–103, 104n238, 116, 137, 184
torts   64, 169
traditional   4, 8, 8n38, 13n61, 14n64, 15n66, 15n68, 17, 22, 26, 27n12, 30n24, 53, 90, 92n191, 121n350, 138, 148, 156, 164n11, 177, 183, 186, 193–194

traditionalism   15n64, 30n24
    traditionalists   26, 29, 40n89, 40–41,
        60–61, 90, 92n191, 120, 163, 176–177
transaction   99, 156, 159–160
transgression   108
tribes   4n14, 4–6, 64, 67, 83, 104, 108,
    122n351, 142
Tunisia   8, 8n36, 11, 27, 91n188, 91–92, 145n108,
    163n9, 164n11, 165n16, 194, 207, 212
Turkey   11, 25n4, 92, 187n135, 196

ulama   xii, 60n190, 210
'Umar   13n60, 40n84, 42, 42n99, 53n159, 88n166,
    88–89, 94, 96, 116, 119, 122n351, 122–123,
    123n358, 147, 147n119, 147n123, 158n189, 171
Umayyad   42n100
    Umayyads   31, 31n31, 42n97
ummah   xii, 36n68
unbelievers   13n59, 37n71, 37n73, 43n101, 47
uncleanliness   13n59
unilateral   xii, 33n47, 112, 184
un-Islamic   10, 27, 86
unjust   12, 131, 182–183, 183n119, 185, 189, 194
unlawful sexual intercourse   89, 96n209
'urf
    custom   xii, 49n135, 50n136, 206
usul al-fiqh
    legal theory   x
'Uthman   35, 42, 104n238, 124
'Uzza   43n101, 69

veiling   15, 20, 77, 79–80, 118–122

wajib   xii
wakil   60, 152, 189
ward   3, 125, 128, 134n52, 134–135, 151n147,
    190–191
Western   8, 11, 34, 59n183, 93, 121n350, 148,
    168, 174n61, 175n67, 178n89, 178n92,
    179n97, 187, 208–209
widow   2, 71, 110, 111n283, 153n157
wilaya
    guardianship   xii, 125, 127n12, 127n13,
        128n17, 129n22, 129n26, 134–135,
        135n53, 137–138, 152, 153n156, 153n162,
        155n178, 190, 193n1, 193n2, 212
will of God   23, 25n7, 29, 83, 94, 177
witness   95, 98, 100–101, 103n236, 117,
    121, 169
    witnessing   4
women's rights   7, 11, 13, 15n66, 17, 17n71, 19,
    21, 70, 108, 132, 135, 192
wujub   xii

Yemen   25n4, 27n12, 105, 117n319

Zaidi   25
Zeinab bint Djahsh   119
zina
    adultery   xi, xii, 89

Printed in the United States
by Baker & Taylor Publisher Services